BREAKING THE SLUMP

For Ann, my favorite not-for-credit student Charles Alexander 5-14-'06

BREAKING THE SLUMP

Baseball in the Depression Era

Charles C. Alexander

COLUMBIA UNIVERSITY PRESS
NEW YORK

Columbia University Press
Publishers Since 1893
New York   Chichester, West Sussex

Copyright © 2002 Charles C. Alexander

Library of Congress Cataloging-in-Publication Data
Alexander, Charles C.
Breaking the slump : baseball in the Depression era /
Charles C. Alexander.
p. cm.
Includes bibliographical references and index.
ISBN 0-231-11342-0 (cloth : alk. paper)
1. Baseball—United States—History—20th century. I. Title.
GV863.A1 A37 2002
796.357'0973'09043—dc21
2001052994

∞

Columbia University Press books are printed on permanent
and durable acid-free paper.
Printed in the United States of America
c 10 9 8 7 6 5 4 3 2 1

*For the more than three thousand people
who've studied American baseball history
with me at Ohio University*

CONTENTS

Preface   ix

PREFACE

THIS BOOK is about what happened with and within the sport and business of American baseball in the period beginning with the collapse of the nation's financial market late in 1929 and ending in the general economic recovery that characterized the last year of peace before the United States formally entered World War II. So it's mainly about baseball in a period dominated by what economists and economic historians have called the Great Depression, and ordinary Americans were more likely to call "hard times."

Anyone who peruses my bibliography will become aware of the large amount of published work—general histories, team histories, oral histories, reminiscences, autobiographies, biographies—dealing in one way or another with baseball in the period 1930 to 1941. Yet to my knowledge this is the first extended effort to examine those years as a unit—as a distinct span of time, strikingly different from what had gone before or would come after.

Although it was generally a period of anxiety and austerity for the "National Pastime" (as baseball was still generally regarded), the years 1930 to 1941 also brought an array of changes that did much to define the structure and operation of professional baseball well into the post–World War II decades. As of 1941, the geography of the two "major" leagues remained what it had been forty-eight years earlier, and at that level and throughout "Organized Baseball"—the majors and the officially recognized "minor" professional leagues—racial segregation remained in place. Yet the Depression years saw the advent and rapid spread throughout the minor leagues of night baseball and then, starting in 1935, the grudging movement toward limited nighttime play at the major-league level. Rather less grudgingly, baseball owners came to terms with the still-new communications technology of radio and, like everybody else, wondered at the first experiments with baseball on television.

The circumstances of the Great Depression also created a growing disposition on the part of major-league teams to follow the lead of the St. Louis Cardinals in building a network of minor-league "farm clubs" that would become the chief source of big-league talent. And while Kenesaw Mountain Landis, baseball's first commissioner, was still in office in 1941 and still able to act with more power than any of his successors, baseball's "czar" encountered growing resistance to his authority in the 1930s, especially on the issue of farm systems.

What I've wanted to do in this book is to convey a sense of what baseball was like in those hard times. What was it like for young men trying to make their way as professional ballplayers in an economy that offered few prospects for them otherwise? What kind of conditions did they have to deal with in terms, for example, of playing facilities, transportation, lodging, and relations with their employers? And what kind of baseball did they play? Was baseball (as I suggest) a tougher, more demanding, more dangerous, and perhaps more desperate game in the years of the Great Depression than it would be in later times?

I've focused on professional baseball, more specifically on Organized Baseball (as defined earlier), and still more specifically on the National and American Leagues—both on what was happening season by season and on major developments in the off-season months from October to March. That of course was the baseball that people followed in the biggest eastern and midwestern cities (where all the major-league teams were located) and the standard by which people everywhere measured the game at whatever level they watched or played it. Yet I've tried not to lose sight of the minor leagues—the baseball that was physically closest to most people across the country. I'm especially concerned with how the minors struggled, adapted, survived, and, from the late 1930s on, revived.

I've also sought to attend to another part of 1930s baseball: that played by African Americans on the other side of what was still called the "color line." A recent generation of baseball researchers has discovered the rich history of black professional baseball—generically referred to as the "Negro leagues"—and we now know far more of that history than we did even as recently as twenty years ago. Without the work of the many other people who've directed their energies to uncovering the hitherto little-known events and personalities in black baseball history, I wouldn't have been able to include in this book a chapter on the Negro leagues.

Yet it's only one chapter, which may not satisfy some readers. My rationale is simply that for all the outstanding teams and players in the Negro leagues in the 1930s, their baseball received little coverage in the white-owned press and possessed little significance for the great majority of Americans (who were then close to 90 percent white). Of course, what happened in the Negro leagues was acutely important for black baseball fans, especially those living in northern cities and informed by black-owned newspapers. But in the vast universe of 1930s baseball, the Negro leagues were always marginal—always in the shadows of the National Pastime.

As abhorrent as that would appear to later generations, the reality is that in 1941—as the United States prepared for a war that would be portrayed as a struggle for the preservation of freedom and democracy against totalitarian doctrines of racial supremacy—white Americans still understood baseball at the highest level as a white man's game. So for that matter did substantial numbers of black Americans, who (as black newspapers frequently complained) were more likely to patronize white major-league ball than black professional teams.

Apart from chapter 1, which provides an introduction to the overall baseball situation in the 1930s, and chapter 8, which looks at the lives of professional ballplayers, my treatment is essentially chronological. Baseball has always been a cyclical thing—a season-by-season, career-by-career experience for both those playing and those following the sport. One best understands baseball history, I'm convinced, by treating it the way people understood it as it was happening.

. . . . .

AGAIN it's been a pleasure to work with Bill Strachan, director of Columbia University Press, my editorial overseer for more than a decade, and I again extend my thanks to Gerry McCauley, my longtime literary agent. Thanks go also to Steve Gietschier of the *Sporting News* and to Bill Burdick of the National Baseball Library. For the suggestion of my title, I'm indebted to Marah Eakin, a student in my "American Baseball Since 1930" course at Ohio University. Of the many people whose contributions have helped me put this book together, I'm especially indebted to such oral-history researchers as Rick Van Blair, James Riley, Norman Macht, Richard Bak, Rich Westcott, Brent Kelley, John Holway, Anthony J. O'Connor, Donald Honig, Lawrence Ritter, and the late Eugene C. Murdock. Their diligence in locating and preserving the recollections of old ballplayers—nearly all of whom are now gone—has made it possible for us to understand, in ways we otherwise couldn't, what the game used to be like.

Finally, for love, support, and understanding in just about everything I've ever tried to do that turned out well, I'm grateful to JoAnn Erwin Alexander (B.S.) and Rachel C. Alexander (B.S., D.V.M.)

Charles C. Alexander
Athens, Ohio

BREAKING THE SLUMP

CHAPTER 1

Past Times

WE CAN BEGIN with the monumental truism that the economic debacle of the 1930s—what came to be known as the Great Depression—was unprecedented in its magnitude and duration, the worst
thing to happen to the American people since the calamitous Civil War.
Recall the familiar images of the thirties: apple sellers on street corners,
lines of people outside soup kitchens, darkened factories and decaying
towns, Dust Bowl sandstorms, sit-down strikes, the aimless wanderings of
hitchhikers and hoboes. From the perspective of the twenty-first century,
however, what also strikes us is how much smaller, in that long-ago time,
were so many things in American life.

The Union itself was smaller by two states, with Alaska and Hawaii
remaining under territorial governments. The 1930 census put the United
States' population at 122,775,046, less than half what it would be at the
end of the twentieth century. Apart from San Francisco and Los Angeles,
its northeastern quadrant held the country's largest cities, led by New York,
with nearly 7 million inhabitants; Chicago, with close to 3.5 million; Philadelphia, almost 2 million; and Detroit, 1.6 million. Over the next half-
century, each of those northeastern cities—as well others such as Cleveland, St. Louis, Boston, Pittsburgh, Washington, Cincinnati, Buffalo,
Milwaukee, Newark, and Jersey City—would experience substantial population losses at the same time that their metropolitan surroundings were
mushrooming.

While professional baseball in the 1930s was played across the North

American continent—from Canada's Maritime Provinces to southern California and from British Columbia to Florida—the geography of the two major, or "big," leagues was still limited to only sixteen teams located in ten cities. Except for St. Louis, which sprawled along the Mississippi River's western bank, all those cities were east of the Mississippi and north of the Potomac and Ohio rivers. Not only was the northeastern quadrant the most densely populated part of the United States, but it had the most extensive and efficient system of railway transportation. Although a few teams had tried air travel by the end of the decade, the big leagues and upper minors continued to rely almost exclusively on the railroads, while teams in the lower minors usually covered shorter intraleague distances in bumpy buses.

An eight-team-per-league setup was the generally accepted model followed in nearly all of "Organized Baseball"—the far-flung structure incorporating the major leagues and the varying number of so-called minor leagues to which the majors gave official recognition. Competition within leagues was top to bottom, one through eight (or in some lower minor leagues, one through six), so the term "division" related not to intraleague alignments but to whether a ball club finished in the upper or lower half within the league: in the "first division" or "second division."

The major leagues and most of the upper minors played 154-game schedules, with teams meeting each other twenty-two times, eleven at home and eleven in the opponent's home city.[1] But of the sixteen big-league baseball franchises, only five—Cleveland, Washington, and Detroit in the American League; Pittsburgh and Cincinnati in the National League—had their home cities all to themselves. Chicago, Philadelphia, Boston, and St. Louis had entries in both leagues, while teams operated in three of New York City's five boroughs: the American League's Yankees in the South Bronx; the National League's Giants in upper Harlem on Manhattan Island; and, across the East River, in the southwestern part of Long Island, the National League's Brooklyn Robins/Dodgers.

Although the St. Louis Cardinals under Branch Rickey's inventive genius already operated a highly productive and steadily expanding system of minor-league "farm teams," at the beginning of the 1930s most franchises within Organized Baseball were still owned individually or in partnership. Investing in a baseball team had never been a highly profitable venture, but the modest return (if any) from operating a franchise had its rewards in high civic visibility, the sense of providing wholesome recreation for the general public, and—for most of the entrepreneurs who put their money into baseball—the satisfaction of being close to players, fans, and something most of them genuinely loved.

One measure of that closeness was that in the 1930s almost all the baseball facilities in use—usually called "parks" or "fields," sometimes "stadiums"—had been built with private capital and often bore the name of the men who'd financed their original construction or subsequent renovation and expansion. For example, Detroit had Navin Field; Chicago, Wrigley Field and Comiskey Park; Philadelphia, Shibe Park and Baker Bowl; Washington, D.C., Griffith Stadium; Cincinnati, Crosley Field; Brooklyn, Ebbets Field.

The most conspicuous exception was the huge Yankee Stadium, opened in 1923 and standing majestically in the extreme South Bronx, directly across the Harlem River from the Polo Grounds at 157th Street and Eighth Avenue, home of the New York Giants. Yankee Stadium was popularly referred to as "the house that Ruth built" because of the money that Babe Ruth's exploits had made for the Yankees in the early 1920s. In fact, it was mostly the inherited fortune and robust hubris of the Yankees' multimillionaire owner, "Colonel" Jacob Ruppert (so addressed because he'd been made an honorary colonel in the New York State guard), that had wrought the nation's most famous sports facility.[2]

With a seating capacity of 65,000 to 70,000, Yankee Stadium was bigger by about 15,000 seats than the Polo Grounds. Whereas Yankee Stadium's playing field was somewhat parabolic, the Polo Grounds was shaped like a horseshoe—or a bathtub. Thus both ballparks had short foul lines (301 feet to left, 295 feet to right at Yankee Stadium; 279 feet to left, 257 feet to right at the Polo Grounds) and huge distances from left-center field around to right-center field.

The only major-league plant with symmetrical dimensions was Comiskey Park, home of the American League Chicago White Sox. Its seating capacity was nearly as great as that of the Polo Grounds, but otherwise (and until the opening in 1932 of Cleveland's cavernous Lakefront Stadium, with which the local Indians would have an on–off relationship) major-league baseball venues in 1930 were smaller than they would be later in the century. The ballparks occupied by the Boston, Brooklyn, Pittsburgh, Chicago, and Cincinnati teams in the National League, the Boston, Detroit, Washington, and Philadelphia American Leaguers, and the two St. Louis teams, which shared Sportsman's Park, were all in the 28,000 to 42,000 range. League Park, home of the Cleveland Indians most of the time, seated only about 22,000, while Baker Bowl, where the Phillies played (usually without success), was the oldest and smallest facility in the majors. No more than 18,500 could find seats at Philadelphia's Baker Bowl.

Whatever their size, the ballparks of the era were situated relatively close to commercial districts and always near subway, elevated railway, or streetcar lines. Built in a period when most people got around cities using some form of mass transportation, they made little, if any, provision for the arrival of great numbers of customers in private automobiles. In the 1930s, as automobile ownership continued to increase despite the Depression, the absence of adequate parking accommodations would be a growing head-ache for both club owners and fans.

Admission to regular-season games ranged from fifty cents for bleacher seats to between $1.50 and $1.75 for field-level boxes. (As the Depression worsened, much was made of the fact that Yankee Stadium offered 20,000 cheap seats, the most in any ballpark.) Once inside, fans could buy peanuts, hot dogs, and a few other food items and wash them down with soft drinks but never with beer. It was, after all, the Prohibition era still: since January 1920, under the Volstead Act, which implemented the Eighteenth Amend-ment to the U.S. Constitution, anything with more than 0.5 percent alcohol content had been illegal everywhere throughout the country. With varying difficulty and in widely varying quality, liquor was obtainable in all the big cities, but not until 1933 would beer, which had been closely associated with baseball almost from its beginnings as a professional sport, again ap-pear as a ballpark concession.

After 1930 the seating capacities of baseball parks—whether major or minor league—were rarely taxed to their limits. While the prosperous times most Americans had enjoyed for the past several years were clearly over by mid-1930 and many minor leagues were in financial trouble, the Great Depression worked a delayed reaction on big-league baseball. In 1930 at-tendance in the majors reached an all-time peak of about 10.1 million, but from then on the hard times that had already hit most other segments of the economy caught up with all of baseball. The early thirties brought sparse crowds, deficits, a dramatic contraction in minor-league operations, and relentless retrenchment throughout the baseball business. Major-league attendance revived considerably starting in 1934 and 1935, and largely as a result of a general conversion to nighttime baseball, the minors experienced a strong comeback. But the decade as a whole—up until the national economy began to gear up for U.S. participation in another world war—was one of hard times for what had long been hailed as America's National Pastime.

Yet for all its difficulties in the Depression era, baseball did hold its place as the National Pastime. From the time spring training got under way in the belt of states from Florida to southern California until the conclusion of the annual World Series in October, baseball was the sport more people watched, listened to on radio, read about, and argued over than any other—probably more than all the others combined.

With a following that did not extend far from a few northeastern and midwestern cities, professional football struggled to gain a solid financial footing and build a national fandom, while professional basketball consisted of a few traveling teams and a few company-sponsored industrial leagues. Tennis and golf were still dominated by nonprofessionals; both remained basically elite sports, lacking mass followings. Prizefighting, while occasionally generating huge interest, especially for heavyweight championship bouts, had never shaken free of its bloodsport and underworld associations. College basketball was still distinctly small-time (the National College Athletic Association didn't stage a championship tournament until the late 1930s), and college football, if supreme on campuses, nonetheless flourished in an environment that remained inaccessible to most Americans. So even though other sports would increasingly encroach on baseball's popularity with the sports-minded public, at the end of a decade of hard times baseball remained Americans' favorite form of athletic competition.

That was true as much for black Americans as for whites. Yet throughout its history, baseball had closely reflected dominant American social values and practices, both good and bad. And throughout the 1930s, baseball, like the larger society, remained sharply divided according to color and racial ancestry. What social commentators termed the "color line" and black citizens commonly called "Jim Crow" still dictated the course of American race relations, whether as law in the southern states where slavery had once prevailed or as extralegal practice in the rest of the country. Since the end of the nineteenth century, baseball had been part of an overall American pattern of racial discrimination and exclusion.

Relatively prosperous in the previous decade, black baseball in organized league form briefly disappeared altogether in the early Depression years. Although the economic crisis hit African Americans even harder than it did most whites, a new group of black baseball capitalists, often men closely tied to the urban black underworld, financed the creation of a new Negro National League in 1933 and, four years later, a Negro American League. More than ever, baseball was a vital element in the lives of African Americans, especially for the vast number of twentieth-century emigrants from the southern states who had settled in the swelling black districts of northern cities.

It seems a plausible conjecture that the professional baseball of the

1930s, while still played on opposite sides of the color line, featured more good players and more good play than at any time before or since in the sport's long history. Today's conventional wisdom holds that with a doubled national population, the breakdown of racial barriers, and the entry into the sport of steadily rising numbers of non-U.S. citizens, especially from Central America and the Caribbean, baseball's talent pool has become much bigger than it was sixty or seventy years ago. Later generations of athletes have also benefited from better diet, sophisticated physical conditioning regimes, and remarkable advances in the treatment of injuries and illnesses.

That's all true enough, but a few demurrers seem in order. First, excellence in baseball requires a greater variety of skills and greater refinement of those skills than is the case with any other form of competitive sports. In baseball, size and strength have never been the determining factors; bigger and stronger people don't necessarily make better ballplayers.

The second demurrer is fairly obvious. Mainly because of television, many other sports—not only football and basketball but, among others, tennis, golf, auto racing, and more recently soccer—have become thoroughly professionalized, big-time money attractions, and many gifted young athletes who in past times would have sought careers in professional baseball now focus their talents elsewhere from an early age.

Is today's baseball talent pool actually that much bigger than was the case in the 1930s? That's questionable. One should keep in mind the immense baseball universe that used to exist outside Organized Baseball. Once upon a time, baseball was king, for both spectators and participants. (Even if in the thirties nighttime recreational softball, playable under minimal outdoor lighting, was rapidly gaining in popularity among both men and women.) Baseball was still the game American children played everywhere (usually without today's omnipresent adult supervision), and millions of adult men continued to play—often into middle age—in organized "semipro" leagues in cities or in loosely structured competition between small towns and rural communities. So not only relatively but in absolute numbers more Americans were probably playing baseball in the 1930s than at any time since. Baseball's presence in American life was one thing that wasn't smaller back then.

But ballplayers were smaller. Consider the rosters for the New York Yankees—a team traditionally thought to favor big men—from 1936 and from 2000.[3] Then, as now, pitchers tended to be bigger on average than what today are termed "position players." The 1936 Yankees pitching staff averaged 6 feet and 186 pounds; that of 2000, 6 feet 3 inches and 204 pounds. The Yankees' 1936 catchers averaged 5 feet 11 inches and 180 pounds versus 6 feet 2½ inches and 200 pounds in 2000.[4] Seven infielders in 1936 averaged 5 feet 11 inches and 171 pounds; seven 1936 outfielders, 6 feet and 180 pounds. The 2000 Yankees listed seven infielders averaging nearly 6 feet 1 inch and 190 pounds and five outfielders averaging 6 feet 3 inches and a hefty 206 pounds. So the average 1936 Yankee stood slightly under 6 feet and weighed 181 pounds, whereas his counterpart in 2000 was 6 feet 2 inches and weighed 200 pounds.

If players were physically smaller in the 1930s, what they were paid for their services was even smaller, in both relative and absolute terms. After reaching an average salary of about $7,500 in the previous decade, with a very few men such as Babe Ruth, Rogers Hornsby, and Ty Cobb drawing a great deal more, major leaguers saw their pay slashed by an average of about 25 percent during the lean early Depression years. The limited economic recovery that began in 1934 made for modest gains, although salary levels never returned to pre-Depression levels until the post–World War II years.

Yet even with the cuts they had to take, big-league ballplayers were still paid much better than wage earners in the general population—as had always been the case. A player earning only $3,000 in, say, 1932 was still making more than twice as much as the typical industrial worker (if that worker had somehow managed to hold on to a job), and at $3,000 one paid federal income taxes at the rate of about 1 percent annually. (By 1936 the rate had increased to 4 percent on a $6,000 income.) And if a particular ballplayer saw his salary reduced by 25 percent, he might take some comfort from the fact that from 1930 to 1933 wages nationally fell by more than half.

Rarely could a player gain a sympathetic hearing for his salary complaints in the baseball press. Sportswriters, usually getting by on skimpy pay themselves, had always tended to take the owners' side in salary disputes, and they were more than ever so disposed in the Depression years. The judgment of Ralph Davis, writing in 1934 out of Pittsburgh (where unemployment was particularly severe), was typical: "A ball player in the majors these days—when men in other professions are laboring for a mere pittance—if they are working at all—is mighty well paid for what he does . . . and he should stretch a mite to give service for what he receives." That same year, when Babe Ruth had to settle for $35,000 (after being cut from $80,000 in 1931 to $75,000 in 1932 and $52,000 in 1933), *Baseball Magazine* editorialized that "Babe now knows what millions of others have found out, how it seems to take a fifty per cent cut."[5]

Players had little leverage in their dealings with club owners. Every one of them—from the loftiest stars such as Ruth down to the greenest rookie—was bound by the "reserve clause," which since the 1880s had been a standard provision in players' contracts and had received constitutional sanction in a famous (or infamous) U.S. Supreme Court decision in 1922. Under the reserve clause, a player was obligated to his present franchise ownership as long as the ownership chose to exercise its exclusive option to re-sign the player for the coming season. If a player didn't like the terms offered him, he might return his contract and refuse to sign until he got more money, but he couldn't play for anybody else as long as his employer wanted to re-sign him. "They used to tell you what you're gonna make," remembered National Leaguer Elbie Fletcher, "and if you don't like it, stay home. What the hell could you do?"[6] Even if an exasperated club owner traded a recalcitrant player, the all-powerful reserve clause went with him, because what was traded wasn't actually the player but his contract.

The last effort to organize something akin to a players' union had died out seven years before the Great Depression hit baseball. Besides the inviolate "baseball law" embodied in the reserve clause, players had no legal representation either collectively or individually, no power to appeal fines and suspensions levied by league officials or owners, and nothing resembling a pension plan.

One pioneer sports agent, Christy Walsh, had helped enrich Babe Ruth through fees for product endorsements and personal appearances and also had sequestered much of the Babe's earnings from his profligate impulses. But the idea that baseball players as a class ought to have professional agents not only marketing their names but representing them at contract time would have seemed to everybody—fans, the press, club owners, baseball officialdom, and probably the great majority of the players themselves—as at best unprofessional, at worst pigheaded. In the spring of 1938, for example, when Yankees star Joe DiMaggio reportedly authorized Joe Gould, manager for former heavyweight boxing champion Jimmy Braddock, to represent him, Yankees business manager Edward G. Barrow was irate. "We'd toss the bum out," affirmed Barrow. "It just isn't done in baseball. . . . Owners have always chosen to deal with players directly."[7]

Although Jacob Ruppert allowed Babe Ruth's unprecedented $80,000 per year salary for the 1930 and 1931 seasons to be publicized and sportswriters continually made educated guesses about what other players were paid, both club owners and players usually considered final contract provisions as confidential matters between themselves and nobody else. As Charley Gehringer, Detroit's stellar second baseman, expressed it, "In those days, you didn't know what anybody made and didn't really seem to care."[8]

If players had to take pay cuts from salaries that in most cases were hardly opulent to begin with, then they also played a kind of baseball that they and others who watched it would always insist was hungrier, rougher, and less forgiving than it became in later decades. For one thing, Depression-era men were more likely, in the argot of the game, to "play hurt." Gaining a place on a twenty-five-man big-league roster put one in an elite company of only four hundred such athletes in the world. Then, beginning with the 1932 season, club owners trimmed their rosters by two, thus sparing themselves the expense of thirty-two players' salaries.

The typical ballplayer of the 1930s, finding circumstances within his profession increasingly precarious (especially with many minor leagues folding), wasn't likely to let a nagging or even a bad injury keep him out of the lineup. In the first week of September 1934, as the Detroit Tigers drove for the American League pennant, shortstop Billy Rogell broke his ankle. He had it wrapped tightly and thickly and continued to play through the World Series. "Hell," said Rogell, "in those days you didn't want to get out of the lineup. Someone might take your job."[9]

What would later be called "sports medicine"—the specialized treatment of sports-related injuries—was still in its infancy. While all major-league and most upper-minor-league teams employed trainers, such men possessed little knowledge of physical conditioning or the treatment of players' ailments beyond massage and Mercurochrome. Licensed physicians hadn't yet arrived at specific diagnoses of such subsequently familiar injuries as herniated discs, hamstring pulls, and rotator cuff and anterior cruciate ligament tears. Surgical procedures rarely had the effect of rejuvenating players' careers, although an extraordinary number of physicians prescribed the removal of teeth and/or tonsils as the remedy for sore throwing arms.

In the circumstances of the thirties, few ballplayers had much in the way of options for making a living outside baseball. Cleveland pitcher Mel Harder, who won 223 games over a twenty-year career in the majors, knew how much better off he was than most. "People were begging and out of work," he recalled. "I'd go back to Omaha, some of my best friends were pushing a rake or a shovel for the WPA [Works Progress Administration], making a dollar a day. And glad to get it."[10]

The game on the field was rougher—at least it seems that way when one reads the frequent press accounts of basemen badly spiked by hard-sliding runners, of batters (in a time before batting helmets or forearm guards) hit by pitches and sometimes hospitalized, of genuine fistfights between players, players and managers, and occasionally even players and umpires.

Old-time ballplayers and sportswriters frequently lamented that short-tempered umpires had taken much of the hustle and fight out of players. As Owen "Donie" Bush, manager of the struggling Cincinnati Reds, complained in 1933, "Man, these umpires are getting terrible! If you open your mouth, you're out of the park. They're taking the spirit out of the game."[11] Yet in fact contemporary umpires appear to have been far less confrontational and far more patient with obstreperous players and managers than would be the case several decades later.

Moreover, umpires called a strike as it was specified in the rule book—anything over the 17-inch-wide home plate between the knees and the shoulders. National League umpires, wearing their chest protectors inside their coats, could stoop lower behind catchers and thus were more likely to call "low strikes" than their American League counterparts, who wore big inflatable protectors outside. But for umpires in both leagues, letter-high fast balls were strikes.

Baseball in the 1930s may not have been as chronically rowdy as that in the 1890s, but much of what happened in the Depression decade makes today's game appear downright genteel. For example, while batters have never liked it when pitchers throw "high and tight," in the thirties few questioned the prerogative of the man on the mound to keep the batter from crowding the plate. Nobody was supposed deliberately to throw at an opponent's head; pitchers suspected of intentional "beanings" or "skullings" were roundly condemned in the baseball press. But sixty or seventy years ago, batters simply expected to be knocked down and were prepared to duck.[12]

In 1932 outfielder Tom Oliver of the Boston Red Sox expressed the common view: "I don't hold it against a pitcher who makes a batter hit the dirt every once in a while. He's out there to keep a batter from hitting and if he thinks he may do it by creating a mental hazard, that's up to him." Catcher Harry Danning, who came up with the New York Giants in 1934, was less amenable but equally resigned: "I'm Jewish so I got called every name in the book and was thrown at a lot. You just accepted it and played. You couldn't let them show that it bothered you or you'd get more of it."[13]

Sometimes even a cantankerous teammate might throw at a hitter. When Roger "Doc" Cramer was a rookie in spring training with the Philadelphia Athletics at Fort Myers, Florida, in 1930, he faced Robert "Lefty" Grove, the team's ace pitcher, in an intrasquad game. His first time at bat, he lined a home run between Grove's outfielders; his next time up, Grove hit him squarely in the back with a fastball. After the game, as Cramer held an ice pack to his back, Grove came over and said, "You didn't hit that one, did you, busher."[14]

Umpires also readily accepted high-and-tight pitches as a necessary tool in the pitcher's repertoire. They were under no orders from league officials to issue warnings to pitchers, and they rarely tried to judge pitchers' intentions and themselves take the responsibility for such warnings. Norman Macht, who grew up in New York City and followed all three of the city's teams in the thirties, has sardonically noted that "in those days umpires hadn't yet learned to read pitchers' minds, and the brushback pitch was not considered ground for banishment, or a breach of etiquette like putting your elbows on the supper table."[15] Again judging from contemporary press coverage, the majority of fights on the field were triggered not by knockdown pitches but by collisions and spikings on the base paths or by what somebody had said to somebody else—in a period when "jockeying" and "riding" opposing players was an accepted part of the game.

If pitchers could throw at hitters with relative impunity, they were also expected to start what they finished—at least most of the time. It was long before the advent of pitch-count meters or even pitching coaches per se. By the late thirties, managers were increasingly utilizing specific pitchers as late-inning "relievers"; for most of the decade, though, whoever came in to relieve an embattled starter usually did so because he wasn't good enough to be a starter himself.[16] Thus the period saw far more complete games pitched than would be the case five or six decades later. In 1935, for example, the eight American League pitching staffs averaged eighty-seven games started and completed in the 154-game schedule; National Leaguers averaged sixty-seven. By 1941, despite the growing use of relievers, American League staffs still started and completed an average of seventy-one games; National League staffs, sixty-six. (Sixty years later, American League pitchers finished an average of 7.6 games per team; the National League average was eight.)

Fewer interruptions for pitching changes was one big reason that games back in the 1930s usually took considerably less time to complete. In 1934 both the New York Giants' Hal Schumacher and the Cincinnati Reds' Paul

Derringer went the distance in a 4–0 Giants victory, with Schumacher giving up twelve hits and Derringer, eleven. Yet the game was over in one hour and twenty-five minutes! A 1935 survey of 150 major-league games (divided equally between the leagues and limited to nine-inning contests) had National League games averaging one and three-quarters hours, three minutes shorter than games in the American League. The National League's longest game was two hours and forty-one minutes; the American League's, three hours and sixteen minutes. The next year National League president Ford Frick chided the New York Giants for playing the slowest games in the league, at an average time of two hours and twelve minutes.[17]

The baseball of the Depression era paid less, left players essentially at the mercy of club owners, and probably demanded more in the way of physical endurance and tolerance of pain. Yet what comes through again and again in the reminiscences of the men who played back then is their deep and abiding love of the game itself—and their understanding of how truly fortunate they were. Lloyd Waner, who with his older brother, Paul, lined thousands of base hits for the Pittsburgh Pirates, later observed that the routine of ballplayers had them going from hotel to ballpark, back to the hotel, and then onto a train for another city, and that consequently they saw relatively little of the hardships most people were enduring. But at season's end, "my brother Paul and me would go back to Oklahoma, and then we would realize how bad things were. The farms were abandoned, the owners off to Lord knew where. Stores that had been doing business in the spring were boarded up. People were glum and poor. That was the real world."[18]

For young men who possessed exceptional athletic skills but had little else going for them, baseball was more than ever the way to make a decent and perhaps handsome living. In 1937, his first full season in the majors, Elbie Fletcher was paid $3,700, but "I couldn't *believe* you could make that much money having fun." "Listen," said Leon "Goose" Goslin, an eighteen-year American League outfielder and Hall of Famer, "the truth is it was *more* than fun. It was heaven." And Bill Werber remembered one day, before a game at Fenway Park in Boston, sitting between Lefty Grove and catcher Rick Ferrell, both future Hall of Famers. "Can you imagine," mused Ferrell, "gettin' paid for doin' this?"[19]

On the other side of the color line, excluded from Organized Baseball, black professional players had even fewer Depression-era options than whites. And just about everything—from roster sizes, league schedules, and press coverage to the crowds they were able to attract and the money they could make—was smaller still for them. One critical difference between their situation and that of their white counterparts was that while most black players signed contracts to play for a particular team in a particular season, there was no such thing as the reserve clause in black baseball. So baseball for African Americans suffered not only from a shaky financial structure but from chronically high turnover in player personnel—from season to season and even from month to month. Basically at liberty to play for whoever paid the most money, black players commonly became baseball vagabonds, moving from team to team in the United States and migrating to Cuba, Puerto Rico, Venezuela, Mexico, and the Dominican Republic for short-term and sometimes extended employment.

. . . . .

THE UNITED STATES remained at peace in the years 1930 to 1941, but for most of that period the country also remained mired in the worst economic circumstances in its history. The pall of "hard times" (as most people referred to the Depression) hung over nearly everything, including the National Pastime. In 1935, in his review of the recently released *Becky Sharp*, the first feature-length motion picture using the splashy Technicolor process, the *New York Times* columnist Andre Sennwald suggested that the next advance in color would be "to repress color deliberately . . . and to recite films in . . . the subdued colorings of the life which we live in the 1930s."[20]

Subdued colorings—down-and-dirty tones, we might also call them—are what commonly come to mind when we try to visualize what life was like in the Depression years. The times were tough for just about everybody, including the young men who tried to make their way as professional baseball players in a decade of persistently discouraging prospects in most kinds of employment, as well as the older men who tried to make ends meet as operators of baseball franchises. Yet the period featured a galaxy of memorable personalities and some of the most memorable baseball ever played. What follows is an effort to evoke the culture of American baseball in the years of the Great Depression—to convey a greater understanding and appreciation of what the National Pastime and its people were like in that long-past time.

CHAPTER 2

The Last Fat Year, 1930

I N THE SUMMER OF 1929, Paul Krichell, the New York Yankees' ace
scout, traveled up to Massachusetts to look over Henry Greenberg,
recently graduated from DeWitt Clinton High School, in the Bronx, and
now playing first base for Schuster Mills in the semipro Blackstone Valley
League. Krichell liked what he saw in the tall, raw, but powerful youngster
and offered him a $10,000 bonus to sign with baseball's richest and most
glamorous team. But as Greenberg later told it, "I had had a look at Lou
Gehrig, and said no thank you."[1] Instead Greenberg signed with the Detroit
Tigers for $1,000 less.

When the first installment of $6,000 arrived in September, Greenberg's
father invested it all in fast-rising American Tobacco Company stock. It was
all lost a month later in the bull market's Great Crash. The following January, young Greenberg passed up the spring semester at New York University and headed south to the Tigers' Tampa spring-training site, no doubt
covering his travel expenses with some of what was left of his bonus.

By mid-November 1929, some $30 billion in stock-market values had
been wiped out; within another two and a half years, another $15 billion
were gone. Average values on the New York Stock Exchange, which had
reached 311.90 the same September that David Greenberg made his ill-
fated investment, had nosedived to 34.5 by the summer of 1932. (By then a
seat on the New York Stock exchange, which had cost $625,000 in 1929,
could be had for $140,000.) And while economists and historians would long
debate whether the crash precipitated the Great Depression or was itself

14

part of a complex symptomology of ill health in the late-1920s economy, by the middle of 1930 it was hard to deny that a full-scale crisis was at hand.

In the summer of 1929, the *New York Times* index of business activity—based on monthly railroad car loadings; automobile, steel, and lumber production; electrical output; and cotton consumption—had stood at 113 percent of what was considered normal activity. By early 1933, the index was at 63 percent. Total national income, which had climbed to $82.69 billion in 1929, fell to around $68 billion in 1930, then to $53 billion in 1931, and to $41 billion the next year. Industrial production plunged by nearly half; from 1929 to 1932, American wage earners saw their income reduced by some 60 percent, as the Great Depression left between 12 and 15 million people without jobs: at least a quarter of the work force. Corporate profits fell by $3 billion; salaried income dropped by 40 percent; and farm income, which had never recovered from the collapse of commodity prices in the fall of 1920, shrank another 61 percent. For rural America what happened was both an economic disaster and—with the coming of the great droughts and dust storms of the early and mid-thirties—an ecological disaster as well.

All that buoyed the small but determined Communist Party of the United States (CPUSA). As early as March 1930, the CPUSA was able to organize a rally in Manhattan's Union Square that brought out what police estimated to be 35,000 demonstrators. When Communist leader William Z. Foster called for a march on city hall and a group of women and children waving placards and singing "The Internationale" formed a vanguard, police commissioner Grover Whalen commanded his mounted constabulary to charge the crowd. Amid cries of "Cossacks!" the marchers scattered. Meanwhile, in Washington, D.C., police fired tear gas to disburse a crowd of radical protesters from the front of the White House, where President Herbert Hoover privately fretted over the economy's downward trend while publicly reassuring the citizenry of its fundamental soundness.

If the smell of revolution (and sometimes tear gas) was in the air for much of the thirties, what was perhaps even scarier for middle-class Americans who had worked hard to accumulate savings was the epidemic of bank failures—4,377 in all—from 1930 until March 1933. In the absence of any kind of depositors' insurance system, runs on banks became a commonplace feature of American life. Some of the most heart-rending scenes of the early Depression years show bunches of stricken people gathered outside padlocked banks, their life savings having vanished.

Although major-league baseball players saw more cash income than the great majority of their fellow citizens, their financial acumen usually wasn't much greater. A few handled their money wisely, such as Edd Roush, a crotchety National League center-field star for fifteen years (not including 1930, when he refused his New York Giants contract and sat out the whole season). Roush reported that he'd stayed out of the stock market and put his money in "good bonds. . . . The market didn't hurt me a bit."[2]

Other baseball people were ravaged by the near-collapse of the country's financial system. Gordon "Mickey" Cochrane, the Philadelphia Athletics' superb catcher and team leader, lost heavily in the market, as did Connie Mack, the Athletics' venerable manager and co-owner. Cochrane, so rumor had it in the fall of 1931, also lost $80,000 in a Philadelphia bank failure. Cincinnati's Harry Heilmann, a four-time American League batting champion with Detroit in the twenties, saw his investments in stocks, real estate, and an insurance business wiped out, while Yankees second baseman Tony Lazzeri lost everything when a San Francisco bank went under. The collapse of Security Home Savings in Toledo wiped out the reserves of the American Association's Toledo Mudhens. One Mudhen player, DeWitt "Bevo" LeBourveau, took the precaution of distributing a $10,000 inheritance among five Toledo banks—of which four failed. Al Simmons, the Athletics' slugging left fielder, barely escaped disaster when he forgot to deposit two checks for $3,000 each in a Philadelphia bank that failed the next morning.

Then there was the case of the picturesque Art Shires, who had come up to the Chicago White Sox in 1928, at the age of twenty-one, determined to gain fame and fortune one way or another. Touting himself as "Whattaman" and "The Great Shires," the native of Italy, Texas, had a fistfight with his manager, tried an off-season of professional pugilism (until Commissioner Landis put a stop to it), and was a .300 hitter and a decent first baseman until a knee injury sidelined him in 1930. Once asked for his advice to the nation's youth, Shires pronounced, "Do something; say something; get yourself known."[3]

Although Shires's baseball skills would never match his ego, for a while he generated considerable press attention. So much so that in the off-season of 1930/1931 (by which time he was back in the minor leagues), he went to Hollywood to make a couple of comedy one-reelers. He later related that he'd lost $7,000 of the $7,500 he'd been paid for these movies in a bank failure, as well as $20,000 in a real-estate venture.

. . . . .

YET FOR ALL SUCH TALES of personal woe, the 1930 season, in the first full year of the Depression, found major-league baseball more popular than ever with ticket buyers and in good financial shape overall. Baseball, suggested *Baseball Magazine*, might just be "an impregnable industry . . . strongly entrenched and . . . vitally necessary to the public welfare."[4] The two-year contract for $80,000 per season on which Babe Ruth and Jacob Ruppert settled that spring would pay the Babe twice the salary the Chicago Cubs paid Rogers Hornsby, the National League's dominant hitter in the 1920s and its highest-salaried player. But while Ruth and Hornsby were above everybody else, quite a number of other topflight performers were also doing quite well.

Among them were pitcher Arthur "Dazzy" Vance and outfielder Floyd "Babe" Herman of Brooklyn; Yankees first baseman Lou Gehrig; Giants first baseman Bill Terry; Cardinals second baseman Frank Frisch; Al Simmons, Lefty Grove, and Mickey Cochrane of the Athletics; and Hornsby's teammate Lewis "Hack" Wilson, a slugging outfielder who stood only 5 feet 6 inches and had short arms and the smallest feet in the majors but also a massively muscled upper body and an ability to hit home runs in clusters. All those men drew salaries in the range of $15,000 to $25,000 per year. Rookies and substitutes, though, still received about $3,000 to $3,500 for a season's work; with no official salary minimum, some were paid even less.

Profiting from Ruth's epic batting prowess and magnetic popular appeal, winners of six pennants and three World Series in the 1920s, and playing at home in baseball's biggest physical plant, the Yankees had cleared something like $1 million over the past decade. Although Edward G. Barrow, Ruppert's thickset, bushy-browed business manager, was a rugged negotiator at contract time, the Yankees still carried a payroll of $300,000 to $350,000. They profited not only by annually drawing a million or more fans into Yankee Stadium but also by being the majors' biggest attraction on the road, where they both made money for the other American League clubs and took their entitled 25 percent of ticket sales.

Over in the National League, the most thriving franchises were the New York Giants and the Chicago Cubs. The Giants had won ten pennants and three World Series since the arrival in 1902 of manager John McGraw, baseball's pugnacious, profane, and hugely respected "Little Napoleon," although they hadn't made it to the Series since losing to Washington in 1924. Like the Yankees and various other big-league franchises, the Giants gained revenue not only from selling baseball tickets but from renting their ballpark for professional and college football, outdoor prizefights, and, increasingly in the thirties, black professional baseball.

The Giants' owner was Charles Stoneham, a grossly fat, bug-eyed onetime dealer in bogus securities who'd purchased the franchise in 1919 in partnership with McGraw (who bought his minority interest with a loan from Stoneham) and Francis X. McQuade, a city magistrate. As of 1930 McQuade was still pressing an ultimately unsuccessful suit against Stoneham and McGraw for the salary he'd lost a few years earlier when his erstwhile partners forced him out as Giants treasurer.

The Cubs' principal owner was William Wrigley Jr. A native of Germantown, Pennsylvania, who'd dropped out of school to work in his father's soap factory, Wrigley arrived in Chicago in the 1880s with an idea for making a gum flavored with spearmint that could be enjoyably chewed. By the 1920s, the sale of Wrigley's Spearmint and other flavored gums—a business that proved Depression-proof—had made Wrigley one of the richest people in the country. Besides steamboats, tugs, yachts, hotels, and estates in Wisconsin and Arizona, he owned the Los Angeles Angels of the Pacific Coast League as well as nearby Santa Catalina Island, where his Cubs did their spring training in surroundings unmatched for luxury and natural beauty.

A 1929 study put the total value of the Cubs franchise—ballpark, equipment, and players—at $4 million. The Cubs' payroll roughly equaled the Yankees'. Wrigley Field, where the Cubs played their home games, seated about 38,000 and was often referred to as the most physically attractive ballpark in the majors (although its signature ivy-covered outfield walls wouldn't appear until a renovation in the late thirties). Wrigley and William Veeck Sr., a onetime sportswriter who ran day-to-day operations as franchise president, had sought both to build a winning team and, as Wrigley put it, to "make the game alluring to the large sections of the public not . . . baseball-minded."[5] They had been able to do that by spending freely for talent ($400,000 in the off-season of 1928/1929 alone, including $200,000 in cash plus several players for Rogers Hornsby), allowing any interested local radio stations to broadcast play-by-play accounts of Cubs games, giving youngsters free admission to the bleachers on Mondays through Thursdays, and staging the majors' most popular Ladies' Days on Fridays, when women fans entered Wrigley Field without charge. By 1929 the Cubs were a powerhouse that finished well ahead of the rest of the National League and, playing before 1,485,000 home customers, set a major-league attendance record.

Baseball's poor relations included the National League's Philadelphia Phillies and Boston Braves and the American League's Boston Red Sox, Chicago White Sox, and St. Louis Browns. The Phillies had won only one pennant (1915) in their fifty-year history and had finished as high as fifth only once in more than a decade. Because of a Pennsylvania law dating back to the eighteenth century, the Phillies, like the American League Athletics and the cross-state Pittsburgh Pirates, were deprived of home playing dates on Sundays, when other teams usually drew their biggest crowds. On Saturdays and weekdays the Phillies played in Baker Bowl (named for owner William F. Baker), which not only had the majors' smallest seating capacity but also was distinctive for a high right-field fence, covered in tin, that was only 280 feet from home plate down the line and no more than 320 feet to the "power alley" in right-center. Thus the Phillies featured left-handed power hitters, of whom the foremost was Chuck Klein, who in 1929 pounded forty-three home runs and forty-five doubles, mostly over and against that fence.

Throughout the 1920s, the Braves and Red Sox had offered New England fans consistently bad baseball. Until 1929, moreover, Massachusetts law also forbade games on Sundays. Owned by Emil Fuchs (called Judge Fuchs because he'd once been a minor New York City magistrate), the Braves played in a fine ballpark that accommodated 42,000 and was the second-newest in the majors (behind Yankee Stadium). But with annual home attendance in the 200,000 to 250,000 range, Fuchs repeatedly had to sell off his best players, most notably Rogers Hornsby after the 1928 season. The group that owned the Red Sox operated pretty much the same way and also skimped on the maintenance of Fenway Park.

While the Cubs prospered on Chicago's North Side, the South Side White Sox had never recovered from the Black Sox scandal, which followed the fixing of the 1919 World Series, and the subsequent banishment by Commissioner Landis of eight players. Charles Comiskey, tight-fisted but well respected by his peers and the baseball press, had built Comiskey Park with his own money in 1910 and later expanded it into the third-largest plant in the majors. Like William Wrigley, he gave away broadcasting privileges to local stations and let women in free once a week. But his perennially down-and-out teams failed to generate much interest or revenue.

The St. Louis Browns had never won a pennant since the formation of the American League in 1901. In 1930 Philip de Catesby Ball had plenty of money and could withstand an estimated $500,000 in losses over the previous three years. But Browns home games at Sportsman's Park, which Ball owned and rented to the National League Cardinals, usually took place before meager crowds and in what one writer called "a funereal atmosphere."[6]

Despite being handicapped by Pennsylvania's Sunday law, the Pitts-

burgh Pirates operated profitably at Forbes Field, which, when inaugurated
in midseason 1909, was the second (after Philadelphia's Shibe Park) "modern" baseball facility entirely of steel-and-concrete construction. Owned by
Barney Dreyfuss, a German-Jewish immigrant who'd made his fortune in
the liquor trade, the Pirates had been World Series victors over Washington
in 1925 and two years later victims of a four-game sweep by the Yankees.
Featuring the Waner brothers in the outfield, Harold "Pie" Traynor at third
base, and a capable supporting cast, the Pirates were usually National
League contenders (although 1930 would prove a lackluster season).

But Barney Dreyfuss wasn't known for loose purse strings. When, near
the close of the 1930 season, shortstop Dick Bartell demanded railroad fare
to return home to Alameda, California, as his contract specified, Dreyfuss,
still smoldering from Bartell's holdout the previous spring, turned him
down and then fined and suspended him for the final four games of the
season, publicly denouncing his "impertinence." "I'll trade you to some
place where they won't hear you when you ask for more money," Dreyfuss
threatened. By the next spring, Bartell was with the last-place Phillies.[7]

The Brooklyn National Leaguers hadn't won anything since 1920, but
despite (or maybe because of) their zany baserunning and frequent fielding
lapses, the people of the borough loved them. Called Trolley Dodgers,
Bridegrooms, and Superbas at various times in their history, they were
currently the Robins. That was the nickname Brooklyn writers had be-
stowed in honor of rotund, bespectacled Wilbert Robinson, who, along with
John McGraw and Connie Mack, directed his team from the dugout in
street clothes. "Uncle Robbie," as he was known to Brooklynites, had been
a teammate of McGraw on the legendary Baltimore Orioles in the 1890s;
unlike McGraw, he was easygoing and popular with his players. According
to one observer, Robinson's team "was really run on the order of a soviet.
Uncle Wilbert was supposed to be manager . . . but the team ran the team."[8]

From 1926 to 1929, Robinson also served as Brooklyn president while
two factions of heirs feuded bitterly. By 1930 the feudists had finally made
peace, and the Robins were pulling more than a million customers into
Ebbets Field. But within a few years, the franchise would be heavily in
debt to the Brooklyn Trust Company.

Other big-league franchises—Washington, Cleveland, Cincinnati—
had drawn 500,000 to 700,000 per season during the twenties and, with
modest payrolls, had broken even or shown profits. In 1929 the Cincinnati
Reds came under the ownership of Sidney Weill, a local automobile mo-
gul. After losing heavily in the Great Crash, Weill came to the sad reali-

zation that it had been a most inopportune time to put his money into big-league baseball.

. . . . .

AT THE START of the 1930 season, the reigning World Series champions were the Philadelphia Athletics. The previous October, after finishing sixteen games ahead of the Yankees, the Athletics had disposed of the Cubs in five games, making World Series history by scoring ten times in the eighth inning of game four to overcome an 8–0 Chicago lead. At the age of sixty-seven, manager Connie Mack was on top of the baseball world, once again hailed as the "Tall Tactician," as he'd been before he dismantled a team that won four pennants and three World Series from 1910 to 1914. Always attired in dark suit, starched collar, and fedora (or straw hat in midsummer), Mack sat on the Athletics bench, waving his scorecard to position his outfielders. "We called Mack the best outfielder in the league," said Roger Cramer, his center fielder from 1933 to 1936, "'cause he'd always move us just right with that scorecard."[9]

Early in 1930, Mack received the Edward W. Bok Award of $10,000 as the person who'd done most for Philadelphia over the past year; the *Philadelphia Record*'s Bill Dooly even compared him with Abraham Lincoln. In the previous season, the Athletics franchise, of which Mack was co-owner along with the Shibe brothers, had profited handsomely from a franchise-record attendance of 839,176.

Although Mack and various of his players were hit hard by the Great Crash, the Athletics looked to be baseball's dominant team for the foreseeable future. They were in fact one of the strongest outfits ever assembled, with a pitching staff that featured the best threesome in baseball and an everyday lineup that listed three future Hall of Famers. George Earnshaw, a big right-hander, had been a twenty-four-game winner in 1929; Lefty Grove had won twenty; and George "Rube" Walberg, another left-hander, had posted eighteen wins. Mickey Cochrane, widely regarded as the best ever behind the plate, was one of the fastest catchers in history and an excellent left-handed hitter. Left fielder Al Simmons, a right-handed hitter, had an awkward batting style, pulling his left foot toward third base— "in the bucket"—as he swung. But with his 37-inch bat, the Milwaukee-born Polish American had little trouble with outside pitches and slammed the ball to all fields with plenty of power. Jimmie Foxx, not especially big at 5 feet 11 inches and 190 pounds and only twenty-two, was a heavily muscled hitter whose snaplike right-handed swing generated tremendous upper-body force.

After a decade of bad teams, Mack had painstakingly rebuilt the Athletics by purchases of minor-league talent and a few astute trades, which was the traditional way big-league teams tried to put together winners—if they possessed the wherewithal. That of course was the basic difficulty for franchises such as the Phillies, Browns, Red Sox, and Braves, which found themselves in a cycle of money troubles necessitating player sales, which in turn made for poorer teams, smaller crowds, still more money troubles, and still more player sales.[10]

The same had once been true of the St. Louis Cardinals, at the beginning of the 1920s a downtrodden, financially strapped operation with little prospect for improvement. But the Cardinals' fortunes had undergone a dramatic reversal, principally as a result of the creative vision of Wesley Branch Rickey. Born in 1881 on a farm in southern Ohio, Rickey worked his way through Ohio Wesleyan College, put in a few years as a run-of-the-mill catcher (including 156 games in the majors), and coached athletics to pay his way through the University of Michigan law school. Stricken by tuberculosis, he spent several months at a treatment facility at Saranac Lake, in northern New York State, and managed a full recovery from that period's most dreaded disease.

In 1913 Rickey went to work for the St. Louis Browns, first as field manager and then as vice president and business manager. Rickey, who remained a pious Methodist throughout his life, didn't get along with the rough-edged, frequently sacrilegious Phil Ball, who purchased the Browns in 1915; in turn, Ball was contemptuous of his prolix, Scripture-quoting, teetotaling subordinate. So in 1917 Rickey moved over to the Cardinals, first as president and then as vice president and business manager after Sam Breadon, a transplanted New Yorker who'd built a string of auto dealerships, acquired a majority of Cardinals stock. From 1919 to 1925, when he was succeeded by Rogers Hornsby, Rickey also was the team's field manager.

Rickey realized that the Cardinals, operating in a city that really wasn't big enough to support two big-league teams, could never match the financial resources of such franchises as the Yankees, Giants, and Cubs. Moreover, by the terms of the National Agreement of 1921 the three top-level minor leagues as well as two lesser leagues had exempted themselves from the annual player draft and thus could hold on to players as long as they wished—or until big-league clubs paid the right price.

By the time he left the dugout and went back to the front office full time, Rickey had well under way a program to make the Cardinals competitive despite the franchise's limited treasury and the scarcity of draftable minor leaguers. In the early twenties, he persuaded Breadon to buy a controlling interest in the International League's Syracuse club (later moved to Rochester) and then to acquire Houston in the Texas League and subsequently a string of lower minor-league franchises. By 1930 the Cardinals owned outright or had close working agreements with seven minor-league teams. Although other big-league clubs had often formed tie-ups with particular minor-league outfits, as of 1930 only the Detroit Tigers had shown any real interest in following the Cardinals' example in building a true farm system.

Rickey's grand design also included hiring more scouts than anybody else, combing the country for prospects, signing youngsters for little if any money, and then keeping close tabs on how they did in the Cardinals' growing minor-league configuration. "Out of quantity comes quality" was one of Rickey's many axioms. The Cardinals went into the Depression with a system that had already produced a pennant and World Series triumph over the Yankees in 1926 and, despite the departure of the irascible Hornsby, another pennant (followed by a Yankees sweep) in 1928.

With the Cardinals remaining in front of everybody else—but with everybody else following them sooner or later—farm-system baseball would transform the minor leagues during the thirties. Many people—from owners and sportswriters to players and fans—had strong reservations about the trend toward farm systems. Nobody opposed that trend more vehemently than Commissioner Kenesaw Mountain Landis.

Late in 1920, in the aftermath of the Black Sox revelations and with the majors' existing governing apparatus no longer workable, the owners had hired Landis and given him almost absolute power to "clean up baseball." As a U.S. district court judge in Chicago since 1905, Landis had often ruled high-handedly and inconsistently; as baseball's "czar," he operated pretty much the same way. Yet while he riled owners and irked some sportswriters, his standing with the public and most of the baseball press as the man who'd restored the integrity of the game remained lofty.

With considerable justification, Landis objected on two major grounds to the establishment of farm systems. First, he believed that the foundation of the minor leagues was local franchise ownership; local fandom ought to be able to know and identify with whoever operated the local ball club. Second, Landis was convinced that the way the Cardinals system functioned—with players controlled for years from St. Louis and kept out of the reach of potential purchasers in the majors or high minors—served to keep deserving players from advancing as quickly as they should. For example, Landis could point out that while the average age for all rookies going to spring training with the sixteen big-league clubs in 1931 was twenty-three years, seven months, the average Cardinals rookie was nearly three years older.

Rickey's counterargument was that with so many minor-league teams in financial trouble, it was to their advantage to tie up with big-league teams and receive vital cash assistance. Rickey would go to his grave convinced that the expansion of farm systems—especially his own—had saved the minors in the worst of the Depression. But he also pointed out that the Cardinals sold or traded away quite a number of players who'd matured on their farm clubs. By 1940, in fact, nearly one in five players on big-league rosters had once been Cardinals "farmhands." What Rickey didn't like to talk about was that he received a 10 percent commission on each and every sale the Cardinals made. That, together with an annual salary that by 1934 was $35,000, made him the most remunerated front-office man in baseball.

The conflict over farm systems and how they ought to be operated—intensely personalized in two aging, hard-willed men—would persist through the Depression decade and beyond. Despite Landis's best efforts, time and economic circumstances were on Rickey's side.

. . . . .

THAT THE MINOR LEAGUES needed help was beyond dispute. Although Landis's authority extended over all Organized Baseball, the minors had their own governing body, called the National Association of Professional Baseball Leagues, which at the start of the 1930 season oversaw the affairs of a total of twenty-three circuits. The minors were organized into six classes, from Class AA down to Class D, with league memberships roughly corresponding to population. Minor-league cities ranged in size from Los Angeles in the Pacific Coast League (AA), at nearly 1.5 million, to Rayne, Louisiana, in the Evangeline League (D), at little more than 4,000.

Whether farm-system baseball saved the minors in the Depression era will always remain debatable. What can't be doubted is that the advent of nighttime baseball made for crowds that were sufficiently bigger to keep conditions—as bad as they were—from becoming a lot worse. Although experiments with baseball under a variety of lighting systems had been tried going back to the 1880s, it wasn't until April 28, 1930, that a regular-season night game was played in Organized Baseball. On that evening Independence, Kansas, defeated Muskogee, Oklahoma, 13–2 in a Western Association (Class C) game illuminated by clusters of lights developed by the Giant Manufacturing Company of Omaha and mounted on poles temporarily set in the ground inside the playing field.

That game didn't really make history; history-making events are whatever people want to make them. A week later, under six permanently set 90-foot-tall Giant Company light towers, what would go down as Organized Baseball's first night game took place in Des Moines, Iowa, where the Class A Western League Demons beat the Wichita Aviators 13–6. The overflow assemblage of 10,000 (which waited until ten o'clock for the first pitch, a scheduling decision intended to maximize illumination in full dark) included Commissioner Landis and a number of other dignitaries, as well as a bevy of visiting press people. A National Broadcasting Company radio crew was on hand to pick up the action at midnight (in the fifth inning) and send a play-by-play account of the rest of the game to much of the United States and, by short wave, to South America, South Africa, Australia, and parts of Europe. Lee Keyser, president of the Des Moines franchise, predicted over NBC that with nighttime play "baseball in the minor leagues will now live."[11] Keyser's electric bill for the event was $25.

Generally acclaimed a success, the Des Moines game precipitated the rapid spread of baseball under lighting systems purchased from Giant and later from General Electric. By midsummer 1930, the *New York Times* was reporting more night than day games in the minors; all told, thirty-eight minor-league teams in fourteen leagues had installed lights. In the Pacific Coast League—six of whose teams converted to lights—attendance for night games averaged about three times that for day games. By the end of that season, the generally conservative *Baseball Magazine* could proclaim: "From a small beginning in the Prairie States beyond the Mississippi, night baseball has spread like a veritable conflagration."[12]

Meanwhile the Kansas City Monarchs, the leading black professional team in the Midwest, traveled with a portable system consisting of lights mounted on poles that could be cranked into vertical position from flatbed trucks. In the spring of 1930, the Monarchs introduced night baseball in five states. Typically, the Monarchs parked their trucks behind canvases stretched along the foul lines and around the outfield. A noisy, smoke-spewing gasoline generator set up in center field and burning fifteen gallons per hour powered the system. The Monarchs not only used the system for their own games but sometimes rented it out to minor-league teams, as they did for a May 8, 1930, game between Alexandria and Baton Rouge in the Class D Cotton States League.

Other teams operating outside Organized Baseball also adopted lights. The bewhiskered and long-haired House of David team, formed in the 1920s to advertise the religious colony of the same name at Benton Harbor, Michigan, traveled from one end of the country to the other, playing as many as 180 games against black and white teams alike and, beginning in 1930, bringing along a portable lighting setup similar to the Monarchs'. In the borough of Queens, on Long Island, Max Rosner, who operated the Bushwicks in the strong semipro Metropolitan Baseball Association, put up wooden light towers at Dexter Park and staged night games on Wednesdays and Fridays from June to September. In 1931 Rosner installed steel towers and, with increased wattage, attracted some 350,000 to Dexter Park. That was more customers than four big-league teams drew that season.

Yet the obvious appeal of night baseball failed to convert baseball's top officaldom or any of the big-league owners. National League president John Heydler; franchise presidents Barney Dreyfuss of Pittsburgh, Clark Griffith of Washington, and Robert Quinn of the Boston Red Sox; business manager Billy Evans of Cleveland; and manager Bob Shawkey of the Yankees were among the many prominent baseball people who disdained the notion that big-league ball should be played at night. Heydler's view was typical: "I find that there is no demand in the majors to get away from baseball . . . and get it into the show business, which, after all is said and done, is all that night baseball is or can be." Editor J. G. Taylor Spink, whose St. Louis–based *Sporting News* served as baseball's weekly trade paper, even worried about the health of night-ball fans: "The man who goes to night baseball after he has eaten a hearty meal is apt to have indigestion if he is nervous or excited; the disturbed and misanthropic fan will not sleep well after a night game."[13]

One might have assumed that the needier big-league franchises would be more receptive to night ball. *Baseball Magazine* reported "many gloomy forebodings . . . at St. Louis with muttered threats of a transfer of a local club to some more appreciative city."[14] All big-league teams played two games on Memorial Day (or Decoration Day, as it was then called), the Fourth of July, and Labor Day; rainouts frequently necessitated additional doubleheaders. But by midseason 1930, the Cardinals were resorting to what critics called "synthetic doubleheaders." These involved pairing a scheduled Thursday or Monday single game with a Sunday game, on the assumption (almost always correct) that offering "two for the price of one" on Sunday would outdraw a weekday single game. But while Breadon was quite willing for lights to be installed at Houston's Buffalo Stadium and the ballparks of other Cardinals farm clubs and in 1932 booked the House of David with its portable lights for a game with the Cardinals at Sportsman's Park, neither he nor the Browns' Phil Ball was interested in nighttime regular-season games.

· · · · ·

SO IN 1930 major-league baseball operated pretty much as it always had, apparently with little inkling of the hard times ahead. On Monday, April 13, President Herbert Hoover—not yet reviled for his supposed indifference and inertia while the masses suffered, as he would be within another year or so—followed the custom established twenty years earlier by President William Howard Taft and threw out the first ball to open the season in the national capital. Hoover, a genuine baseball fan, stayed for the whole game, which Walter Johnson's Senators lost to Boston, 4–3. It would be one of only fifty-one winning occasions for the 1930 Red Sox, who contrived to lose one hundred games for the fourth time in six seasons.

The seven opening games (with one rainout) drew an aggregate 205,112, topped by some 50,000 at the Polo Grounds for the Giants' win over Boston. At Shibe Park in Philadelphia, a capacity turnout of 32,000 went home happy with a victory over the despised Yankees when Al Simmons, a holdout all spring who'd just signed for $30,000, hit a home run and won Lefty Grove's game. Twelve days later, the Yankees opened at home before 66,000 by losing again to the defending World Series champions.

About a third of the way into the season, a couple of things had become pretty clear: more people than ever were clicking the turnstiles at major-league ballparks, and they were witnessing more potent offense than ever. Free-swinging, power-oriented baseball—mostly influenced by Babe Ruth's success on the field and at contract time but also blamed on a livelier baseball and a variety of other factors—had been the dominant mode of play since the early 1920s. Nearly every big-league team had assembled an array of batters who hit for distance and usually for high averages as well. As batting averages, runs scored, and especially home-run totals had grown, so had pitchers' earned run averages (ERAs). Conversely, such stratagems as base stealing, the hit-and-run and squeeze plays, and sacrifice bunting had largely fallen into disuse. It was a kind of baseball that Ty Cobb and other luminaries of the pre-1920 "dead-ball era" repeatedly decried, but it was also what people had come out to see in unprecedented numbers during the prosperous twenties.

What happened in 1930, though, often dismayed even full-fledged converts to Ruthian-style baseball. Typical of what became commonplace that season, particularly in the National League, was a game at the Polo Grounds on April 29. Before a good weekday crowd of around 20,000, the Giants and Brooklyn Robins amassed thirty-four runs on forty-one hits. Brooklyn led 13–2 after two innings, only to see John McGraw's team score nine runs in the third and eventually win 19–15, with right fielder Mel Ott, who'd tied Chuck Klein for league home-run honors the previous year, hitting two. The Giants then left on their first western trip, where they scored ninety-nine runs on 154 hits in nine games.

Meanwhile, in the other league, the Cleveland Indians made 25 hits, including thirteen doubles into an overflow crowd in the League Park outfield, in beating the Athletics 25–7. On Friday, May 23, at Philadelphia, Ruth hit two homers in the opener of a doubleheader and another in the second game; Lou Gehrig homered three times in the nightcap, as did Jimmie Foxx; and the Yankees won both games, 10–1 and 20–13, with a total of 39 hits. Two days later (after the idle Pennsylvania Sabbath), Ruth homered twice more in another doubleheader sweep of the Athletics, 10–6 and 11–1. In the six-game series, of which New York won five, Ruth totaled eight home runs.

Although Ruth, Gehrig, and company bombarded Connie Mack's pitchers in that series and the Athletics played inconsistently over the first half of the season, by early July they'd moved into the lead over Washington. The Washington Senators—whose regular lineup had future Hall of Famers Joe Cronin at shortstop and outfielders Sam Rice and Henry "Heinie" Manush (obtained in June from St. Louis for Goose Goslin, another Hall of Famer)—didn't hit many home runs playing half their games in spacious Griffith Stadium. But they batted .302 as a team, took seventeen of twenty-two meetings from the Yankees, and won ninety-four games to rise from fifth place in 1929 to second in 1930.

For much of the season, Ruth's home-run pace was ahead of that of 1927, when he established his long-standing record of 60. He ended up with forty-nine to Gehrig's forty-one, batted .359 to Gehrig's .379, and drove in 153 runs to Gehrig's 174. As a team the Yankees batted .309, knocked 152 homers, and scored 1,062 runs, a major-league high for the twentieth century. But with shaky pitching and fielding and, over the last part of the season, a rumored breakdown of discipline under manager Bob Shawkey, they finished at 86–68, in third place. More people than ever came to watch them, though. The 1.6 million who paid their way into Yankee Stadium surpassed baseball's previous attendance record, set by the Cubs only a year earlier. Nobody would equal that for another sixteen years.

In 1930, American Leaguers as a whole hit 673 home runs, batted .288, and scored 6,670 runs. Thirty-three American League batters hit for better than a .300 average. American League pitchers' collective earned run average swelled from 4.24 to 4.65. All of that represented a substantial increase in offensive output over the league's totals for the previous year. But if American League pitchers struggled, National League moundsmen often seemed helpless in the face of an unprecedented batting barrage.

The way National League hitters assailed the ball that season was positively phenomenal, especially given the fact that since big offense had come into vogue ten years earlier, the American League had generally been considered the heavier-hitting circuit. In 1930 the entire National League averaged above .300, led by the .319 mark of the Giants, who also hit a majors'-best 171 homers. Only seventh-place Cincinnati and sixth-place Boston failed to average .300, although Braves rookie Wally Berger totaled thirty-eight homers, thereby setting a record for first-year players that wouldn't be tied until 1956 (by Frank Robinson) or broken until 1987 (by Mark McGwire). Forty-five National Leaguers—nearly a quarter of the league's playing personnel—batted at least .300.

No kind of lead, it seemed, was ever really safe, as teams repeatedly rallied from deficits of eight, ten, or even twelve runs to win games. Pitchers trudged to the mound, threw their best stuff, watched it knocked all over the ballpark, and gave up an average of 4.97 runs per nine innings—highest in the majors since 1924 and in the National League since 1894.

People who'd followed baseball since before the turn of the century could remember the batting surge in the National League (the sole major league at the time) that followed the lengthening of the pitching distance to 60.5 feet in 1893. But while batting averages and scoring had soared for the next few years, the rubber-centered baseballs supplied exclusively by the firm of A. G. Spalding and Brothers simply didn't carry as well as Spalding's rubber-and-cork-centered balls, introduced late in the 1910 season and then—so experienced baseball people insisted, despite Spalding's disclaimers—given considerable added bounce and carry in 1920 and 1921. So while 1890s players had hit lots of singles and doubles, they hadn't battered pitchers with three- and four-base blows as hitters had done for the past ten years or so—and as they were doing with greater regularity than ever in 1930.

John McGraw, who'd been the master of pre-1920s, closely played, run-at-a-time "inside baseball," shook his head in disgust at what he saw game after game. "I don't care what the manufacturers of the ball . . . say," protested McGraw. "It is lively, and every sensible baseball man knows it. Why, most of the pitchers are scared to death when they are sent to the mound. The home run slugging has taken the heart out of them." Bill Klem, serving his twenty-fifth year as a National League umpire, had had some legendary run-ins with McGraw, but on the subject of the ball he was in full agreement with the Little Napoleon. "I'm telling you," Klem said, "they will have to get it out of there. It is making the game ridiculous." But if all this heavy hitting was so bad, asked John Kieran, the *New York Times*'s urbane sports columnist, "what of the thousands who are demonstrating their disapproval by rushing through the turnstiles in a way that bids fair to set a new attendance record for both leagues?"[15]

The Philadelphia Phillies' season was maybe the strangest any big-league team ever had. Defending National League batting titlist Frank "Lefty" O'Doul hit .383, Chuck Klein matched O'Doul's average in addition to hitting forty homers and driving in 170 runs, and Arthur "Pinky" Whitney batted .342 and drove in 117 runs. As a team, the Phillies averaged .315 and scored 944 runs. But they won only fifty-one games and finished buried in last place, forty games out of first. They led the majors with 239 errors and yielded 1,199 runs, an average of close to eight per game.

Phillies pitching was simply abominable. Grover Cleveland Alexander—once the team's ace, later star of the Cardinals' 1926 World Series win over the Yankees, and winner of 373 big-league games, but now broke and alcoholic—began the season back with his old club but drew his release after three starts and three losses. Following a short stay in the Texas League, Alexander ended the season traveling with the House of David. Other Phillies moundsmen included Claude Willoughby, who won four and lost seventeen games with an ERA of 7.59, and Les Sweetland at 7–15 and 7.71. ("My country 'tis of thee / Sweetland and Willoughby / Of thee I sing," a bibulous Philly sportswriter would intone as he settled in for still another afternoon of sacrificial pitching.)[16] Visiting teams batted .350 at Baker Bowl. So many balls banged against the high tin fence in right field that Klein was able to throw out forty-four runners—an assist record never likely to be equaled.

A couple of miles away, on Philadelphia's north side in upscale Shibe

Park, the Athletics played their home games before 118,000 fewer spectators than in 1929, but they maintained their standard of baseball excellence. On September 18, Mack's team clinched its second-straight pennant, winning a 14–10 slugfest at Chicago, with Foxx and Simmons hitting homers. When the season closed, Philadelphia led the stubborn Washington club by eight games. Lefty Grove won twenty-eight games, the most since Dazzy Vance registered the same number six years earlier; Grove also led the majors in strikeouts, with 209, and, in that robust season for hitters, allowed only 2.54 earned runs per nine innings. Frequently used by Mack in late-inning relief, Grove appeared in a total of fifty games and saved nine for his fellow moundsmen. Big George Earnshaw, a Swarthmore College graduate from an affluent Philadelphia-area family, added twenty-two victories. Al Simmons led the league with a .381 average, hit thirty-six homers, and drove in 165 runs; Jimmie Foxx batted .335, with thirty-seven homers and 156 RBIs; and Mickey Cochrane batted a career-high .357.

The National League pennant race proved far more competitive. Into September it was still a four-team battle among the Giants, Cubs, Robins, and Cardinals. The Cubs had such a potent batting order that they hardly missed Rogers Hornsby, who had broken his ankle in May and was disabled for more than two-thirds of the season. But chunky Hack Wilson hit fifty-six homers, more than anybody besides Babe Ruth up to then, and batted in 191 runs—a record still in place into the next century. The Giants' even stronger lineup had first baseman Bill Terry leading the majors with a .401 batting average (plus twenty-three homers and 129 RBIs); right fielder Mel Ott at .349, with twenty-five homers and 119 RBIs; and third baseman Fred Lindstrom at .379, with twenty-two homers and 106 RBIs.

Brooklyn had the National League's best pitcher in Dazzy Vance, who'd finally made the majors to stay in 1922 at the age of thirty-one, and then led both leagues in strikeouts for seven straight seasons. Vance had lost some of his speed, and in 1930 he was repeatedly plagued by poor support afield and often at bat. But he still led the Brooklyn staff with seventeen wins, was runner-up to St. Louis's "Wild Bill" Hallahan in strikeouts, and posted a 2.36 ERA, the best in the majors and more than two and a half runs better than the National League average.

Vance's teammate Babe Herman had gained a well-deserved reputation for miscreant conduct on the base paths and in right field, but the tall, left-hand–batting Californian was also one of baseball's great natural hitters. In 1930 Herman enjoyed his finest year: a .393 batting average, thirty-five homers, 130 RBIs. But the Robins also got plenty of offense from shortstop

Glenn Wright (.321, twenty-two homers, 126 RBIs) and first baseman Del Bissonette (.336, sixteen homers, 113 RBIs). The St. Louis Cardinals' 104 homers were only the fifth-highest total in the league, but with ten players who went to bat at least two hundred times hitting at least .303, led by second baseman Frank Frisch's .346, they scored a league's-best 1,004 runs.

After being in first place for weeks, Brooklyn lost three times at St. Louis on August 11 and 12, while in Chicago the Cubs took four of five games from Boston and moved into the lead. On that western trip, the Robins dropped fifteen of eighteen games, including five straight to lowly Cincinnati. But then Uncle Robbie's team regrouped, won eleven games in a row, and on September 16, as they began a series with the Cardinals at Ebbets Field, led St. Louis by one game and Chicago by a game and a half, with the Giants having fallen well off the pace.

On the Monday night before the next afternoon's series opener, Flint Rhem, who'd been a Cardinals starter for five years and was scheduled to pitch one of the games at Ebbets Field, mysteriously disappeared, only to reappear on Wednesday with a yarn that nobody, least of all manager Charles "Gabby" Street, was prepared to believe. Rhem claimed he'd been standing outside the Alamac Hotel in midtown Manhattan when he was kidnaped at gunpoint by gangsters, taken to a hideout in New Jersey, and forced to swallow cup after cup of bootleg whiskey. Whatever had actually happened, people familiar with the rustic South Carolinian's personal habits had grave doubts that Rhem would have had to be forced to drink anything alcoholic.[17]

That same night Bill Hallahan, the Cardinals ace left-hander, managed to smash a hand—fortunately his right one—in a car door. The next day, working with a painful gloved hand and in front of a capacity crowd, Hallahan beat the Robins and Vance 1–0 in ten innings, in one of that season's few old-fashioned pitching duels. Meanwhile, over at the Polo Grounds, the Giants' Carl Hubbell shut out Chicago; at day's end the Cardinals, Robins, and Cubs were only a game apart.

From that point, Brooklyn couldn't win another game in ten tries and ended up in fourth place. New York finished third, five games out. The Cardinals, winning twenty-one of their last twenty-five games, held on to the lead despite the continued pounding of Hack Wilson and company. St. Louis clinched the pennant on September 26 by beating Pittsburgh 10–5 at Forbes Field behind the veteran Jess Haines. Two days later, in the Cardinals' season closer, a gangling nineteen-year-old Arkansas share-cropper's son, recently brought up after winning a combined twenty-five games in the Western and Texas leagues, defeated Pittsburgh 3–1. It was the big-league debut for Jay Hanna Dean, who subsequently decided that his name was actually Jerome Herman Dean and whose minor-league antics had already earned him the nickname "Dizzy."

Meanwhile William Wrigley Jr., in a move that surprised people who weren't close to the situation, fired Joe McCarthy, his manager since 1926. Although McCarthy had brought the Cubs in first a year earlier, their World Series loss to the Athletics had been a bitter disappointment for the chewing-gum magnate, whose life's ambition was to win it all. Besides, Wrigley was convinced that McCarthy had allowed too much celebrating following the 1929 pennant clincher and generally had lost control of his team. So with the Cubs still only two and a half games behind St. Louis and coming home to Wrigley Field to end the season with four games versus seventh-place Cincinnati, Wrigley announced that McCarthy was out. Rogers Hornsby—whom Wrigley greatly admired and respected despite that native Texan's cold, hard-bitten personality and incorrigible horse-playing—took over as Cubs manager. A sweep of the hapless Reds did no good, because the Cardinals won all five of their remaining games.

. . . . .

BY 1930 the World Series had become an annual radio event, but both the National Broadcasting Company and the newer Columbia Broadcasting System could still carry the games free of charge. Over NBC's national hookup Graham McNamee, a veteran of Series play-by-play, and sportswriter Ford Frick would do every game, while CBS, which had Ted Husing to cover the action, opted to devote Sunday, October 5, to previously scheduled programming. Despite radio's growing presence, many people would still follow the play-by-play on message boards outside newspaper offices and elsewhere. New Yorkers, for example, could gather in Madison Square Garden to watch the progress of games on an electric board projected on a 40-foot screen.

On Wednesday, October 1, President Hoover and five members of his Cabinet were among the chilled 33,000 who packed Shibe Park for the Series opener. Several thousand more paid the occupants of row houses to watch from roofs and top-floor windows across narrow Twentieth Street, which ran behind the right-field fence. Before the game, the ballpark's loudspeaker system played recorded martial music, and the comedy duo of Al Schacht and Nick Altrock, who doubled as Washington's coaches during the season, regaled the gathering with their pantomimes. J. Roy Stockton of the *St. Louis Post-Dispatch*, discounting Wrigley Field, called Shibe Park, with its superior playing field and accommodations for customers, "the best equipped and cleanest baseball plant in the big leagues."[18]

Following the season's hitting onslaught, the World Series featured some of the best pitching in the history of postseason play. The Athletics, solid favorites with gamblers, won the first game 5–2, Al Simmons and Mickey Cochrane homering and Lefty Grove scattering nine hits. Thirty-seven-year-old Burleigh Grimes, one of only three remaining hurlers exempted from the ban on spitball pitching adopted ten years earlier, was the loser. The next day, the Athletics won even more easily, driving out Flint Rhem in the fourth inning and cruising behind George Earnshaw, 6–1. Cochrane homered again, as did St. Louis's George Watkins; and Frank Frisch's forty-second hit in World Series play, a first-inning double, set a new record.

After the long train ride west, the Series resumed on Saturday in St. Louis, a city whose economy was already in a bad way. A local reporter estimated that of the thousands waiting through the night to get in line when the bleachers ticket window opened at 7:30 A.M., one in ten intended to sell his place for the $1 ticket price. Some of the waiting men, lacking anything to eat or drink, joked that they were "living on prosperity"; one, who gave his name as Paul Blay, said he'd been working only one day a week.[19] When Blay failed to sell his place and found himself at the ticket window, he had to step aside in favor of somebody who could pay the tariff. (Meanwhile, in Cleveland's Public Hall, President Hoover spoke to the annual convention of the American Bankers Association; outside, motorcycle police used tear gas to disperse a crowd of Communists and sympathizers.)

On Saturday, October 4, Hallahan threw a seven-hit shutout, besting Rube Walberg 5–0. Every seat in Sportsman's Park was occupied, including temporary field boxes that extended from the regular first- and third-base stands and obliged players and managers to sit outside their dugouts on benches. Then, on Sunday, the Cardinals tied the Series when Jess Haines pitched a four-hit, 3–1 gem, holding the Athletics hitless after the fourth inning. Although Grove gave up only five hits himself, a fourth-inning throwing error by third baseman Jimmy Dykes led to two Cardinals runs, which proved enough. On Monday the pitching was even better. Earnshaw allowed three hits and no runs; Grimes gave up only five hits, but in the top of the ninth inning he walked Cochrane and then hung a curve ball to Foxx, who sent it far back into the left-field bleachers.

Back in Philadelphia on October 8, Earnshaw took the mound with only a day's rest and, getting homers from Foxx and Dykes, took a 7–0 lead into the ninth inning, when outfielder Charles "Chick" Hafey doubled in infielder Andy High for the Cardinals' only run. Hallahan started for St. Louis and left trailing 2–0 in the second; as his three successors yielded five more runs, a brass band in the Shibe Park upper deck played "The St. Louis Blues," and Connie Mack savored his fifth World Series championship.

Neither team had been able to do much with the other's pitching. The Cardinals batted .200 to Philadelphia's .197, but they were outscored almost two to one, and their strongest hitters—Frisch, Hafey, and first baseman Jim Bottomley—combined for only twelve hits over the six games. The Series drew 212,019 paying customers and receipts of $953,772. The players' individual shares (figured of course for only the first four games) came out to $5,038 per winner, $3,536 per loser.

The Series money cushioned some of the losses that Mack, Cochrane, and others had suffered in the past year's financial disaster. Although the Athletics' home crowds had fallen off over the second half of the season, for the majors as a whole—especially for the National League—it had been a very good year. Some 5.25 million paid to see National League games, an increase of 500,000 over 1929; nearly as many bought tickets in the American League. The combined income of big-league franchises in 1930 was close to $2 million ($629,000 above the previous year); the average profit margin grew from 11.3 percent to 16.4 percent. The Cubs broke their own league attendance record; the Yankees drew even more.

The 1930 season, though, would be major-league baseball's last fat year for a decade. Ahead was a succession of lean years that would be still leaner for the faltering minors. Then would follow somewhat better times, years in which the American people found their relationship to their national government undergoing profound and permanent transformation under President Franklin D. Roosevelt and the New Deal.

CHAPTER 3

Lean Years, 1931–1932

A WEEK AND A HALF after George Earnshaw throttled the Cardinals to close out the World Series, Joe McCarthy succeeded Bob Shawkey as manager of the New York Yankees, as he'd been expected to do since his firing by William Wrigley Jr. the previous month. McCarthy and "Colonel" Jacob Ruppert staged the signing ceremony in Ruppert's paneled office suite in his Third Avenue brewery (which, like many other breweries in the Prohibition years, had been producing near beer and other legal malt beverages). As he took the fountain pen to sign his $25,000-per-year contract, a nervous McCarthy confused Ruppert with Colonel T. L. Huston, who'd co-owned the Yankees with Ruppert until they quarreled and Ruppert bought Huston's holdings late in 1922. "Ruppert. Ruppert," prompted the honorary colonel. "Oh yes, my mistake," McCarthy said quickly. Then McCarthy beamed into the camera flashes and said, "I am the happiest man in the world. . . . If I could beat the Cubs with my new team, I would be willing to jump off the Brooklyn bridge."[1] In another year McCarthy would get just that chance.

McCarthy's signing with the Yankees got more press attention, but of far greater import for Organized Baseball as a whole were the doings at the annual winter meetings of the major and minor leagues. Under a new National Agreement, all the minors, including those that had opted out of the process in 1921, accepted a return to an annual universal draft in exchange for increases in prices for drafted players (up to a maximum of $7,500 for a player taken from Class AA). Moreover, each big-league club could now option fifteen players to the minor leagues, an increase of seven per club, and could send a player down to the minors as many as three times (versus the former limit of two) before the player became draftable. In actuality, that made it possible for a player to be held for four years on farm clubs, then optioned out three times, and thus controlled by one big-league organization for seven years, regardless of what Commissioner Landis or anybody else might think.

If Landis hadn't liked the previous minor-league draft exemptions, he abominated farm systems. In fact, the new National Agreement turned out to be a considerable setback for Landis's efforts to thwart the growth of "chain-store baseball," as he sneeringly called Branch Rickey's handiwork. And it also signaled the growing willingness of club owners to stand up to the man who would appear less and less czarlike as the decade moved along.

At the majors' meetings in New York, the consensus among club officials was that something had to be done to help the besieged pitchers and quell explosive offenses. Not surprisingly, nonpitchers suspected that such efforts would provide a justification for owners to impose salary cuts. While a number of big-league teams had enjoyed record attendance and profits the past season, the continuing economic slide in the winter of 1930/1931 prompted growing apprehension among people in all lines of commercial activity, including baseball.

Some observers, though, reasoned that if people really liked high-scoring games and watching "jackrabbit" balls clear the fences—which evidently they did, judging from 1930 attendance figures—then what needed to be fixed? Early in 1931 the monthly *Baseball Magazine* asked its readers—people who presumably would be pretty astute in baseball matters—what they thought. The result was a 957 to 451 verdict against doing anything to deaden the baseballs currently in use. Eddie Collins, whose distinguished career as an American League second baseman had spanned both the dead- and lively-ball eras, also spoke out in favor of the "modern" game. In "old-style" baseball, quipped Collins, "you sat in the stands and admired what didn't happen and concluded that you were witnessing phenomenal pitching."[2]

Nonetheless, the owners, with the Yankees the sole dissenter, voted to instruct the Spalding company to change the baseballs for the 1931 season. Both leagues wanted raised and longer stitching and coarser thread for the covers, all of which would supposedly give pitchers a better grip and help them snap off sharper curve balls. But the National League also directed Spalding to thicken the horsehide covers, an alteration that was expected to have a deadening effect on the baseballs.

None of that required any action by the joint league rules committee.

But that body did adopt a rule change as well as a scoring change that would affect home-run hitting as well as overall batting statistics. Up to then, balls that bounced over fences had counted as home runs. Even balls hit inside the foul lines that then bounced into the seats in foul ground entitled the batter to four bases.

How many such "fluke homers" (as Babe Ruth called them) had been hit over the years had never been calculated, but they did happen from time to time. Rogers Hornsby's first major-league homer (of 301 for his career) occurred in 1916, at old National League Park in St. Louis, when he lined a ball over third base that twisted into foul ground and landed in the field boxes. And on June 6, 1930, at Brooklyn's Ebbets Field, three of four homers hit by the Cubs in a 12–9 loss to the Robins were on drives that hopped over the 2-foot fence in front of the left-field bleachers. As of 1931, though, home runs would have to clear the playing field on the fly; balls that bounced over fences would give the batter only two bases.

The scoring change eliminated the sacrifice fly, whereby fly-ball outs on which runners tagged up and advanced to the next base weren't counted against hitters as times at bat.[3] From now on, fly balls that advanced runners would be registered as ordinary outs, although batters would continue to receive a run batted in on flys that scored a runner from third base.

The American League clubs also voted to have all their players wear numbers on the backs of their uniform shirts, as the Yankees and Senators had been doing since 1929. Numbering players may have seemed like a harmless way to help people in the stands identify the men on the field, but such a change had long been resisted on the grounds that (1) it depersonalized the players and (2) true baseball fans would already be familiar with their favorites. So with John McGraw, among others, continuing to speak out against numbering, National Leaguers voted to keep the backs of their players' uniforms vacant.[4]

More grumbling than usual and a fair amount of tough talk went on in the early months of 1931, as most club owners tried at least to hold the line on payrolls and as players—in many instances coming off their best seasons—sought more money. Edd Roush still wouldn't sign his contract, and McGraw sent him back to Cincinnati, whence he'd been acquired four years earlier. Bill Terry, who more than seventy years later would still be the National League's last .400 hitter, finally signed for $22,500 and joined the Giants at Memphis when they came through on the way north from their San Antonio training site. But relations between McGraw and the dour, money-wise Tennessean would remain distant at best. The Cardinals'

Chick Hafey wanted $18,000, had a succession of bitter exchanges with
Sam Breadon and Branch Rickey, and finally signed for $12,500, with a few
hundred dollars deducted for games missed at the start of the season.
Chuck Klein signed a three-year contract for $15,000 per year, but that was
$3,000 less than the annual pay he'd sought.

Al Simmons and Hack Wilson were notable exceptions to the owners'
Depression-prompted tightfistedness. Simmons agreeably signed for three
years at $33,000 per season, while Wilson was happy to become the second-
highest-paid man in the National League (behind only player-manager
Hornsby), signing for the same amount as Simmons for one season.

. . . . .

LATE IN MARCH, Ernest S. Barnard, the American League's president,
died at the age of fifty-six. Sixteen hours later, in St. Louis, Byron Bancroft
"Ban" Johnson, that league's founder and president up to 1927, died at
sixty-seven. Within another seven months Charles Comiskey, originally
Johnson's close ally in making the American League a success but later his
bitter foe, would also be gone (at seventy-two), leaving the White Sox franchise in the uncertain hands of his obese son. Comiskey's death would be
followed within a few months by that of Barney Dreyfuss, the little immigrant from Freiburg, Germany, who, largely through baseball, had actually lived the American dream of rising from obscurity to wealth and
prominence.

Each of those men had helped to make baseball history, but the Brooklyn
Robins made some history of their own that spring by taking a steamer from
Miami to Havana and exhibiting their skills before big crowds in five intrasquad games at Tropical Stadium. The veteran pitcher Adolfo Luque, a Havana resident, and Al Lopez, a young second-year catcher who'd grown up
in Tampa's Cuban district, were the main attractions for the *fanáticos*. Meanwhile, in Brooklyn, work was nearing completion on the renovation of Ebbets
Field. When Uncle Robbie's men arrived, they would find a ballpark enlarged
by around 10,000 seats, with new double-decked stands extending down the
left-field line and across left field to join the high fence across right field. A
12-foot concrete wall had replaced the little bleachers fence.

Although the Giants and White Sox had been willing on March 21 to
play a nighttime exhibition game in Houston in cold and gathering fog
before about five hundred people, as yet nobody at the major-league level
wanted anything but all-daylight baseball. But the minors would continue

their rapid transition to nighttime play, even if only sixteen leagues began the 1931 season, seven fewer than a year earlier. All the Pacific Coast League parks now had lights, including San Francisco's brand-new Seals Stadium, the first baseball plant to be built for night baseball. Night ball would be played in all the remaining fifteen leagues, although the greatest number of night games was scheduled in the lower minors. Half the International League clubs would play most of the time at night, but in the American Association only Indianapolis had installed a lighting system.

The eight home openers in the majors drew a record total attendance of 247,162. The first Sunday of the season turned out even more people, with an officially reported 80,403 overflowing Yankee Stadium for a Yankees–Athletics contest. Wrote Fred Lieb of the *New York Evening Post*, "Perhaps the public is tired of talking depression and welcomes the opportunity to change the conversation to Babe Ruth's homers, Bill Terry's quest for new batting championships and Babe Herman's antics in the outfield." Proclaimed the same city's *Herald-Tribune*, "Better not sell baseball short this season!" The *Chicago Herald and Examiner* was sure that "no one in the crowd of 46,000 at the opening game [at Wrigley Field] was aware that any area of depression existed within a thousand miles of the baseball park. . . . This should be a great baseball year."[5]

That it would be, at least in terms of the caliber of baseball being played. But those big early crowds proved deceptive; as the season progressed, it became impossible to deny that the Great Depression had finally caught up with big-league baseball. Overall attendance fell by 18 percent, net income for the sixteen clubs was only $217,000, and their aggregate profit margin shrank to 2.3 percent.

At least fewer baseballs would have to be paid for. Within a month of opening day, National League hitters were groaning about the deadened ball and the insistence of the umpires—presumably as directed by league headquarters—on keeping in play balls that had become stained, scuffed, and softened. The 1931 season saw total National League home runs cut by almost half, the league's batting average drop by twenty-six points, and the league's earned run average diminish by more than a run per nine innings. Bill Terry's average fell to .349, but he still almost won another batting title: Chick Hafey beat him out by only a fraction of a point. Chuck Klein, who'd hit forty homers and batted in 170 runs in 1930, hit thirty-one and batted in 121 in 1931. Mel Ott hit twenty-nine homers; no other National Leaguer had as many as twenty.

By late May, National League president Heydler was bragging about a recent game in his league in which only ten baseballs had been used. The changes in the ball, Heydler said, "have brought about . . . the very result at which we aimed when we adopted the new ball in February." While batting averages were down, "it has given us closer and better games." Later in the year Heydler proclaimed that "the era of slugging is over, as far as the National League is concerned."[6]

Al Lopez, who batted .309 in 1930 but struggled to hit .269 in 1931, remembered how "balls that I had been hitting up against the walls or even into the stands were all of a sudden just easy lazy fly balls."[7] Nobody suffered more from the deadening of the ball than Hack Wilson. Wilson rarely pulled the ball; nearly all his home runs were hit in the arc from right-center to left-center field. As what would have been homers the previous year now fell harmlessly into outfielders' hands, Wilson became more and more frustrated; as he did, he caroused, drank too much, and infuriated Rogers Hornsby, his teetotaling manager. The new ball, said the Giants' Fred Lindstrom in August, "killed off Hack Wilson, and Hack was a colorful home-run hitter with a contending club. That made him a league asset."[8] After homering only thirteen times and driving in sixty-one runs in 112 games, Wilson ended the season suspended without pay and with Hornsby and Cubs president William Veeck determined to get rid of him.

The pitchers, though, thought the new ball was just fine. As Burleigh Grimes put it, "It's a step in the right direction. It's given the pitchers a little encouragement. It's made them feel that the problem of pitching a good game isn't altogether hopeless."[9]

In the American League, where offenses had been somewhat less potent in 1930, the less deadened ball produced less dramatic changes in batting figures. The Yankees again scored more than 1,000 runs and topped the majors with 155 homers, Babe Ruth and Lou Gehrig tying for individual honors with forty-six apiece.[10] Ruth drove in 163 runs, while Gehrig's 184 RBIs broke his own league record. As a team the Yankees batted .297, even as the league average fell by eleven points.

With all their batting power, the Yankees again couldn't contend with the mighty Athletics and especially with Connie Mack's superb pitchers. Aside from Charles "Red" Ruffing, a husky right-hander acquired in a trade with Boston during the previous season, who won sixteen games, and Vernon "Lefty" Gomez, who pitched twenty-one victories in his first full big-league season, New York's pitching was spotty.

Although Gomez, a garrulous young Californian of Irish-Protestant and Spanish-Catholic ancestry, could throw the ball with plenty of speed, at 6 feet 2 inches and 155 pounds he looked so frail that the Yankees had most of his teeth extracted (per the medical wisdom of the time), made him drink three quarts of milk per day, and even gave him an unlimited meal allowance on road trips. Apparently it all worked, because Gomez also had the league's second-lowest ERA.

The stingiest pitcher of all again was Lefty Grove, who was close to unbeatable in 1931. Despite missing at least two starts in May because of a heavy cold, the tall native of the little mining town of Lonaconing, Maryland, pitched thirty-one wins, lost only four, and held opponents to slightly more than two runs per nine innings. He completed twenty-seven starts, saved five games in relief, struck out 209, and walked only sixty in 288.6 innings. Sixteen of his wins came in a row, which tied the American League record.

The streak came to an end on Sunday, August 23, in St. Louis, where some 15,000 people—an extraordinary turnout for a Browns home date—were on hand for a Sunday doubleheader. In the fourth inning of the first game, Grove gave up a bloop single, followed by a drive that outfielder Jimmy Moore, subbing in left field for Simmons (who was at home in Milwaukee nursing an ankle injury), misplayed into a triple. That scored what turned out to be the game's only run. Grove gave up only five other hits and no runs, but Browns left-hander Dick Coffman worked the game of his life, shutting out the hard-hitting Athletics on three hits. Afterward, Grove, a man of few words but a ferocious competitor and notoriously tough loser, ripped off his uniform; threw bats, balls, and gloves in every direction; and then did his best to destroy the Sportsman's Park visitors' locker room. As teammates ducked and dodged, he broke chairs and tore apart locker partitions. It didn't help his mood that the Athletics proceeded to pound the Browns 11–0 in the second game, with veteran right-hander Waite Hoyt the beneficiary of the outburst. The next day Grove blamed not young Moore for his misplay but Simmons, because, he said, "If Simmons had been here and in left field, he would have stuck that ball in his back pocket. What the devil did he have to go to Milwaukee for?"[11]

Grove went on to win his next five decisions, as the Athletics pulled away from the rest of the American League. They won 107 times, thus becoming the first American League team to reach the hundred-win mark for three consecutive seasons, and finished thirteen and a half games ahead of New York and fourteen ahead of Washington. Besides Grove's thirty-one, George Earnshaw and Rube Walberg each won twenty, Roy Mahaffey won fifteen, and onetime Yankees ace Hoyt added ten. Jimmie Foxx had a subpar season, batting only .291, with thirty home runs and 120 runs batted in; but Mickey Cochrane averaged .349, and Simmons led the majors at .390, with twenty-two homers and 128 RBIs.

Yet another relatively easy pennant—clinched on September 15 at Shibe Park, the Athletics' seventeenth-straight win and twentieth in their last twenty-one games—didn't make any money for a franchise carrying one of the majors' fattest payrolls. Crowds dwindled as Mack rested his regulars, prompting John Kieran to observe that "there were days when it seemed that Connie was using casual tourists in the outfield and total strangers on the mound."[12] Overall attendance at Shibe Park fell to 627,464; as early as August, rumors began to circulate that Mack intended to break up his team after the season.

The defending National League champion Cardinals attracted a few big home crowds, notably a huge overflow of 45,715 for a July 12 doubleheader with Chicago. They won the opener 7–5 and then lost the farcical nightcap 17–13, with thousands of outfield standees pushing in toward the infield and making for twenty-three ground-rule doubles. The two games, played under what the *Sporting News* called "unspeakable conditions," were "more like country fair exhibitions than major league contests."[13]

For the season, though, the Cardinals drew a couple of thousand fewer people than the Athletics. Like Mack's team, Gabby Street's well-balanced outfit took the suspense out of the pennant competition early. After sweeping an August 23 doubleheader at Braves Field, in Boston, behind the veteran Syl Johnson and rookie Paul Derringer, the Cardinals led New York by eight and a half games, the Cubs by three more. They clinched a day later than the Athletics, beating the Phillies at Sportsman's Park while the hopes of the ailing John McGraw for just one more pennant collapsed in a doubleheader loss to last-place Cincinnati.

As it turned out, the 1931 Cardinals didn't need the audacious Dizzy Dean, who had insisted the previous fall that if he'd pitched they'd have won the World Series and then announced in spring training that they would win another pennant if they kept him. Gabby Street and Branch Rickey had decided that the young right-hander would profit from another stay at Houston. There he won twenty-six games, struck out 302 batters, and regaled the local press with his boasts and rustic wit. Sparked by Dean and a slugging young outfielder named Joe Medwick, the Buffalos easily won both halves of a split season. Along the way Dean married Patricia Nash, a bosomy brunette several years his senior.

At season's close the Cardinals, the first National League team in eighteen years to win one hundred games, led the New York Giants by thirteen. The Cubs, with Rogers Hornsby's potent bat absent much of the time while the manager rested his weak ankle and sore heel, trailed by seventeen. Brooklyn finished a very distant fourth; Wilbert Robinson, under fire in the local press, complained that he had "only 19 enemies in the world and all of them are newspapermen."[14]

The last three weeks of the season featured several exhibition matchups intended to raise money to help the unemployed. On September 9, for example, 60,549 were at Yankee Stadium for a Giants–Yankees game that raised $59,643 for the mayor's unemployment fund; the next day, at Comiskey Park, 34,865 watched as the Cubs and White Sox also played for charity. (Before that game, Charles "Gabby" Hartnett, the Cubs' affable catcher, was photographed signing a scorecard for the son of gangster boss Al Capone and chatting with Capone and his cronies—a gesture that brought a sharp rebuke from Commissioner Landis.) On September 25 the Giants, Yankees, and Brooklyn played a round-robin doubleheader before 44,119 at the Polo Grounds. Other charity games involved the Browns and Cardinals, Phillies and Athletics, and Red Sox and Braves. A few players did their bit individually, such as Frank Frisch, who made a radio appeal for donations of old clothes for St. Louis's Citizens Committee on Relief and Unemployment. Reflecting the persistent belief that helping the needy ought to remain essentially local and voluntary, such well-intentioned early Depression events did little to ease the distress of the jobless and their families.

The Cardinals were hardly the scoring machine of 1930. Although Hafey led the league in batting and Frisch and Jim Bottomley put in solid years, the Cardinals' overall average fell by nearly thirty points, and they hit only sixty home runs and scored almost two hundred fewer runs. But St. Louis's staff ERA was the second-lowest in the majors; six pitchers won as many as twelve games, led by Hallahan's nineteen, Derringer's eighteen, and Grimes's seventeen.

· · · · ·

STILL, the Athletics were again odds-on favorites to take their third World Series in a row. That they didn't had to do with a number of factors, but the one player who would always get the biggest credit for the defeat of Mack's great team was Johnny Leonard Roosevelt "Pepper" Martin.

Twenty-seven years old, a high-school dropout, and a seven-year minor leaguer from Osage County, Oklahoma, Martin finally made it to the big time to stay in 1931 and, playing mostly in center field, batted an even .300 in 123 games. In the spring he'd scrimped on travel expenses by hitchhiking and riding freight trains for five days to reach the Cardinals' Bradenton, Florida, training site, arriving hungry and filthy. His personal appearance never improved much. Stockily built, barrel-chested, hawk-nosed, with thinning hair, he wore the dirtiest uniforms on the team and seemed perpetually disheveled off the field. (According to teammates, he also did without underwear.) Very fast, Martin ran the bases intrepidly and stole sixteen times, in a period when base stealing had ceased to be much of an offensive tactic. (Frisch led the National League that year with twenty-eight steals.) Martin also used a crowd-pleasing, belly-flopping slide, whereas the conventional method was a feet-first, fallaway or hook slide. The 1931 Series would make him something of a national hero.

It was the most competitive World Series since 1926, when player-manager Rogers Hornsby led the St. Louis National Leaguers to a dramatic victory over the Yankees in seven games. At Sportsman's Park the Athletics won the opener behind Grove, who gave up two runs in the first inning and then held the Cardinals scoreless from then on, despite being touched for twelve hits overall. Philadelphia scored four times on Derringer in the third and finished off the big right-hander with Simmons's two-run homer in the seventh. Martin doubled in St. Louis's second run, singled twice, and worked a double steal with Hafey. The next day the Cardinals evened it on Hallahan's three-hit shutout, which beat Earnshaw, even though he gave up only six hits. Martin singled and doubled, stole two bases, and scored both Cardinals runs.

After two off days—Saturday for travel, Sunday for Pennsylvania Sabbatarian observances—the Series resumed in Philadelphia, with President Hoover arriving to hear cries of "We want beer!" from the Shibe Park assemblage. Whereas the National League's deader ball was used in St. Louis, the American League ball was put into play at Shibe Park. That proved rather more to the liking of the Cardinals than the Athletics. They knocked around Grove and Mahaffey for twelve hits and five runs, Martin singling and doubling and scoring twice. Grimes allowed only two hits, held the Athletics scoreless until Simmons's two-run homer in the ninth inning, and drove in two runs himself. Nicknamed "Old Stubblebeard" because he usually pitched with a couple of days of thick facial growth, Grimes was also, as described by one National Leaguer, "the meanest man I've ever seen. He'd knock you down with a spitball."[15]

Game four saw the Athletics even the Series again. After Simmons doubled in two runs off Syl Johnson in the first inning, Earnshaw needed nothing else, pitching a three-hit shutout. Martin was again the star in game five, with three runs driven in on three hits, one a two-run homer. Hallahan scattered nine hits and gave up one run; the Cardinals made twelve hits and five runs off Hoyt, Walberg, and Eddie Rommel.

On the train back to St. Louis, Martin, batting .667 for the Series, was congratulated by Commissioner Landis, who remarked that he'd love to trade places with the Oklahoman. "It's all right with me, Judge," replied Martin. "I'll trade my $4500 for your $50,000 a year any day."[16] (Actually, Landis was still drawing a $65,000 salary, for which he was increasingly criticized.)

Back in Sportsman's Park, with the National League ball, the see-saw Series evened again. The Athletics broke a scoreless tie with four fifth-inning runs off Derringer and went on to win 8–1. Grove held the Cardinals to five hits—none by Martin—and a single run. But the next day—Saturday, October 10—the Cardinals ended the National League's four-year losing streak with a 4–2 victory before only 20,805. After Earnshaw's wild pitch gave St. Louis one run in the first inning, outfielder George Watkins scored when Cochrane dropped a third strike, pegged to first to retire the batter, and Foxx's return throw to Cochrane was wide of home plate. Watkins then made it 4–0 with a third-inning two-run homer. Grimes, fighting an appendicitis attack, allowed no runs until the ninth inning, when pinch hitter Roger Cramer singled in two Athletics. With two out, Hallahan came in to get Max Bishop to lift a fly ball to center field, where Martin grabbed it to close out the Series.

While the Athletics went home with $2,985 apiece in losers' shares, each Cardinal received $4,484, which meant that Martin almost doubled his season's pay. He picked up a few thousand more with two weeks on the vaudeville circuit, beginning his turn even before the Series was over at St. Louis's Ambassador Theatre the night before game seven.[17] For the Series, he'd batted an even .500, stolen five bases, driven in five runs, scored five more, and hit one of the Cardinals' two homers. Although some speculated that Cochrane's financial losses had affected his play behind the plate, Martin later revealed that he recognized very early that Athletics pitchers weren't adept at holding runners on base, so he ran almost at will. "Really," said Martin, "I felt sorry for Cochrane. But it wasn't his fault."[18]

The Cardinals' Series upset was especially popular in the central South, the Southwest, and the southern plains—areas impoverished by the Depression and already suffering from a drought that would worsen year by year and provoke the migration of tens of thousands of people from America's Dust Bowl. Then, as now, commentators were prone to freight up sports personalities and events with symbolic meanings. Pepper Martin would never be a great player. But it's understandable that with his humble, mid-American origins, long toil in the minors, and hell-bent style of play, he would appear to symbolize the gritty struggle so many Americans faced in those years.

· · · · ·

COCHRANE, Simmons, and Grove wouldn't have long to brood over their defeat: within the week after the Series ended, they joined a baseball expedition to Japan. It was organized by the sportswriter Fred Lieb and by Herb Hunter, an ex-ballplayer who'd already promoted a couple of smaller excursions to that country, and financed by *Yomuri Shimbun*, Japan's most powerful newspaper. The party also included Lou Gehrig, Lefty O'Doul, Frank Frisch, eight other big leaguers, and several spouses.

Relations between the United States and Japan were strained; Japanese national pride was still smarting from the Washington Treaty of 1922, which had assigned Japan a naval-construction ratio inferior to that of the United States and Britain. Moreover, just the previous month Japanese forces had launched a full-scale invasion of Manchuria, an action the Hoover administration strongly condemned.

But the tour went well. Although there was no professional baseball in Japan, the country was baseball-crazy, with collegiate competition exciting huge followings. The Americans met teams of collegians and former collegians in seventeen games, winning all and playing before some 450,000 people. Over their two-month stay, the players and their wives traveled from city to city, were hosted by officials of the imperial household, and generally had a fine time, especially Braves shortstop Walter "Rabbitt" Maranville, a twenty-year major leaguer whose 5-foot 5-inch height and antic ways made him a big hit with the crowds. Long afterward, Lieb could look back on the venture as "an artistic and financial success."[19] The fourteen players who made the trip included seven future Hall of Famers.

· · · · ·

BACK HOME, belt-tightening was more than ever the order of the day. Pestered by sportswriters, Connie Mack declared, "No, emphatically no, I am not going to dismember [this] gallant team."[20] But Branch Rickey was determined to reduce the Cardinals' payroll, even if it meant weakening the team's chances for another pennant. He rewarded Burleigh Grimes for his Series heroics by trading him to Chicago for the forlorn Hack Wilson and a second-line pitcher and then sold Wilson to Brooklyn for $45,000 and a minor leaguer. Rickey also unloaded Chick Hafey's salary, sending the reigning batting champion to Cincinnati for two players and a few thousand dollars.

At the same time, as one minor league after another adopted reductions in rosters and monthly payrolls, Rickey continued to look for likely additions to the Cardinals' farm system. It numbered eight teams by the fall of 1931 and now included Columbus in the American Association, headed up by Leland Stanford "Larry" MacPhail, a dynamic, red-haired World War I veteran and lapsed attorney-at-law who'd tried various business ventures before Rickey hired him to rejuvenate the moribund Columbus franchise.

The Yankees, having spent somewhere around $400,000 in recent years for minor-league talent—with mixed results—were ready to follow Rickey's example. That fall Jacob Ruppert and Ed Barrow began to build their own farm system, negotiating the purchase of the Newark franchise in the International League, including the ballpark that would later be renamed Ruppert Stadium. They also hired George Weiss, the thirty-six-year-old president of the Baltimore Orioles in the same league, to become baseball's first officially titled farm-system director, as well as president of the Newark franchise. Within a few months, Weiss had started to build a network of Yankees farms, purchasing outright the Springfield, Massachusetts, franchise in the Eastern League.

At the December meetings of the National Association at West Baden, Indiana, and major-league executives in Chicago (where the first-class Drake Hotel was charging $3 for single rooms, $5 for doubles), jobless baseball people stood, sat, and sprawled around lobbies in the hope that something might turn up. A writer covering the West Baden gathering noted "the army of unemployed—three free agents for every vacancy." The owner of the Denver Western League team had interviewed ninety-two men who wanted to become his new manager.[21]

In Chicago cost cutting went forward determinedly. A joint resolution to reduce salaries met with general approval in the baseball press. *Baseball Magazine* editor F. C. Lane proclaimed an end to "the golden age of inflated player income. . . . When gigantic corporations everywhere are cutting salaries, from the president's office down, while incomes shrivel and dividends disappear, baseball players can no longer claim immunity." The weekly magazine *Outlook* had no sympathy for "the well-fed, bankroll-padded baseball holdout." Added H. G. Salsinger of the *Detroit News*, "Never before has the owner had such a break in salary arguments."[22]

Ultimately the club owners voted to cut roster sizes by two positions, from twenty-five to twenty-three: an overall reduction in playing personnel from 400 to 368. The umpiring staff was cut from twelve per league to ten, which meant that each day during the regular season, two games in each league would be worked by only two umpires.

National League executives voted to retain the deader baseball used the previous season and again refused to put numbers on their players' uniforms, and both leagues accepted the recommendation of the joint rules committee to continue the ban on the sacrifice fly. Somebody figured out that if the sacrifice fly had still been legal in 1931, Al Simmons would have batted .403; Babe Ruth, .389; and Bill Terry, .359.

As spring training got under way, people across the country, including ballplayers, read with dismay of the kidnapping of Charles and Anne Morrow Lindbergh's baby from their New Jersey home and the subsequent discovery of the baby's corpse. But still more dismaying for many players were the salary slashes they were expected to absorb.

Hack Wilson's Brooklyn contract was for $15,000, less than half his 1931 salary. If Wilson would no longer have to toil under Rogers Hornsby's stern rule, he also wouldn't be playing for the indulgent Wilbert Robinson, who'd been fired in favor of Max Carey. Dazzy Vance, one of Uncle Robbie's favorites, had his salary cut by $3,000, while Babe Herman was traded to Cincinnati along with Ernie Lombardi, a ponderous young catcher. John McGraw finally talked Bill Terry into taking a $5,000 cut, but Terry reported two weeks late for spring training in Los Angeles and refused to speak to McGraw. Lefty Grove neither took a cut nor got a raise—in 1931 he'd received $19,000 in salary plus $500 for each win over twenty, for a total of $31,000—but he did sign a two-year contract for $25,000 per season.

Jacob Ruppert said publicly that Babe Ruth would have to take a big reduction from what he'd drawn for the past two seasons. "Ruth hasn't a chance to get $80,000 in 1932," declared Ruppert, "nor any other year in the future. Never again will any player get that much money for a year's pay."[23] The Babe finally signed for one year for $75,000, while Joe McCarthy began his second season as Yankees manager making a third as much.

. . . . .

ROGERS HORNSBY—whose baseball savvy William Wrigley had valued more than he had McCarthy's—hadn't given Wrigley a pennant in 1931, and now he never would get the chance. The chewing-gum magnate died on January 26, 1932, leaving Hornsby to deal with several players who didn't like him and, in William Veeck, a franchise president of limited patience now in full authority. Hornsby wouldn't last past August 2, when Veeck decided he'd had enough of the Texan's uncivil, ill-tempered ways, his betting losses and borrowings from players, and his inability to keep his team in first place.

For Joe McCarthy, though, it would be a very good year indeed. As a player, McCarthy had been a career minor leaguer who'd made it to the majors as Cubs manager after six years managing Louisville in the American Association, where his teams won two pennants. With William Wrigley's money, he quickly built the Chicago team into a contender and then a pennant winner. Ironically, it was Wrigley's conviction that McCarthy had been too lenient with Hack Wilson and other high-living Cubs that had gotten him fired.

If that had been the case in Chicago, McCarthy evidently learned his lesson, because in New York he built a reputation as a tightly organized, no-nonsense leader who expected his men not only to play like big leaguers but to act and dress that way as well. When McCarthy entered the clubhouse, remembered Ed Wells (who pitched for the Yankees from 1929 to 1932), "frivolity and fun" came to an end.[24] His players were to wear jackets, ties, and hats off the field, although an exception was made in the case of Ruth's famous camel's-hair cap. A dedicated cigar man, McCarthy had an aversion to pipe smokers, convinced that such players were too self-satisfied (although Lou Gehrig occasionally puffed on a pipe).

McCarthy also advised his men against beer drinking, which "went to the legs"; if they drank at all, they should stick to whiskey. McCarthy was hardly a teetotaler himself; in fact, Bill Werber, who was briefly with the Yankees in 1930 and again in 1933, found him not only aloof and unfriendly but "sometimes imbibing of too much whiskey."[25] That last trait never made it into public print during McCarthy's lifetime, although some people knew and others suspected that his occasional absences—when he might be reported as confined to his hotel room with the flu or at home in Buffalo with a gall-bladder flareup—were in fact drinking binges.

But McCarthy also possessed, as Joe Williams of the New York World-Telegram put it, "an understanding of human nature, a high talent for dealing with miscellaneous personalities and temperaments." He had to be especially careful with Ruth, who since his second marriage in 1929 had mostly abandoned his wastrel ways and settled into a well-ordered, monogamous lifestyle. But besides still being the greatest player and biggest box-office attraction in history, the Babe thought he could manage the Yankees better than "busher" McCarthy. In his first season in New York, McCarthy told Ben Chapman, a speedy outfielder, that he could try to steal a base whenever he thought he could. One day, when Chapman was thrown out at second and Gehrig followed with a home run, Ruth grumbled, "Somebody ought to tell that guy McCarthy base-stealing went out of style when Ty Cobb quit."[26] Ruth never respected McCarthy and continued to nourish his own managerial ambitions, but in 1932 the Babe generally kept those feelings to himself and had what turned out to be his last big season.

Second baseman Tony Lazzeri was a wholly different problem. Like Grover Cleveland Alexander, whom McCarthy had sent to St. Louis on waivers in 1926, Lazzeri was an epileptic, although the hard-hitting San Franciscan had nothing like Alexander's addiction to drink. Long before anticonvulsant medications, Lazzeri experienced frequent seizures, always in the morning, according to Ed Wells, and never during games. On train trips, Wells was assigned a seat across the aisle from Lazzeri, who told Wells that if he felt a seizure coming on, Wells was to put a wet towel on his forehead, hold his tongue down, and not get upset if his mouth began to foam; it would be over in four or five minutes. After Wells left the team, others would look after Lazzeri on trains, as would his roommates in hotels.

. . . . .

EARLY IN APRIL, in a full-page advertisement in the New York Times and other major daily newspapers, Walter P. Chrysler, president of the automobile company that bore his name, declared that the Depression had "made me THINK. And being forced to think, we have overcome many obstacles." The 1932 Plymouth—available for as little as $495, with a 65-horsepower engine, hydraulic brakes, and 112-inch wheelbase—was a product of Depression-born exigency. "In prosperous times," said Chrysler, "we could never have done it."[27] Later that month the board of governors of the Federal Reserve System issued a self-congratulatory announcement that in March the number of bank failures across the country had fallen to 45, from 122 in February and 342 in January.

If baseball ticket prices had seemed out of reach for many would-be customers the previous season, they were even more so in 1932 with the addition of a 10 percent federal amusements tax. At any rate, with the Yankees opening out of town in Philadelphia, the eight season inaugurals drew only 121,000, with the Yankees and Athletics playing before 16,000 in Shibe Park and no more than 7,000 showing up in St. Louis to watch the Cardinals begin defense of their World Series title. Things didn't improve with the second round of home openers: a month into the season, overall attendance was down about 45 percent from the same point in 1931. As the various indices of economic activity continued to worsen, so did baseball patronage. At season's end, big-league owners collectively had lost $1,201,000, for a loss margin of 15 percent.

Meanwhile, even with the spread of night ball, the minors continued to contract. Nineteen circuits started play; fourteen would finish out the season, with several teams disbanding within the leagues that survived. One of the few success stories that year was Columbus, Ohio, where Larry MacPhail raised the money for a new lighted ballpark that opened in June with Commissioner Landis on hand. Staging a variety of promotions and giveaways, MacPhail attracted a minors'-best 310,000 people to watch a second-place team stocked with Cardinals farmhands, including Dizzy Dean's younger brother, Paul.

As for Dizzy Dean himself, despite being hit hard in his Florida outings, he remained with the Cardinals and by midseason had established himself as a coming star. While injuries multiplied, nearly everybody slumped at bat, and the team sagged all the way to sixth place, twenty-one-year-old Dean won eighteen games and led the National League with 286 innings pitched and 191 strikeouts. Readily accepting his role as Gabby Street's workhorse, late in August he pitched two complete-game wins over New York within three days.

As the Cardinals fell out of the race early, the Giants fell even farther— all the way to last place by the beginning of June. On Thursday, June 2, at the age of fifty-nine, John McGraw ended his thirty-year reign as Giants manager and turned the team over to Bill Terry, with whom he hadn't exchanged words for months. Way overweight, worn down by travel and worry, and annually plagued by acute sinusitis from May to September, McGraw had actually been on the Giants' bench only about two-thirds of the time for the past seven or eight years. But especially in the New York press he was still venerated as the game's master manager. And despite his infirmities, he'd lost little of his combativeness—something he showed in May in the last of many memorable run-ins with Bill Klem, this one after Klem refused to call off a Giants–Reds game played in a downpour in Cincinnati. Under Terry the team managed to finish in a tie for sixth with the Cardinals.

With St. Louis and New York floundering, Pittsburgh, managed by former Pirates catcher George Gibson, led most of the season. Pittsburgh's pitching was only so-so, but the Waner brothers in the outfield, Pie Traynor at third base, and Floyd "Arky" Vaughan, a twenty-year-old rookie shortstop, all hit at least .318.[28]

Paul Waner, who'd already garnered one National League batting title and would win two more in the years ahead, collected 215 hits, for a .341 average. Older than his Oklahoma brother by three years, he was almost exactly the same size at 5 feet 8½ inches and 155 pounds. Contemporaries have remembered him as one of the biggest boozers in the league, but they've also named him as the best hitter they ever saw: a left-hander with steel-strong wrists who lined the ball in every direction. Said Giants center fielder Joe Moore of Paul Waner, "No telling what he would have done if he had taken care of himself."[29]

If Depression-induced roster pruning and salary cuts didn't actually make players more desperate, the times may have made them more contentious and truculent. In any case, the 1932 season featured what seemed to be an unusual number of player melees and also a legendary brawl involving an umpire and several players.

In mid-May, for example, Cincinnati shortstop Leo Durocher drew a three-day suspension for decking Dick Bartell, his Phillies counterpart, after Bartell tagged him harder than Durocher thought appropriate. Then on Independence Day, in Washington, D.C., Senators outfielder Carl Reynolds rammed into Yankees catcher Bill Dickey and scored a run that eventually ended Lefty Gomez's eleven-game winning streak. As Reynolds got to his feet and headed for the home team's dugout, Dickey swung a haymaker right, fracturing Reynolds's jaw in several places. American League president William Harridge slapped a $1,000 fine and thirty-day suspension on the catcher. Jacob Ruppert called that "excessive"; Joe McCarthy contended that Dickey had been the target of aggressive runners all season—

that he'd been knocked unconscious by Boston's Roy Johnson in one game and flattened by Washington's Heinie Manush in another.[30]

A month earlier, Harridge had had to deal with an even uglier episode at Cleveland's League Park. After the Indians beat the White Sox 12–6 in the opener of a Decoration Day doubleheader, Chicago manager Lew Fonseca and his players spatted with plate umpire George Moriarty all through the nightcap. When Moriarty wouldn't call a third strike on Earl Averill in the bottom of the ninth and Averill followed with a triple that won the game 12–11, several angry White Sox followed the umpire from the field down the tunnel leading to the locker rooms. Moriarty, a husky former Detroit infielder known for his quick temper and foul language, turned and challenged the players to fight him one at a time or all at once and then floored pitcher Milt Gaston with one punch. Whereupon Fonseca and catchers Charley Berry and Frank Grube threw him down and pummeled and kicked him until several Cleveland players intervened to stop the brawl. Treated at a local hospital for spike wounds, bruises, and a broken right hand, Moriarty was in no condition to umpire the next day.

Harridge went from his New York office to Cleveland to investigate the matter personally. After hearing from all sides, he reprimanded Moriarty and, despite Fonseca's insistence that Moriarty had cursed him and his players, fined the White Sox manager and Gaston $500 each, Berry $250, and Grube $100 and suspended coach Johnny Butler for ten days for his own bad language. As it turned out, the banged-up Moriarty would miss most of the rest of the season.

A few weeks later, Jersey City manager Charley Moore knocked out Newark manager Al Mamaux when the two got into a dispute during a game at Newark. Chicago Cubs rookie outfielder Marvin Gudat traded punches with Pittsburgh's Arky Vaughan, and Cubs shortstop Billy Jurges punched and tussled in the infield dirt with Brooklyn's Neal "Mickey" Finn. The *Sporting News* wasn't happy with all the diamond combat, observing that "in this season, more than in any season in several years, some players of the major leagues have been acting like mean and sour-tempered boys." Fred Lieb commented that he'd thought John McGraw's retirement broke "the last link between baseball as it was played in the gay 'nineties and today. . . . I apparently spoke too soon. We seem to be back in the baseball period of '95."[31]

Early in July, Billy Jurges encountered mayhem of a wholly different kind. The ballplayer had tried to break off a relationship with a young divorcée who danced and modeled under the name Violet Valli. After downing quite a lot of bootleg gin and writing a note in which she declared she didn't want to live and intended to "take Billy with me," she went to Jurges's room in his hotel near Wrigley Field, armed with a small revolver. As Jurges struggled with the woman, her pistol discharged three times, the bullets breaking her wrist, grazing his finger, and glancing off his ribs and exiting near his right shoulder. Jurges wouldn't press charges, and the Chicago police eventually dropped their own charge of attempted murder, but the shortstop was out of the lineup for three weeks.[32]

By the time Jurges was ready to play, Rogers Hornsby was on his way out as Cubs manager, and first baseman Charley Grimm, popular with teammates and fans, was about to take charge of the ball club. At that point, the National League race had become a four-team matter; by Sunday night, August 14, only four games separated Chicago, Pittsburgh, the Brooklyn Dodgers (as they were now again called), and the astonishing Phillies, who were finally getting a little decent pitching. Within a week, though, the Pirates, having lost seventeen of their last twenty games, had fallen into third place, while the Phillies also sagged out of contention. Charley Grimm's team, getting superb pitching from young Lon Warneke and veterans Guy Bush, Perce "Pat" Malone, and Charley Root, swept a three-game series from Brooklyn at Wrigley Field; the Dodgers' collapse continued with a doubleheader loss at St. Louis that put them eight and a half games behind Chicago.

Grimm's club ran up a fourteen-game winning streak before Dizzy Dean stopped them on August 31. Chicago sportswriters gave much of the credit for that surge to Mark Koenig, who'd been the regular shortstop for the champion 1926 to 1928 Yankees and then had drawn his release at Detroit and caught on in the Pacific Coast League. Purchased in mid-August from Los Angeles, Koenig took over from the light-hitting Jurges and batted .353 in thirty-three games.

While the Cubs were leaving behind the rest of the National League, Rogers Hornsby's gambling history—at least some of it—was making headlines. Prompted by a *Chicago Daily News* story that the ex-Chicago manager and his players had operated a horse-race betting pool, Commissioner Landis traveled first to Pittsburgh to talk with Bush, Malone, coach Charley O'Leary, and infielder and team captain Elwood "Woody" English and then to St. Louis for another conference with those men and with Hornsby, who resided in that city.

What Landis learned was what other newspapers had already reliably publicized: there had been no team betting pool, but Hornsby had borrowed heavily—up to about $12,000—from O'Leary and various players, who in some instances had also cosigned bank notes for him. Hornsby denied that his borrowings had been to cover gambling losses, but neither Landis nor anybody else was prepared to believe that story. Some of the money had been repaid; the remainder, according to what William Veeck and Hornsby had agreed to, would come out of the $17,000 the club still owed Hornsby on his twelve-month manager's contract. That apparently satisfied Landis. Hornsby was no longer Cubs manager, his creditors would get their money back, and that was that.

In September the Pirates righted themselves, but by then it was too late. Winning thirty-seven of fifty-five games under Grimm's leadership, the Cubs clinched the pennant on September 20 with a 5–2 victory over Pittsburgh in the first game of a Wrigley Field doubleheader. Before an overflow crowd in misting rain, Bush won his nineteenth decision on a three-run triple by outfielder Hazen "Kiki" Cuyler. The game was played in an hour and twenty-one minutes.

The Cubs finished with a record of 90–64, four games better than Pittsburgh. They weren't a great ball club, but they did have five future Hall of Famers: rookie second baseman Billy Herman, who made 216 hits and batted .314, plus Cuyler, Gabby Hartnett, infielder Stan Hack, and Burleigh Grimes (although the old spitballer could do no better than a 6–11 record in 1932).

As usual, the American League didn't offer much of a pennant race. With the stalwart threesome of Grove, Earnshaw, and Walberg combining for sixty-one victories; Al Simmons having another productive year (.322, thirty-five home runs, 151 RBIs); and Jimmie Foxx coming within two homers of Ruth's record sixty besides batting .364 and driving in 169 runs, the Athletics won ninety-four games. In many seasons that would have been enough, but this year the Yankees were unstoppable. In breaking Philadelphia's three-year American League reign, New York won 107 games and, despite losing Bill Dickey for a month, had little to worry about after July. Joe McCarthy thus became the first man to direct pennant winners in both major leagues.

Lefty Gomez compiled a 24–7 record; Red Ruffing won eighteen; George Pipgras posted sixteen; and Johnny Allen, a young, hot-tempered, jut-jawed right-hander, won seventeen while losing only four. (Once asked if he would knock down his own grandmother, Allen replied, "No, but I wouldn't give her a good ball to hit.")[33] Ruth batted .341, homered forty-one times, drove in 137 runs—and then scared everybody by having an appendicitis attack in mid-September. (Briefly hospitalized in New York, the Babe rejoined the team in Philadelphia for a season-closing series.)

Tony Lazzeri, whom the Yankees seemed to want to replace every spring, batted in 115 runs, and Ben Chapman drove home 107 more, while Lou Gehrig hit .341 and had 151 RBIs.

Of Gehrig's thirty-four homers, four were struck consecutively on June 2 at Shibe Park, in a twenty-run assault on Connie Mack's pitchers. That hadn't been done since 1894, but in what had become something of a leitmotiv in Gehrig's career, somebody—usually Ruth—always seemed to be upstaging him. In this case it was John McGraw, whose resignation dominated the sports pages the next day.

Washington finished a strong third, only a game behind Philadelphia, and had the majors' top winner in Alvin Crowder, with twenty-six. Walter Johnson, who in his long career had won more decisions than anybody besides Cy Young, was universally esteemed as a person, but after fifth-, second-, third-, and third-place finishes, some people questioned his managerial worthiness. "He was a nice guy," remembered Monte Weaver, himself a twenty-two-game winner for the Senators in 1932, "Everybody liked him. But he didn't seem to be in the game. He wouldn't think ahead. Situations would come up and he wouldn't be ready for them."[34]

Cleveland ended up fourth, nineteen games out of first. The Indians' season wouldn't have been particularly notable except for their debut in the city's enormous new stadium on the Lake Erie shore on Sunday, July 31. Financed through a bond issue approved by local voters in a futile effort to attract the 1932 Olympic Games, the stadium saddled the city with heavy debt at the worst time. But it was the nation's first publicly financed, multipurpose facility intended to accommodate baseball as well as other attractions. After New York's Empire State Building and Rockefeller Center, it was possibly the most imposing structure going up in the early Depression years.

On that Sunday afternoon, a paying crowd of 76,979 and a thousand or more guests—including Landis, both league presidents, Ohio governor George White, and Cleveland mayor Ray Miller—saw a brilliant pitchers' duel between Philadelphia's Lefty Grove and Cleveland's Mel Harder. In the eighth inning, Mickey Cochrane singled in Max Bishop for the game's only run. The Indians played the rest of their 1932 home games at Lakefront Stadium and then renewed their lease for 1933.[35]

. . . . .

AT YANKEE STADIUM, now baseball's second-biggest venue, only 41,450 were present on September 28 for the World Series opener. Joe Vila of the

New York Sun attributed the disappointing turnout to Landis's edict that, as in the past, reserved seats had to be sold in three-game strips. Commented Vila, "Times have been such around here this year that not many people are in a position to lay out $16.50 or $19.80 on the line and think nothing of it."[36] Those on hand, though, could now identify the Cubs players by the numbers on their backs—an innovation that National League club officials had finally agreed to in midsummer.

Two-to-one favorites with bookmakers, the Yankees went into the Series both confident of themselves and carrying a grudge against the Cubs. That Charley Grimm and his players hadn't voted any part of their Series money to Hornsby concerned the Yankees not at all, but that they'd voted only a one-third share to Mark Koenig—without whom, many believed, the Cubs wouldn't have made it into the Series—roused the ire of Ruth and other former teammates of Koenig. "Cheapskates," "tightwads," and "nickel nursers" were among the more gentle aspersions the Yankees used on their opponents, who came back with jibes about Ruth's girth and physiognomy, Gomez's and Lazzeri's ancestry, and whatever else came to mind. The two teams may have set something of a record (at least up to then) for sheer volume of dugout billingsgate.

If any of that fazed anybody, it must have been the Cubs. The Yankees won in four games, an outcome that was immensely satisfying for Joe McCarthy, who found himself with little to do but make out the lineup cards, order an occasional pitching change, and watch his men batter Chicago's pitchers, starting with Guy Bush. Nicknamed "Mississippi Mudcat" but also known as an off-field fashion plate, Bush retired the first nine Yankees and took a 2–0 lead into the fourth inning, when Gehrig unloaded a three-run homer. Bush and then Grimes gave up nine more runs, while Ruffing yielded ten hits but struck out a like number and coasted in, 12–6. The next day about 51,000 were present as both Gomez and Warneke went the distance. The Cubs got runs in the first and third, but Gomez shut them down the rest of the way, while the Yankees reached Warneke for two runs in the first, two more in the third, and another in the fifth.

Game three, in Chicago two days later, took place before a capacity gathering of nearly 50,000, including 10,000 sitting in temporary bleachers built above the regular bleachers in right and left field. Sharing a field box with Chicago mayor Anton Cermak was New York governor Franklin D. Roosevelt, who was campaigning in the Midwest as the Democratic Party's presidential candidate. Supported by his son James's arm, the smiling, paraplegic Roosevelt stood and tossed out the first ball. (The following February, in Miami, Cermak would be fatally wounded by an assassin's bullet intended for president-elect Roosevelt.)

The game Roosevelt witnessed would go down in baseball legend. In the first inning Ruth hit a two-run homer, and Gehrig followed with another; then Kiki Cuyler hit a two-run shot off Pipgras in the third to tie the game at 4–4. When Ruth again faced starter Charley Root in the fifth, spectators threw lemons onto the field, and the Cubs yelled insults and obscenities from the third-base dugout. What happened then became a matter of endless dispute and a central ingredient in the mixture of Ruthian fact and folklore that would long outlive the Babe.

Most of the accounts seem to agree that after taking two balls and two called strikes, Ruth held up or waved two fingers at the Cubs dugout to indicate that he still had a strike coming. But whether the Babe then "called his shot" by actually pointing to center field, whether he pointed at Root himself, or whether, as he said years later, he just "waved to the fence" and "didn't point to any particular spot," he sent Root's next pitch on a great soaring arc to the base of the flagpole in the open area between the end of the right-field bleachers and the big scoreboard in center.[37]

As he neared third base in his characteristically mincing trot, the grinning Ruth gestured with both hands for the Cubs to sit down and shut up. Which is pretty much what they did, especially after Gehrig followed Ruth's blast with a rising line-drive homer of his own that landed in the upper bleachers in right field.

That was all for Root, who was succeeded by Pat Malone and later two more Cubs pitchers. Another Yankees run in the ninth made it 7–4; in the bottom of the inning, after Gabby Hartnett hit one of Pipgras's pitches into the left-field bleachers, Herb Pennock came in to retire the next three Cubs without further damage. Afterward, in the clubhouse, Ruth acknowledged that a pretty stiff wind, blowing across the diamond toward right field, "was with us, that's all." But he added, "Boy, I'd like to have just one season playing in this park. I'd hit a million."[38]

Taciturn Tony Lazzeri might have wished for the same thing, because the next day he homered twice and drove in four runs in a 13–6 rout, as the Yankees completed their third sweep in their last three Series appearances. The Cubs drove out Johnny Allen with four first-inning runs, but Wilcey Moore and Pennock held them to two runs from then on, while center fielder Earle Combs also homered, and the Yankees scored eight times over the last three innings. Bush lasted only one-third of an inning; he and four successors surrendered nineteen hits. For the Series as a whole, the Yankees batted .313, hit a record eight home runs, and made thirty-seven runs on forty-five hits. It was also a very loosely played Series, with the Yankees committing eight errors, and the Cubs, six.

In the winners' locker room, coach Art Fletcher led the players in singing "The Sidewalks of New York," and, despite the swelling in his right arm where Bush had plunked him in the first inning, Ruth roared with pleasure over the beating that he and his mates had given the Chicago tightwads. While the Cubs took home $4,245 apiece, the Yankees split their portion of Series receipts into twenty-six shares; each player plus McCarthy and his two coaches came out with $5,011.

On the Twentieth Century Limited back to New York, the Yankees celebrated with champagne or whatever other illegal beverages they favored. While the popular black tap dancer Bill Robinson, a dedicated Yankees fan, did his steps in the Pullman aisles, Ruth, clad only in a blanket, led his teammates in a pajama-tearing ritual that included an assault on the dignified Ruppert. Lefty Gomez was about to marry June Schwarz, who, under the stage name June O'Dea, danced and sang in the Gershwins' long-running Broadway musical *Of Thee I Sing*; Bill Dickey would wed Violet Arnold, another New York showgirl. Both Gomez, only twenty-two, and Dickey, twenty-five, could anticipate long careers with the Yankees and several more World Series checks.

· · · · ·

BUT FOR Al Simmons, Jimmy Dykes, and center fielder George "Mule" Haas—all key men in the Athletics' three-year reign at the top of the American League—whatever they achieved from here on would be in new surroundings. While the Yankees were demolishing the Cubs, long-suffering South Side Chicago fans were surprised and buoyed by the news that Connie Mack had sold the threesome to the White Sox for $100,000 in cash. With a 1932 home attendance of only 405,500—less than half what it had been three years earlier—Mack and his associates saw no alternative than to dispose of high-salaried players for indispensable operating cash.

That Mack had started to break up the second great team he'd put together, sustained through three championships, and paid well was one of the most telling consequences of the Great Depression for the National Pastime. But if the times were hard, the worst was yet to come—for baseball and the rest of American society.

CHAPTER 4

The Leanest Year, 1933

I N 1932 nobody in the major leagues except the two pennant winners
had made any money. The Chicago Cubs' 990,000 led the majors in attendance, although that was a drop of more than 500,000 from 1930.
The St. Louis Cardinals, who'd won everything the previous October, drew
some 333,000—only 20,000 or so more than what their Columbus farm
club, under Larry MacPhail's direction, was able to attract. Again led by
Chuck Klein (.348, thirty-eight homers, 137 RBIs), the Philadelphia Phillies
topped the majors in team batting average and the National League in runs
and soared to fourth place, their best showing in many years. Yet they
enticed little more than 206,000 people into little Baker Bowl. Even those
figures would have looked good to Phil Ball, sole owner but co-occupant
of Sportsman's Park, whose 1932 St. Louis Browns played at home before
a grand total of 82,000—give or take a few hundred.

In Washington, D.C., Clark Griffith saved some money by firing Walter
Johnson and, as he'd done eight years earlier, naming a "boy manager." In
1924 it had been Stanley "Bucky" Harris, a twenty-seven-year-old second
baseman who led the Senators to back-to-back pennants. Now Griffith
turned to Joe Cronin, his hard-hitting shortstop, timing the announcement
for Cronin's twenty-sixth birthday on October 12. Already a five-year American Leaguer, the broad-shouldered San Franciscan would never be more
than a passable shortstop, but he was one of the top run producers ever to
play the position, with 368 runs batted in over the past three seasons. Young
Cronin didn't see anything particularly complex about his new duties.

"All a manager can do is keep his players hustling," he said. "Any player able to get into the majors knows what it's all about."[1]

Cleveland business manager Billy Evans put the average annual cost of operating a major-league team at $535,000, with at least $235,000 of that going for players' salaries. Spring-training costs ran to about $10,000; rail transportation, hotel rooms (usually $5 per night for doubles), and meals (usually $3.50 to $4.00 per player per day), another $30,000; scouting expenses, $50,000; and purchases of new players, $50,000. Evans estimated that a team would have to draw 500,000 at home and another 500,000 on the road to break even. But in 1932, while the Yankees had still turned a profit, Evans put the losses of the other seven American League franchises at $50,000 to $150,000.

Losses in the minors had been heavy as well; night baseball hadn't been enough to save many teams in the lower-classification leagues, nor had resorting to such attractions as raffles, beauty pageants, chicken chases, and cow-milking contests. The three AA leagues remained intact at the end of the 1932 season, and a few franchises, such as Columbus and Newark, had drawn well, but overall it had been another bad year for the minors.

In December, at the National Association's convention in Columbus, President William G. Bramham again urged economy. The delegates voted to reduce Class AA rosters from twenty to eighteen, Class A rosters from eighteen to sixteen, B and C rosters from seventeen to fifteen, and D rosters from sixteen to fourteen. At the urging of Pacific Coast League owners, AA clubs would have no mandatory salary limits. Class A, though, would observe a monthly maximum of $2,450; B teams, $2,000; C teams, $1,800; and D teams, $1,500.

Branch Rickey continued to pick up franchises here and there for his farm system, but other majors clubs were backing off minor-league affiliations in the belief that they cost more than they were worth. Cleveland, for example, ended its working agreement with Toledo (American Association), Brooklyn cut its brief connection with Jersey City (International League), and the Cubs were content for Reading to be dropped from the International League and not to seek another top-minors tie-up.

"The overhead must come down," pronounced the Cardinals' Sam Breadon. "Club owners, in view of the times, realize that something must be done to give us all a chance to break even. This means still greater reductions in the pay of players than was the case [for] 1932." But when Jacob Ruppert was asked whether the prosperous Yankees might not help the weaker clubs, he replied imperiously, "I found out a long time ago that there is no charity in baseball, and that every club owner must make his own fight for existence."[2]

Although Breadon's proposal for twenty-man rosters wasn't adopted at the majors' winter meetings, both leagues voted to move back the date on which teams had to reach the twenty-three-man limit from June 15 to May 15, thereby saving a month's pay for several players per club. Salary trimming and the sale or trade of higher-paid players continued, so that by the start of the season the average major-leaguer's annual pay was $6,500, down a full $1,000 from three years earlier. After much public complaining, Babe Ruth finally signed for $52,000, taking a whopping $23,000 cut; Lou Gehrig, at the peak of his marvelously consistent career, quietly accepted a reduction from $25,000 to $22,000. Although Hack Wilson had staged a considerable comeback the previous season with Brooklyn, for 1933 he was offered $11,000—and eventually he took it.

Most teams also reduced or eliminated altogether their coaching staffs. The Browns, Cardinals, Detroit, White Sox, Cubs, Cincinnati, and even Yankees each dropped a coach, which in the case of the White Sox and Reds meant that Lew Fonseca and Donie Bush, respectively, would have to get along with no assistants at all. At the same time, William Benswanger, who'd succeeded the late Barney Dreyfuss as Pittsburgh president, gave a sinecure coaching job and later organized a series of benefits for fifty-nine-year-old John "Honus" Wagner, eight-time National League batting champion and the greatest player in the franchise's history. With his Pittsburgh sporting-goods store in receivership, Wagner had become almost destitute.

The foremost player transactions of the off-season had outfielder Goose Goslin returning to Washington from the Browns in exchange for outfielders Carl Reynolds and Sammy West; Jim Bottomley moving from the Cardinals to Cincinnati for a couple of players (and taking a $5,000 pay cut); and, for four benchwarmers sent to Cincinnati, Babe Herman joining the Cubs, who sought more batting punch after totaling only sixty-nine homers in 1932. Fred Lindstrom, who thought that he rather than Bill Terry should have succeeded John McGraw as Giants manager, asked to be traded. Lindstrom went to Pittsburgh as part of a general housecleaning by which Terry got rid of fourteen of the twenty-three men on the 1932 New York roster.

Two big-league franchises changed hands as well. Gerald Nugent purchased a majority interest in the Philadelphia Phillies from William Baker's heirs, and Thomas A. Yawkey bought the Boston Red Sox from Robert Quinn and associates, with Eddie Collins leaving his Athletics coaching job to become Red Sox business manager and Yawkey's junior partner. A graduate of Yale University and Sheffield Scientific School, Yawkey had just turned thirty and come into the balance of a fortune of about $8 million—based in mining, timber, and paper mills—inherited from his adoptive parents. He also inherited a debt-ridden franchise, a last-place team that in 1932 had finished sixty-four games out of first, and a ballpark in disrepair.

. . . . .

EARLY IN MARCH 1933, as the annual rites of spring training began from southern Florida to California, the contingents of players, managers, coaches, sportswriters, and fellow travelers all found themselves directly and immediately affected by the most critical development yet in the on-going financial crisis. On a chilly and overcast Saturday, March 4, Franklin D. Roosevelt took the presidential oath of office in the midst of an almost complete breakdown of the nation's banking and currency system. The next day he called the Congress into special session and the day after that, stretching constitutional authority to the limit and beyond, issued an executive order closing all banks for the next four days and ordering citizens to turn in to the Treasury Department all their gold coins, notes, and certificates.

The "bank holiday" left millions of people suddenly with little, if any, ready cash. At St. Petersburg, covering the Yankees, Rud Rennie of the *New York Herald-Tribune* had $8.75 to live on—for how long he didn't know. In Tampa, Sidney Weill received telegrams from Reds players in Arizona, Texas, and Massachusetts explaining that with their funds stuck in closed banks, they hadn't been able to join the team. Within four days, however, most banks affiliated with the Federal Reserve System had reopened; within six weeks, three-fourths of all banks that had survived the Depression were certified as sound and back in business.

As the great banking crisis came and passed, natural disaster hit southern California and especially Long Beach, killing at least 110 people and doing damage estimated at $50 million. At Wrigley Field in Los Angeles, where the Giants were again training, the grandstand swayed and the ground shuddered at intervals during an exhibition game with the Cubs. A couple of nights later, when the players were shaken out of their beds at the Biltmore Hotel by another trembler, Bill Terry threatened to move his team out of the area, although he soon calmed down along with the elements and the Giants finished their scheduled stay.

By the time the season opened, the Congress had effectively ended the thirteen-year experiment with nationwide prohibition by passing what was popularly called the Beer Act, which sanctioned beverages up to 3.2 percent alcohol content in all the states (but not the District of Columbia). The Congress had already submitted a constitutional amendment to repeal the federal ban on liquor and return the question to the states; by December 5, 1933, the necessary three-fourths of the states had ratified the Twenty-First Amendment. Roosevelt had been elected on a platform calling for prohibition repeal; the Depression, by shriveling tax revenues, had given repeal advocates the powerful argument that legalizing and then taxing liquor would substantially boost both employment and government income at all levels.

Although repeal proved disappointing on both counts, on April 11 and 12, 1933, beer was sold in major-league ballparks for the first time since October 1919, except in Washington, Philadelphia, and Pittsburgh. (Of course, Yankee Stadium, opened in 1923, had never had beer sales, nor for that matter had Cleveland's big stadium.) Thus the historic connection between beer and baseball was again legitimized, if not yet made wholly respectable.

That spring, as the Yankees played their way circuitously northward from St. Petersburg, the pall of the Depression hung over everything. Rud Rennie remembered that "we came home . . . through Southern cities which looked as tho they had been ravaged by an invisible enemy. People seemed to be hiding. They even would not come to see Babe Ruth and Lou Gehrig. They simply did not have the money to waste on baseball games or amusements." Once the season began, "all over the major-league baseball circuits one saw stores for rent, silent shops, idle factories, half-empty hotels, and slim crowds in the ball-parks, night-clubs, and places of amusement."[3]

The *Sporting News* thought baseball's ills had less to do with the Depression than with the game itself. Apparently having forgotten the brawls of the past season, the trade weekly editorialized that baseball could do much to bring people back to the ballparks by promoting more aggressive play, such as one saw at college football games. Overbearing umpires had forced on players a "pink-tea brand" of baseball, a lack of enthusiasm among fans, and "the absence of spirit among the players. Restoration of the old fire would help a lot." Or, as *Baseball Magazine* put it six months later, "There is an element of wholesome roughness about the national game which should not be suppressed." John Heydler seemed to agree. "Action and hustle, and still more action and hustle, are needed," he declared in an unprecedented directive to all National League teams just before the opening games. The coming season, he added, would "put to the acid test the popularity of our national game and directly affect your livelihood as a player."[4]

· · · · ·

AVERAGE ATTENDANCE for the first eight home openers was 19,191, which, with the Yankees opening at home, was an increase of a couple of thousand from a year earlier. It was an obvious sign of the hard times that the Yankee Stadium bleachers, filled with 20,000 fifty-cent customers, accounted for half the opening-day crowd. At Fenway Park, in Boston, however, another 20,000, the biggest opening-day turnout in nine years, came to see if the Red Sox would be any better under their new ownership. (In fact, they were, improving by twenty games and featuring the league's batting champion in first baseman Dale Alexander, but still finishing seventh, ahead of only the hapless Browns.)

A mixture of young players and veterans, the Yankees were favored to return to the World Series. Lazzeri, Dickey, and Chapman had solid seasons, while Gehrig was only a little off his 1932 performance—despite having to worry about reconciling his doting, overbearing mother to his engagement and impending marriage to Eleanor Twitchell of Chicago. But Lefty Gomez lost game after game one way or another and ended with an abysmal 9–14 record; only the St. Louis and Chicago pitching staffs allowed more earned runs within the league.

Ruth—who at age thirty-eight reported overweight at 232 pounds and was out of the lineup a good deal of the time with various complaints— batted .301 in 459 official times at bat, hit thirty-four home runs, and drove in 103 runs. Those may have been solid numbers by most players' standards, but they were a sizable letdown for the Babe. On the Yankees' last western trip, he batted only .167 and was, as described by Marshall Hunt of the *New York Daily News*, "a pathetic, starched figure in the outfield."[5] On the last day of the season, however, Ruth again demonstrated why he was the most talented all-around athlete in the game's history. As he'd done to close the 1930 season, the man who was once the American League's premier left-hander entertained the Yankee Stadium faithful by pitching a complete-game victory over Boston.

The Philadelphia Athletics, the other dominant team over the past eight years, won only five games more than they lost and dropped to third place.

That happened even though Jimmie Foxx led the league in batting (.356), home runs (forty-eight), and runs batted in (163) and Lefty Grove led the majors with twenty-four victories, including an August 2 shutout that ended the Yankees' streak of 308 games without being held scoreless. But Mack's team missed the big bat of Al Simmons (who complained throughout his first season in Chicago about having to hit in the bigger distances of Comiskey Park, although he batted .331 and drove in 119 runs), while Rube Walberg and George Earnshaw went into sharp decline. After winning nineteen games in 1932 and seeing his salary cut from $17,500 to $6,500, Earnshaw reported overweight and never got into playing shape. Mack sent him home from Detroit and then later fined him $500 and suspended him "for reporting at the park today in no condition to play ball."[6] If Mack needed an excuse for getting rid of Earnshaw after the season, the big pitcher had given it to him.

Under Walter Johnson, Washington had been no more than a respectable also-ran. But in June 1933, as the hitherto-unemployed Johnson succeeded Roger Peckinpaugh as Cleveland manager, his old ball club won fifteen of sixteen games and took over first place from New York. There they stayed, clinching the American League pennant on September 21 before a weekday home crowd of 20,000, when Walter Stewart outpitched the Browns' Irwin "Bump" Hadley, 2–1. After the clubhouse merrymaking, bachelor Joe Cronin donned his street clothes and dashed across the field, trailed by a posse of adoring women. Expecting to find his automobile waiting behind a door in the right-field fence, the Senators' young manager found nothing, ran to the center-field fence and through another door, finally reached his automobile on Fifth Avenue, and sped away from his female pursuers.

Throughout the season Cronin led by example, batting .309 and driving in 116 runs. He hit only five homers, and the whole team only sixty, but the Senators led the majors with a .287 batting average and were second to the Yankees in runs scored. Right-hander Alvin Crowder won twenty-four games; left-hander Earl Whitehill (known almost as much for his darkly handsome looks as for his pitching ability) won twenty-two. Used by Cronin almost exclusively in relief, Jack Russell came out of the bullpen on forty-seven occasions, saving thirteen games and winning twelve for himself.

Bad blood between the Senators and the Yankees carried over from the Dickey–Reynolds affair of the previous season. At Griffith Stadium on April 23, with the Yankees already ahead 16–0, Ben Chapman slid into second

baseman Charles "Buddy" Myer with spikes high; they scuffled, both were
ejected, and when Chapman left the field through the Washington dugout
(entrance and egress for both teams), he and Whitehill got into another
fight. American League president Harridge hit Chapman, Whitehill, and
Myer with five-day suspensions and $100 fines. From then on, Washington–
New York relations remained hostile, although the Senators also had trouble in Detroit, where Whitlow Wyatt hit Myer with a pitch and put him in
a local hospital.

Late in May the Philadelphia Phillies, with Chuck Klein on his way to
another outstanding year, were surprise leaders in the National League,
but that wasn't expected to last and didn't. Hardly anybody thought that
Bill Terry's rebuilt Giants had any pennant prospects, especially after a pitch
broke Terry's right wrist two weeks into the season. Sam Leslie filled in for
Terry until he was traded to Brooklyn in mid-June for Watson Clark, a
twenty-game winner in 1932, and Lefty O'Doul, the reigning National
League batting titlist. O'Doul contributed some timely hits in part-time
duty, and although Clark was ineffective, the remainder of the Giants' staff
turned out to be so good that his help wasn't needed.

Giants pitchers had a collective earned run average of 2.71, the lowest
in either league since 1919. Young Hal Schumacher posted nineteen wins;
veteran Fred Fitzsimmons, sixteen; and Roy "Tarzan" Parmelee, thirteen.
Terry's ace was Carl Hubbell, a bony left-hander from Oklahoma who at
age thirty, in his sixth big-league season, emerged as one of the premier
hurlers in the game's history. Hubbell possessed excellent control, a respectable fast ball and curve, and a baffling "screwball," which he threw
with an inward wrist snap that caused the ball to break opposite to the arc
of a curve. In 1933 he won twenty-three games, lost twelve, saved five more,
and averaged a meager 1.66 runs per nine innings.

Hubbell also pitched ten shutouts and in one stretch didn't allow a run
for forty-five innings. On July 2, in the first game of a doubleheader at the
Polo Grounds, he and St. Louis's James "Tex" Carleton dueled for sixteen
scoreless frames. After Carleton retired, Hubbell blanked the Cardinals for
two more innings, while the Giants finally put across a run in the top of
the eighteenth. (The nightcap was another 1–0 classic, Parmelee besting
Dizzy Dean.) Once asked how he'd lasted through that and other marathon
outings (such as a seventeen-inning loss to Parmelee, by then with St. Louis,
three years later), Hubbell noted simply, "When you're in a game, there's
a sort of nervous energy which keeps you going all the way."[7]

Much of the credit for the Giants' superb pitching went to catcher

Gus Mancuso, a smart, agile Houstonian obtained in the off-season from St. Louis. But aside from their mound staff, the Giants weren't a memorable ball club. Although they led the National League with eighty-two homers, that was the smallest power output for a Polo Grounds–based team in seven years. Terry returned to the lineup in July and batted .322, but hit only six homers; Mel Ott led the club with twenty-three, but struggled to bat .283. Although the Giants lacked speed, trailing the majors with thirty-one stolen bases, they played sound defense and, in something of a throwback to the dead-ball era, used sacrifice bunts and hit-and-run plays to good effect.

Terry was generally popular with his players but had little time for journalists (especially the rare female of the species) or anybody else hanging around the team. A onetime minor-league pitcher who'd reluctantly given up a full-time office job with Standard Oil to reenter professional baseball, Terry was a solid family man, reserved and colorless (except during eruptions with umpires)—quite unlike the volatile, domineering John McGraw. Whereas McGraw had tried to control everything his players did both on and off the field, Terry held a loose rein and, as Harry Danning later put it, "let us play and we learned from that and got better." (Terry was also a fussy dresser. Edward F. Doyle worked for a Philadelphia tailor named Twer, who pressed suits for visiting players during games at Baker Bowl. Doyle remembered that Terry's suit "was never pressed to his satisfaction, and Mr. Twer invariably had to press it again for nothing.")[8]

Most observers considered the whole Giants team to be every bit as colorless as their leader—"the say-littlest club that ever won a pennant," cracked Dan Daniel of the *New York World-Telegram*.[9] (As if to commemorate the passing of the roistering old-time ballplayer he'd portrayed in his fiction, Ring Lardner died in late September at East Hampton, Long Island, at the age of forty-eight.)

The Giants were in first place for the last 123 days of the 1933 season. On September 19, during a game in St. Louis, New York sportswriters traveling with the team signaled from the press box that Pittsburgh had lost at Philadelphia, giving Terry's club the pennant. At 91–61, they finished four games ahead of the Pirates, six ahead of the disappointing Cubs, and nine and nine and a half ahead of Boston and St. Louis, respectively. The day after clinching in St. Louis, the Giants found a crowd estimated at 10,000 waiting to greet them at Grand Central Terminal, and the day after that they rode in a parade from city hall to the Polo Grounds.

Aside from the Giants themselves, the league's most surprising team was the Boston Braves. Managed by wizened Bill McKechnie, who'd directed pennant winners at Pittsburgh in 1924 and St. Louis in 1928, the Braves were actually serious pennant contenders until the Giants entered Braves Field at the beginning of September. A swarming overflow of more than 50,000 on Saturday, September 2, was the biggest turnout that had ever come to Braves Field—or ever would. Hubbell and Fitzsimmons downed the locals in both games; New York went on to take four of five decisions with one tie, thereby quashing the hopes of Boston's long-unrequited National League fandom.

The Cardinals went through another frustrating season. Rogers Hornsby, signed to a $15,000 player's contract the previous fall, was supposed to bring a formidable bat to their lineup, but the "Rajah," as St. Louis writers had dubbed him years earlier, could no longer do the job in the field. In May, after Branch Rickey traded Paul Derringer to Cincinnati for Leo Durocher, a light-hitting but combative and slick-fielding shortstop, Frank Frisch could move from shortstop back to second base, and Hornsby found himself relegated to pinch-hitting duties.

Gabby Street may have worried that Hornsby wanted to manage the Cardinals, despite Hornsby's insistence that he would "dig ditches before I'll take that job."[10] But with the Cardinals in sixth place on July 24, it was Frisch whom Sam Breadon and Rickey picked to replace Street, making the announcement between games of a doubleheader. Two days after that, with Branch Rickey acting as intermediary, Hornsby signed a three-year contract with Phil Ball to manage the St. Louis Browns.

From his home in Joplin, Missouri, Street unloaded his resentments over what had happened at St. Louis. Frisch, Street complained, had been a demoralizing influence all through the 1932 season. He'd urged Breadon to lay a heavy fine on Frisch, but the Cardinals' owner replied that he was afraid Frisch would quit the team, as in fact he'd done with the Giants in 1926 after a tongue-lashing by John McGraw. When Breadon "refused to back me up," said Street, Frisch "had me where he wanted me and he could do as he pleased." When told of Street's accusations, Frisch's only comment was, "The old buck must have gone goofy."[11]

Frisch—who signed as manager under a standard player's contract that obliged Breadon to give him only ten days' notice of his termination—was in for plenty of personnel troubles of his own, especially with Dizzy Dean. With considerable justification, Dean already believed himself the finest pitcher in the history of the St. Louis franchise. During the 1933 season he won twenty games, and while he also lost eighteen he led the league with 199 strikeouts, logged a 3.04 earned run average, and on July 30 struck out seventeen Chicago Cubs—a new big-league record.

At least in and around St. Louis, Dean had become a major celebrity—known to people of all classes and types. One evening in July, he entered a pharmacy near his hotel and found himself looking down the barrel of a pistol held by one man; another man kept a clerk at gunpoint while he rifled the cash register. After they cleared out, a somewhat shaken Dean returned to his hotel, where a few mornings later he received a telephone call from a man who identified himself as one of the pair who'd robbed the pharmacy. The robber wanted to assure Dean that it hadn't been anything personal and told the pitcher that to make sure there wouldn't be any hard feelings, he was having a half-dozen new neckties sent over to Dean's hotel.

But Dean also had a quick temper and the idea that he ought to be able to do pretty much as he pleased. In Cincinnati he had angry words and tussled with Paul Derringer (before Derringer was traded to the Reds) until Dazzy Vance (obtained the previous February from Brooklyn) broke things up by sitting on both combatants. Later in the season, Dean drew a $100 fine for passing up an exhibition game in Elmira, New York, and choosing instead to travel with the pitchers and catchers en route from New York to begin a series in Pittsburgh. Great days were ahead for Dean, as well as quite a lot of Dean-related headaches for Frank Frisch.

. . . . .

AT TWENTY-TWO, Dean was one of eighteen National Leaguers and a like number of American Leaguers chosen by popular balloting—with the ballots made available in newspapers, ballparks, and other places—to participate in a midseason all-star game at Comiskey Park, Chicago. Arch Ward, sports editor of the *Chicago Tribune*, had hatched the idea of having elected teams from the two leagues play a game that would be a feature of the Century of Progress Exhibition, which Chicago's business and financial leaders had determined to launch despite the prevailing hard times. Proceeds from the game would help fund a charity for indigent old ballplayers. Ward first sold the plan to American League president William Harridge, who in turn convinced a skeptical Commissioner Landis to give it his sanction.

The *Tribune* named Connie Mack and John McGraw to manage the two teams. The game was set for Thursday, July 6, an off day in the schedule, with no accommodation for travel time before or afterward. Thus most of the players had to finish a game on Wednesday, then catch a late-afternoon train to get to Chicago, and then catch another train to wherever their teams were playing on Friday. For their troubles, they received only expense money.

Some 49,000 people, producing $51,000 in net revenue for the players' charity, nearly filled Comiskey Park. Before the game the tall, thin Mack and the short, rotund McGraw—veterans of countless diamond struggles, including three World Series matchups with each other—posed obligingly for hordes of photographers. At seventy, Mack had managed his last pennant winner; at sixty, McGraw had only eight months to live.

Played in bright sunshine and ninety-degree heat, the game lived up to expectations. In what was really his last big moment in the national spotlight, Ruth tagged Bill Hallahan for a two-run homer into the right-field upper deck to put the Americans ahead 3–0 at the end of three innings. In the sixth the Nationals' Lon Warneke scored on an infield out, and Frisch followed with a homer to make it 3–2; then Earl Averill touched Warneke for a single in the bottom of that inning, scoring Joe Cronin. Hubbell and Lefty Grove held the opposition scoreless the rest of the way. Fittingly, Ruth saved the game for the Americans when he ran back and leaped against the right-field wall to take Chick Hafey's drive. Afterward, while players from both teams sought autographs from the two managers, McGraw called it "a splendid game" and praised Ruth: "He was marvelous. That old boy certainly came through when they needed him."[12]

Originally intended as a one-time-only spectacle showcasing the best talent in the two leagues, Arch Ward's invention proved such a success both financially and artistically that both baseball writers and fans around the country expected it to become an annual event. Despite the early complaints of some club owners and a few players, that was what it would become: an annual midsummer baseball extravaganza scheduled during a three-day break in the regular schedule.[13]

. . . . .

IF THE WORLD SERIES remained unrivaled as the nation's foremost sports attraction, that of 1933, pairing two distinctly unglamorous ball clubs in the worst year of the Great Depression, appeared to excite considerably less than the usual interest. No Series game was a sellout, even though the Giants made grandstand and field-box tickets available on a game-by-game basis rather than in the usual strips of three. On October 3, a Polo Grounds crowd of 46,672—about 7,000 short of capacity—saw the Giants win the Series opener 4–2. Hubbell threw a five-hitter and struck out ten; Ott made four hits, including a homer, and drove in three runs; and Buddy Myer helped the Giants with three errors. Left-hander Walter Stewart was the loser. The next day, only 35,461 were on hand to watch Hal Schumacher again hold the Senators to only five hits. The Giants scored six times in the sixth inning off Alvin Crowder, the key hit being a two-run pinch-hit single by Lefty O'Doul. Washington's only run came on Goose Goslin's third-inning homer.

President Roosevelt—driven onto the field through the right-field gate and then helped from his automobile so he could make his way on crutches up a wooden runway to his first-base box—was an unpaying spectator at Griffith Stadium for game three. After a morning of rain, a paying crowd of 23,737 was on hand for Washington's only victory of the Series: a five-hit shutout for Whitehill over Fitzsimmons, who gave up nine hits and four runs. Myer led Washington's attack with a double, two singles, and three RBIs.

On an ideal day, Roosevelt remained in the White House, but an additional 4,000 people did turn up for game four, which lasted eleven innings. In the fourth inning, Terry hit one of Weaver's pitches into the temporary seats in the triangular area in center field to make it 1–0 New York. Two innings later, the Senators reached Hubbell for the tying run, and in the next inning Heinie Manush became one of the few players ejected from a World Series game, when he wouldn't quit arguing with umpire Charley Moran over being called out at first base. In the top of the eleventh, sore-legged Travis Jackson beat out a bunt, was sacrificed to second, and scored on shortstop John "Blondy" Ryan's single. The Senators loaded the bases on Hubbell with one out in the bottom of the inning, only to see pinch hitter Cliff Bolton ground into a double play, Ryan to Hughie Critz to Terry.

The Series ended on Saturday, October 7. As a near-capacity crowd of 28,434 filtered in, Al Schacht and Nick Altrock again did their pregame comic routines; once the game started, however, Schacht took seriously his duties as the Senators' third-base coach and Joe Cronin's principal aide. By the end of the sixth inning, with the score tied at three, Crowder had given way to Jack Russell, and Schumacher to forty-three-year-old Dolf Luque (picked up on waivers the previous year from Brooklyn).

Both relievers held the opposition scoreless until the top of the tenth inning, when Ott drove one of Russell's pitches to deep center field. Washington's Art Schulte (who'd tied the game with a three-run homer in the sixth) dashed to the 3-foot railing in front of the temporary bleachers and leaped for the ball, which ticked off his glove as he tumbled in among the spectators. While Ott waited on second base, umpires Moran, Cy Pfirman, Emmett "Red" Ormsby, and George Moriarty discussed whether Schulte had deflected the ball into the bleachers on the fly or whether it had hit the ground first. Finally they waved Ott home, as Cronin and several other Senators jumped around and gesticulated in protest, to no avail. In the bottom of the inning, Luque put two men on base with two out, whereupon Joe Kuhel swung futilely at Luque's curve ball, which broke in the dirt. The last World Series in the history of the Washington Senators franchise was over.

Each Giant took home about $4,700; each Senator, about $3,400. Bill Terry's Giants, consistent with their low-key image, confined themselves to a few 3.2 beers and minimal horseplay on the train ride home. At Penn Station they hurried through the couple of thousand faithful who greeted their arrival and proceeded to the Hotel New Yorker for a celebration staged by owner Charles Stoneham. The next day, before he left with his wife and sixteen-year-old Bill Jr. for a visit to Niagara Falls and then the Chicago fair, Terry met with Stoneham and signed to manage the Giants for the next five years at an annual salary of $27,500.

. . . . .

JOHN MCGRAW, who'd sat in the Griffith Stadium press box munching peanuts throughout the victorious finale, rode back to New York with Terry and his players, no doubt thinking about a return trip from Washington nine years earlier, when his Giants had lost game seven of a memorable Series to Bucky Harris's ball club. The following February 25, at a hospital in New Rochelle, New York, McGraw died of prostate cancer and uremic poisoning, six weeks shy of his sixty-first birthday.

William Veeck Sr. and Phil Ball had already preceded McGraw. Veeck died in Chicago on October 5, apparently of leukemia; seventeen days later Ball succumbed to blood poisoning in St. Louis. Nineteen-year-old Veeck Jr., still limping from a broken foot sustained at Kenyon College that summer when he fell out of a window, left school to go to work for the Cubs; Philip K. Wrigley, heir to the Chicago franchise, now reluctantly had to accept a more active role in its operation. Ball's heirs were content for the Browns to be operated in trusteeship while they waited for a buyer, and Rogers

Hornsby—as much admired by Ball as he'd been by William Wrigley—found himself managing a bad ball club that drew abysmally few people (79,000 for the whole 1933 season) and had little prospect for anything better.

The 1933 Cincinnati Reds, again finishing last, had a home attendance of 218,181. Having lost something like $600,000 over the past four years, Sidney Weill declared bankruptcy and put the franchise in the hands of a local bank. Yet the Reds were about to receive a life-giving transfusion of money and leadership. In Columbus, Larry MacPhail had quarreled with Branch Rickey over player dispositions and embarrassed himself and the Cardinals organization by being publicly drunk. Although Rickey had fired him during the 1933 season, the teetotaling Methodist still thought enough of MacPhail's abilities to recommend him to the Cincinnati bankers as somebody who might help restore the Reds franchise to solvency.

Hired as the Reds' business manager, MacPhail was able to persuade Powel Crosley, a multimillionaire electrical-appliance manufacturer and radio-station owner, to purchase a controlling interest in the franchise. Believing that radio coverage of Reds games would build fan interest, MacPhail brought in Mississippi-born Walter "Red" Barber from Gainesville, Florida, to do play-by-play re-creations of all Cincinnati road games and thirteen home games over Crosley's station, WSAI. MacPhail also charged stations WFBE and WKRC $2,000 apiece for broadcasting rights under the same schedule.

As the Reds' prospects seemed to brighten, those of the Philadelphia Athletics continued to dim. After another attendance decline (to less than 400,000) and heavy financial losses ($300,000, according to one source), Connie Mack continued to jettison players from his championship teams of 1929 to 1931. George Earnshaw, who won only five games and was virtually an outcast by season's end, went to the White Sox along with reserve catcher Charley Berry for $20,000 and a player of no consequence. But the deals that left Philadelphia fans bereft involved the departure of Lefty Grove and Mickey Cochrane. Grove, along with Max Bishop, was dealt to Boston for two players and $125,000; Cochrane was sold to Detroit, where automobile-manufacturing tycoon Walter O. Briggs, who'd recently acquired a major bloc of stock in the franchise, put up the $100,000 with which Tigers president Frank Navin made the deal. Navin then named Cochrane to succeed Bucky Harris, who in turn signed to manage the Red Sox. As manager and, by consensus, still the game's best catcher, Cochrane was given a contract for $30,000.

Connie Mack had long complained that "we cannot meet our payrolls playing on seventy-seven weekdays at home."[14] For 1934, however, the Athletics as well as the Phillies and Pirates could at least look forward to playing at home on Sundays. On November 7, 1933, at the same time they ratified the amendment repealing national prohibition, Pennsylvania's voters also approved a local-option law that repealed the state's historic ban on Sabbath commercial amusements. Neither the Athletics nor the Phillies, however, could persuade Philadelphia's city council to permit beer sales at their ballparks.

As Detroit's new manager, Cochrane was one of the most visible figures at pre-Christmas major-league meetings at the Palmer House in Chicago. (It was the first such gathering since 1919 where liquor was openly purchasable, although most of the drinking still took place in private rooms.) Cochrane was able to deal outfielder Jonathan Stone to Washington for Goose Goslin, who hadn't gotten along with manager Cronin. Meanwhile the Cubs, with Babe Herman having been something of a disappointment, again sought more batting power. They gave new Phillies owner Gary Nugent three players and $125,000 in sorely needed cash for Chuck Klein.

About six weeks before his death, William Veeck, watching Cubs attendance shrink by about 400,000, had come out in favor of a series of mid-season games between American and National League teams. Presidents Alva Bradley of Cleveland and Stephen W. McKeever of Brooklyn had declared themselves definitely in favor of the idea; the Cardinals' Sam Breadon and the Pirates' William Benswanger said it was worth considering. Fred Lieb had endorsed the proposal in the *New York Evening Post*, and late in the year editor F. C. Lane of *Baseball Magazine* also advocated interleague play, although he thought that it ought to take place during the closing weeks of the season.

Nothing that radical came out of the Depression-plagued Chicago gathering, but the big-league moguls did vote to adopt a "uniform ball" for 1934. That actually meant that the American League's ball, which had been somewhat livelier than the National's since 1931, would now be used in both leagues. While approving of the change, Lane cautioned against returning to the "rabbit ball" of 1930. "A too lively baseball," said Lane, "is like a debased currency. It upsets established values and creates a new set of values of unknown stability."[15]

At the annual meeting of the National Association, in Galveston, Texas, President William G. Bramham, while acknowledging that farm systems were here to stay, inveighed against violations of league-imposed salary limits and cover-up practices whereby a major-league team could control a player longer than the draft provisions specified. Fourteen leagues had made it through the season, but the lower minors—at B, C, and D classifications—had dwindled to only seven circuits, nine fewer than in 1930. Organized Baseball had largely disappeared from small-city America.

Besides offering night baseball and promotional gimmicks, most of the minors had tried to sustain fan interest and generate additional revenue by various provisions for postseason play. Some used a split-season format that matched first- and second-half winners; others scheduled series between pennant winners and runners-up; and two leagues staged what in effect was a postseason tournament involving the four top finishers. Proposed early in 1933 by Frank Shaughnessy, president of the International League's Montreal franchise, and instituted that year in Shaughnessy's league as well as in the Texas League, such postseason competition arrayed the first- and fourth-place teams and the second- and third-place teams in opening-round series and then pitted the winners against each other in a championship matchup. That arrangement proved so popular that within a few years four-team "Shaughnessy playoffs," like night ball, would become standard practice throughout the minors.

If Frank Shaughnessy's idea derived from the hard times of the early 1930s, still another form of postseason play, long antedating the Depression, produced modest additional revenues for club owners and a couple of hundred dollars apiece for participating players. As far back as 1904, the American Association and International League winners had inaugurated a Junior World Series, which was played intermittently until it became an annual event in 1920. That same year saw the first Dixie Series between Texas League and Southern Association champions. By 1927 there were as many as seven such interleague postseason series, but by 1933 only the Junior World Series, the Dixie Series, and a Midwest Series between the Western League and Mississippi Valley League victors took place.

Aggregate minor-league attendance in 1933 was about 3.5 million, while the major leagues totaled 5,965,000—in both cases, a drop of 40 to 45 percent from 1930 numbers. Major-league franchises collectively lost $1,651,000, which averaged out to a loss margin of 23.9 percent. The St. Louis Browns, Cincinnati Reds, Philadelphia Phillies, and Boston Braves were in really bad shape; if something besides the railroads had been available for transporting teams to distant destinations, it's likely that at least a couple of big-league franchises would have relocated, perhaps to California. As it was, the majors' poor relations would have to stick it out and hope for better times, while the few franchises still on sound financial footing would continue to grumble about barely meeting travel and meal expenses on their visits to various big-league cities.

Yet as another season rolled around, the worst part of the Great Depression—for baseball and for most other segments of the American economy—was in the past. Full economic recovery—by which people usually meant not significant future expansion but simply regaining the lost (if limited) prosperity of the 1920s—would remain elusive for the remainder of the decade. But by 1934, with Franklin D. Roosevelt's New Deal operating in high gear, there finally was reason to believe that better times were ahead.

CHAPTER 5

New Deal Baseball, 1934–1935

ABE RUTH shouldn't have gone to Hawaii. At the end of the 1933 season, Detroit Tigers president Frank Navin was genuinely interested in hiring Ruth to replace Bucky Harris, who'd quit with two games left and the Tigers in sixth place. But the Babe already had a contractual commitment to play a series of exhibition games in Honolulu, so, despite Ed Barrow's warning that he was making a mistake, the Babe left without meeting with Navin. When he finally called Navin from Hawaii (reportedly at 2:00 A.M. Detroit time), the Tigers' president was so irritated that he put off Ruth and two months later acquired Mickey Cochrane to be his player-manager.

That was as close as Ruth would ever come to a managing job. He absolutely refused to manage in the minor leagues (unlike his illustrious contemporaries Walter Johnson and Tris Speaker, both of whom had managed Newark in the International League), and he had no chance of displacing Joe McCarthy as Yankees field boss. Jacob Ruppert and Ed Barrow really didn't know what to do with Ruth, who was still too valuable a property to release outright and too expensive for anybody to buy. After a meeting with Ruppert at his brewery, "Root" (as the Germanic Ruppert always pronounced the Babe's name) seemed reasonably happy to sign for $35,000. That was $45,000 less than he'd been making only three years earlier, but it kept him as the majors' highest-salaried player.

Meanwhile Lou Gehrig, who after a long courtship and engagement had finally married Eleanor Twitchell, again agreed to $23,000. And after leading the American League in nearly every offensive category and being named its Most Valuable Player by both the *Sporting News* and the Base Ball Writers Association of America, Jimmie Foxx learned that the Athletics wanted to cut his salary from $16,300 to $11,000. Eventually he signed a one-year contract for $18,000, but Philadelphians were left to wonder just how far Connie Mack and associates might be willing to go in their cost-cutting campaign.

Although Foxx and major leaguers in general were being paid far more than most people could even hope for, by the spring of 1934 a lot of Americans had money in their pockets that they hadn't had a year earlier. The economy had experienced no massive surge toward recovery, but the federal government's multiplying efforts under the New Deal—especially its limited relief and work programs under the Federal Emergency Relief Administration, the Civil Works Administration, and the Civilian Conservation Corps (CCC)—had improved the circumstances of several million people, at least temporarily.

One of the most popular and durable New Deal programs, the CCC housed young American men in rural work camps and paid them $22 per month to put out forest fires, clear brush, plant trees, and undertake other small-scale conservation projects. It also gave them the chance to play baseball after work and on weekends. By the late 1930s, more than a few minor leaguers had once worked for the CCC.

Moreover, widespread pre–New Deal reductions of working hours in business and industry designed to "spread the work"—largely standardized in the summer of 1933 under the National Recovery Administration's wages and hours codes—had made the five-day week the common work regimen, especially for wage earners. So for many baseball fans across the country, baseball had become both somewhat more affordable and a good deal more accessible.

· · · · ·

THAT SPRING, the World Series champion New York Giants were cocky and confident. Not caring to risk any more southern California earthquakes and guaranteed a $10,000 subsidy by Miami's mayor, the Giants decided to move their spring-training base to the other side of the United States. In an interview in New York a couple of weeks before he left for Miami, Bill Terry said he expected St. Louis, Chicago, and Pittsburgh to be the teams to beat in 1934. Somebody mentioned Brooklyn. "The Dodgers?" replied the Giants manager. "Why—are they still in the league?"[1]

The Dodgers had finished sixth in 1933 under the entertaining but un-inspiring leadership of Charles Dillon "Casey" Stengel, who'd succeeded Max Carey even though Carey had a year remaining on his contract. Stengel had played the outfield for Brooklyn and four other National League clubs, including three seasons under John McGraw, and had managed a year in the Eastern League and three years at Toledo before being hired as a Brooklyn coach. Although conceded to be one of the funniest men around, at forty-three Stengel hadn't yet impressed anybody as a big-league man-ager.

He also hadn't perfected the uniquely convoluted, non-sequitur mode of speaking that would later be known as "Stengelese"—although he was getting there. One day, as his infielders went through a nifty pregame prac-tice, he exclaimed, "Look—did you see that play? Those boys of mine look just like professionals out there." He didn't much care for the nickname "Dodgers," he mused on another occasion, and he wished somebody would come up with another one, but not "Caseys," because that would remind everybody of "that guy that struck out."[2]

As of 1934, though, Stengel's speech was relatively coherent most of the time. "The first thing I want to say," he told reporters at Brooklyn's Clear-water, Florida, training site, "is that the Dodgers are still in the league." But when Bill Terry watched Stengel's players twice get mixed up on the bases in a game in Florida, he cracked, "They're in midseason form already."[3]

Terry and his men also referred to the St. Louis Cardinals as "coolies," a reference to the salaries that Sam Breadon paid his players and the in-frequency with which he had their uniforms laundered. But like the Cardinals and seven other big-league franchises, the Giants saved money by having the team managed by an active player. The mid-1930s featured the biggest concentration of player-managers since the early years of the century.

Branch Rickey, ever sensitive to charges by Commissioner Landis that the Cardinals kept young players from progressing as fast as they ought to, pointed out at a local businessmen's luncheon in Greensboro, North Caro-lina, that thirty-three former St. Louis players or farm-system products were currently on the rosters of other National League clubs; eleven more were playing in the American League. What Rickey neglected to say was that in 1933 he'd made $14,970 on commissions from player sales and that the Cincinnati Reds still owed the Cardinals $50,000 for past player trans-actions.

That spring, as the baseball teams moved north from Florida, signs of better times were evident. Southern stores and banks that had been closed a year earlier were again doing business; at least some of the shut-down mills and factories were again fouling the atmosphere with thick black smoke—a commonly understood symbol of prosperous times. From New Orleans to Baton Rouge to Meridian to Memphis, the touring Giants and Cleveland Indians drew full houses. Other teams also saw the biggest crowds in years, as local people again took the rare opportunity to see big leaguers in the flesh.

When they got back to Cleveland, the Indians again opened for business full time in little League Park, having spent a desultory season and a half playing at home in the immenseness of Lakefront Stadium. There the team batting average had dropped by thirty-five points and run production by 22 percent. Except perhaps for American League pitchers, everybody seemed to agree with Babe Ruth's judgment when he first saw Lakefront: "The new park here is too big for the players, too big for the public—well, it's just too big."[4]

In Boston, Tom Yawkey and Eddie Collins were determined to turn around the fortunes of the Red Sox. In the off-season, they had spent about $250,000 on renovating and generally sprucing up Fenway Park. Among other changes, they had the slope in front of the left-field wall eliminated and replaced the wooden wall with a tin-covered fence topped by netting, thereby increasing the total height of the barrier by 12 feet but also shortening the distance down the line from 320 to 312 feet. (It wasn't yet the "Green Monster," though, because for another twenty years the wall would be covered in advertisements.)

Yawkey, Collins, and new manager Bucky Harris naturally expected much from Lefty Grove and Rube Walberg, the two off-season acquisitions from the Athletics. But Walberg proved ineffective as a starter and would spend most of the time in the Boston bullpen, while Grove, who'd won 185 games in eight seasons with Philadelphia, developed a sore shoulder in spring training. Sessions with the team's trainer were unproductive, so physicians looked into Grove's mouth and, sure enough, concluded that three abscessed teeth were the cause of his arm trouble. "Let the teeth fall where they may," quipped Grove in an uncharacteristically puckish moment.[5] Out came the teeth, and later Grove's tonsils as well, but he still had trouble throwing the ball with any speed. The season became a thoroughly frustrating one in which Grove pitched in only twenty-two games and finished with an 8–8 record and a horrendous 6.50 earned run average.

Despite Grove's travail, the Red Sox had their best season since winning their last pennant in 1918. They finished in fourth place with a 76–76 record, seven games better than the eviscerated Athletics. That improvement had much to do with the arrival from Cleveland of Wes Ferrell, who now joined older brother Rick, acquired from the Browns in 1933, to form a siblings' battery. A rival to Earl Whitehill as the majors' most handsome man and probably the best-hitting pitcher in baseball history (besides Babe Ruth), the tall North Carolinian had won 101 games since 1929. But he hadn't gotten along either with Roger Peckinpaugh, Walter Johnson's predecessor as Cleveland manager, or with Johnson himself, and he refused to sign for $5,000 following a poor 1933 season in which he'd been paid $12,000. As fiercely competitive on the mound and as ill-tempered in defeat as Grove, Ferrell once became so disgusted with himself that he sat on the bench tearing apart his glove with his teeth. In March 1934 Ferrell told Alva Bradley that he wanted to buy out his own contract; when Bradley set the price at $25,000, Ferrell gave up on that and became a holdout. Late in May, Bradley dealt Ferrell to Boston for two players and (coincidentally) $25,000. Ferrell proceeded to rack up fourteen wins in only twenty-three starts.

· · · · ·

THE SIXTEEN HOME OPENERS registered an attendance gain of nearly 63,000 over 1933, with 33,336 packing new-edition Fenway Park. President Roosevelt was cheered lustily by the near-capacity throng in Washington, where he threw out the first ball, ducked a foul drive as Secret Service men scrambled to cover him, and stayed until a downpour arrived in the fourth inning. About 18,000 chilled Chicagoans watched Detroit defeat the White Sox 8–3 in Mickey Cochrane's managerial debut, while in St. Louis, Dizzy Dean pitched a 7–1 victory over Pittsburgh in ideal weather. Yet only 7,500 paid their way into Sportsman's Park that day; fewer than half as many were on hand for the Browns' home opener. Not just the Browns but the Cardinals as well had become considerable drags on their respective leagues.

So, for that matter, were Cincinnati, Philadelphia, and to some extent Brooklyn in the National League and, in the other league, the Chicago White Sox and even the defending league champion, Washington. Attracting only 236,559 paying fans, the White Sox had a miserable season despite Al Simmons's last strong year (.344 and 104 runs batted in), George Earnshaw's respectable 14–11 record, and the arrival of rookie first baseman Henry "Zeke" Bonura, a native New Orleanian who batted .302, with twenty-seven homers and 110 RBIs. Bonura made only five errors and would always show a high fielding percentage, but his lack of range afield dismayed Jimmy Dykes (who succeeded Lew Fonseca in May) and a succession of later managers. Edward Burns of the *Chicago Tribune* dubbed his manner of waving at balls as they went past "the Bonura salute." Bonura's trouble, remarked the acerbic Dykes, was that he hadn't "found out that you can't get killed with a batted ball."[6]

Relatively speaking, Washington's year was even more miserable. What had been a superb Washington pitching staff in 1933 virtually fell apart; at 14–11, Earl Whitehill alone showed a winning record. Alvin Crowder, winner of fifty games over the past two seasons, nursed a variety of discontents that included being away from his ill wife in North Carolina. Finally put on waivers, he was claimed by Detroit. Washington's pitching situation got so bad that, in August, Griffith even gave a brief trial to a House of David pitcher named Allen Benson. Johnny Stone suffered a broken ankle; Joe Kuhel missed much of the season with a broken leg; manager Cronin slumped to .287 (although he still drove in 101 runs) and sat out the last few weeks with a broken arm; Cecil Travis, a good-looking rookie infielder, was hospitalized with a severe concussion after a beaning by Cleveland's Thornton Lee; and various other Senators went down with injuries and illnesses. Ending up in seventh place and trailing even Rogers Hornsby's Browns, Cronin's team performed one of the worst one-season turnarounds in big-league history.

Cronin did have a pleasant midseason interlude when, as manager of the previous season's American League champion, he led twenty of his league's top players into the second All-Star Game versus Bill Terry's twenty National League standouts. Played at the Polo Grounds, in New York, before 48,363, the game would always be remembered for Carl Hubbell's stunning feat of striking out five future Hall of Famers in a row: Babe Ruth and Lou Gehrig to end the first inning; Al Simmons, Jimmie Foxx, and Joe Cronin in the second. That Hubbell's successors were pounded in the middle innings, that Cleveland's Mel Harder shut down the Nationals with one hit over the last five frames to preserve a 9–7 victory, or that the American League's entire starting lineup consisted of future Hall of Famers—all that would forever be overshadowed by what Hubbell did.[7]

. . . . .

THE LOSING PITCHER in the All-Star Game was a big South Carolinian with the singular name of Van Lingle Mungo, who toiled for Brooklyn. Although Mungo led the majors in 1934 with 315 innings pitched, won eighteen games, and convinced many batters than he was the fastest pitcher in baseball, Casey Stengel's outfit again could do no better than sixth place.

The Phillies, after climbing into the rarefied atmosphere of fourth place in 1932, had fallen back to seventh in 1933, even though Chuck Klein, like Jimmie Foxx, led his league in batting, homers, RBIs, and nearly everything else and, like Foxx, was named its Most Valuable Player. With Klein gone to Chicago, the 1934 Phillies were even worse, although they still managed to finish ahead of Cincinnati.

A footnote to the Phillies' season was that it was the end of the road for Hack Wilson. Released by Brooklyn, the onetime terror of the league's pitchers caught on with the Phillies, played a few games, couldn't hit, and again was released. Released yet again in 1935 by Albany in the International League, Wilson would then begin a thirteen-year slide into alcoholism, poverty, and finally death at age forty-eight.

Despite the best efforts of Larry MacPhail in the front office and, successively, Bob O'Farrell, Burt Shotton, and Charley Dressen in the dugout, the Cincinnati Reds lost ninety-nine times and played before only 206,773 customers at what was now called Crosley Field. Paul Derringer, who'd known better days as a Cardinals rookie, lost twenty-one games; Syl Johnson topped that by one. In June, though, the Reds made history by becoming the first baseball team to travel by air. MacPhail chartered an American Airlines DC-2 to fly O'Farrell and his players—except for a fainthearted few who who preferred the train—from Chicago back to Cincinnati.

The 1934 Boston Braves were again a respectable team, again finishing in fourth place, higher than they would finish for another twelve years but still far out of the running—and as unattractive to local fans as they'd been before their pennant flirtation the previous season. Bill McKechnie's club won a few more games than Pittsburgh, which fell to fifth, with Pie Traynor, who replaced George Gibson a third into the season, becoming the majors' ninth player-manager. Paul Waner won his second batting title at .362; Arky Vaughn, at .333, was the majors' best-hitting shortstop.

As usual, the Giants and the Cubs were contenders in the National League. But the Cardinals, down for two years, experienced a resurgence under the leadership of Frank Frisch. A Fordham University graduate and an infield star on John McGraw's four-time pennant winners in the early 1920s, Frisch had fallen out of McGraw's favor and come to St. Louis following the 1926 season in exchange for Rogers Hornsby. A fast base runner, an excellent fielder, and the majors' foremost switch-hitter (or "turn-around batter," in contemporary parlance), Frisch had quickly won over fans furious with Sam Breadon for having traded the great Hornsby and become the sparkplug of teams that won three pennants in five years and dethroned the mighty Athletics in the 1931 World Series.

The son of a well-to-do Bronx linen manufacturer, Frisch, as described by the St. Louis sportswriter Bob Broeg, "was born with a silver spoon in his mouth, yet talked as if he'd cut his teeth on a cuspidor." He was "sarcastic, funny, and extremely profane, especially when arguing with umpires."[8] If Frisch had earlier undermined Gabby Street's authority (as Street charged), then Frisch himself sought to avoid a similar situation by shipping the veteran catcher Jimmie Wilson to the Phillies, where the Philadelphia native could fulfill managerial ambitions of his own as well as catch about half the time.

But if Frisch thought that Wilson's departure would solve his problems, he reckoned without the growing self-importance of Dizzy Dean. In 1934 "Diz," as he'd come to be known, had his finest year, starting thirty-three games, completing twenty-four, relieving in seventeen others, winning thirty (the last National Leaguer to do so), losing only seven, and striking out 195. Paul Dean, Diz's junior by two and a half years, joined the Cardinals' staff after two outstanding seasons in Columbus and pitched nineteen victories, including a no-hitter in Brooklyn during the nightcap of a September 21 doubleheader (after Diz had shut out the Dodgers in the opener). In Florida, Diz had predicted that "me 'n Paul" would win forty games between them. The forty-nine they did win accounted for more than half the Cardinals' 1934 victories; together they pitched in nearly 60 percent of their team's games. For their labors, Diz was being paid $8,500; Paul, a princely $3,000.

Temperamentally, the Dean brothers were almost complete opposites. Paul Dean, who turned twenty-one in July, had little to say, content to let his loquacious brother do the talking and make most of the decisions. But Dizzy Dean—like Babe Ruth (and also Art Shires, by 1934 relegated to the Texas League) but unlike many other athletes of limited education and sophistication—absolutely gloried in the spotlight.

Supremely confident in his own abilities, Diz went out of his way to attract attention, as on one day at Sportsman's Park in hundred-degree heat, when he built a paper fire in front of the dugout, wrapped himself in a blanket, and performed a war dance. Later, at Braves Field in Boston, he did a pantomime of a man shaving and scattered sneezing powder in front of the home team's dugout. On still another occasion, he went into the visitors' locker room at Sportsman's Park, sat down, and cheerfully proceeded to instruct Bill Terry and his Giants on how he intended to pitch to them. Dizzy Dean, thought the New York journalist Tom Meany, "has made Ring Lardner come true. Dean [is] the kind of ballplayer Lardner wrote about."[9]

But Diz also still showed a surly and fractious side. On June 1, in Pittsburgh, he sat in the grandstand on a one-game "strike" to protest Paul's low salary. Told by Frisch that he couldn't do anything about his brother's pay, Diz returned to the mound the next day and beat the Pirates. Then in mid-August, he and Paul refused to accompany the team from St. Louis to Detroit for an off-day exhibition game following a Sunday doubleheader in which they'd both pitched. The side-trip exhibition was the kind of thing all the big-league clubs did at various times during the season to make extra money, but the Cardinals scheduled more such games than any other team—and that was a persistently sore point with Cardinals players and whoever happened to be managing them. When the team got back to St. Louis, Frisch told Diz that he was fined $100 and Paul $50, whereupon Diz threw a tantrum, kicking things around the clubhouse and then tearing his two Cardinals home jerseys to shreds. For that, he received a ten-day suspension.

Sam Breadon and Branch Rickey backed Frisch's action, and Paul Dean, in a rare show of independence, paid his fine and gained reinstatement on August 17. Meanwhile Diz traveled to Chicago to put his case to Commissioner Landis in the presence of Breadon, Rickey, and Frisch. When Landis endorsed Dean's suspension, all the unhappy pitcher could do was serve it and pay up. All told, he was out $486 in fines, compensation for the shredded jerseys, and lost salary. "There are ten million people out of work in this country," grumbled Frank Frisch, "yet Dizzy Dean is willing to sacrifice a daily income of approximately $50 to fill the role of a play-boy."[10] But Frisch was happy to have his ace back; on August 26, in his first start since being suspended, Diz shut out the Giants on five hits for his twenty-second win.

By the time both Deans were reestablished in Frisch's pitching rotation, the Cardinals and Cubs were jockeying for second place behind the Giants, who seemed to have a comfortable lead. Although Roy Parmelee was disabled for much of the season after an appendectomy (and resentful that Terry pressured him to return to the mound too soon), Hubbell, Schumacher, and Fitzsimmons won sixty-two games among them. "King Carl"

Hubbell had twenty-one victories and led the majors with a 2.30 ERA, while "Prince Hal" Schumacher racked up twenty-three. Terry put in a full season and batted .354; Mel Ott batted .326 and led the league in homers (thirty-five) and RBIs (135); center fielder and leadoff man Joe Moore batted .331; and Travis Jackson, dividing his time between shortstop and third base, drove in 101 runs.

But while the Cubs started to slip back, the Cardinals, with the Deans carrying most of the pitching load, continued to nibble away at the Giants' lead. On September 8, after losing two out of three games at the Polo Grounds, the Cubs had fallen eight games back and were all but finished. Eight days after that, in a Sunday doubleheader before a record Polo Grounds crowd of 62,573, Dizzy Dean, with help from Tex Carleton, was the winner over Parmelee and Schumacher by a 5–3 score; and Paul Dean, who'd beaten the Giants in twelve innings three days earlier, topped Hubbell 2–1 in eleven. That gave the Cardinals four wins in their five-game series with Terry's team and left them only three and a half games out of first place. After another ten days, the Cardinals had closed to within a half game, and on September 28, when Dizzy Dean shut out Cincinnati while New York was idle, they moved into a tie.

The Giants would close the season at the Polo Grounds in two games with Brooklyn, while the Cardinals had two left in St. Louis versus Cincinnati. The sixth-place Dodgers had drawn only about 435,000 at Ebbets Field, but on Saturday, September 29, about half the 13,774 people at the Polo Grounds were Brooklynites, many ringing cowbells and waving placards reading "Yes! We're Still in the League." In Cincinnati, Joe Medwick homered and tripled and drove in three runs, and Paul Dean shut down the Reds 6–1 for his nineteenth win. In New York, Van Lingle Mungo gave the Giants only five hits and one run, while the Dodgers drove out Parmelee with five tallies. St. Louis now led by one game.

So far in 1934 the Cardinals had played before few big crowds at home and would total only 334,821 for the season, but on Sunday, September 30, Sportsman's Park was jammed with 37,402 fans. James "Ripper" Collins, the Cardinals' stocky, switch-hitting first baseman, hit his thirty-fifth homer; Leo Durocher hit his third; and Dizzy Dean cruised to his thirtieth win, 9–0.

Playing an hour later than the game in New York, the Cardinals learned in the ninth inning that the pennant was theirs. Word came down from the press box that in the tenth inning, with the score 5–5, Hubbell had relieved Schumacher with the bases loaded. Again at least half the crowd—a full house on this decisive day—rooted for the visitors. An error, a fly ball, and a single gave Brooklyn three runs before Hubbell could retire the side; Johnny Babich, Stengel's fourth pitcher, then disposed of Hughie Critz, Bill Terry, and Mel Ott in order. Dodgers fans waved their placards, stomped on the roof of the Giants' dugout, threw things at the Giants as they climbed the steps to their clubhouse in center field, and carried Stengel and catcher Al Lopez up the steps to the opposite-side visitors' quarters.

The Giants had lost their last five games and thirteen of their last twenty; Ott had failed to hit in his last twenty-five times at bat. Terry had no alibis. "For the mistakes we made," he said, "I'll take the full responsibility."[11] A few days later, when he returned home to Memphis, Terry saw signs in shop windows again reminding him—as if he needed reminding—that Brooklyn was still in the league. For the rest of his life, somebody would always be bringing up his ill-advised preseason putdown.

The famed New York journalist Damon Runyon described the 1934 Cardinals as "a warrior club, with warrior spirit, and its vanguard is the redoubtable Jerome 'Dizzy' Dean, the most colorful character the game has produced in many years." Yet a lot more than the mound heroics of Diz and his diffident younger brother went into the Cardinals' success. Tex Carleton won sixteen games; Ripper Collins batted .333 and drove in 128 runs to go along with his league's-best thirty-five homers; and Frisch, who'd turned thirty-six by the end of the season, batted .305. Although Pepper Martin, now stationed at third base, would never play as spectacularly as he had in the 1931 World Series, he'd become a solid big leaguer, fast enough to lead the league regularly in base stealing. And while Leo Durocher wasn't much at bat, many thought him the league's best shortstop, as well as Dizzy Dean's superior as a loudmouth. "If there were prizes for bashfulness," observed John Kieran, "Leo wouldn't get to first base. He doesn't get there often, anyway."[12]

Frisch's outfield wasn't distinguished, apart from twenty-two-year-old Joe Medwick, who batted .319, with eighteen homers and 106 RBIs. Powerfully muscled at 5 feet 10 inches and 180 pounds, the New Jersey–born son of Hungarian immigrants was a notorious "bad-ball hitter" who swung at anything near the strike zone but was still hard to strike out. Obviously one of the game's rising stars, Medwick was also, according to Burgess Whitehead, his teammate for three years, "very self-centered," seemingly more concerned with his own statistics than the team's fortunes. For example, with Pepper Martin in a protracted slump, the St. Louis Globe's Ray Gillespie spread hairpins (widely thought to bring good luck) in front of the Cardinals' dugout. Along came Medwick to scoop them up. "The hell with Martin and his slump," snapped Medwick. "Let Martin find his own base hits."[13]

. . . . .

IN COMPARISON WITH the down-to-the-wire National League race, the American League's lacked much suspense. In the friendlier surroundings of League Park and despite the departure of Wes Ferrell, Walter Johnson's Cleveland Indians improved to 85–69, good for third place. Mel Harder was a twenty-game winner; Californian Montgomery Marcellus "Monte" Pearson won eighteen. Hal Trosky, a big first baseman, had an outstanding rookie season, batting .330, slamming a franchise-record thirty-five home runs, and driving in 142 runs, while Earl Averill put in his customary productive year (.313, thirty-one homers, 113 RBIs) and hometown boy Joe Vosmik batted .341 in his fourth big-league season.

The Yankees again were runners-up, even though a rejuvenated Lefty Gomez led the majors with twenty-six victories, Red Ruffing won nineteen, and rookie Johnny Murphy, like Frisch a Fordham University product, both started and relieved to gain fourteen wins. Lou Gehrig had one of his greatest seasons, winning what sportswriters would later dub the "Triple Crown" by batting .363, hitting a career-high forty-nine homers, and driving home 165 runs. He also showed a Ruthian .706 slugging average on 409 total bases.

Ruth himself, though, came to bat only 365 times in 125 games, most of which he wasn't able to complete. Sore-legged and ponderous, bothered mightily by record heat in the western cities, he put up his poorest numbers since becoming a full-time player in 1919: a .288 batting average, twenty-two homers, eighty-eight RBIs. As he struggled afield and at bat, Ruth came to resent Joe McCarthy more and more, and he was also on bad terms with various teammates, particularly Gehrig, who'd once been his admiring friend and something of a protégé. Inasmuch as everybody assumed that it was the Babe's last year as a player, the Yankees' final stops around the league brought out bigger-than-usual crowds to bid farewell to the man who not only had been baseball's greatest player and its most compelling, magnetic personality, but had actually changed the game itself.

Besides Ruth's deteriorated skills, the Yankees were afflicted by a variety of other misfortunes. In June, Earle Combs, their center-field stalwart for a decade, crashed into a concrete outfield wall in St. Louis and suffered a broken collarbone and skull fracture that kept him hospitalized for weeks and ended his season. Although he would try a comeback in 1935, his career was essentially over. Bill Dickey was disabled for a time with a broken finger, Ben Chapman went out with a knee injury, and Johnny Allen developed arm trouble and pitched in only thirteen games.

But despite a broken toe and teeth extractions, Gehrig again was in the lineup every day, as he'd been since June 1, 1925.[14] In view of what would later befall him, one reads ominous portents into his reported bouts of "lumbago"—then pretty much a generic term for back troubles. Convinced that Gehrig's ailing back was a result of sleeping on air-conditioned Pullmans, McCarthy decreed that his players would have to sleep without the innovation that some railway lines had recently installed to provide relief from the midsummer heat, not to mention the coal dust that blew into open Pullman windows.

At the end, the Yankees were seven games in back of the Detroit Tigers, who hadn't won anything since 1909 and had been nobody's preseason pick. But on Sunday, July 15, at Detroit's Navin Field, the Tigers beat the Yankees 8–3 and moved into first place to stay. They went on to record 101 victories and lead the majors in attendance, attracting 919,161 fans to Navin Field. That was triple what they'd drawn the previous year and a full one-third of all the people who paid to see American League games in 1934.

Baseball writers in Detroit and around the majors mainly credited Mickey Cochrane with the Tigers' rise to the top of the league following a sixth-place showing in 1933 under Bucky Harris. Still just thirty-one, the Bridgewater, Massachusetts, native and onetime Boston University football star not only caught 120 games and batted .320 but proved a fiery, tough, and seemingly indomitable leader. "You know how Mike is when he's losing a ball game," remarked Jimmy Dykes about his former teammate. "He'd yank an arm off you and whack you over the nose with it."[15]

But those qualities wouldn't have brought Cochrane's team home in first place if not for the fact that several of his veteran players had what would later be called "career years," and a couple of younger men came into their own as front-rank big leaguers. At shortstop, for example, switch-hitting Billy Rogell batted better than he ever had or would again (.296, with one hundred RBIs), as did Marvin Owen at third (.317, ninety-six RBIs). Second baseman Charley Gehringer, a quiet, methodically excellent nine-year veteran, enjoyed his best year up to then: .356 with 127 RBIs. Left fielder Goose Goslin, whose salary Clark Griffith had unloaded the previous December, was a .305 hitter and drove in an even one hundred runs, while Ervin "Pete" Fox, Gerald "Gee" Walker, and Joyner "Jo-Jo" White shared the remaining two outfield posts, batting .285, .300, and .313, respectively.

(Walker, an ebullient young Georgian and a favorite of Navin Field fans, was a good hitter and capable outfielder, but he specialized in base-running gaffes. Perhaps his most bizarre had occurred a couple of years earlier, when he managed to swallow his chewing tobacco and, as he gagged and stumbled, was tagged out between first and second. Walker's antics on the bases prompted occasional fines and more than a few anguished moments for his exacting young manager.)

The big man in the Detroit lineup, both literally and figuratively, was Henry Greenberg. Back in the spring of 1930, at the Tigers' Tampa training camp, Bucky Harris had looked over Greenberg and told reporters: "We've got one we think pretty good, and we got him from within a block of the Yankee Stadium. . . . He's been murdering the ball down here."[16] By the time he reached the Tigers in 1933 after three seasons in the Tigers-affiliated minors, notably at Beaumont in the Texas League (and after exhausting what remained of his father's ill-timed investment of the youngster's bonus money), he'd acquired the nom de jeu "Hank."

For some 2 percent of the U.S. population, Greenberg was the most important big-league player so far, because he was the first truly outstanding Jewish player to come along. He was also a big, handsome guy—at 6 feet 4 inches and about 215 pounds in his prime—and thus a standing refutation of commonly heard jokes that began "There was this little Jew. . . ." In 1933 Greenberg had assumed the regular first-base job and batted .317; as the powering force behind the 1934 pennant drive, he hit .339, belted twenty-six home runs, and drove in 139 runs.

For gentile Americans, many of whom harbored varying degrees of anti-Semitic prejudice, it was hard to comprehend the fervor with which American Jews embraced Greenberg as their hero. As a retired Detroit realtor put it many years later, "I don't think anybody can imagine the terrific importance of Hank Greenberg to the Jewish community. He was a God, a true folk hero. That made baseball acceptable to our parents, so for once they didn't mind if we took a little time off from the big process of getting into college."[17]

Or as Greenberg himself said, "Being Jewish did carry with it a special responsibility. . . . If I had a bad day, every son of a bitch was calling me names so that I had to make good. I just had to show them that a Jew could play ball." It was a heavy burden for a twenty-three year old, especially in

Greenberg's particular circumstances. In the mid-1930s, anti-Semitism was especially virulent in and around Detroit. While a resurgent Knights of the Ku Klux Klan and the counterpart Black Legion recruited followers from Detroit-area auto workers, Father Charles Coughlin proclaimed to several million listeners of his nationally syndicated radio talks, broadcast from his Royal Oak parish, that an international Jewish financial conspiracy was responsible for the Depression. It was tough going to bat every day and, as Greenberg phrased it, "have some son of a bitch call you a Jew bastard and a kike and a sheenie and get on your ass. . . . If the ballplayers weren't doing it, the fans were. Sometimes I wanted to go up in the stand and beat the shit out of them."[18]

Greenberg would always be slow afoot, but otherwise the 1934 Tigers had plenty of speed. Besides batting .300 as a team and leading the majors with 958 runs, they led everybody with 124 stolen bases, nearly twice as many as the supposedly daredevil Cardinals. Cochrane relied on five sturdy pitchers, led by Lynwood "Schoolboy" Rowe, Arkansas's fourth gift (besides the Deans and Lon Warneke) to big-league mound fame. After a shaky start in his first full season, the 6-foot 5-inch, 210-pound right-hander went on a sixteen-game winning streak. Although he lost his last two outings, Rowe ended up with a 24–8 record and batted .303 in 109 times at the plate. Tennessean Tommy Bridges, slightly built but the possessor of a superb curve ball, won twenty-two games; Eldon Auker, who'd suffered a shoulder injury playing football at Kansas State College and subsequently developed a three-quarter-underhand or "submarine" pitching motion, won fifteen, as did the veteran Fred "Firpo" Marberry, used frequently in relief. Alvin Crowder won five of six decisions after being virtually given away by Washington.

. . . . .

FOR VARIOUS REASONS, the Tigers–Cardinals matchup excited an extraordinary amount of national interest. For one thing, it would be the first World Series since 1919 that didn't involve an eastern seaboard city. Both St. Louis and Detroit were heartland cities that had been especially ravaged by the Depression: Detroit as a result of massive layoffs prompted by a plummeting automobile market; St. Louis because of the collapse of the Plains wheat-belt economy and the decline of Mississippi River traffic, among other factors. Some people might have thought it appropriate that in the first full year of the New Deal, two cities that desperately needed its help should make it into the Series. Then, too, the teams possessed an abundance of color and verve, with the Cardinals featuring such personalities as Dizzy Dean, Frisch, Durocher, and Medwick; the Tigers, Cochrane, Greenberg, Rowe, and Gee Walker.

When the Cardinals' train pulled into Detroit early on the morning of October 2, Dizzy Dean stepped off "with a regal air and with Mrs. Jerome on his arm," in the description of one writer. As a waiting crowd yelled "We want Dean!" Diz, with wife and brother in tow, waved his big hat and proceeded to the Book-Cadillac Hotel, where he hobnobbed with such celebrities as Mae West and Will Rogers and held court for reporters and admirers.[19]

The next afternoon, 43,000 people filled Navin Field, including 12,000 or so crammed into huge temporary bleachers that rose above left field. As he warmed up, Diz paused to be photographed with anybody who asked, including the ever-present Al Schacht, who, clad in a Tiger robe, climbed up on the pitcher's back. "Hey, Mose!" Dean yelled at Greenberg. "What makes you so white? Boy, you're a-shakin' like a leaf." As J. Roy Stockton observed in later years, "One of Dean's weaknesses was that he never differentiated between those who could be insulted freely . . . and those who should have been treated with courtesy."[20]

For the home team, the Series opener was something of a debacle. Over the first three innings, the Tigers committed five errors behind Crowder. Medwick cracked a home run and three other hits, and although Dean yielded eight hits, including a homer to Greenberg, and threw 150 pitches, he came out the winner, 8–3. That evening, at a local affiliate of the Columbia Broadcasting System, Dean talked by short wave to the explorer Richard Byrd, who was commanding an expedition at the South Pole. "Howdy there Dick Byrd down at the South Pole," bellowed Dean. When Byrd asked about the game, Diz replied, "I didn't have nary a thing on the ball. . . . It was a lousy, tick-flea-and-chigger-bit ball game."[21]

The hosting of the sharecropper's son continued the next morning, when, accompanied by the movie comedian Joe E. Brown, Diz, Paul, and Patricia Dean ate breakfast with Henry Ford at the Ford mansion outside Detroit; got a tour of Greenfield Village, Ford's re-created nineteenth-century hamlet; and then roared back into the city with a motorcycle-police escort.

A few hours later, Rowe took the mound before another full house, while Frisch chose the battle-tested Bill Hallahan. Both men pitched well for eight innings, and then Gee Walker's single in the ninth tied the game at 2–2. While Rowe continued to set down the Cardinals, Bill Walker, another left-hander, relieved Hallahan and gave up a game-winning single to Goslin in the bottom of the twelfth. At that, people poured out of offices and stores in downtown Detroit to celebrate the Tigers' first Series victory in twenty-five years.

With no scheduled off days, the Series picked right up again on October 5 in St. Louis. Sportsman's Park was full as Paul Dean gave up eight hits and five walks but pitched eight shutout innings, while the Cardinals got to Bridges and Elon Hogsett for four runs, with Pepper Martin doubling, tripling, and scoring three times. The Tigers' only run came in the ninth.

In the fourth game of the Series, five St. Louis errors (three by Martin) helped the Tigers score ten times, Rogell driving in four runs and Greenberg, three. Tex Carleton started for the Cardinals, but Bill Walker was the loser, victim of a five-run outburst in the eighth inning. Auker went the distance for Detroit despite giving up ten hits and four runs. Losing the game was bad enough for St. Louis fans, but in the fourth inning the whole Series appeared lost. It started when Virgil "Spud" Davis's pinch-hit single sent Durocher to third. Whether Frisch then sent Dizzy Dean in to run for Davis or whether Diz ran out to first base on his own would never be entirely clear. In any case, Martin followed with a perfect double-play grounder to Gehringer, who tossed to Rogell coming across the bag to force Dean, who didn't slide. Rogell's throw hit Dean squarely in the forehead; he dropped like a rock, and 38,000 people fell silent as their pitching mainstay was carried from the field. Few seemed to notice that as the ball bounced off Dean's head and into short right field, Durocher scored what was then the tying run.

Within a week, tens of millions of American moviegoers had watched newsreels of the incident, which looked a lot worse than it turned out to be. While the game got away from his teammates, Dean regained consciousness in the locker room and announced that he intended to pitch the next day, because "you can't hurt no Dean by hittin' him on the head." "I saw thousands of stars and all kinds of animals," he added, "but I still can't see them Tigers."[22]

But before a capacity-plus 38,536 he was outpitched by Bridges, 3–1. Each man allowed seven hits, but the game was decided when Gehringer bounced a two-run homer off the right-field pavilion roof in the sixth. The teams quickly entrained for Detroit, with the couple of hundred writers covering the Series generally agreeing that it would probably end with game six.

But it didn't, because Paul Dean not only held the Tigers to three runs but got the decisive hit himself. Rowe went the distance and pitched well enough to win, but a critical play in the sixth inning, when catcher Bill DeLancey grabbed Goslin's bunt and threw out Cochrane at third, blunted what might have been a big Tigers rally and limited them to one run. A few minutes later Durocher, on a rare hot day at bat, got his third hit, a double, and Paul Dean won his own game with a run-scoring single.

It was a rough-and-tumble game, especially for Mickey Cochrane. Ernie Orsatti knocked him over on a tag-out at the plate, and he received a bad spike wound in a collision with Paul Dean at first base. Cochrane spent an overnight in a local hospital; the next morning's *Detroit Free Press* carried a front-page photo of the supine manager, his leg in bandages, under the headline *our stricken leader*. That only gave the Cardinals' bench jockeys more to work with.

Cochrane heard their jeers throughout game seven, which he failed to finish behind the plate. By the time the banged-up Detroit manager limped to the dugout and gave way to Ray Hayworth, the score was 11–0, St. Louis. That's how the most lopsided Series game up to then mercifully ended. A few more than 40,000 were present to see the Cardinals jump all over Auker in the third inning. "I thought I had better stuff," the Kansan reminisced nearly sixty years later. "I was faster but the ball wasn't moving."[23] With Dizzy Dean getting two hits in the inning, seven Cardinals scored. Two more came home in the sixth, and another two in the seventh, as Cochrane waved in five more pitchers—including all three of Detroit's previous Series starters—in a vain effort to quell St. Louis's seventeen-hit assault. Dean pitched an almost leisurely game, permitting six hits, striking out five, and holding the Tigers completely at bay.

Besides the score, the game was unique in that it featured the only removal of a player at the order of baseball's commissioner. In the top of the sixth inning, Medwick drove home Martin with a triple between the outfielders. As Medwick slid into third with spikes high, he and Marvin Owen got their feet tangled. Medwick jumped up, a little pushing ensued, and the two squared off before umpire Bill Klem stepped between them. Medwick jogged home on Collins's single to make the score 7–0 at that point.

When the Cardinals were retired and Medwick went back out to left field, the masses in the bleachers became a howling mob. Over the wire bleachers fence soared a limitless variety of missiles: fruit, eggs, vegetables, bottles, anything people within throwing range could get their hands on.

Medwick retreated toward the infield and, with Dizzy Dean and the rest of the Cardinals, stood and watched the continuing barrage. When the four umpires asked Frisch to remove Medwick, the Cardinals' manager flatly refused, whereupon umpire-in-chief Harry Geisel ran over to Commissioner Landis's box near the Tigers' third-base dugout. Landis then summoned Medwick and Owen and, as Frisch, Cochrane, and Bill Klem stood by, talked briefly with the two belligerents. With St. Louis already far ahead and Dean clearly in control, Landis ordered Medwick out of the game. Escorted by police, the St. Louis outfielder disappeared into the visitors' dugout. With the bleachers finally quieted, the game proceeded to its inevitable conclusion.

But with still other angry Detroiters menacing the front entrance to the Book-Cadillac Hotel, the Cardinals had to use the service entrance. Two plainclothes police followed Medwick to his room and stayed with him for hours while his teammates were out celebrating. Said Medwick afterward, "Gee, I felt rotten—but safe."[24]

On the afternoon of October 10, when the Cardinals' train arrived at St. Louis's Union Station, Dizzy Dean emerged on the platform wearing a paper pith helmet and waving a rubber toy tiger. The Cardinals then piled into automobiles and were paraded through the business district. Meanwhile recruiters at the U.S. Army's Whitehall Street station in Manhattan hung a poster that alluded to Diz's brief army service in 1929 and claimed "The Army Trained Him."[25]

The Dean brothers' post-Series festivities had to be cut short, because the next day they flew to Oklahoma City. That night, Diz pitched for his All-Stars—his brother plus assorted minor leaguers and semipro players—against the Kansas City Monarchs. That was the start of a grueling barnstorming itinerary that would take them to Chicago, Cleveland, Columbus, and Pittsburgh, in the course of which Dizzy Dean and Satchel Paige (fronting a contingent of Negro leaguers) opposed each other on a couple of occasions. Also on the Deans' postseason schedule was a series of appearances at the Roxy Theatre in Manhattan, for which together they were to receive about $3,000. Then Diz traversed the continent to pitch briefly in the California Winter League, including another matchup with Paige.

For the first time, Series broadcasting rights had been sold, with the Ford Motor Company paying major-league baseball $100,000 for exclusive advertising. That helped make the players' money pool the biggest thus far: each Cardinal received $5,941; each Tiger, $4,313. Dizzy Dean's Series share—on top of his season's salary, $3,000 for product endorsements and

a local weekly radio appearance, and $8,000 for his barnstorming and the-
ater appearances—would put his 1934 income in the neighborhood of
$25,000 to $26,000.

That didn't include whatever the Dean brothers were paid for a two-
reel movie they made in Hollywood for Vitaphone Pictures. Called *Dizzy
and Daffy*, the film had them clowning around with Shemp Howard (later
known as "Moe" of the Three Stooges). As his pitches raise smoke from
Howard's catcher's glove, it suddenly occurs to Diz that he ought to be
called "Dizzy," to which Paul adds, "Yeah, when I get through with 'em,
it'll be daffy." "Dizzy and Daffy Dean!" exclaims Howard. "What a name!
What a moniker!"[26] (The movie failed to gain consideration in the Academy
Awards short-subject category.)

Patricia Nash Dean was resolved that her husband must cash in for all
he could while he could. After interviewing her at the Deans' Forest Park
Hotel apartment, Marguerite Martyn of the *St. Louis Post-Dispatch* wrote
that "except when she is talking about money there is nothing hard about
Mrs. Dean." But where money was concerned, she didn't mince words. "I
simply will not see money thrown away," she told Martyn. "I am determined
Dizzy shall not end his career on a park bench."[27]

But as the Deans cashed in, the aftermath of the Series found a player
and an umpire somewhat reduced in funds. Landis fined Bill DeLancey
$50 for cursing plate umpire Clarence "Brick" Owens in game four and
Bill Klem a like amount for what the commissioner termed "over-ripe
words" to Goose Goslin in the Book-Cadillac lobby before game six, when
Goslin tried to apologize for a clash they'd had in St. Louis.[28] Klem finally
accepted his Series check, although he initially sent it back to Landis when
it arrived with the $50 deduction. Never one to carry a grudge lightly,
Landis would refuse to have Klem in another Series until 1940, when the
sixty-six-year-old umpire was about to retire.

· · · · ·

IN THE FALL OF 1934, as the Deans were putting themselves on display
both outdoors and indoors in this country, on the other side of the world
other baseball travelers were exhibiting their skills in Japan and later in
Shanghai and Manila. Led by seventy-one-year-old Connie Mack, the party
consisted entirely of American Leaguers, including Ruth, Gehrig, Gomez,
Gehringer, Foxx, Whitehill, Averill, seven other players, an umpire, a
trainer, and a number of players' wives. On hearing of the trip, Ed Barrow

fretted over what might happen to Gehrig and Gomez (but not Ruth): "Suppose the ship sinks? Suppose there is a wreck, an accident or something. Whereinhell would the Yankees be?"[29]

If Barrow no longer cared what happened to Ruth, many millions still cared about him deeply—not only in his own country but over much of the world. More than anything else, the trip to the Orient (as it was still called in those days) was a triumph for the Babe. After a stopover in Hawaii (where Ruth insisted on spreading cheer among the residents of the leper colony on Molokai), the party sailed for Japan. In Tokyo, Ruth was practically mobbed by worshipful throngs shouting "Banzai Babe Ruth!" Editorialized *Baseball Magazine*, "No foreign potentate could have evoked a more royal welcome."[30]

Japan's outpouring of affection for the American ballplayers, added the baseball monthly, ought to receive more publicity in the United States than "scareheads of Japan's increasing navy and supposed militaristic aims."[31] In fact, Japan was a country in political turmoil; two months after the Americans departed, Matsutara Shoriki, the Tokyo publisher who'd sponsored the visit of the big leaguers, would be stabbed almost to death by militant young nationalists.

As in 1932, enormous crowds turned out in Tokyo and other cities to watch top-flight American ballplayers in action against teams of Japanese collegians and ex-collegians. Moe Berg, a Princeton University and Columbia Law School graduate, a multilinguist, and a journeyman catcher brought along because he knew Japanese, spent much of his time wandering around Tokyo with a camera. (The eccentric Berg would later promote the myth that photos he took from a hospital roof were of vital use in the targeting of the United States' carrier-based bombing raid on Tokyo in April 1942.)[32]

Some Japanese observers contrasted the dignified and respectful behavior of the Philadelphia Royal Giants, a group of black professionals who'd visited the country in 1927 and 1931, with the way the Americans burlesqued the one-sided games. But on the whole, the trip seemed a resounding success—especially for Ruth, who hit thirteen homers in seventeen games.

The baseball over, some of the players and wives traveled on around the world. When Gomez and June O'Dea arrived back in New York, he signed a two-year contract for $20,000 per year. The Yankees sought to buy Buddy Myer from Washington and arrange a trade for Heinie Manush, but neither deal materialized. But they did give the Pacific Coast League's San Francisco Seals $25,000 and transfer five players from their Newark farm

club for outfielder Joe DiMaggio, who'd already gotten quite a lot of national publicity by hitting in sixty-three straight games in 1933. Tom Laird
of the *San Francisco News* hailed this son of a local Sicilian fishing family
as "potentially as great an all-around ballplayer as there in the national
pastime today, bar none."[33] Because of misgivings about an earlier knee
injury, the Yankees decided to leave the twenty-year-old with the Seals for
another season.

Bill Terry, determined to strengthen his infield, paid the Phillies $75,000
of Charles Stoneham's money and included four players in a deal for Dick
Bartell. Branch Rickey dealt Tex Carleton, who didn't get along with either
Dizzy Dean or Joe Medwick, to the Cubs for a couple of hangers-on and
cash; in turn, the Cubs sent Babe Herman and Guy Bush to Pittsburgh for
Fred Lindstrom and left-hander Larry French, as part of a housecleaning
whereby Charley Grimm got rid of ten players from his 1933 roster.

But the most-talked-about transaction of the off-season was the sale of
Joe Cronin to Boston (with infielder Lyn Lary as a throw-in) for $250,000,
a record amount of cash. Cronin had recently married Clark Griffith's niece,
but the "Old Fox," as the press called him, wasn't one to mix kinship with
finance. Still only twenty-eight, Cronin signed a five-year contract to succeed Bucky Harris as Red Sox manager; the peripatetic Harris now returned to Washington to manage a team that wouldn't be going anywhere.

Griffith had run a substantial deficit in 1934, as had at least five or six
other big-league franchises. In an unprecedented act, Larry MacPhail
called a press conference to make public that the Reds had lost $229,161
the past season. (It soon became apparent that MacPhail's detailing of Reds
money problems was part of his campaign for night baseball.) Philip K.
Wrigley subsequently revealed that the Cubs had lost about $600,000 since
1932, adding that inasmuch as Babe Herman (gone) and Chuck Klein (re-
tained) had failed to deliver the offense they were supposed to, the club
would have no more $25,000-per-year players. Nonetheless, the Cubs re-
mained one of baseball's wealthiest operations—as well as the most solic-
itous of fan comfort and convenience. In the off-season, Wrigley had the
ballpark's old grandstand seats removed and new, wider ones installed,
thereby reducing its seating capacity by 2,000.

Despite various teams' persistent money ills, baseball had done better
in 1934 than in any year since 1930. Overall American League attendance
was up by nearly 1 million. Besides Detroit's record turnouts, the Yankees
increased their attendance by some 230,000; the Giants did considerably
better than in 1933; and even though the Cardinals' regular-season patron-

age continued to be disappointing, by clearing about $145,000 in World Series receipts Sam Breadon was able to balance his books. His and Rickey's talks with an Oklahoma City oilman named Lew Wentz about selling the franchise came to an end.

At December's major-league meetings, at the age of sixty-five, John Heydler submitted his resignation as National League president, concluding sixteen years in the office. The eight club executives voted to replace Heydler with forty-year-old Ford C. Frick, a former sportswriter, one of Babe Ruth's favorite ghostwriters, and the league's publicity director for the past nine months.

The immediate issue before the National League was Larry MacPhail's proposal that the Reds be permitted to play up to seven night games at Crosley Field. Although Landis reportedly told MacPhail, "Not in my lifetime will you see a baseball game played at night in the majors," the "roaring redhead" managed to gain the positive approval of six of the other seven club representatives—with Charles Stoneham abstaining. Stoneham vowed that the New York Giants would neither have lights themselves nor play at night elsewhere. "With pitchers like Dizzy Dean, Roy Parmelee and Van Lingle Mungo throwing at night," he explained, "we may have serious injuries to batsmen. Besides, baseball is strictly a daytime game."[34]

As for Diz himself, he finally exacted a big raise from Sam Breadon and Branch Rickey, signing for $19,500 and then, accompanied by a bodyguard, going to New York to receive the Base Ball Writers Association award as the National League's Most Valuable Player. But when Lou and Eleanor Gehrig returned to their New Rochelle home from their around-the-world travels, a contract was waiting for $23,000, the same salary the Yankees' slugger had drawn for the past two seasons. Bolstered by his strong-minded wife, for once Gehrig demanded more—and after a couple of weeks, the Yankees gave in. Late in February, Gehrig met with Ruppert at his brewery (now running full blast) and signed for $31,000, which would make him baseball's highest-paid player.[35]

The day after Gehrig signed, Ruth drew his release. Nobody in the majors wanted the Babe as a manager, and again he'd turned down Ruppert's offer of a managing job at Newark. Thanks to the financial guidance of Christy Walsh, his press agent and business manager, Ruth had kept his money out of the stock market and put it into annuities, so that he and Claire Hodgson Ruth could simply have walked away from baseball and settled into a comfortable retirement. But the Babe wasn't ready for that—not yet.

So on February 25, nineteen days after his fortieth birthday, he signed a contract with the Boston Braves as a player and as vice president and assistant manager. The two titles were meaningless, meant to pump up Ruth's self-importance and mislead him into thinking that in 1935 he would replace Bill McKechnie as Braves manager. In fact, Braves president Emil Fuchs—who was behind on his rent on Braves Field and had recently tried to put a dog-racing track in the ballpark (until Landis and Ford Frick vetoed the idea)—just hoped that the Babe could draw enough people locally and around the league to get him out of debt.

· · · · ·

WHEN THE BRAVES met the Cardinals in an exhibition game in St. Petersburg, an overflow crowd of 6,467 showed up to watch Dizzy Dean pitch to Babe Ruth for a couple of innings. Diz took it easy on the Babe, but in Miami Beach, after Bill Terry declared the Giants' clubhouse off limits to Dean and admonished his players not to engage in pregame banter with him, he repeatedly threw at Terry and other Giants until umpire Cy Pfirman made him stop it. It was all good showbiz; about 3,500 people, a local record, paid to get in despite inflated tourist admission prices as high as $2.20.

In Florida and on exhibition stopovers on the way north, Ruth played first base most of the time, struck out a lot, and had trouble running the bases, but he hit a few homers, including two in Newark. And in a chilled season opener at Braves Field, 27,000 New Englanders were ecstatic when he singled in one run and then clouted a 430-foot homer off Carl Hubbell for a 4–3 victory. But it soon became apparent that Ruth was far over the hill. Although his throwing arm was still strong, he couldn't move more than a few feet in any direction in the outfield, and he rarely made solid contact at bat.

The Babe enjoyed one last big day, on May 25 at Forbes Field, Pittsburgh. After homering off Charles "Red" Lucas in the first inning, he hit another off Guy Bush, then singled, and then in the seventh drove Bush's pitch over the double-decked right-field grandstand and completely out of Forbes Field—something nobody had done in the ballpark's twenty-six-year existence. But the Braves lost the game 11–7 and sank deeper into the National League cellar.

That classically Ruthian home run in Pittsburgh was the Babe's 714th in regular-season play. Five days later, in Philadelphia, he twisted his knee running after a fly ball and limped off the field. Ruth wanted to be put on the voluntarily retired list and stay on with the Braves in some capacity, but Fuchs insisted that he continue as a player. Then they quarreled over whether Ruth could take leave to attend a party celebrating the arrival in New York of the *Normandie*, France's huge new ocean liner. At that Fuchs, up to his ears in unpaid bills, was ready to unload Ruth, his $25,000 salary, and his .181 batting average. Ruth and his wife returned to their spacious apartment on Manhattan's Upper West Side, with the Babe still hopeful that somebody in the majors would ask him to manage.

The team he left behind was as bad without him as with him—a 115-game loser that drove Fuchs to sell his holdings in the franchise to co-owner Charles F. Adams, who made Bill McKechnie its president and started looking for buyers. Just two years earlier, things had looked so promising for Boston's National League franchise.

· · · · ·

BABE RUTH'S last try at doing what he'd once done better than anybody else was one thing that gave the start of the 1935 season a distinctive quality. Another was the fact that for the first time since the spitball was developed and widely adopted early in the century, nobody in either league could legally throw it. Just before the season began, Burleigh Grimes—the last spitball pitcher in the majors and one of an original seventeen exempted from the ban on "trick pitches" adopted in 1920—was released by the Yankees, the fourth club with which he'd tried to hang on over the past year and a half. From then on, nobody could apply spit or smear, stain, scuff, cut, or otherwise alter the baseball—at least not within the rules. Of course, plenty of pitchers would continue to "load up" one way or another; umpires would continue to police them, with varying degrees of success.

At the beginning of the 1935 season, thirteen of sixteen major-league ballparks were equipped with loudspeaker systems, from which resounded not only information about lineups and lineup changes but phonograph music and advertisements. Although the *Sporting News* worried about excessive use of such amplifying apparatus, in the years and decades ahead ballparks would be filled with an increasing amount of manufactured noise.

The eight opening days drew 11,509 fewer people than in 1934—an outcome attributed to generally foul weather in the eastern United States. But as the season progressed, it became apparent that baseball was experiencing an attendance turnaround paralleling an increasingly discernible turnaround in the nation's economy. At last, the New Deal's unprecedented peacetime spending programs were affecting the myriad ordinary ways by which Americans did business. Yet accompanying the hesitant economic resuscitation was the growing militance and power of American wage earners, whose efforts to form unions and exact collective-bargaining rights from employers gained blanket federal sanction that year under the Wagner Act.

Suddenly Leo Durocher found himself personally affected by what had happened in Washington, D.C. The Central Trades and Labor Union in St. Louis announced a boycott of the Cardinals because Durocher had had a woman picketer arrested when she harassed Grace Dozier, his wife, as Dozier crossed a picket line in front of a dress shop where she worked as a designer. Durocher subsequently apologized, and the boycott was called off, but the episode could serve as a footnote to the changing circumstances of American life under the New Deal.

The 1934 Cardinals acquired the nickname "Gas House Gang" retrospectively; it actually didn't appear in the press until midsummer 1935. Who first used the phrase would remain in question, but it quickly caught on as a fitting label for such a scrappy, unkempt, rollicking band of ballplayers. Yet for all their color and drawing power (more on the road than at home), the 1935 Cardinals couldn't repeat their championship season.

The National League that year would belong to the Chicago Cubs, rebuilt almost as thoroughly by Charley Grimm as the Giants had been by Bill Terry two years earlier. The season was only two weeks old when the Cubs proved themselves as combative as anybody. At Wrigley Field, Pittsburgh's Harry "Cookie" Lavagetto slid hard into Billy Jurges at second base; as they rolled around and punched at each other, Grimm ran toward the melee, and Guy Bush, resentful at being traded from his old team, headed for Grimm but landed a blow instead on pitcher Roy Joiner before the umpires got things under control. In his first such disciplinary action, league president Frick fined Jurges $50 and suspended him for three days; Bush had to pay a like amount and was suspended for five days. Somehow Lavagetto got off free.

The Giants moved out to an early lead over St. Louis, with Pittsburgh and Chicago staying fairly close. The Pirates' pitching never measured up to that of the National League's three other consistent contenders, but in 1935 Darrell "Cy" Blanton, a rookie right-hander who two years earlier had struck out 284 batters in the Western League, posted eighteen wins, led the majors with a 2.58 ERA, and moved all too easily into the Pirates' company of hard drinkers. With a succession of line-drive hitters tailored to spacious Forbes Field, the Pirates usually led the league in triples; of the ninety they hit in 1935, shortstop Arky Vaughan collected ten, en route to leading the majors with a .385 batting average.

Carl Hubbell, with twenty-three wins, was again the Giants' main man on the mound, but Hal Schumacher won nineteen (including a stretch of eleven in a row); Roy Parmelee, fourteen; and newcomer Clydell Castleman, fifteen. Dick Bartell stabilized the left side of the New York infield and enabled chronically gimpy Travis Jackson, still effective at bat, to move to third full time. In his last full season, Bill Terry batted .341, while Mel Ott put in another fine year (.322, thirty-one homers, 113 RBIs), and Hank Leiber, a broad-shouldered native Arizonian, became Terry's full-time center fielder and batted .331, with twenty-two homers and 107 RBIs.

Joe Medwick and Ripper Collins again led the Cardinals' attack—Medwick with a .356 average, twenty-three homers, and 126 RBIs, and Collins with .313, twenty-three homers, and 122 RBIs. But the aging Frank Frisch became a part-time player, catcher Bill DeLancey's career ended when he developed tuberculosis, and rookie Terry Moore, although playing a sparkling center field, couldn't provide much offensive punch.

Although lefties Bill Hallahan and Bill Walker both pitched effectively, with 15–8 and 13–8 records, respectively, the Dean brothers again carried most of the St. Louis pitching load. Between them they appeared in ninety-six games, won forty-seven, saved ten, and worked 595 innings. Diz won twenty-eight times; Paul again won nineteen. But while the St. Louis writer Dick Farrington hailed Diz as "the new gate god, [Ruth's] successor to the throne of public appreciation and idolatry," the elder Dean's ego continued to get in his and others' way.[36]

On June 9, in Pittsburgh, Dean became incensed by a succession of errors behind him and started lobbing the ball to the Pirates batters, who started teeing off. Removed by Frisch, he had a shouting match in the dugout with Medwick and Collins and then a scorching session with Frisch in the locker room. On July 5 he and Paul refused even to leave the dugout and wave to about 10,000 people who'd come to Lexington Park in St. Paul for a Cardinals–St. Paul Saints exhibition game.

Afterward Dean, besides pointing out that he'd pitched in Chicago the day before (his twelfth win) and that Paul would take his turn on the team's return to St. Louis, went on to lambast Breadon and Rickey for scheduling so many exhibition dates. Six weeks later, the Boston Braves canceled a home game with the Cardinals on Tuesday and rescheduled it as part of a doubleheader on Wednesday, so both teams could travel 150 miles to play an exhibition game in Lewiston, Maine. Paul Dean begged off that trip, claiming a sore hip; Diz went along on the excursion but would only sit on the bench in street clothes.

While the Giants, Cardinals, Cubs, and Pirates had been winning most of the time, the Reds and Phillies, two chronic losers, had met in Cincinnati in major-league baseball's first regular-season night game. On Friday, May 24, at 9:00 P.M., President Roosevelt threw a switch that sent electric current from the White House 450 miles west to flood Crosley Field in light. Ford Frick, subbing for Landis, threw out the first ball; American League president Harridge and numerous other dignitaries from baseball and public life were on hand, as were 20,433 paying customers—about six times as many as usually attended Reds weekday games. Manager Charley Dressen started Paul Derringer but held the veteran Jim Bottomley as well as Ernie Lombardi, his star catcher, out of the lineup (presumably out of concern for their safety); Joe Bowman pitched for the Phillies. The night air was chilly and damp, and by the time the well-pitched and errorless game ended at 10:55 in a 2–1 Reds victory, locomotive smoke from a nearby rail yard had settled over the field. That convinced the *Sporting News*'s Edgar Brands of "the impracticability of holding night games until warm weather arrives."[37]

But Larry MacPhail wasn't waiting for midsummer. The next Reds night game took place only a week later, versus Pittsburgh. Those first two nighters and the five that followed (concluding with a second game with the Phillies on September 8 that drew only about 11,000) produced an aggregate attendance of 123,991 and net receipts in excess of $150,000. The haughty Giants missed out on a nice visitors' share, but the Cardinals received a hefty dividend on the night of July 31, when an overflow crowd was on hand to see Dizzy Dean in action. St. Louis won the game, but toward the end, as people crowded up toward home plate, it took on a farcical aspect. At one point, a young woman grabbed a bat and occupied the batter's box as Dean shook with laughter on the mound.

The Reds were a better team in 1935, rising to sixth place. Economic conditions in and around Cincinnati were also somewhat improved, so the Reds' season attendance of 448,000 and $50,000 profit couldn't be attributed solely to night baseball. Nonetheless, it was obvious that many people would attend night games who couldn't or wouldn't be there in the daytime. Yet ingrained caution, a sense of tradition, and, in the case of St. Louis, an inability to agree on which franchise would pay for a lighting system kept the other big-league teams from following the Reds' lead. When the next franchise turned on the lights, it would again be at the initiative of Larry MacPhail.

Regarding another innovation of the Depression era, however, the major-league club owners seem to have been won over. By 1935 the All-Star Game had proved both an effective way to raise money for a worthy charity and, as a midsummer spectacle, something fans across the country and most of the baseball press wanted to see continue. The third All-Star Game took place in Cleveland's huge stadium, a rather peculiar circumstance inasmuch as the Indians were still playing all their home games at League Park. Nearly 70,000 were on hand for the American League's third-straight victory. Jimmie Foxx's two-run homer off Bill Walker in the first inning provided all the runs the Americans needed, although they later scored two more while Lefty Gomez and Mel Harder held the Nationals to four hits and a single run.

At that point, the Giants held first place in the National League. But the Cardinals were in the midst of a fourteen-game winning streak that, before Brooklyn's Johnny Babich stopped it on July 19, put them within a half game of New York. Within another nine days, the Cubs, having themselves won twenty of their last twenty-three, were only a game and a half out of first. In August the Giants stretched their lead back by a few games, only to yield it to St. Louis by the end of the month. At the conclusion of the Labor Day doubleheaders, St. Louis led by two games over New York, and two and a half over Chicago.

Two days later, on September 4, the Cubs began a long home stand by defeating Philadelphia 8–2 behind Larry French. They didn't lose again until September 28, after twenty-one consecutive victories. That streak propelled them past the Giants (who fell to third and stayed there) and finally the Cardinals. On Wednesday, September 25, leading St. Louis by two games, they began a five-game set at Sportsman's Park that would determine the pennant and end the season.

That day, first baseman Phil Cavaretta—a nineteen-year-old signed the previous year out of Chicago's Lane Technical High School—homered for the game's only run, as Lon Warneke's two-hitter overcame Paul Dean for Chicago's nineteenth consecutive win. A rainout on Thursday necessitated a Friday doubleheader, which the Cubs swept on a cold, dark day before 16,694. Bill Lee clinched the pennant by holding the Cardinals to two runs while a tired Dizzy Dean gave up fifteen hits and six runs, including homers to Fred Lindstrom and Stan Hack. That put Chicago up by four games, with only three to play. Charley Root and little Roy Henshaw combined to beat the Cardinals 5–3 in the nightcap, pushing the streak to twenty-one. It ended in a meaningless Saturday game, when Joe Medwick homered in the eleventh inning off little-used Fabian Kowalik.

The Cubs finished with an even one hundred victories, four more than the Cardinals, who'd actually won one more game than in 1934. Down the stretch, Chicago's pitching staff, shaky earlier in the season, solidified into a remarkably balanced and consistent group of hurlers. Bill Lee—a big, handsome right-hander from Plaquemine, Louisiana, and a former Cardinals farmhand whom Branch Rickey had unwisely sold for $20,000—was a twenty-game winner in his second year in the majors. Lon Warneke also won twenty; Larry French and Tex Carleton won seventeen and eleven, respectively, for their new club; Charley Root was still good for fifteen; and the 5-foot 8-inch Henshaw posted thirteen wins—the high point of an otherwise undistinguished career.

Although they topped the league with a .288 team average and 847 runs, the 1935 Cubs weren't a powerful outfit. Chuck Klein led the team with twenty-one homers, as he, Lindstrom, and Al Demaree shared time in center and right fields. Grimm's everyday left fielder was Californian Augie Galan, whose first full big-league season—in which he batted .314 and led both leagues with 133 runs scored—was the best of his sixteen in the majors. Billy Herman batted .341 and played the league's best second base, and the redoubtable Gabby Hartnett hit .344, drove in ninety-one runs, and still showed one of the strongest catcher's arms ever.

. . . . .

AS USUAL, the American League race wasn't anything special. Jimmy Dykes's Chicago White Sox didn't hit much, but they played surprisingly well in the early going and ended up in fifth place, their strongest showing in eight years. Joe Cronin's Boston Red Sox had even more trouble scoring runs, but they again finished fourth, largely on the strength of Wes Ferrell's twenty-five wins along with twenty by Lefty Grove. Mysteriously recovering his arm strength, Grove threw 273 innings, allowed only 2.70 earned runs per each nine, and completed twenty-three starts. Cleveland again finished a fairly remote third; in August, Alva Bradley gave up on Walter Johnson, firing the game's second-winningest pitcher and giving his job to Steve O'Neill, a former Cleveland catcher who'd been managing at Buffalo. Mel Harder won twenty-two games for the Tribe, and, with most of his teammates slumping at the plate, Joe Vosmik batted .348 but lost the American League batting title by one point to Washington's Buddy Myer.

Although the Ruthless Yankees led at the All-Star break, by the end of the month Detroit had moved ahead by two and a half games. Most of the Yankees' regulars went into a batting slump; during one stretch, they scored one run for Red Ruffing in twenty-two innings and did little better for Gomez, who won only twelve times with the league's fourth-best ERA. With Ruth gone, opposing moundsmen now often pitched around Gehrig, with the result that he walked more times (132) than anybody in either league. Occasionally leaving games because of "lumbago attacks," Gehrig batted thirty-four points lower, hit nineteen fewer homers, and drove in forty-six fewer runs than in 1934. (Ed Barrow attributed the subpar performances of Gomez and Gehrig to their being worn down by their off-season global travels.)

Gomez later pinpointed the deciding moment in the 1935 race: a mid-August game at Yankee Stadium before more than 70,000, when he blew a 5–0 lead in the sixth inning, with Tony Lazzeri barely missing Marvin Owen's bloop hit down the right-field line that scored the go-ahead runs. After that, the Tigers pulled away, winning twenty-two of twenty-seven games on a long home stand and building an eight-game lead. They clinched on September 21 with a doubleheader sweep in St. Louis, although by losing a season-closing doubleheader at Chicago, they ended up only three games better than the Yankees.

"Say, this master-minding business is a lot of bunk," cracked Mickey Cochrane as his Tigers neared their second pennant in a row. "What it takes to win ball games is hitting, pitching, throwing, and fielding—not deep thinking."[38] Cochrane's 1935 team had all those qualities in plenitude. The Tigers again topped the majors with 919 runs, of which Hank Greenberg drove in 170; Goose Goslin, 109; and Charley Gehringer, 108. Pete Fox became Cochrane's everyday right fielder and batted .321, while Cochrane himself hit .319 in 115 games. (Ray Hayworth, his backup, batted .309 for the hard-hitting Detroiters.) Not the sensation he'd been in 1934, School-boy Rowe nonetheless led the staff in innings pitched (276) and posted a 19–13 record. Tommy Bridges was Detroit's top winner with twenty-one; Eldon Auker won eighteen times, and Alvin Crowder, sixteen.

The Tigers again led everybody in attendance, surpassing the 1 million mark for the first time in the franchise's history. They could have packed in bigger crowds on a number of occasions if Navin Field's regular capacity had exceeded 32,000. Again the ballpark underwent a postseason expansion, but for the 1935 World Series the left-field bleachers were built in as well as up, so that the distance down the line diminished from 339 feet to 300 feet, with a 20-foot wire fence fronting the bleachers.

. . . . .

AGAIN, Ford Motor Company paid $100,000 for Series advertising rights. Besides NBC, for which Hal Totten and Ty Tyson would do the play-by-play, and CBS, which employed France Laux and Jack Graney, the new Mutual Broadcasting System would carry the games, with airtime divided between Chicago's Bob Elson and Quin Ryan and young Red Barber from WLW in Cincinnati.

For the second year in a row, the World Series began in the American League city.[39] As things played out, this year's "fall classic" wouldn't have the drama of last year's, although a person sitting close to the field in the $6.50 boxes could hardly have questioned the players' pugnacity. If for nothing else, the 1935 Series would be remembered for the torrent of really nasty bench jockeying that went on, especially by the Chicago Cubs. As one commentator has written of the Cubs, "They picked on physical features, ethnic background, religion, weight, embarrassing incidents—anything to get a player flustered or angry."[40]

Early in game one, first-base umpire George Moriarty called time and went over to the nearby visitors's dugout to lecture the Cubs on the need to quell their harassment of Hank Greenberg—"pants' presser" being one of the milder epithets he'd heard directed at the big slugger. From that point on, the Chicago players also yammered away at Moriarty.

As for the opening game itself, it proceeded briskly to a 3–0 outcome in favor of Chicago. Lon Warneke threw a neat four-hitter, while the Cubs scored twice in the first inning on Rowe, who made a critical throwing error, and again with Frank Demaree's ninth-inning home run. Every seat at Navin Field was filled that day, as was the case for game two, which Detroit won 8–3 behind Bridges. Charley Root was routed after facing only four batters and giving up four runs, including a two-run homer by Greenberg. But in the seventh inning, Greenberg slid into home plate and suffered what X rays revealed to be a broken wrist.

For game three, the next day, the Series moved to Chicago. Again Wrigley Field's capacity had been enlarged by the construction of wooden bleachers above the regular stands in right and left fields. Marvin Owen moved over to first base; reserve infielder Herman "Flea" Clifton took over at third. With Greenberg's big bat lost to the Tigers, Chicago seemed to have the advantage, but the Detroiters took the Series lead with a 6–5 victory in eleven innings. Larry French—who'd relieved Warneke, who in turn had taken over from Bill Lee and given up four runs in the eighth— lost the game when Jo-Jo White singled in Owen after Fred Lindstrom, playing third base, fumbled what should have been a double-play ball. Auker started for Detroit and gave way to Elon Hogsett, who was relieved by Rowe after the seventh inning. Rowe let the Cubs tie the game in the bottom of the ninth but managed to hold on through the tenth and eleventh.

It was a ragged game, marked by wobbly pitching and shoddy fielding— and by continual verbal exchanges between Moriarty and the Cubs dugout. After Moriarty ejected manager Grimm for arguing too vigorously over a call at second base, reserve outfielder Tucker Stainback and Woody English, Chicago's bench-riding captain, also got the thumb, with Moriarty standing over the dugout occupants and giving them something of a clinic in profanity. Both Commissioner Landis and Ford Frick were sitting close enough to hear most of it; Frick declared that no National League umpire would be allowed to talk that way.

The next morning Landis summoned Grimm, English, Billy Herman, Billy Jurges, and Moriarty to his little Michigan Avenue office. Grimm avowed that he'd "never heard an umpire abuse members of a ball team with the language Moriarty used yesterday to Herman, to Jurges, to English, and to me, and then to the entire bench." Landis asked Herman to repeat what Moriarty had said. "I have always prided myself on a command of lurid expressions," Landis said years later. "I must confess that I learned from these young men some variations of the language even I didn't know existed."[41]

That afternoon, before nearly 50,000 at Wrigley Field, Alvin Crowder pitched superbly, allowing five hits and a single run—Hartnett's second-inning homer. Clifton scored what proved to be the winning run in the sixth, when Galan dropped his fly ball and Jurges let Crowder's roller get through him. Tex Carleton left after seven innings, behind 2–1 in what should still have been a tied game.

Down three games to one, the Cubs came back to win game five in a matchup of hard-throwing Arkansans. Warneke pitched six innings of shut-out ball with an aching right shoulder and then turned the game over to Lee with Chicago ahead 2–0 as the result of a two-run homer by Chuck Klein (in his only Series start) off Rowe in the top of the sixth. Herman doubled in another run in the seventh; Lee got through that inning and the eighth and then gave up a run on three straight singles to start the ninth before retiring the next three batters to preserve Warneke's victory. (In the Chicago clubhouse, while trainer Andy Lotshaw applied heat to his shoulder, Warneke sat listening to the game's progress on radio, chewing tobacco and smoking cigarettes at the same time.)

Because he'd had to use Lee for three tough innings the day before, Grimm gave the ball to French in the hope that the left-hander could prolong the Series, while Cochrane relied on Bridges to end it. Pete Fox doubled in Cochrane in the first inning, but the Cubs tied it in the third. Detroit scored again in the fourth; then, in the top of the sixth, Herman put Chicago into the lead again with a two-run homer. But in the bottom of that inning, Marvin Owen got his only hit of the Series, driving in Billy Rogell with the tying run. Meanwhile Moriarty continued to wrangle with the Cubs, who were all over him after he called out Stan Hack for veering out of the baseline and then ruled Jurges out at second when he tried to stretch his hit into a double.

Hack led off the ninth inning with a triple, but three outs later he was still standing at third base and the score was still 3–3. With one out in the bottom of the ninth, Cochrane singled and then advanced to second as Cavaretta knocked down Gehringer's line drive and stepped on first base. As Goose Goslin took his stance in the left-hand batter's box with 48,237 roaring for a hit, he told umpire Ernie Quigley, "If they pitch that ball over this plate, you can go take that monkey suit off."[42] The Goose connected with French's second pitch, lifting a soft line drive that fell in right-center field; Cochrane raced home with Detroit's first World Series championship.

Jubilant Tigers fans waited to cheer each player as he left the Detroit locker room, while downtown the streets were clogged with shouting, laughing, frequently tipsy, but generally orderly celebrants. Frank Navin rewarded Cochrane with a $15,000 bonus to go with his $30,000 annual salary and his $6,100 Series share. Tommy Bridges took $1,040 of his Series money and purchased a new Cadillac. "We thought he'd gone crazy," recalled Auker, "spending a thousand dollars for a new car."[43]

Each Cub's share was $4,198, although Grimm, Herman, Jurges, and English would discover that Landis had deducted $200 apiece in fines from their checks; umpire Moriarty's Series pay was reduced by the same amount. "There isn't an ounce of fear in [Moriarty]," wrote John Kieran. "But a few ounces of discretion inserted above his shoulders would have saved a lot of useless and boisterous bickering."[44]

Frank Navin had lost a fortune in the Great Crash and on bad picks at the race tracks and had been forced to borrow money to send his team to spring training in 1931. To keep going, he'd had to rely increasingly on the wealth of Walter O. Briggs, whose company manufactured automobile bodies for Ford and Chevrolet. By 1935 Briggs owned 50 percent of the Detroit franchise, and he became full owner after November 11, 1935, when at age sixty-four Navin suffered a fatal heart attack while horseback riding. One of Briggs's first acts was to make Cochrane vice president of the Detroit franchise.

Following two successful seasons on the playing field and at the ticket windows, that franchise was financially solid, operating in a city that had weathered the worst of the Depression. Now, although epic labor–management struggles lay ahead, the automobile assembly lines were humming again, and people were going back to work. The weekly magazine *Time* even suggested that Cochrane was at least partly responsible for Detroit's improving economy, noting that his arrival from Philadelphia "coincided roughly with the revival of the automobile industry and the first signs of revived prosperity." Cochrane's "determined, jolly New England–Irish face grinning from newspapers" had seemed to herald better times for the city.[45]

Long afterward, as he looked back on his twenty-one-year professional career, Goose Goslin pronounced Detroit "the best baseball town I ever played in and for. . . . The fans there were great."[46] Detroit would always be a splendid baseball town, but the happy days for the Tigers were over for a while. Cochrane, his players, and Tigers fandom were about discover just how wrong things could go and how little anybody could do—either in the American League or in the World Series—to stop the most powerful Yankees aggregation so far.

CHAPTER 6

Toward Recovery, 1936–1937

URING THE 1935 SEASON, the Brooklyn Dodgers drew 470,517 people to Ebbets Field and managed to meet expenses but again finished in sixth place under Casey Stengel. The franchise was still way in debt. All in all, it wasn't much of a season to remember except for one truly macabre episode—something that many contemporaries assumed could happen only with the Dodgers. John Kieran was moved to advise his readers that *Idiot's Delight*, Robert E. Sherwood's hit Broadway play, had nothing to do with the Brooklyn ball club.

Len Koenecke was a thirty-one-year-old outfielder—a Wisconsinite who'd first come up to the New York Giants from Indianapolis in 1932, then been sent back to Indianapolis, and then drafted by Brooklyn. Koenecke had a good first year with the Dodgers, but in 1935 his hitting fell off, and Stengel put him in the lineup less frequently. Koenecke apparently drank a lot, at least enough that on September 17, in St. Louis, Stengel decided to hand him his unconditional release.

With two other players (both in good standing), Koenecke was supposed to return by air to New York, but in Detroit he was put off the regular commercial flight for being drunk and obnoxious. Koenecke then chartered a private aircraft to fly him to Buffalo. En route he got into a fight with pilot William Mulqueeney; unable to subdue him otherwise, copilot Irwin Davis grabbed a fire extinguisher and beat the ballplayer senseless. When they made an emergency landing at Toronto, Koenecke was pronounced dead. After a brief inquiry, both Mulqueeney and Irwin were exonerated.

If baseball followers, especially Brooklyn loyalists, were shocked at reading of the Koenecke episode, at least by late summer 1935 most of them
would also have been better able to afford a daily newspaper as well as a
few other nonessentials. Baseball shared in the generally improving economic conditions; major-league attendance for 1935 reached a little more
than 6 million, quite a comeback from the bottom times two years earlier.
Twenty-one minor leagues began the season; not only did they all complete
their schedules, but there was a notable absence of the franchise foldings
and relocations that had especially plagued the lower minors. The Atlanta
Southern Association franchise was one of 1935's success stories; under the
energetic presidency of young Earl Mann, the Crackers set a new league
attendance mark of 330,795.

By the second half of 1935 the federal government was massively and
unprecedentedly involved in putting people back to work and pumping
money into the economy. Despite the Supreme Court's invalidation of the
National Recovery Administration and subsequently (in January 1936) the
Agricultural Adjustment Administration, the New Deal's centerpiece recovery programs, the Civilian Conservation Corps, remained in business,
and other federal programs were taking people by the millions off the
unemployment rolls. Established in 1933, the Public Works Administration
(PWA) contracted for large-scale construction projects such as airports,
schools, highways, and major bridges. But while the PWA was supposed to
be the New Deal's biggest spender, under Secretary of the Interior Harold
L. Ickes's tightfisted direction the agency never provided the massive stim-
ulus to recovery that its framers had anticipated.

As it turned out, the Works Progress Administration (WPA)—created
in a second big burst of New Deal legislation in 1935—spent more money
than the PWA and put more people to work, albeit on what were supposed
to be temporary and relatively small-scale projects. By early 1936, more
than 3 million previously unemployed Americans were drawing up to $40
per month from the WPA for doing everything from digging drainage
ditches and building roadside parks to painting post office murals and playing in orchestras. And by then, the New York Times's index of business
activity had climbed to 95 percent of normal.

Meanwhile the Communist Party of the United States, which up to 1935
had been militantly anticapitalist and anti–New Deal, followed directions
from Moscow and initiated a broad coalition that brought together Communists, fellow travelers, independent radicals and liberals, labor unions,
and assorted other progressive elements in an antifascist Popular Front.

Besides recruiting carefully screened volunteers to fight for the Spanish Republic in its civil war against rightist rebels, the CPUSA took a leading role in the newly created Congress of Industrial Organizations (CIO), as the CIO sought to organize workers industry by industry in such mass-production segments of the economy as automobiles, steel, rubber, and textiles. So, as the Depression-era economy improved, American wage earners became increasingly demanding and confrontational, determined to redress the historic imbalance between labor and capital.

. . . . .

ALL OF WHICH AFFECTED professional baseball players little, if at all. They made no effort to unionize, to attack the reserve clause, or to change the basic elements of labor–management relations. Like other still-employed professional people in the 1930s, they were happy to be getting paid to do what they wanted to do, even if their lives in professional baseball usually lasted no more than five or ten years. So, within their limited maneuverability vis-à-vis their employers, they sought to make as much as they could while they could.

For many of them, that meant barnstorming ventures and other forms of postseason competition before crowds who rarely, if ever, had a chance to see big leaguers in the flesh. On Sunday, October 13, for example, the semipro Metropolitan Baseball Association provided a final venue for both Babe Ruth and Dazzy Vance (who'd spent 1935 with Brooklyn). Ruth was in the lineup for the Bay Parkways; Vance was on the mound for the Bushwicks. Before some 16,500, the Babe hit one of Vance's no-longer-fast pitches out of Dexter Park and did a last tour of the bases.

On the same day, at Yankee Stadium, Dizzy Dean collected $1,400 for beating the Kansas City Monarchs 3–0 and then took his All-Stars to Chattanooga and New Orleans (where he refused to pitch because of small crowds) and on to Dallas, where he threw five innings versus Schoolboy Rowe.[1] From Dallas, Dean's tour headed for Los Angeles for games there and at Santa Monica with a collection of black professionals playing as the Brooklyn Royal Giants. Dean, now backed by an assortment of Pacific Coast Leaguers and California-based big leaguers, fared well against the Royal Giants, who included such standouts as Satchel Paige, Chet Brewer, Norman "Turkey" Stearns, George "Mule" Suttles, and Raleigh "Biz" Mackey. Larry French, however, lost twice to the Royal Giants.

Meanwhile Connie Mack's son Earle led a team of major leaguers on an expedition to Mexico City, with expense-raising stopovers for games with

Texas semipros. Including Jimmie Foxx, Earl Whitehill, the White Sox's Ted Lyons, Heinie Manush, and Rogers Hornsby (still listed on the Browns' active roster), the big leaguers played sixteen games in eighteen days, mostly against Mexican professionals and teams of picked amateurs. But on October 25, 26, and 27 they met the Pittsburgh Crawfords, who'd just defeated the New York Cubans for the Negro National League championship.

One of the top teams in black baseball history, the Crawfords featured Oscar Charleston, William "Judy" Johnson, James "Cool Papa" Bell, the mighty Josh Gibson, and Leroy Matlock, who'd won eighteen games without defeat in league competition that year. After a hotly debated 6–6 tie, the white players won 11–7 and 7–2 behind Lyons and the Browns' Jack Knott. Although the interracial series in Mexico City occasioned sparse coverage in the American press, it was a hard-fought, memorable encounter featuring a galaxy of future Hall of Famers—from both sides of the color line.

By the time Heinie Manush and Jimmie Foxx got back home with the $800 apiece the touring white players had cleared after expenses, they discovered that they were both likely to be moving to new ball clubs. At the December league meetings, Manush went to the Red Sox from Washington in exchange for outfielders Roy Johnson and Carl Reynolds, and Connie Mack dealt Foxx and pitcher Johnny Marcum to the same team for $175,000 of Tom Yawkey's cash and a couple of throw-in players.

The departure of Foxx, who'd been with the Athletics since he was seventeen years old, completed the dismemberment of Mack's champion clubs of 1929 to 1931. With a $23,000 contract, Yawkey assuaged whatever regrets (if any) Foxx may have had about leaving surrogate father Mack and his bad ball club. (A few weeks later, Mack also sent Roger Cramer and infielder Eric McNair to the Red Sox for a couple of expendables and more sorely needed cash.)

Al Simmons, the other heavy hitter on the champion Athletics, made his third stop in the majors when the White Sox sold him to Detroit for $75,000. Mickey Cochrane was delighted with the deal, which, as Tigers vice president as well as player-manager, he'd negotiated. "We have all we had last year," Cochrane enthused, "and the big Polack added."[2]

Also at the December gatherings Johnny Allen, whose temperamental behavior and arm troubles had tired Joe McCarthy, went to Cleveland in exchange for two pitchers: right-hander Monte Pearson, an eighteen-game winner in 1934 but no better than 8–13 during the past season, and minor leaguer Steve Sundra. And with Hughey Critz retired, Bill Terry traveled to the National Association meeting in Denver, dickered with Branch Rickey, and gave up Roy Parmelee plus another player and cash for Burgess

Whitehead, a capable second baseman besides being a Phi Beta Kappa graduate of the University of North Carolina.

Again operating on the premise that Tony Lazzeri was about washed up, Ed Barrow and Joe McCarthy made a strong play for Washington's Buddy Myer, reportedly offering Clark Griffith as much as $100,000 for the reigning American League batting champion. Then, too, having missed out on Hank Greenberg, the Yankees apparently sought to land a Jewish player good enough to appeal to the big Jewish population in the Bronx. The fact that Myer was a native of Ellisville, Mississippi, a graduate of Mississippi State Agricultural College, and a thoroughgoing Southerner didn't seem to enter into anybody's thinking. In any case, Griffith wanted more than the Yankees were willing to give, and Myer remained in Washington, where injuries and illness would keep him out of the lineup for two-thirds of the coming season.

Even without Buddy Myer, Jacob Ruppert expected improving economic conditions to bring more people to Yankee Stadium. Besides finally having a loudspeaker system installed, he decided to enhance the comfort as well as the safety of the stadium's bleacherites by taking out the original wooden bleachers and having new concrete open stands built. That cut the distance to straightaway center field by about 25 feet.[3]

Charles Stoneham, Ruppert's closest counterpart among the major-league owners, died in Hot Springs, Arkansas, early in the new year, at the age of fifty-nine. Succeeding him as head of the New York Giants franchise was his thirty-two-year-old son, Horace. Whereas the elder Stoneham had made his fortune through tough, marginally criminal methods, the cherubic Horace liked things soft and easy. Bill Terry would have a stronger hand than ever in Giants operations.

The Boston National League franchise acquired both new ownership and a new nickname when Charles F. Adams finally found a group of local investors to take it off his hands. The new owners hired Robert Quinn, who'd had a long career as a baseball executive with many teams, most recently Brooklyn, to serve as franchise president and, in a further effort to put new life into the organization, changed the team's nickname from Braves to Bees. That may actually have helped: the 1936 Bees would win thirty-three more games than the 1935 Braves and climb to sixth place.

. . . . .

SPRING TRAINING 1936 in St. Petersburg brought the arrival of Joe DiMaggio, who was coming off a third season in San Francisco during which he batted .398, scored 173 runs, drove in 154, hit thirty-four homers, and absorbed the baseball savvy of Lefty O'Doul in the first season of O'Doul's long managing career in the Pacific Coast League. The object of the biggest publicity buildup any rookie had ever received, DiMaggio had become such a sensation that Charley Graham offered to buy the youngster back for $35,000—$10,000 more than the Yankees had paid Graham for him in 1934.⁴ Ed Barrow wasn't at all interested.

DiMaggio, a tenth-grade dropout, was painfully shy and sparsely communicative, with a dead-pan demeanor that New York writers compared with that of the brilliant young heavyweight boxing contender Joe Louis. Yet the twenty-one-year-old left no doubt that he was out to make as much money as he could, as quickly as he could. With older brother Tom acting as his financial adviser, he'd mailed two contracts back to Barrow before agreeing to a third—for $7,500, extraordinary pay for a first-year man. Reaching St. Petersburg from San Francisco after a weeklong automobile trip with fellow San Franciscans Tony Lazzeri and Frank Crosetti alternating behind the wheel (DiMaggio couldn't drive), the youngster was immediately impressive at bat and afield. In his first exhibition game, he hit three singles and a triple off three Cardinals pitchers.

Dizzy and Paul Dean remained unsigned, although within a couple of weeks Diz and Branch Rickey would agree on a salary of about $24,000 for himself and $10,000 for brother Paul. So the Deans missed not only DiMaggio's debut but four earlier games that the Cardinals had split in Havana with teams made up of Cuban professionals and Negro leaguers who'd been playing in the Cuban winter league.

Meanwhile Larry MacPhail had gone the Cardinals one better, sending the Reds by boat to Puerto Rico for the first few weeks of spring training before they relocated to their regular site at Tampa. After a couple of days of practice, one group of Reds flew to the Dominican Republic and won from teams representing Escojido and Licey. The rest of the Reds' contingent remained at San Juan, where they split with still another team of wintering black professionals and lost to the Havana Reds, led by the great pitcher-outfielder Martin Dihigo. The *Cincinnati Enquirer's* Tom Swope described the Cubans and the American black pros he saw in San Juan as "high class players, most of whom come up to big league, or at least, Class AA requirements."⁵

Later, in Tampa, John Kieran talked with Reds manager Charley Dressen about his players. Much was expected of a big left-handed pitcher from California named Lee Grissom, who'd already gained a reputation as something of an eccentric—a "flake," in baseball parlance. Two years earlier, on hearing about Lefty Grove's having his teeth pulled, Grissom had decided that whatever was good for Lefty would be good for him, too. So he had two teeth extracted—"two perfectly good teeth," according to Dressen. "When the Doc asked him which ones to pull, he says, 'Just pull the nearest ones.' He does whatever the big shots do. . . . No head, but a great arm."[6]

Mature beyond his years, Hank Greenberg was anything but a flake. After his superb 1935 season, he demanded $20,000 and got it on March 26, after a long, contentious session with Mickey Cochrane and Walter O. Briggs in Lakeland, Florida, the Tigers' spring base. Another major holdout was the Yankees' Red Ruffing, who wanted more than the $12,000 he'd been paid for winning sixteen games and batting .339 in 109 at bats, including eighteen pinch-hitting calls. The contract Ruffing finally signed contained a $1,000 raise, or so he claimed. Barrow and Ruppert denied it.

Also that spring, National League umpire Albert "Dolly" Stark became the first of his profession to stage a holdout. Stark had been making $9,000, which was about $1,200 above the average for major-league umpires; in the off-season, he also coached Dartmouth College's basketball team. Although umpires couldn't hope for salaries as big as what star players made, they did have an established pension program, something the players wouldn't gain for another decade. After fifteen years of big-league service, an umpire could receive an annual pension of $1,500; after twenty years, $2,000. But Stark wanted more money, and he was willing to jeopardize not only his pension but his whole future as an umpire. National League president Frick wouldn't agree to a raise, so Stark would spend the 1936 season announcing Athletics and Phillies games for a Philadelphia radio station.

That spring, the Yankees' prize rookie established what would become a recurrent pattern of not being ready to start the season. In St. Petersburg, Earl "Doc" Painter, the Yankees trainer, somehow forgot to take Joe DiMaggio out of a diathermy machine in which he was treating a sore heel; by the time he remembered, the youngster had suffered a severe heel burn—so severe that when the Yankees reached Atlanta on the way north, McCarthy sent him ahead to New York (which DiMaggio had never seen) for medical treatment.

· · · · ·

SO ON APRIL 14, while Frank Crosetti played shortstop with a broken nose suffered in Knoxville, DiMaggio sat out the season's first game, in Washington. With President Roosevelt looking on, Lefty Gomez lost 1–0 to the Senators' Lewis "Buck" Newsom, just as he had a year earlier to Wes Ferrell. At the Polo Grounds, Babe Ruth was among some 56,000 on hand for the Giants' 8–5 victory over Brooklyn. Asked how it felt not to be on the field, the Babe seemed bemused: "Feels funny, funny. It's been a long time since I missed an opener." Fiorello LaGuardia, New York City's diminutive, effervescent mayor—a nominal Republican elected in 1933 by a pro–New Deal coalition—threw out the first ball.[7]

Dick Coffman—claimed on waivers the previous fall after a fistfight aboard a train with Rogers Hornsby and banishment from the St. Louis Browns—pitched three scoreless innings for the Giants to save Hal Schumacher's game. Despite Coffman's reputation in the American League as a boozer and troublemaker, the *New York Times*'s John Drebinger thought that he would behave himself for Bill Terry, because "the Giants as a whole are such a quiet, orderly lot . . . that a gay blade soon wears himself out looking for company."[8]

Before the season the consensus among sportswriters was that neither the Yankees nor the Giants were likely to do any better than third place. As things turned out, they met in the World Series for the first time since 1923, the inaugural year of Yankee Stadium. For the Giants, it was something of a struggle; for their American League counterparts on the other end of the Harlem River bridge, it proved to be a relatively easy route to the franchise's eighth pennant.

Detroit, the consensus favorite in the American League, fell into a sea of troubles. The reunion of Al Simmons and Mickey Cochrane turned sour, with Simmons resenting his former buddy's authority and Cochrane resenting Simmons's presumption of favored treatment. Simmons put in another good season, batting .327 and driving in 113 runs, but by September it was generally understood that he would be elsewhere in 1937.

Tommy Bridges had his best year, leading the league with twenty-three wins, but Schoolboy Rowe began the season with a hurting shoulder, and while he won nineteen games he also had a fat 4.51 earned run average. Eldon Auker was even more generous, giving up nearly five earned runs per nine innings and winning only thirteen games while losing sixteen. Alvin Crowder pitched in nine games and then, plagued by ulcers, quit baseball for good. Hank Greenberg was off to a strong start when, on April 29 in Washington, he reached for a throw and collided with the Senators' Alvin "Jake" Powell. Greenberg's left wrist—the same wrist cracked in the previous fall's World Series—was broken again. The season was over for the big slugger.

Worse was still to come. On June 4 the Tigers played the Athletics at Shibe Park, where Connie Mack had ordered a 20-foot extension—"Mack's spite fence," critics called it—built atop the right-field wall to block the view from the Twentieth Street row houses. In the third inning, Cochrane legged out a bases-loaded, inside-the-park homer and then went to the visitors' locker room and collapsed. It soon became apparent that his exhaustion was more emotional than physical—that in fact the Tigers' highstrung, fretful catcher, manager, and vice president had broken under the stress of his multiple duties. Cochrane was away from the team for more than a month, spending most of the time resting at a friend's Wyoming dude ranch. By the time he rejoined the Tigers for their eighty-seventh game of the season, the Yankees had a ten-game lead, and the pennant race was all but decided.

Indicative of how the Tigers' season went was that on July 24, when they gathered in center field to raise their 1935 championship flag, the rope broke, the flag fluttered to the ground, the brass band playing "Hail to the Chief" fell silent, and the ceremony ended. Detroit lost to Boston that day, with the crowd at Navin Field booing even the venerated Charley Gehringer when he committed two errors.

Joe DiMaggio finally made his regular-season debut on May 3, tripling and singling twice in a 14–5 pounding of Rogers Hornsby's hapless Browns before a Sunday crowd of 23,430 at Yankee Stadium. Of course, despite his own proletarian background and like ballplayers in general, DiMaggio was totally indifferent to New York City's charged political and ideological atmosphere. Two days earlier, on the traditional international working-class holiday, Communists and other Popular Fronters had marched to Union Square in lower Manhattan to protest fascism at home and abroad; with the Giants on the road, the anti-Communist wing of the Socialist Party had rented the Polo Grounds for its own rally.

With the addition of DiMaggio and the departure of Johnny Allen and, in June, the touchy Ben Chapman, traded to Washington for Jake Powell, Joe McCarthy had the kind of post-Ruth team he wanted. Personified by the bellwether brilliance of Lou Gehrig, it was an outfit that went about its business with deadly efficiency. The 1936 Yankees batted an even .300, scored 1,065 runs, had 573 extra-base hits, set a new major-league record with 182 homers, and showed the league's lowest earned run average. Ruffing was the staff's only twenty-game winner, but Pearson, Gomez, Bump Hadley, Cubs discard Pat Malone, and Yale University graduate Johnny Broaca won from twelve to nineteen games apiece.

Gehrig again led the Yankees' attack, batting .352, driving in 152 runs, and equaling his career high in homers with forty-nine. Bill Dickey came back from a kidney injury to bat .362, hit twenty-two homers, and drive in 102; Robert "Red" Rolfe batted .319 and played the league's best third base; outfielders Powell and George Selkirk were also .300 hitters; and Tony Lazzeri, whom the Yankees wanted to replace every off-season, drove in 109 runs and hit fourteen homers, including two with the bases loaded in a 25–3 slaughter in Philadelphia on May 24.

DiMaggio fulfilled every expectation, batting .323 with twenty-nine homers and 125 RBIs—and proving the power of his arm with a majors-leading twenty-two assists. Until August, McCarthy positioned him in left field, where Italian Americans in the bleachers behind him waved huge national flags to show their ethnic pride, despite widespread public hostility toward the regime of Benito Mussolini—especially among black Americans—following Italy's invasion of Ethiopia the previous fall. DiMaggio also had the distinction of being the first ballplayer to appear on the cover of *Time*, which hailed him as "the American League's most sensational recruit since Ty Cobb."[9] His two homers in one inning at Chicago on June 24 stirred considerably greater interest than Chuck Klein's feat of hitting four in the Phillies' ten-inning victory at Pittsburgh three weeks later. As Klein's teammate Pinky Whitney put it many years later, "In my day you had to be humble if you played for the Phillies."[10]

DiMaggio's worst day of the season came, ironically, during the All-Star Game, played at what was now called National League Park (sometimes the "Beehive") in Boston. Before a disappointing 25,534, the National League won for the first time, 4–3. Joe Medwick's fifth-inning RBI single and Lon Warneke's relief pitching were the deciding factors. The first rookie All-Star, DiMaggio not only went hitless in five at bats, each time leaving men on base, but misplayed Billy Herman's single, allowing him to take second and then score on Medwick's hit.

When the regular season resumed—with temperatures climbing above one hundred degrees and dust blowing from the drought-stricken central United States as far eastward as Philadelphia and Washington—the Yankees continued to build on their lead over Detroit, Chicago, Washington, and Cleveland, which remained bunched together. Nobody was really capable of challenging them.

The Cleveland Indians were again playing in the big stadium on the Lake Erie shore, but only on holidays and other special occasions. One such occasion was Sunday, August 5, when 63,345 sat through a sixteen-inning tie with the Yankees in a game promoted in connection with the city's ongoing Great Lakes Exhibition. Led by Hal Trosky and Earl Averill, the 1936 Cleveland club fielded a hard-hitting lineup that averaged .304, but apart from Johnny Allen, who won twenty games (and wrecked a Boston hotel corridor with a fire extinguisher after one tough loss), Steve O'Neill's pitching staff was mostly ineffective.

But it did include a seventeen-year-old farm boy who'd only finished his junior year at Van Meter, Iowa, high school. Unveiled in a July exhibition game with the Cardinals, Bobby Feller became an immediate sensation. Throwing a fastball that was overpowering when it found the strike zone (which frequently it didn't), Feller appeared in fourteen regular-season games, winning five and losing three. In sixty-two innings, he struck out seventy-six batters but walked forty-seven. On August 27, at Cleveland's League Park, he fanned fifteen St. Louis Browns, coming within one strike-out of the American League record (set by Rube Waddell in 1908) and within two of Dizzy Dean's major-league mark, set in 1933. Then, at League Park on September 13, Feller was matched against Philadelphia's Randy Gumpert, an eighteen-year-old just graduated from Douglasville, Pennsylvania, high school. The Indians scored twice on an error to win 5–3; Feller walked nine but struck out seventeen to equal Dean's record.

Not only did nearly everybody assume future greatness for Feller, but the boy seemed to assume as much for himself. Billy Sullivan, a Cleveland catcher that year, recalled that when the Indians checked into the Wardman Park Hotel in Washington on Feller's first road trip, he and Feller were billeted together. When Sullivan came back to the room about 8:00 P.M. and Feller let him in (wearing an old-fashioned long nightshirt), on a table Sullivan discovered an old baseball, on which the teenager had been prac-ticing writing his autograph!

Nothing much happened to enliven Washington's generally lackluster season except for the arrival from the Southern Association of nineteen-year-old John "Buddy" Lewis, who'd left Wake Forest College the previous year to play for Chattanooga. Lewis took over third base and, with twenty-two-year-old Cecil Travis at shortstop, gave the Senators long-term stability on the left side of the infield. Bucky Harris got decent mound work from Buck Newsom, Earl Whitehill, and a one-time wonder named Jimmy DeShong, who led the staff with eighteen wins. But as usual, the Senators lacked power, totaling only sixty-two homers. That was two more than were hit by Jimmy Dykes's White Sox, although shortstop Luke Appling batted .388 to lead the majors, and left-hander Vernon Kennedy won twenty-one games. The White Sox's third-place finish was their best showing in the post–Black Sox years.

For all the money he'd spent, Tom Yawkey had to watch his Red Sox sink to sixth place, ahead of only St. Louis and Philadelphia. With player-manager Cronin injured much of the time, "Yawkey's millionaires," as the press dubbed them, scored fewer runs than anybody in the league besides the Athletics, even though Jimmie Foxx delivered as expected (.338, forty-one homers, 143 RBIs). Lefty Grove and Wes Ferrell pitched more than half of Boston's victories, Grove winning seventeen times and posting the league's lowest ERA, and Ferrell winning twenty. But Ferrell liked working for Joe Cronin even less than for Walter Johnson, and on August 21, at Yankee Stadium, he simply walked off the mound in the midst of a New York rally. For that stunt, Ferrell drew a $1,000 fine—subsequently remitted when the temperamental North Carolinian won his next two starts.

On September 9 the Yankees clinched the pennant on the earliest date in American League history, when they knocked out Mel Harder and beat Cleveland 11–3 behind Monte Pearson to take an eighteen-game lead over Chicago, which was temporarily occupying second place. In the League Park clubhouse, Joe McCarthy told his team, "Boys, I knew from the start that you would win the pennant. As soon as I sized up the squad at St. Petersburg, I knew we had the flag."[11] Finishing with a record of 102–51, the New Yorkers led Detroit by nineteen and a half games, with the Tigers, Chicago, Washington, and Cleveland separated by only three.

As always, Lou Gehrig insisted on starting every remaining game of a season that had been decided with three weeks to go—although from time to time he took himself out after a few innings to rest his aching back. Asked how he could stay in the lineup day after day, Gehrig said simply, "Damned if I know." But then he wondered, "How will it be when I can't bend for the ball or do the club any good at the plate? They'll have to take me out, won't they."[12]

. . . . .

IF THE MAIN FASCINATION in the 1936 American League season was watching the Yankees overpower the other seven teams, the National League again gave baseball fans a real race. For the first half of the season, the Giants and Cubs contended for the lead with Pittsburgh, St. Louis, and even Cincinnati, which went on a seven-game winning streak and got up to fourth place before the Cubs stopped them on July 2 in front of an overflow night crowd of 33,469. Finishing as high as fifth for the first time since 1928, Charley Dressen's Reds drew 129,000 at night, more than 500,000 for all their home games, and returned a $200,000 profit. Night baseball had proved its utility, conceded the *Sporting News*, because "the easy-money days of before 1929 are gone, and . . . the present generation may as well forget about them."[13]

For the Cardinals, Dizzy Dean was again in top form both on and off the field. The victor in eleven of his first thirteen decisions, Diz seemed to be enjoying himself in every way. Late in May, for example, when the Cardinals stayed at the Bellevue-Stratford Hotel in Philadelphia, Dean, Pepper Martin, and utility infielder Henry "Heinie" Schuble were inspired to don coveralls and workmens' caps and parade through the lobby, dining room, and kitchen—all the while chattering about needed repairs to light fixtures, boilers, and other objects—and then invade a convention of the United Boys Clubs of America and stage a mock fight.

For Diz's younger brother, however, it was anything but a carefree time. Paul Dean struggled all season with a lame arm, pitched only ninety-two innings, and could win only five games. Late in July, after being out of action for more than three weeks, he was driven from the mound by a shoe-company team in an off-day exhibition in Randolph, Massachusetts. Manager Frisch decided to send him back to St. Louis to be examined by team physician Robert Hyland. "I'm no good around here," said young Dean, trying not to sob. "There's something wrong with my shoulder. I can't get anything on the ball."[14]

Despite Paul Dean's ineffectiveness, the Cardinals were in the race for most of the season. As usual, they were a scrapping, umpire-baiting outfit, apparently determined to live up to their Gas House Gang image. In May, for example, Leo Durocher and Casey Stengel scuffled following a game at Ebbets Field. In an August game at Sportsman's Park, Dizzy Dean left the mound to square off with Tex Carleton before resuming business and defeating the Cubs 7–3. The next day, when Durocher was called out at first by umpire Bill Stewart, the Cardinals hurled bats and gloves from the dugout. Stewart chased Durocher and three others and then had to struggle through the angry crowd that poured onto the field at the end of the game, which Chicago won 6–4. The Cardinals even fought among themselves; in September, Joe Medwick and pitcher Ed Heusser traded punches in the Cardinals' dugout when Heusser accused his teammate of not hustling. At one point, Ford Frick summoned Frisch, Durocher, and coach Clyde "Buzzy" Wares to explain why, by his tabulation, the Cardinals had wrangled with umpires in sixty-three of sixty-seven games. Piped Frisch afterward, "I don't know what was the matter with us in those other four games. It sorta spoiled our record."[15]

After sweeping a doubleheader at Pittsburgh on August 16, with Dean winning for the twentieth time, St. Louis led New York by two games, and Chicago by a half-game more. But the Giants, sparked by the return of Bill Terry, bad knee and all, to the everyday lineup in place of Sam Leslie, were in the midst of winning fifteen straight games and twenty-one of twenty-two. That hot spell, in combination with St. Louis's four losses at home to the Boston Bees, launched New York into a three-game lead over Chicago, while the Cardinals dropped to third place.

That's the way they finished. The Giants clinched on September 24 by winning the opener of a doubleheader with Boston in ten innings, Hal Schumacher topping the owlish Danny MacFayden 2–1, while Pittsburgh's Cy Blanton blanked the Cubs. St. Louis swept two from Cincinnati, to no avail. New York's record for the season was 92–62; both Chicago and St. Louis were at 87–67; Pittsburgh, at 84–70.

Mel Ott continued to be the National League's most consistent power hitter, slamming thirty-three homers and driving in 135 runs, although Joe Medwick topped him in RBIs by three. Medwick batted .351, and Chicago's Frank Demaree hit .350, but Paul Waner—hung over much of the time though he may have been—won his third (and last) batting crown with a .373 average.

Dizzy Dean was more than ever the Cardinals' workhorse, totaling 315 innings and pitching in fifty-one games (including four appearances in five games over three days in mid-September). Besides winning twenty-four, he saved eleven for an otherwise mediocre staff.

But it was really Carl Hubbell's year. The quiet-spoken Oklahoma lefty registered a 2.31 ERA, lost only six games, and was the victor in twenty-six, including his last sixteen decisions and a classic 2–1 duel with Dean on July 21. Even the left-wing weekly *Nation* acclaimed Hubbell, who, as Heywood Broun described him, "moves through the world with . . . self-effacement" and "gains his effects with a minimum of effort and with precision rather than power."[16]

. . . . .

JOE DIMAGGIO'S MOTHER, Rosalie, and brother Tom crossed the country to be part of the crowd of 39,419 at the Polo Grounds for the

World Series opener on Thursday, October 1. On a raw, rainy day the Yankees lost to Hubbell, who allowed only a single run—George Selkirk's homer. Dick Bartell hit a two-run shot in the fifth; aided by two Yankees errors, the Giants put it away with four runs off Red Ruffing in the eighth. After a rainout on Friday, the Series resumed on a fine day, especially for the Yankees. Most of the crowd of 43,543 watched in dismay and then tedium as the Yankees battered Schumacher and four successors for seventeen hits and eighteen runs, while Lefty Gomez held the Giants to six hits and four runs. Lazzeri homered with the bases loaded; Dickey, whose left hand had been broken a couple of weeks earlier by an Athletics pitcher, hit one with a man aboard. It was the most one-sided game in Series history and, at two hours and forty-nine minutes, the longest for nine innings. Remarked Giants pitcher Gene "Gabbo" Gabler, "Well, nobody was killed."[17]

President Roosevelt sat through the second-game debacle until two were out in the bottom of the ninth inning. At that point, the public-address announcer asked the spectators to remain in their seats as the president's open automobile came in through a gate in center field, veered around DiMaggio, and pulled up to Roosevelt's box near the Giants' dugout. Only when Roosevelt and entourage disappeared through the gate did play resume, with DiMaggio going back to take Hank Leiber's long fly and then bound up the clubhouse steps.

The next two games, at Yankee Stadium, each set new Series single-game attendance records. In game three, 64,842 saw an excellent pitching duel between Bump Hadley and Fred Fitzsimmons. They gave up one run apiece over the first seven innings—the Yankees' score coming on Gehrig's second-inning homer, and the Giants' on a sixth-inning drive by Jimmy Ripple. Then, in the bottom of the eighth, Frank Crosetti's bounder eluded Fitzsimmons, and Jake Powell came home on the scratch hit. Pat Malone, who'd saved nine games during the season, came on to close it out. The next day, the Yankees dealt Hubbell his first loss since July 13. They scored three times in the third inning on Crosetti's single, Rolfe's double, and Gehrig's homer and added another in the eighth off Gabler, while Pearson held the Giants to two runs on seven hits. The crowd on a bright Sunday afternoon numbered 66,669.

Game five ran for ten innings, played over two hours and forty-five minutes. Schumacher walked six Yankees and gave up ten hits and four runs but also struck out ten and held on until Malone, pitching his fourth inning in relief of Ruffing, gave up a double to Joe Moore, who took third base on Bartell's sacrifice bunt and scored on Terry's long fly ball. A paying crowd of 50,024, most of whom expected the Yankees to end it in five games, was on hand for one of the more tenacious pitching performances in Series history.

The Yankees did end it on Tuesday, October 6, before 38,427 at the Polo Grounds. Terry sent Fitzsimmons back to the mound with only two days' rest, but this time "Fat Freddie" gave up a two-run homer to Powell and lasted only until the fourth inning. Gomez didn't have his best stuff, either, throwing a home-run pitch to Ott and, with his team ahead 5–4, leaving in the seventh in favor of Johnny Murphy. The Yankees added another run in the eighth, as did the Giants on Moore's homer; then, in the top of the ninth, Terry's pitching collapsed, as Dick Coffman and Harry Gumbert gave up seven runs on five hits and four walks. It ended 13–5 when pinch-hitter Harry Danning hit a bounder to Gehrig, who calmly stepped on first base, put the ball in his pocket, and ran for the clubhouse.[18]

The 1936 World Series—the Yankees' first ever without Babe Ruth—broke the attendance record for a six-game set. Each Yankee's share came out to $6,440; each Giant got $4,656. (Mark Koenig, who'd appeared in forty-two Giants games as a utility infielder, picked up his fifth Series check for his third different team.)

. . . . .

JOE DIMAGGIO returned to San Francisco with his mother, brother, and more money than anybody in his eleven-member family had ever seen, and moved back into the three-residence house on Taylor Street where he'd grown up. DiMaggio's main off-season activity would have to do with opening Joe DiMaggio's Grotto Restaurant in partnership with brother Tom.

Meanwhile Christy Walsh, who'd become Lou Gehrig's press agent after Ruth's retirement, sought to promote him as the movies' "new Tarzan," having the muscular Yankee pose for photographers wearing a leopard skin and waving a bludgeon. Joked Johnny Weismuller, the reigning Tarzan, "I guess they'll be making me a ball player next."[19] Gehrig in leopard skin didn't impress Hollywood, but he did impress the Base Ball Writers Association enough to gain his second Most Valuable Player Award, while Hubbell got the honor in the National League.

Jacob Ruppert looked over the Yankees' season's attendance of about 980,000 paid and, as always, directed that most of his profits go back into franchise operations. Ruppert approved plans for the extension of Yankee Stadium's right-field triple-decked grandstand from the foul line into right-center field—a project that would eliminate about 5,000 spaces in the new concrete bleachers but achieve a net gain in overall stadium capacity of about the same number. At the same time, Ruppert and Ed Barrow authorized farm director George Weiss to establish a working agreement with Kansas City of the American Association, which proved preliminary to outright purchase of the franchise the following summer. As of the 1937 season, the Yankees' organization would have grown to ten minor-league franchises.

At last the Giants accepted the necessity of having a farm system of their own. With Terry taking on the added title of farm-system director, Horace Stoneham purchased control of the Albany International League franchise and moved it to Jersey City, where Mayor Frank Hague had succeeded in getting the Public Works Administration to build a big new sports facility, to be christened Roosevelt Stadium. Travis Jackson, who'd been unable to cover much ground at third base in the Series, ended his big-league career to become player-manager at Jersey City.

In a September 10 speech at Charlotte, North Carolina, President Roosevelt, all but assured of reelection in November, had pronounced the Depression conquered. At that juncture, the *New York Times*'s business index had reached 102.8, only a little more than ten points below the high reached at about the same date in 1929. Major-league baseball attendance had climbed to approximately 8 million, with nine of the sixteen franchises showing profits.

One of those profit-showing franchises was Cincinnati, which had come back from the doldrums mainly because of Larry MacPhail's initiative and imagination. But MacPhail, a chronically restless sort, relished challenge more than the fruits of success. So as early as September 19, he announced that he was resigning as Reds vice president and general manager. To succeed him, Powel Crosley and associates hired Warren Giles, who'd been head of the Cardinals' Rochester farm team for the past eight years.

Giles kept Charley Dressen to manage the Reds, but after Brooklyn's drop to seventh place (and despite the biggest crowds at Ebbets Field since 1930) Casey Stengel had finally worn out his welcome. As with Max Carey, the Dodgers still owed Stengel for another year under his contract; like Carey, Stengel would be paid ($15,000 in his case) for doing nothing. It was a situation that John Kieran compared with the New Deal's strategy of paying farmers not to plant crops.

While Stengel and his wife, the former Edna Lawson, acted on the advice of Dodgers outfielder Randy Moore and invested in the Moore family's oil holdings in the great northeast Texas field, the Dodgers hired Burleigh Grimes to direct the team.[20] Grimes's Louisville team had done no better than seventh place in 1936, but Old Stubblebeard had apparently impressed somebody in Brooklyn's muddled hierarchy by getting himself thrown out of numerous games and engaging in a memorable on-field fist-fight with Toledo manager Fred Haney.

Dizzy Dean's pop-off proclivity reasserted itself while he was again barn-storming in Oklahoma and Kansas. Dean complained about "minor league support for a guy who pitched his arm off" and declared that whatever money the Cardinals offered him for 1937, "it wouldn't be enough." That irked at least two of his teammates. From his Rochester, New York, home Ripper Collins noted that "our bush league outfit was good enough to win 24 games for Dean," while in a radio interview in St. Louis, Terry Moore, "speaking as one busher to another," said he hoped to live long enough to see Dean pitch like Carl Hubbell.[21] Collins, displaced at first base by young Johnny Mize, was about to learn that he wouldn't have to put up with Dean as a teammate after all. In the biggest deal of the off-season, he and Roy Parmelee were swapped to the Cubs for Lon Warneke.

But an even bigger transaction that might have happened never did, because Commissioner Landis decided to uphold Cleveland's rights to Bobby Feller, despite clear evidence that the Indians had violated an ex-isting rule prohibiting major-league teams from signing precollege amateur players. General manager Cyril B. Slapnicka had done some creative record keeping to make it appear that Feller had actually been signed by Fargo-Moorhead, South Dakota, with which Cleveland had a working agreement, and then sold to New Orleans, also connected to the Indians. In fact, none of that had taken place; Slapnicka had signed Feller and brought him di-rectly to Cleveland the previous June.

Landis had every reason to rule that Cleveland had signed Feller ille-gally, thus making him a free agent, but the commissioner was convinced that a bidding war for the young phenom—the Red Sox had already offered $200,000—would be bad for baseball. So he ordered the Indians to pay $7,500 to the Des Moines franchise, in whose territory Feller had been signed; Feller then signed a 1937 contract with Cleveland for $10,000—far more money than any ballplayer of his age had ever been paid.

In January 1937 heavy rains and an unusually early thaw caused rivers and creeks throughout the Northeast and in the Ohio and Mississippi river valleys to overflow their banks. When the swollen Ohio backed up into Mill Creek, Crosley Field in Cincinnati was all but submerged. Whereupon Lee

Grissom, in town to sign his contract, found a rowboat somewhere and, with Reds groundskeeper Matty Schwab, rowed from the first-base grandstand over the left-field fence. A photographer was on hand to record the stunt for the ages. (The flood brought lesser but more laudable notoriety to another pitcher, the Athletics' Harry Kelley. When the St. Francis River inundated a large area of eastern Arkansas, Kelley, who owned a farm near Wynne, fitted two boats with outboard motors and, piloting one boat himself, rescued several stranded families.)

That spring, as advance parties of pitchers, catchers, and rookies converged on training sites from Florida to Catalina Island, some writers thought they detected a new obstinacy about salary on the part of veteran players. Perhaps, they suggested, players had caught the militant spirit of workers, who seemed to be striking everywhere—in a whole range of industries from aluminum, smelting, and lumber to tobacco products, shoes, and softdrinks but most of all in the automobile industry. The first months of 1937 brought historic sit-down strikes at a succession of Michigan plants, as the CIO-affiliated United Auto Workers struggled to unionize the giant industry.

Of course, notions of working-class militance carrying over into professional baseball were fanciful. As skilled professionals, ballplayers expected to be paid on performance—and on what club officials thought they could afford. Jacob Ruppert maintained that the Yankees' net profits had never exceeded $160,000 in any year—a 2 percent return on a franchise value he estimated at $8 million. Ruppert and Ed Barrow not only saw winning, in Dan Daniel's words, "as a to-be-expected development," but assumed that their players ought to be satisfied with their World Series shares and not make inordinate salary demands.[22]

So while the Yankees were paid handsomely by the standards of the time, they didn't do as well as they might have if, for example, they'd worked for Tom Yawkey. Although second-year man Joe DiMaggio, again negotiating by long distance, got his salary doubled to $15,000, Bill Dickey, an eight-year veteran coming off his most productive season, had to hold out for a $2,500 raise that brought him up to DiMaggio's level. Lou Gehrig was another holdout; no longer the diffident and submissive employee he'd once been, Gehrig finally agreed to $36,000 plus a $750 signing bonus. He didn't get into an exhibition game until March 20, his latest-ever spring appearance. Twenty-game winner (and .291 batter) Red Ruffing remained unsigned until May 4. He came into the fold for $15,000, although Barrow docked him for the fraction of a season he'd missed.

Dolly Stark also had to come to terms with the baseball establishment. When his broadcasting contract wasn't renewed in Philadelphia, Stark let it be known that he was ready to get back into his blue serge suit and cap and resume his umpiring career. Early in May, when fifteen-year veteran Ernie Quigley became critically ill, the National League rehired Stark, presumably at the same $9,000 salary he hadn't been willing to take a year earlier.

After the 1936 Series, Bill Terry had retired as a player, but as Giants manager as well as general manager he dealt smoothly with his players, most of whom had never been hard to deal with anyway. Carl Hubbell, baseball's best pitcher in 1936, got a $5,000 raise, to $22,500; Mel Ott, a chronically underpaid great player who was being asked to shift to third base (a position he'd never played), compliantly settled for $17,500.

Not so Dizzy Dean, who now lived with his wife in Bradenton, Florida, where he'd purchased a gas station. Despite his bluster of the previous fall, Dean was willing to sign, but only after much haggling at the Cardinals' Daytona Beach training site with Sam Breadon and Branch Rickey over both money and their insistence on inserting a good-conduct clause in his contract. He finally accepted both the clause and a 1937 salary of $25,500.

A couple of weeks later, Diz and his teammates, still in uniform, returned to the Tampa Terrace hotel after a game with Cincinnati. There they encountered tubby Jack Miley of the *New York Daily News*, who during Dean's holdout had written that "for a guy picking cotton for 50 cents a day a few years ago, Diz has an amusing idea of his own importance." "I don't want a $120-a-week man writin' about me," Dean yelled at Miley. "I don't want you ever to mention my name again." When Miley shot back that he didn't like writing about "bush leaguers" anyway, Dean threw a punch. Irving Kupcinet of the *Chicago Daily News* intervened; Joe Medwick swung at him. Medwick or somebody blackened Kupcinet's eye, someone else hit Miley over the head with a pair of spikes, and somehow Frank Frisch ended up under a sand urn and lamp. Afterward, Frisch declared that that was it—he wasn't standing for any more of such shenanigans. "Shucks," said Dean, quickly back in good humor, "there ain't no doubt about it, it's still the gas house gang."[23] So much for good conduct.

If Dean could take pride in the antic Gas House image, Bill Terry's Giants perpetuated their own image of low-keyed professionalism. But as defending National League champions, they found themselves awkwardly disadvantaged in a series of games from late February to early March in Havana, where they began spring training with the idea of attracting enough people to games with Cuban teams to pay their expenses and maybe show a profit.

As with the Cincinnati Reds' games in Puerto Rico and the Dominican Republic a year earlier, the Giants' stay in Havana became a showcase for Latin American baseball talent. The Havana Reds and the Almendares club, thought the *New York Times*'s John Drebinger, "were in far better trim than any big-leaguers [the] Giants could play at that time." The Giants managed one win (mostly pitched by Hubbell) but lost four and tied one. Terry was especially impressed by Almendares's Ramon Bragana, who beat the Giants 6–1 and then battled them to a twelve-inning, 1–1 tie. Terry called Bragana, a Negro National Leaguer in the summer months, "just about as great a pitcher as I ever saw." Drebinger wondered whether "there must be something fishy about calling a world series in New York a clash between the best the game has to offer."[24]

The crowds in Havana had been good, but an even bigger payoff for the Giants, as well as for the Cleveland Indians, came when the teams hooked up in New Orleans on an exhibition tour that had them playing twelve games in seven states and sleeping nearly every night aboard Pullman cars. At every stop, the locals insisted on seeing Hubbell and Bobby Feller in action, beginning in New Orleans, where they both pitched five innings before a crowd of 11,000. Although neither allowed a run, Feller walked six and hit Hank Leiber in the head. Hospitalized for a week, the big outfielder experienced blurred vision and dizziness when he tried to play again. He would miss two-thirds of the season.

A final Hubbell–Feller matchup at the Polo Grounds drew a remarkable preseason crowd of 31,486 to watch them pitch eight innings apiece. For its April 19 issue, *Time* made Feller the second ballplayer to grace its cover. The season ahead, though, would be a frustrating one for the eighteen-year-old Iowan, because in his first start, after striking out eleven St. Louis Browns in six innings, he had to leave the game with a hurting elbow. Feller didn't take the mound again for more than two months (during which time he returned to Van Meter for his high-school graduation). When he came back, he was the staff's workhorse, pitching in twenty-six games, striking out 139 batters in 143 innings, and winning nine games while losing seven.

Over the winter, Schoolboy Rowe had undergone a tonsillectomy in hopes of reinvigorating his arm. It didn't work; after pitching in only five games, he left for what a half-century later would be called a "rehab assignment" at Beaumont, Detroit's Texas League farm club. Paul Dean, Rowe's World Series adversary three years earlier, started once and exited in the first inning; had arm surgery in St. Louis; and then, as stipulated by a clause in his $12,500 contract, took a salary reduction to $400 per month until he could pitch again. Later he refused reassignment to Houston and went back to his Texas farm.

When he reported to St. Petersburg, Joe DiMaggio discovered that during the past year he'd grown an inch and a half, to almost 6 feet 2 inches, and gained about fifteen pounds. But in Florida he also developed a lame throwing arm, and while he kept his teeth, on April 16 he submitted to a tonsillectomy. The arm came back, but his first appearance of the season didn't come until May 2.

Shortly after DiMaggio got into the lineup, substitute outfielder Roy Johnson ruined himself with Joe McCarthy. Following a loss in Chicago, McCarthy huffed into the locker room and happened to overhear Johnson say, "What does that guy expect to do—win every game?" McCarthy immediately told Ed Barrow, "Just get him out of here."[25] Johnson was quickly put on waivers; when (probably through Yankees influence) the other seven American League clubs passed on him, he was sold to the Boston Bees for the waiver price.

With Johnson gone and Jake Powell disabled by an appendectomy, the Yankees called up young Tommy Henrich from Newark. Whereas the previous fall Commissioner Landis hadn't been willing to declare Bobby Feller a free agent, in mid-April 1937 he decided that Cleveland had sought to keep Henrich out of the minor-league draft by illegal methods. Henrich signed at his Massillon, Ohio, home with Yankees scout Johnny Nee for $20,000 plus a $5,000 salary for 1937. In sixty-seven games after joining the champions, the left-handed Henrich batted .320.

· · · · ·

FOR DICK BARTELL, what one New York writer called "the post-depression baseball business" began with a tomato, thrown with precise accuracy from the Ebbets Field upper deck, that hit the Giants' shortstop squarely in the chest when he led off the season opener.[26] The Giants won that game behind Hal Schumacher and quickly found themselves in their usual pennant tangle with Chicago, St. Louis, and Pittsburgh. Hubbell won his first eight decisions to run his streak to twenty-four in a row in regular-season play. It ended in the opener of a Memorial Day doubleheader before an overflow 61,756 at the Polo Grounds, when Brooklyn drove him out in the fourth inning and went on to win 10–4. The great left-hander then lost three more starts before struggling to an 8–4 win at Wrigley Field—to the sound of jackhammers and drills, as work went forward on new concrete bleachers that would enclose the outfield.

Meanwhile Dizzy Dean began the season with twenty scoreless innings and won his first five starts. The fourth was an easy outing in which he laughed and chattered his way to an eleven-strikeout, 13–1 win in Boston. Four times he fanned Vincent DiMaggio, who'd knocked around the Pacific Coast League for five years before being drafted by the Bees. Two years older than his celebrated brother, Vince DiMaggio hit with power but always had trouble making contact in the majors. In 1937 and in five subsequent seasons, he would lead the National League in strikeouts.

Dean lost for the first time on May 14 to Pittsburgh, which had moved out to an early lead in the pennant race. Five days later, an extraordinary weekday turnout of 26,000 at Sportsman's Park (including nearly 4,000 youngsters let in free) was present for a Hubbell–Dean matchup. They saw Hubbell make ninety-three pitches, throw seventy strikes, and win his twenty-second decision in a row. They also saw Dean make a complete fool of himself.

Before the game, the umpires conversed with Terry, Frisch, and the two pitchers about Ford Frick's recent order that the existing balk rule— according to which, with a runner on first or second base, a pitcher had to come to a complete stop before delivering the ball—be strictly enforced. In the sixth inning, with Burgess Whitehead on second, Bartell's pop fly was caught by shortstop Durocher, but plate umpire George Barr ruled that Dean had balked, waved Whitehead to third, and directed Bartell back to the batter's box. Pepper Martin in right field then dropped Bartell's liner, and Whitehead scored. After center fielder Terry Moore misplayed Lou Chiozza's fly, Joe Moore singled in both Bartell and Chiozza to give the Giants a 4–1 lead.

From that point on, Dean threw at every Giants batter except Whitehead, a former teammate, and Hubbell, who of course could throw at Dean—but didn't. As John Drebinger described it, "the Giants went up and down at the plate like duckpins."[27] In the top of the ninth, Jimmy Ripple decided to retaliate in a time-honored way, by dragging a bunt between first and second and forcing Dean to cover first. Second-baseman Jimmy Brown fumbled and then threw late to Dean, who tried to throw a hip into Ripple. When the Giants outfielder swung wildly at the pitcher, the benches emptied. After order was restored, the umpires inexplicably allowed Dean and Ripple to remain but tossed out Gus Mancuso and

Cardinals rookie catcher Arnold "Mickey" Owen, neither of whom had been in the game.

When the mild-mannered Mel Ott took his position in right field, he was showered with bottles until two mounted policemen flanked him so the game could proceed, with Hubbell striking out Johnny Mize and Joe Medwick to seal the Giants' victory. Afterward, Dean seemed to profess his innocence: "Hellfire, nobody, not even a great pitcher like me, could keep from bein' wild once in a while. What are them Giants hollerin' dusters for?"[28] Dean got off with a $50 fine, as did Ripple.

Dean wouldn't let it go at that. A couple of weeks later, speaking to a church group (!) at Belleville, Illinois, he called Frick and George Barr "the two greatest crooks in baseball," after which Frick notified the reckless pitcher that he was suspended indefinitely. When the Cardinals reached New York, Frick called in Dean and Frisch and listened to Dean deny what, in a Belleville newspaper in front of the league president, he was reported to have said. When Frick demanded that he sign a statement of apology, Dean shouted, "I ain't signin' nothin."[29] In fact, he didn't, but when he repeated his denials in front of a group of reporters, who then signed their own statement attesting that he had, Frick agreed to lift Dean's suspension after three days.

Still roundly miffed, Dean first threatened not to take part in the All-Star Game, to be played on July 7 in Washington, and then arrived after everybody else and by chartered aircraft. He explained that he hadn't wanted to make the long train ride from Chicago (where the Cardinals had just lost a doubleheader), "so I thought I'd stall until the only way I could make it was by flyin' in."[30]

He should have stayed in St. Louis. Dean and Lefty Gomez were the starting pitchers; Gomez pitched three shutout innings, and Dean held the American Leaguers scoreless until two were out in the bottom of the third, when DiMaggio singled and Gehrig drove the ball over Griffith Stadium's high right-field fence. Earl Averill followed with a vicious line drive that broke Dean's left big toe and ricocheted to Billy Herman, who tossed to Johnny Mize for the third out.

The American Leaguers went on to win their fourth All-Star Game by a score of 8–3. Terry used Dean and five other pitchers; McCarthy simply had Gomez, Tommy Bridges, and Mel Harder work three innings apiece. But even though the roster sizes had been expanded to twenty-three, McCarthy kept his eight starting position players—four of them Yankees—in place for the entire game. Afterward, in the Americans' locker room, Yankees coach Art Fletcher led the players in a round of jokes and jeers about "the great Dizzy Dean."

Few people in the capacity-plus crowd of 32,000 (including President Roosevelt) were even aware that Dean had been hit; sixty years later, Oscar Eddleston recalled watching Dean walk to the third-base dugout, his All-Star stint concluded, "without any visible indication of injury."[31] Yet from that moment on, Dean's career would be mostly downhill.

With the Cardinals in the midst of another hot race, Sam Breadon, Branch Rickey, and Frank Frisch obviously wanted their ace back on the mound as soon as possible. Whether it was their insistence or Dean's own towering hubris that caused him to try to pitch too soon will never really be known. Whatever the case, when he tried to come back with toe unmended, he couldn't pivot properly off his left foot. Altering his motion in an effort not to put weight on his toe, he wrenched his pitching arm.

On July 21, in his first post–All Star Game start, Dean lost a tough 2–1 duel to Boston's Johnny Lanning; against Brooklyn eleven days later, he gave up three runs and, limping and complaining of shoulder and arm pain, left in the seventh inning of a game that eventually ended 8–1, Dodgers. Five days after that, he had a 6–3 lead on the Phillies when he asked to be removed; his successors blew the game. With a record of 12–7 at the All-Star break, Dean lost three decisions and won once—a 9–7 struggle at Pittsburgh in which he helped himself with a home run and two singles— over the remainder of the season. In his last outing, on August 26, he lobbed the ball to two batters and walked off the mound.

Rickey was unsympathetic. Dean, he said, ought to "quit now and remain out of baseball all of 1938." Dean had become "a big shot. He has too many interests outside of baseball." Would the Cardinals be willing to sell him? "Dizzy is definitely not on the market," said Rickey, "for the reason that he has destroyed his own market. Now he must rehabilitate it." Shot back Dean, "Why don't Rickey retire for a year. He's havin' a pretty bad year himself."[32] With a week to go in the season, Dean drew his last paycheck and left for his Florida home.

Dean's inability to pitch effectively doomed St. Louis's pennant hopes. Lon Warneke and left-hander Bob Weiland, an American League castoff, with eighteen and fifteen wins apiece, took up some of the slack; Johnny Mize reached stardom (.364, twenty-five homers, 113 runs batted in); and Joe Medwick had his finest season yet, leading the majors in batting (.374) and the league in RBIs (154) and tying for most homers (thirty-one). But Frisch's ball club fell steadily behind over the last two months. The

Cardinals ended in fourth place with an 81–73 record, only a game better than Boston, for which Jim Turner and Lou Fette, two unlikely rookies at ages thirty-four and thirty, respectively, each won twenty games. Turner also had a league's-best 2.38 earned run average.

As usual, strong batting by the Waner brothers and Arky Vaughan couldn't overcome Pittsburgh's inconsistent pitching, and as the Pirates settled into third place it again was the Chicago Cubs whom the Giants had to beat down the stretch. Roy Parmelee wasn't much help to Charley Grimm, but aging Charley Root was still good as both a spot starter and a reliever, and Bill Lee, Tex Carleton, and Larry French combined for forty-six wins. Chicago led the league in batting (.288) and runs (811), with Billy Herman registering .335; Frank Demaree, .324; and Gabby Hartnett, .354 in 110 games (backed up by Ken O'Dea at .301.)

Hit by injuries in August—most seriously Ripper Collins's season-ending ankle break and Bill Lee's rib-cage tear, which cost him several starts—the Cubs saw their lead over the Giants shrink from seven games on August 3 to none by the end of the month. New York's Labor Day sweep of Philadelphia at the Polo Grounds while the Cubs divided at Cincinnati put the Giants up by three games. Although Chicago subsequently closed to a game and a half, on September 30 the Giants clinched another pennant, despite Larry French's win at Cincinnati before only 630 fans—the Reds' tenth loss in a row. In Philadelphia, Hubbell gave up a ninth-inning homer to Dolph Camilli but then retired the side to gain his twenty-second win, 2–1 over the Phillies' Claude Passeau. When both teams won their season closers three days later, the Giants finished with a 95–57 record, and Chicago with 93–61.

That relatively narrow victory margin gave the Giants their third pennant in five years and carried Bill Terry, just shy of his thirty-ninth birthday, to the apex of his career as a manager. On September 1, amid rumors that Terry might defect to Cleveland in 1938, Horace Stoneham had given him a new five-year contract. Now he would be paid $40,000 annually for bossing the Giants on the field and from the front office—at the same time that he kept his off-season position in Memphis with Standard Oil.

It was a period in which baseball players—and sports figures in general—were often measured by whether or not they possessed an indefinable quality called "color." Of course, Babe Ruth had it, as did Dizzy Dean, and so, hoped New York's sportswriters (although as yet they'd been disappointed), did Joe DiMaggio. As well liked as he was, Lou Gehrig had always lacked it; so had Bill Terry, who wasn't so well liked by the people who covered the Giants. He didn't like most of them, either. Besides often rebuffing their approaches for interviews and photos, he saw no reason why they ought to intrude into his team's locker room, especially after tough losses. But whatever they might think about him (or he about them), the New York press corps had to acknowledge that not only had Terry been a great ballplayer, but he'd more than proved himself as a manager.

Besides getting another splendid season from Hubbell and a surprising one from Cliff Melton, a floppy-eared, 6-foot 6-inch North Carolinian who won twenty games in his rookie year, Terry found his staff to be barely adequate. Having unwisely traded fourteen-year Giant Fred Fitzsimmons to Brooklyn for a nondescript pitcher, he was left with Hal Schumacher, whose record dropped to 13–12; Clydell Castleman, effective in spots, who won eleven; and Harry Gumbert, who could do no better than 10–11.

Nor did the Giants overpower anybody at the plate. Johnny McCarthy was no Terry, batting only .279, and while Mel Ott tied Medwick for league home-run honors with thirty-one, his average dropped to .294 and his RBIs to ninety-five. Jimmy Ripple (.317), Joe Moore (.310), and Dick Bartell (.306) were Terry's only .300 hitters.

·　·　·　·　·

TERRY'S 1937 GIANTS would be considerably less of a match for the Yankees than they'd been a year earlier, but then nobody in the American League had really threatened to unseat the "Bronx Bombers"—as they were now being hailed in the New York press. They won again, matching their 102 victories of the previous year. Clinching the pennant on September 13, they finished thirteen games in front of Detroit.

Up to the All-Star break, Detroit and Chicago stayed in contention, but by mid-July, after winning ten in a row, the Yankees had built six- and seven-game leads on the White Sox and Tigers, respectively. Late in June, after Gehrig was knocked unconscious by a pitch in an exhibition stopover at Norfolk, Virginia (a Yankees farm club), McCarthy persuaded Ed Barrow to cancel four remaining exhibition dates. And he also ordered his players to quit retrieving opposing catchers' masks to save them the trouble. "The Tigers come into the stadium and the fans feel that we hate them," McCarthy said. "Well, we hate them. But in the third inning somebody on our side picks up the mask and with a big, broad smile, hands it over to the Detroit catcher. The man who pays a buck-ten ruffles his brow, and he says to himself, 'Those birds can't be hating each other so much.' . . . So from now on, that stuff is out."[33]

To repeat in 1937, the Yankees had to overcome DiMaggio's and Ruffing's late starts; Powell's appendectomy; injuries to Selkirk, Henrich, and Lazzeri; Pearson's ailing back; a sore shoulder that plagued Spurgeon "Spud" Chandler, a promising right-hander (and former University of Georgia football star); the midseason desertion of maritally troubled Johnny Broaca; and assorted other mishaps. Of course, nothing could keep Gehrig out of the lineup—not broken fingers and an aching back, not even being kayoed in Norfolk. The "Iron Horse," as somebody in the press corps had decided to nickname him, was always ready for the next regular-season game.

It was Gehrig's last big year at bat. In 157 games (including three ties), he made two hundred hits, batted .351, drove in 159 runs, scored 138, and homered thirty-seven times. DiMaggio topped him in RBIs by eight, topped the majors in homers with forty-six, and batted .346, besides ranging over the vast reaches of Yankee Stadium's center field to turn doubles and triples into deceptively easy outs. Although Lazzeri, Crosetti, and Rolfe struggled at bat, McCarthy's outfielders all hit above .300, with the exception of Powell, who partly compensated for his .263 average with fierce postappendectomy play, including two fights with Washington's Joe Kuhel.

Despite domestic strife of his own with June O'Dea, Lefty Gomez was the American League's best pitcher, with a 22–11 record and a majors'-best 2.33 ERA; and despite missing at least three starts, Ruffing again won twenty. With Pat Malone gone, Johnny Murphy became McCarthy's bullpen stalwart, relieving in thirty-five games, saving ten, and getting the win thirteen times. Yet while New York scribes played up the exploits of "Fireman Johnny," the White Sox's Clint Brown became even more the prototype of a later era's relief specialist. A onetime starter for Cleveland, Brown pitched only one hundred innings in 1937 but made fifty-three appearances—all in relief—and saved eighteen games.[34]

Bump Hadley, a native of Lynn, Massachusetts, who claimed early New England ancestry, had never been more than a journeyman pitcher with the Browns, White Sox, and Senators until the Yankees acquired him in 1936. With 14–4 and 11–8 records in his first two years with the New Yorkers, the thickset right-hander proved a reliable fourth or fifth starter for McCarthy. But Hadley would be mostly remembered as the man who ended Mickey Cochrane's playing career.

On May 25, 1937, at Yankee Stadium—after Cochrane had homered on his previous at bat—Hadley threw a high, inside pitch that Cochrane lost sight of. The ball hit Cochrane's right temple; Marvin Owen later said that "it sounded like it hit a sack of sand."[35] Cochrane was rushed to St. Elizabeth's Hospital, where it was determined that he'd suffered a triple fracture of the skull. Unconscious for two days, he was subsequently transferred to Henry Ford Hospital in Detroit, where he remained until July 9. Three weeks later, in street clothes, he returned to the Detroit bench as the Tigers lost at Yankee Stadium. As in 1936, by the time he rejoined his team it was already too far behind the Yankees to have much hope of anything better than a distant second place. On September 13, with the pennant lost and his playing days over, Cochrane again put the Tigers in the care of coach Del Baker and, with his family, boarded an Italian ocean liner for Europe.

The 1937 Tigers were again potent at the plate, batting .292 as a team. Al Simmons was gone—sold to Washington shortly before the season started for only $15,000. But Charley Gehringer won his only batting title with a .371 average, and Hank Greenberg drove in 183 runs (the third-highest total ever), besides clouting forty homers and batting .334. Pete Fox hit .331; Gee Walker continued to have base-path misadventures but also had his best year at bat (.335, eighteen homers, 113 RBIs); and Rudy York, a husky rookie who alternated between catcher and third base, put some life into an otherwise drab Detroit August by hitting eighteen homers—a one-month record. In only 103 games, the part-Cherokee Alabamian totaled thirty-five homers and 107 RBIs. Yet with all that, Detroit's pitching staff showed the highest ERA of any club in either league besides the bottom-dog Browns, Athletics, and Phillies.

Actually, apart from the Yankees' staff, quality pitching was scarce around the whole American League that season. Fourth-place Cleveland's Johnny Allen was a bright exception. After winning twenty games in 1936, Allen didn't pitch for six weeks in 1937 because of an appendectomy but still won fifteen of sixteen decisions. His one defeat—after he'd set a league record with seventeen consecutive victories dating back to the previous September—came in Detroit on the last day of the season, when Hank Greenberg doubled past third baseman Odell "Bad News" Hale to drive in the game's only run. In the dugout, teammates had to restrain Allen from assaulting Hale, who ought to have made the play—or the so the fiery right-hander insisted.

Lefty Grove, with a 17–9 record and a 3.02 ERA for the perennially disappointing, fifth-place Red Sox, was another exception to the pitching dearth. But Wes Ferrell, still spatting with Joe Cronin, had trouble getting people out; in June he and brother Rick, along with Mexican-born outfielder Melo Almada, were swapped to Washington for Ben Chapman and Buck Newsom. For the season Ferrell won fifteen games, but he also lost nineteen and led the league in hits and runs allowed. At twenty-nine, the handsome, hot-tempered right-hander was already on the downside of a career that had produced 173 big-league victories but would yield only eighteen more.

· · · · ·

IF JOE MCCARTHY had any lingering doubts about the wisdom of trading Johnny Allen a couple of years back, he could take plenty of satisfaction in the excellent work his current staff gave him in the 1937 World Series. With the Yankees the prohibitive favorites, the Series generated considerably less interest than had been the case a year earlier. The opening game at Yankee Stadium on Thursday, October 6, was the only one of the Series attracting at least 60,000; plenty of empty seats could be seen in the triple-decked right-field grandstand extension, completed the previous July.

This year Giuseppe DiMaggio, the non-English-speaking patriarch of the DiMaggio clan, had come from San Francisco with Tom DiMaggio for the Series. Sharing their box were two of Joe DiMaggio's legion of newly acquired friends—Jimmy Braddock, who'd lost his heavyweight title to Joe Louis the previous summer, and Braddock's manager, Joe Gould. New York governor Herbert Lehman, former president Hoover, and of course the Babe were among the other celebrities in attendance.

Lefty Gomez was close to his best, throwing a six-hitter and yielding a single run, which the Giants scored in the sixth inning. But in the bottom of that inning the Yankees sent up thirteen batters and scored seven runs on five hits, four walks, and two Giants errors. Replaced by Gumbert, Hubbell was so shaken that he started walking toward the first-base dugout—his team's lodgment at the Polo Grounds but the Yankees' at the Stadium. Lazzeri homered in the eighth off Al Smith for the Yankees' eighth and final run.

The Yankees won game two by an identical count. Although the Giants scored on Ruffing in the first inning, Cliff Melton gave up two runs in the fifth; Gumbert, four in the sixth; and Coffman, two more in the seventh. (The lop-eared Melton came in for merciless razzing from the Yankees' dugout, Gomez calling him "a cab with both doors open" and Jake Powell yelling, "Hey, ump, make that monkey paint his ears green so we can have a background for hittin'.")[36] The bottom part of the Yankees' batting order—Myril Hoag, Selkirk, Lazzeri, Ruffing—did most of the damage, with the hard-hitting pitcher singling, doubling, and driving in three runs.

At the Polo Grounds in game three, with only 37,385 paying spectators present, the Yankees took an unassailable three-game advantage, reaching Schumacher for five runs in five innings with the help of three Giants errors. The Giants managed a run off Pearson in the seventh and, with two outs, loaded the bases in the bottom of the ninth, at which point Murphy came on to make Harry Danning fly out to DiMaggio. But the next day, the Giants survived with a 7–3 win, erupting for six runs off Hadley and little-used Ivy Andrews. Hubbell went the distance, scattering six hits, one of which was Gehrig's tenth home run in Series play.

On Sunday, October 10, at the Polo Grounds, on a field made soggy by an all-night rain, the Yankees won their seventh World Series. Melton, Terry's starter, gave up a home run to Hoag in the second inning and another in the third to DiMaggio, who drove the ball against the facade of the left-field upper deck. In the bottom of the third, Ott tied the score at 2–2 with a homer into the right-field upper deck off Gomez, scoring Bartell ahead of him.

The game was decided in the top of the fifth inning, when Lazzeri bounced a drive against the center-field fence at the 480-foot mark for a triple and scored when Gomez, who joked about his usually inept bat work, dribbled a hit through the infield. Al Smith relieved Melton and gave up a double to Gehrig that brought home the fourth and final run of the game. After that, the Giants kept putting men on base, but Gomez, working deliberately (at one point stepping off the mound to watch a small aircraft pass over the ballpark), kept them from scoring. The insouciant left-hander made the final putout himself, taking Gehrig's toss at first ahead of the lunging Joe Moore. That clean fielding play made the 1937 Yankees the first team to complete an errorless World Series.

In the visitors' clubhouse, while McCarthy extolled Jacob Ruppert's virtues and Art Fletcher led a chorus of "The Beer Barrel Polka," Gehrig sat in front of his locker, quietly puffing on a Camel cigarette. Bill Terry came over to congratulate McCarthy and then told the assembled press people, "They beat us like they beat all of the clubs in their own league."[37] There wasn't much else he could say.

Ford Motor Company had withdrawn its $100,000 sponsorship of the Series, and while all three networks again carried the play-by-play, nobody else had paid for the rights, so the Series shares were considerably reduced. Each Yankee's full share was $4,837, with the players voting, as usual, to cut in men who'd been with the team for only part of the season. Johnny Broaca's whereabouts were still unknown, but the Yankees went ahead and voted to give $1,000 to his wife, who'd filed for divorce in Massachusetts. The Giants consoled themselves with $3,891 apiece.

Prospects for anybody dethroning the Yankees for the next several years were downright discouraging. In the midst of the Giants' nightmare sixth inning in game one, the Philadelphia sportswriter Al Horwitz had yelled to his 450 colleagues in the mezzanine press section, "Bring on Newark!"[38] That was a reference to the Yankees' powerhouse Newark Bears farm club, which had just won the International League pennant by twenty-one and a half games and then, after dropping three games in the Junior World Series, recovered to win four in a row from Columbus, the American Association champions. The consensus in eastern baseball circles was that the Bears were probably the greatest minor-league outfit ever, and that they would have given the Yankees more competition than several American League clubs—and maybe the Giants.

. . . . .

THE NEWARK–COLUMBUS SERIES drew 63,340, which was indicative of the vigorous comeback the minor leagues had made in the past few years. Three-fourths of the minor leagues had adopted the top-four postseason play-off scheme initiated in the International League four years earlier and named for Frank Shaughnessy, now president of that league. Thirty-seven minor leagues started and completed the 1937 season, attracting a total attendance of 13.5 million. Crowds in the Class D Evangeline League—whose eight member cities had a total population of 87,500— exceeded 600,000 for a 135-game season.

Despite another runaway in the American League, aggregate attendance in the majors had increased by about 10 percent, to nearly 9.5 million. The Yankees and Tigers again led, with approximately 1 million each, followed by the Giants and Cubs, at close to 1 million. At the other end of the scale, the Phillies played at home before about 250,000, and the Browns to about 130,000. With Dizzy Dean pitching infrequently over the season's second half, the Cardinals drew only 480,000, which, in light of baseball's widespread attendance gains, again raised doubts about the long-term viability of two big-league franchises in St. Louis.

It had been a year of general recovery in baseball and the economy as a whole. At least it had been for most of the year. On August 22 the *New York Times*'s business index registered a post-1929 high at 110.9; shortly thereafter, the WPA's employment rolls had been reduced to 1,451,112 people—the smallest number since the national work-relief program went into operation two years earlier. As unemployment fell and prices rose, quite a few economists and business analysts began to warn that the mild boom the country was experiencing also carried with it the threat of an inflationary spiral.

Then, in September, the bottom dropped out again, in what quickly came to be called the "Roosevelt Recession." Largely the consequence of massive reductions in New Deal spending as the Roosevelt administration sought its elusive goal of a balanced budget, the sharp downturn in the economy—even sharper than what followed the 1929 crash—brutally demonstrated that whatever the president had said, the Depression was far from conquered.

Like nearly everything else, professional baseball would continue to be affected by a depression that had proved far more obdurate than optimistic New Dealers had foreseen. And the other seven teams in the American League and whoever represented the National League in the World Series would have to deal with the dominating reality of the New York Yankees, who were also proving more obdurate than anybody had foreseen.

Philadelphia Athletics, American League and World Series champions, 1930. *Left to right, front row*: Pinky Higgins, Cy Perkins, Mickey Cochrane, Jimmy Dykes, manager Connie Mack, Al Simmons, Bing Miller, Jimmie Foxx, player-coach Eddie Collins, and coach Kid Gleason; *back row*: Eric McNair, Lefty Grove, Max Bishop, Mule Haas, Joe Boley, Rube Walberg, Wally Schang, Art Mahaffey, Bill Shores, Homer Summa, Jimmy Moore, George Earnshaw, Dib Williams, Jack Quinn, and Eddie Rommmel. The Sporting News

Lefty Grove, 1931.
Baseball Hall of Fame
Library, Cooperstown, N.Y.

New York Yankees, American League and World Series champions, 1932. *Left to right, front row*: Herb Pennock, Roy Schalk, Frank Crosetti, coach Art Fletcher, manager Joe McCarthy, coach Jimmy Burke, Myril Hoag, Ben Chapman, and Bill Dickey; *middle row*: Sammy Byrd, Johnny Allen, Ed Wells, Tony Lazzeri, Lefty Gomez, Babe Ruth, Walter Brown, Lou Gehrig, Earle Combs, Lyn Lary, and trainer Earl Painter; *back row*: Eddie Farrell, Red Ruffing, George Pipgras, Wilcy Moore, Charlie Devens, Danny MacFayden, Arndt Jorgens, Joe Sewell, and Joe Glenn.   THE SPORTING NEWS

Wrigley Field, Chicago, 1932. Babe Ruth's "called shot" home run landed in the outfield at the base of the flagpole to the right of the scoreboard.   BASEBALL HALL OF FAME LIBRARY, COOPERSTOWN, N.Y.

1933 NATIONAL LEAGUE ALL~STAR TEAM

HARTNETT, WILSON, FRISCH, HUBBELL, WALKER, WANER, ENGLISH, SCHUMACHER, TRAYNOR, LOTSHAW.
HALLAHAN, BARTELL, TERRY, McKECHNIE, McGRAW, CAREY, HAFEY, KLEIN, O'DOUL, BERGER.
HASBROOK, MARTIN, WARNEKE, CUCCINELLO.

National League All-Star team, 1933. *Left to right, front row*: batboy Hasbrook, Pepper Martin, Lon Warneke, and Tony Cuccinello; *middle row*: Bill Hallahan, Dick Bartell, Bill Terry, coach Bill McKechnie, manager John McGraw, coach Max Carey, Chick Hafey, Chuck Klein, Lefty O'Doul, and Wally Berger; *back row*: Gabby Hartnett, Jimmie Wilson, Frank Frisch, Carl Hubbell, batting-practice pitcher Bill Walker, Paul Waner, Woody English, Hal Schumacher, Pie Traynor, and trainer Andy Lotshaw. THE SPORTING NEWS

Jimmie Foxx, Babe Ruth, and Lou Gehrig before the All-Star Game at the Polo Grounds, New York, 1934.
REVEREND JEROME C. ROMANOWSKI, LAUREL SPRINGS, N.J.

St. Louis Cardinals, National League and World Series champions, 1934. *Left to right, front row*: Joe Medwick (*standing*), Haley, Bill Walker, Bill Delancey, Ernie Orsatti, Tex Carleton, Chick Fullis, Spud Davis, Ripper Collins, and coach Buzzy Wares; *back row*: unidentified, Miguel Gonzalez, Pat Crawford, Burgess Whitehead, Jim Mooney, Pepper Martin, Dazzy Vance, Paul Dean, manager Frank Frisch, Jess Haines, Bill Hallahan, Leo Durocher, Jack Rothrock, Dizzy Dean, and Henry Pippen.
BASEBALL HALL OF FAME LIBRARY, COOPERSTOWN, N.Y.

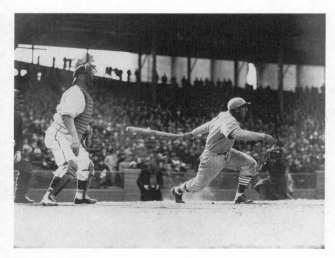

Catcher Gabby Hartnett watching as Pepper Martin lines a hit at Wrigley Field, Chicago, 1935.
BASEBALL HALL OF FAME LIBRARY, COOPERSTOWN, N.Y.

Wes Farrell, 1935.
BASEBALL HALL OF FAME
LIBRARY, COOPERSTOWN, N.Y.

Detroit Tigers, American League and World Series champions, 1935. *Left to right, front row*: Pete Fox, Charley Gehringer, coach Del Baker, manager Mickey Cochrane, coach Cy Perkins, Jo Jo White, Hank Greenberg, and batboy Joe Roggins; *middle row*: Goose Goslin, Billy Rogell, Marvin Owen, Ray Hayworth, Alvin Crowder, Eldon Auker, Schoolboy Rowe, and Flea Clifton; *back row*: Heinie Schuble, Frank Reiber, trainer Denny Carroll, Elon Hogsett, Gee Walker, Joe Sullivan, Tommy Bridges, and Vic Sorrell.   BASEBALL HALL OF FAME LIBRARY, COOPERSTOWN, N.Y.

Chicago Cubs manager Charley Grimm and Detroit Tigers manager Mickey Cochrane talking
for the newsreel cameras before the first game of the World Series at Navin Field, Detroit, 1935.
THE SPORTING NEWS

Joe DiMaggio and Dizzy Dean
before the All-Star Game, 1936.
THE SPORTING NEWS

Doing the old hands-over-hands routine
before the first game of the World Series in
1936 are New York Giants Mel Ott and Joe
Moore and New York Yankees Joe DiMaggio
and Lou Gehrig. THE SPORTING NEWS

Jacob Ruppert in St. Petersburg, Florida,
spring 1937. BASEBALL HALL OF FAME
LIBRARY, COOPERSTOWN, N.Y.

Larry MacPhail and Brooklyn Dodgers
manager Burleigh Grimes in Clearwater,
Florida, spring 1938. BASEBALL HALL OF
FAME LIBRARY, COOPERSTOWN, N.Y.

Johnny Vander Meer of the Cincinnati Reds pitching his second no-hitter, in the first night game played at Ebbets Field, Brooklyn, June 15, 1938.   ASSOCIATED PRESS

Kenesaw Mountain Landis, 1938.
BASEBALL HALL OF FAME LIBRARY,
COOPERSTOWN, N.Y.

New York Yankees, American League and World Series champions, 1938. *Left to right, front row*: Joe Gordon, Bill Knickerbocker, coach John Schulte, coach Art Fletcher, manager Joe McCarthy, coach Earle Combs, Babe Dahlgren, Jake Powell, and Frank Crosetti; *middle row*: Tommy Henrich, Joe Glenn, Bump Hadley, Spud Chandler, batting-practice pitcher Paul Schreiber, Bill Dickey, Red Rolfe, Lou Gehrig, and trainer Doc Painter; *back row*: George Selkirk, Johnny Murphy, Ivy Andrews, Joe DiMaggio, Red Ruffing, Lefty Gomez, Steve Sundra, Arndt Jorgens, Myril Hoag, and Monte Pearson; *in front*: batboy Hennessey. Note the left-sleeve patches advertising the 1939 World's Fair.
THE SPORTING NEWS

World Series action, 1938: Chicago Cubs shortstop Billy Jurges throwing to first base over Joe DiMaggio to complete a double play.
THE SPORTING NEWS

Harry Craft, Bill Dickey, Ernie Lombardi, Joe DiMaggio, Frank McCormick, and George Selkirk before the first game of the World Series at Yankee Stadium, New York, 1939.
THE SPORTING NEWS

Bobby Feller warming up at Comiskey Park, Chicago, 1939.
BASEBALL HALL OF FAME LIBRARY, COOPERSTOWN, N.Y.

Hank Greenberg, 1939.
BASEBALL HALL OF FAME
LIBRARY, COOPERSTOWN, N.Y.

Buzz Arlett as a Baltimore Oriole.
THE SPORTING NEWS

Nick Cullop as a Columbus
Redbird.   THE SPORTING NEWS

Mules Suttles of the Chicago
American Giants, 1938.
BASEBALL HALL OF FAME LIBRARY,
COOPERSTOWN, N.Y.

Ciudad Trujillo Dragones, Dominican Republic champions, 1937. *Left to right, front row*:
Enrique Lantigua, Leroy Matlock, Julio Vasquez, Cool Papa Bell, Sammy Bankhead, Silvio
Garcia, and Chee Chee Correa; *middle row*: Lazaro Salazar, Joe Enrique Ayubar (deputy of
the National Congress and team director), and Satchel Paige; *back row*: Josh Gibson, Harry
Williams, Antonio Caselnos, Rodolfo Fernandez, Bob Griffith, Perucho Cepeda, and Bill
Perkins. BASEBALL HALL OF FAME LIBRARY, COOPERSTOWN, N.Y.

Josh Gibson of the Washington-
Homestead Grays, 1940.
BASEBALL HALL OF FAME LIBRARY,
COOPERSTOWN, N.Y.

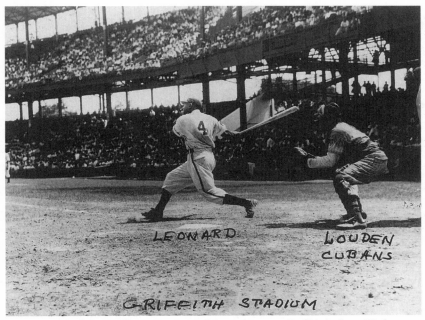

Buck Leonard, of the Washington-Homestead Grays, batting at Griffith Stadium, Washington,
D.C., 1942. The catcher is Louis Louden, of the New York Cubans.   BASEBALL HALL OF FAME
LIBRARY, COOPERSTOWN, N.Y.

Satchel Paige, in New York Black
Yankees attire, warming up at Yankee
Stadium, May 15, 1941.
BASEBALL HALL OF FAME LIBRARY,
COOPERSTOWN, N.Y.

Cincinnati Reds, National League and World Series champions, 1940. *Left to right, front row*: Lew
Riggs, Ival Goodman, Junior Thompson, Morrie Arnovich, coach Hank Gowdy, manager Bill
Mckechnie, player-coach Jimmie Wilson, Bill Werber, Billy Myers, Elmer Riddle, and trainer Dick
Rohde; *middle row*: traveling secretary Gabe Paul, Whitey Moore, Eddie Joost, Ernie Lombardi,
Bucky Walters, Frank McCormick, Paul Derringer, Johnny Hutchings, Bill Baker, and general
manager Warren Giles; *back row*: Jim Turner, Jimmy Ripple, Johnny Vander Meer, Mike McCormick,
Milt Shoffner, Witte Guise, Harry Craft, Lonnie Frey, and Joe Beggs. THE SPORTING NEWS

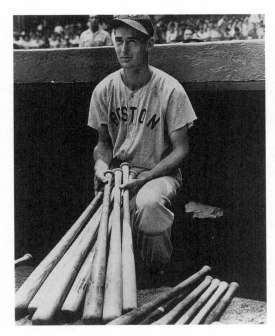

Ted Williams, 1941.
ASSOCIATED PRESS

Brooklyn Dodgers, National League champions, 1941. *Left to right, front row*: trainer Doc Wilson, Cookie Lavagetto, Pee Wee Reese, Pete Reiser, coach Red Corriden, manager Leo Durocher, coach Charlie Dressen, Kirby Higbe, Mickey Owen, and Lew Riggs; *middle row*: Joe Medwick, Curt Davis, Tom Dranke, Larry French, Whitlow Wyatt, Ed Albosta, Luke Hamlin, Newt Kimball, Billy Herman, and Johnny Allen; *back row*: Hugh Casey, Dolph Camilli, George Pfister, Jimmy Wasdell, Herman Franks, Roy Spencer, Pete Coscaret, Fred Fitzsimmons, Augie Galan, and Dixie Walker; *in front*: batboy Jack Bodner. THE SPORTING NEWS

Brooklyn Dodgers manager Leo Durocher and pitcher Whitlow Wyatt arguing balls and strikes with umpire Bill McGowan during the fifth and final game of the World Series in 1941, while Phil Rizzuto of the New York Yankees waits to bat. BASEBALL HALL OF FAME LIBRARY, COOPERSTOWN, N.Y.

Branch Rickey, around 1942. BASEBALL HALL OF FAME LIBRARY, COOPERSTOWN, N.Y.

CHAPTER 7

Pathos and Progress, 1938–1939

B ABE RUTH had never given up hope of getting a managing job—or his insistence that it had to be in the majors. But the two years following his retirement in 1935 saw only one big-league managerial change: Steve O'Neill for Walter Johnson at Cleveland. A rash of firings and hirings began in July 1937, when Donald Barnes, the St. Louis Browns' new owner, ran out of patience with Rogers Hornsby's horse-playing and last-place ball club and paid him off. Jim Bottomley, ending his playing career before the meager turnouts at Sportsman's Park, took over for the rest of the season. That fall, Bottomley's and three other managing jobs became open.

But nothing for the Babe, who remained a celebrity without much to do. "If it wasn't for golf," he told one interviewer, "I think I'd die." "I'm nuts about baseball," he told another visitor to his Riverside Drive apartment. "I like the game and all that goes with it. I love kids and crowds." But as Robert Creamer has observed, "It was not so much out of sight, out of mind as it was out of touch, out of mind. The times were passing Ruth by."[1]

After the Browns straggled to a 21–56 record under Bottomley, Barnes hired Gabby Street. Street had known both good and bad times with the Cardinals; with the Browns he would know one season of little but bad. Charley Dressen, whose Cincinnati Reds had finished an encouraging fifth in 1936 and then fallen back to the bottom the past season, was fired with twenty-five games to go. That fall, Powel Crosley and Warren Giles hired Bill McKechnie away from Boston, where by common agreement Mc-Kechnie had achieved surprisingly good results the past two years with a bunch of run-of-the-mill players. Casey Stengel, who'd spent the past year dabbling in Texas oil, was induced to take over the Bees and to put $40,000 into the penurious franchise. And in Cleveland, Steve O'Neill, unable to improve on Walter Johnson's record, departed in favor of the loquacious Oscar Vitt. Once a light-hitting American League infielder and teammate of Ty Cobb, Vitt had managed the 1937 Newark Bears to their runaway International League championship and Junior World Series triumph.

Approaching the peak of his career, Joe McCarthy signed a new three-year contract, again at $35,000 per annum, while Frank Frisch agreed to a one-year contract but took himself off the Cardinals' active player roster. Brooklyn also renewed Burleigh Grimes's contract, despite the Dodgers' sixth-place showing and Grimes's troubles with Van Lingle Mungo, who drunkenly wrecked a hotel room in St. Louis, drew a $1,000 fine, and ended up winning only eight games.

By the first months of 1938, the Roosevelt Recession had just about wiped out the encouraging boomlet of the past three years. The *New York Times*'s business index sank to 78.1; steel-ingot production was indexed at 48.4 as compared with 125.1 a year earlier; automobile output had fallen from 84.1 to 50.5. The officially recorded jobless now numbered about 11 million, nearly 3 million more than during the previous summer. Works Progress Administration rolls had grown by about 1 million, and in New York City one-third of the people employed in construction were working on projects contracted under the Public Works Administration.

. . . . .

YET THE BAD ECONOMIC NEWS didn't keep various baseball executives from proceeding optimistically. Despite their frustrating season, the Detroit Tigers had led the majors in attendance, with some 1,181,000 paying fans. Now Walter O. Briggs directed the extension of Navin Field's grandstand upper decks all the way across right and left fields, leaving only an uncovered but double-decked center-field section and enlarging the ballpark's capacity to some 52,000. The renovation also shortened the distance to right field by 10 feet and left an inviting upper-deck overhang—or "porch." Briggs then acceded to the renaming of Navin Field as Briggs Stadium.

Meanwhile Philip K. Wrigley—little interested in baseball when he inherited the Cubs in 1932 but now avidly involved in nearly every aspect of franchise operations—oversaw the finishing work on Wrigley Field's new bleachers and had an idea for still another improvement to his ballpark. By the next spring, his ground crew as well as young Bill Veeck Jr. were at work sprigging ivy at the base of the red brick outfield walls; by midsummer 1938 Wrigley Field had acquired its unique decorative effect.

Sportsman's Park, which the Cardinals rented from the Browns' ownership, hadn't undergone much improvement since the mid-1920s, but in his office at the ballpark Branch Rickey continued to scheme to enlarge the Cardinals' farm system. By the start of the 1938 season, it would consist of thirty minor-league franchises that the Cardinals either owned outright or maintained working agreements with—not to mention a number of sub-rosa hookups that had come under Commissioner Landis's suspicious eye. All told, the Cardinals controlled 732 players.

Nobody before or after would have as extensive a system as Rickey built in St. Louis, but for the Yankees, George Weiss had put together a network consisting of thirteen farm clubs, with Kansas City now joining Newark as New York's flagship minor-league enterprises. Detroit also continued to rely on its half-dozen or so farm clubs—headed by the Texas League's Beaumont Exporters—for the development of most of its players. And while Tom Yawkey would always be willing to go out and pay for whatever seemed to be needed, he'd also hired Billy Evans to construct a farm system for the Red Sox; by the end of 1938, the Boston ball club had working agreements with eight minors franchises. Within another year, the Cincinnati Reds had bought a controlling interest in the Southern Association's Birmingham Barons and had tie-ups with franchises in every classification—from Indianapolis (American Association) to Bassett, Virginia, in the Class D Bi-State League. After Donald Barnes bought the Browns, even that downtrodden organization—lacking the wherewithal to purchase control of minor-league franchises—formed working agreements with a dozen or so.

At the major-league meetings in December 1937, the National League executives voted unanimously to discontinue the standard ball in use for the past few years and to adopt a deader ("slower" was the preferred term) type of baseball with higher seams for 1938. At the behest of Jacob Ruppert, American Leaguers voted as a unit to continue using the ball that both leagues had used the previous season. Commented National League president Frick a few months later, "We can't move the walls in our parks back to meet the advanced springiness of the ball, so we do the next best thing and operate on the ball."[2]

For several years, National Leaguers—everybody from league officials to club owners to sportswriters who covered the league's teams—had sought to promote the notion that their league played a faster, more competitive game. In fact, the National League had been far more competitive; since 1930 only one American League pennant winner (Detroit in 1935) had played below .650 ball, while only one National League winner (St. Louis in 1931) had played above .650. The American League, "a seven-team second division," in the phrase of the St. Louis writer J. Roy Stockton, had "plenty of clodhoppers, as you know if you've ever tortured yourself by watching American League base running."[3] National League players—typified, thought Stockton, by Pepper Martin—were mostly faster, played harder, took more chances, and gave spectators a more entertaining show for their money. Maybe so, but that didn't counter the reality that since 1927 American Leaguers had taken eight of eleven World Series.

Of course, now the problem for the rest of the American League was doing something about the Yankees' mastery. Mickey Cochrane sought to strengthen his Tigers by swapping Marvin Owen, the popular Gee Walker, and a young catcher named Mike Tresh to the White Sox for infielder Tony Piet, outfielder Fred "Dixie" Walker, and pitcher Vernon Kennedy—a deal that, as it turned out, didn't do much for either team. But Jimmy Dykes at least could take satisfaction in a trade with Washington: Joe Kuhel, both a reliable hitter and a deft fielder, for Zeke Bonura, who'd averaged .318 and 110 runs batted in during his four years with the White Sox but given too many "Bonura salutes" to ground balls. Besides, Bonura thought he was worth more than the $10,000 or so the White Sox had offered him. And Buck Newsom was on the move again (as he would be many times during his long career), going back to the Browns from the Red Sox in exchange for Joe Vosmik, who joined Roger Cramer and Ben Chapman in what was expected to be one of baseball's best outfields.

Early in 1938 the Brooklyn Trust Company, which held the mortgage on the Dodgers, persuaded Larry MacPhail to leave the banking business (in which he'd marked time the past year) and sign a three-year contract to head the Brooklyn franchise. Almost forty-seven years old, the chain-smoking, hard-drinking, hyperkinetic MacPhail quickly moved to change things around Ebbets Field. For one thing, the Dodgers would start building a farm system, but before that materialized they would make some trades. Brooklyn had already traded four players for Leo Durocher; MacPhail's first player deal came on March 2, 1938, when he rescued Dolph Camilli, a hard-hitting first baseman, from the Phillies for $45,000 and a throw-in player.

Although the American League clubs voted 5–2 against Cleveland's request to play seven home games at night in the big stadium, Cincinnati was about to lose its unique nighttime prerogative. When asked if he planned to have night baseball at Ebbets Field, MacPhail was initially cagey, prompting Dan Parker of the *New York Daily Mirror* to suggest that "the Dodgers should learn to play baseball in the daytime before attempting the more difficult task of playing it in the evening, which is reserved for more pleasant pastimes in Brooklyn."[4] But in the spring, MacPhail announced that lights would be installed at Ebbets Field and the Dodgers would play the seven night games allowed under National League rules.

Meanwhile the Philadelphia Phillies—who in 1937 had yielded the National League cellar to Cincinnati but again trailed the league in attendance—made plans to abandon the cramped and unkempt Baker Bowl and move into Shibe Park as tenants of the Athletics, who of course needed the rent money. After signing a ten-year lease with Connie Mack and sons, the Phillies would debut in Shibe Park on July 4, splitting the Independence Day doubleheader with Boston. (Their new surroundings didn't help; by season's end, they'd totaled only forty-five wins and reclaimed last place, and Jimmie Wilson had drawn his last paycheck from owner Gerald Nugent.)

. . . . .

SO BY THE FIRST MONTHS OF 1938, as the economy worsened again and baseball prepared for its eighth season since the onset of the Depression, various big-league venues had been or soon would be changed. Training sites were changing, too. Bill Terry moved his Giants to Baton Rouge, where they could capitalize on exhibition dates with Cleveland—especially Carl Hubbell–Bobby Feller matchups—before the two teams started what had become their annual spring tour of southern towns and cities. In Baton Rouge, the Giants worked out in the cavernous surroundings of the new Louisiana State University football stadium.

The Cardinals and Bees traded Florida sites, Boston moving to Bradenton and the Cardinals beginning their long-running tenure at St. Petersburg. Both Deans were on hand at Waterfront Park, but when Paul Dean give up nine hits and nine runs to the Bees in three innings, Branch Rickey told reporters, "He showed me nothing and his arm was dead."[5] Finally Paul agreed to reassignment to Houston, at the same time that Rickey was shopping Dizzy around the league.

On April 16 Rickey concluded a deal with the Cubs that was little short of astonishing. The Cubs obtained Dizzy Dean for pitchers Curt Davis and Clyde Shoun, a reserve outfielder, and $185,000 in cash—one of the biggest sums ever paid for any player, let alone a sore-armed pitcher. Rickey and

Sam Breadon were their usual uncharitable selves. Dean hadn't "pleased us altogether since 1934," said Rickey; Breadon opined that the Cardinals would be "a twenty-three-player club now and not a Dizzy Dean club."[6]

But while the Cardinals officials were happy to get the needed cash (and a couple of quality pitchers), they were also trying to digest Commissioner Landis's sweeping invalidation earlier in April of their hold on seventy-four players on the rosters of twenty-five clubs in their farm system. Not only, Landis found, had the Cardinals covered up the transfer of players within the system to protect them from the annual majors–minors draft, but Rickey had contrived to control more than one team in a particular league—in fact, every team in the Nebraska State League.

Breadon hadn't known about some of Rickey's tricks, and the bad publicity that followed Landis's action contributed to a developing rift between the Cardinals' owner and his well-compensated employee. In fact, though, the Cardinals continued to expand their system, which within two years would consist of thirty-two teams and more than six hundred players. And as things turned out, they'd lost only one prize emancipee. Harold "Pete" Reiser, a native St. Louisian who'd spent 1937 with Newport, Arkansas, in the Class D Arkansas-Missouri League, signed with Brooklyn (for a whopping bonus of $100) and within three years would be one of the majors' brightest stars.

Two especially notable rookies traveled to Florida from the Pacific Coast that spring. A tall, thin nineteen-year-old named Ted Williams came from San Diego—where he'd spent the past two seasons as an outfielder with the hometown Coast League Padres—to join the Boston Red Sox at Sarasota. Williams was the classic fresh busher, cocksure and generally off-putting. Introduced to Tom Yawkey, he cracked, "Don't look so worried, Tom. Foxx and me will take care of everything."[7]

But when the left-hand–hitting stringbean stepped in the batting cage, he got everybody's attention. While the youngster was still a poor base runner and weak on fly balls, the *Sporting News* thought he had "perfectly coordinated wrist action and appears to be a natural hitter."[8] But for 1938 Joe Cronin remained satisfied with his veteran outfield of Chapman, Cramer, and Vosmik. So Williams, loudly promising to be back next spring, left to join Donie Bush's Minneapolis American Association ball club, with which the Red Sox had a loose working agreement.

The other rookie was the Yankees' twenty-three-year-old Joe Gordon, an Oregonian who'd been the Newark Bears' hard-hitting second baseman. Tony Lazzeri may have been the star of the 1937 World Series, but at thirty-five, with the flashy Gordon in the wings, Lazzeri finally drew his release and caught on with the Cubs. Joe McCarthy grinned with anticipation as he watched Gordon operate around second base. "There wasn't a lot of sentiment over Lazzeri's loss," remembered Tommy Henrich. "Gordon was just better. It was that simple."⁹

Lazzeri's departure left Lou Gehrig as the surviving member of the Yankees' mighty 1927 outfit. Gehrig's 1938 contract brought him up to $39,000 and kept him as baseball's top-salaried player. Almost universally admired and respected as representing the finest in professional sports, he was honored in the off-season with a dinner in Manhattan at the Harvard Club, given by the city's Young Men's Board of Trade.

Gehrig also spent several weeks in Hollywood doing personal appearances, learning to ride a horse, and starring in a low-budget western entitled *Rawhide*. When Gehrig arrived at Crescent Lake Park to start spring training, Lefty Gomez yelled "Camera!" and George Selkirk, firing cap pistols, rode an old horse placarded "Gehrig Model" onto the field. Heralded by a parade that included both Yankees and Cardinals, the movie premiered on March 23 in St. Petersburg, later ran at the Globe Theatre in Manhattan, and was quickly forgotten.

Twenty-three-year-old Joe DiMaggio missed all that, because he was still in San Francisco, holding out for a lot more money than Jacob Ruppert and Ed Barrow were prepared to give him. Irked that DiMaggio hadn't had the courtesy to touch base with them before he left for the West Coast after the Series, the Yankees' bigwigs weren't about to deal with DiMaggio's crony Joe Gould or anybody else except the ballplayer himself—and they weren't going to pay him more than $25,000. It became the most publicized holdout of recent times, as the weeks passed and DiMaggio remained on the other side of the continent.

Finally, on April 20, two days after the Yankees opened the 1938 season with a loss in Boston, DiMaggio wired Ruppert that he would take the $25,000. He left San Francisco that afternoon; some seventy-six hours later, his train pulled into Penn Station. The next day, flanked by Barrow and Ruppert, DiMaggio signed his contract, after which Ruppert made sure the jam of reporters understood that DiMaggio's salary wouldn't start until he was in shape to play.

. . . . .

DiMAGGIO MISSED the season's first twelve games, which cost him nearly $1,800. When he finally got into the lineup, in Washington on April

30, he was roundly booed in a 4–3 loss and managed to collide with Gordon as they chased a pop fly. Both had to leave the game, but while DiMaggio was back the next day, the Yankees' prize rookie was sidelined for six weeks.

In Washington and wherever else he played—even Yankee Stadium—DiMaggio heard boos from people who failed to understand how a young man of limited education couldn't be satisfied with $25,000 in the midst of the seemingly intractable Depression. Thoroughly chastened, DiMaggio told the press that he'd held out for the last time.

The Yankees urgently needed DiMaggio, because Gehrig was in the worst slump of his career. He wasn't hitting with his usual power—in fact, wasn't hitting much of anything—and was spending time in the diathermy machine with a sore and stiff back. By May 31, when he played in his two thousandth consecutive game (a 12–5 battering of Boston before only 6,917 at the Stadium), he'd managed to hoist his average to .285, but on June 19 he marked his thirty-fifth birthday by going hitless in ten at bats in a double-header with St. Louis. For a few games McCarthy even dropped him to fifth place in the batting order and slotted DiMaggio fourth—the first time Gehrig hadn't batted cleanup in eleven years.

Over the first half of the season, the Yankees as a whole struggled along with Gehrig. On Memorial Day, before a record paid attendance of 81,591 at the Stadium, they swept two games from the Red Sox (the first of which featured a fight between Joe Cronin and Jake Powell) and improved to 19–14. At that point Cleveland—with a heavy-hitting lineup built around veterans Hal Trosky and Earl Averill and rookies Ken Keltner and Jeff Heath and getting decent pitching from Feller, Mel Harder, and Johnny Allen—led New York by three and a half games.

Allen won fourteen games that season and remained his irascible self. In Boston he walked off the field when umpire Bill McGowan acceded to Joe Cronin's protests and ordered the pitcher to change his sweatshirt, which Allen had cut into shreds to create a flapping distraction behind his fastball. Instead of backing up his pitcher, first-year manager Oscar Vitt fined Allen $250. That was the first in a long series of incidents that over the next two years would destroy Vitt's credibility with his players. (Allen later sold the shirt for $50 to a Cleveland department store, which put it in a display window.)

Despite Gehrig's woes, by the All-Star break the Yankees had maneuvered into first place by a small margin over Cleveland and Boston. Detroit stumbled along in fourth; the White Sox, with Luke Appling missing half the season with a broken ankle and other regulars disabled at various times, slipped to sixth, behind Washington.

The Tigers could still score lots of runs: Charley Gehringer was his usually productive self; Rudy York hit thirty-three homers and drove in 127 runs to affirm that the previous August's outburst hadn't been a fluke; and Hank Greenberg homered fifty-eight times, matching what Jimmie Foxx had done in 1932. On the last day of the season, in a doubleheader in Cleveland, Greenberg made four hits but couldn't clear the fences. In the nightcap he struck out twice, as Bobby Feller threw his fastball and a wicked curve past eighteen Detroit hitters to establish a new major-league record. (Feller also walked seven and lost the game, 4–1.)

But if the Tigers scored a lot, they also gave up a lot. Schoolboy Rowe was again demoted to Beaumont to try to get his arm back in shape, and nobody else could pitch with any consistent success. Mickey Cochrane, no longer an active player, couldn't inspire what had become a lackluster team—a fact that Walter Briggs acknowledged on August 8 when he fired Cochrane from both his vice president's and manager's jobs, making his son, Walter "Spike" Briggs Jr., his vice president and Del Baker his full-time field manager. (Out of gratitude, pride, or pique, Cochrane refused to be paid for the remaining year on his contract.)

Although Jimmie Foxx would never equal his own fifty-eight-homer mark, he continued to justify what Tom Yawkey had paid for him. He won his second batting title, at .349, hammered fifty home runs, and drove in 175. Chapman, Vosmik, Cramer, Cronin, and Frank "Pinky" Higgins (still another arrival from Connie Mack's ongoing fire sale) all batted above .300, and twenty-year-old Bobby Doerr, purchased from San Diego the previous year, established himself as one of the majors' top second basemen in his first full season. Always nursing his arm, Lefty Grove couldn't take the mound as often as he once had, but when he did he was still as good as anybody, winning fourteen games and again leading the league with a 3.08 earned run average.

In fact, the 1938 Red Sox, finishing in second place with a record of 88–61, were Boston's best American League entry since Babe Ruth had pitched them to victory in the 1918 World Series. But that still left them quite a distance from a pennant, because over the second half of the season the Yankees' combination of power and pitching carried them into another insurmountable lead. The New Yorkers clinched their third-straight pennant on September 18 and, at 99–53, finished eight and a half games ahead of Boston.

One thing that made memorable still another relatively easy Yankees pennant season was Monte Pearson's no-hitter against Cleveland on August 27—a 13–0 walkover that climaxed three consecutive doubleheaders in which the Yankees took five of six games and crushed the Indians' chances.

Far more memorable than Pearson's no-hitter was the instant tumult created by something Jake Powell said in a radio interview. The leading hitter in the 1936 World Series, Powell since then had become Joe McCarthy's little-used fifth outfielder. But on July 29, at Comiskey Park, WGN's Bob Elson needed somebody for his on-field pregame interview, so when the Yankees finished batting practice, he caught Powell. After a few routine questions about Powell's background and career, Elson asked him about his off-season activities, whereupon Powell blurted that he worked as a policeman in Dayton, Ohio, and kept in shape "crackin' niggers over the head." At that, WGN immediately cut off Elson's interview.[10]

The remark wasn't just stunningly stupid, but also an outright lie, inasmuch as Powell, a native of Silver Spring, Maryland, who spent his winters in Dayton, had never served a day on the Dayton police force. (He'd once applied for a place on the force, but his application was rejected.) The next day, while WGN repeatedly broadcast disclaimers, a delegation of prominent black Chicagoans appeared at Comiskey Park and presented a petition to umpire-in-chief Harry Geisel, insisting that Powell be "barred from professional baseball." While black-owned newspapers in the northern cities echoed that demand, Commissioner Landis summoned both Powell and Joe McCarthy to his office in Chicago. Although Powell denied "saying anything like that at all" and claimed that he had "some very good friends among the Negroes of Dayton," Landis laid a ten-day suspension on the ballplayer.[11]

McCarthy, Ed Barrow, and much of the daily press either made light of the episode or damned the messenger, contending that Powell had meant no harm and, as McCarthy said, radio people shouldn't "pester players for interviews."[12] But given the sizable number of black fans who came up from Harlem to patronize the Yankees (as much as 15 to 20 percent of the admissions on some days) and the tidy sums that the Yankees made from renting the stadium for Negro-league doubleheaders on Sundays, damage control was clearly needed.

So Barrow ordered Powell to make a penitent tour of Harlem bars, lodges, and the offices of the weekly *Amsterdam News*, at the same time that Bill Robinson acted as the Yankees' emissary in trying to smooth things over. That didn't suffice for black fans and sympathetic whites in Washington and Chicago, where on the Yankees' next visits Powell was pelted with bottles and other objects whenever he appeared on the field. *"L'affaire* Powell,"* as the *Nation* magazine called it, pointed up the hypocrisy that while the "baseball magnates . . . would not allow Negroes on their teams," it had become the thing to "denounce Powell's uncouth chauvinism."[13] But in fact *"l'affaire* Powell"* blew over rather quickly in a country that still tolerated the denial of political rights to black citizens in much of the South, as well as other kinds of racial discrimination everywhere—whether de jure from Delaware to Texas and from Missouri to Florida or de facto in the northern states.

For those who were Yankees in 1938, perhaps what would be the most memorable of all was Lou Gehrig's rally during the last part of the season. Although he wasn't able to get his batting average above .295, Gehrig began to hit with much of the old power, ending with twenty-nine home runs and 114 RBIs. It was the twelfth consecutive season in which the Iron Horse had driven in at least that many.

Gehrig's reduced output didn't hurt the Yankees a great deal, because collectively they hit 174 home runs and scored 955 runs. DiMaggio led the way with a .324 batting average, thirty-two homers, and 140 RBIs; Dickey hit .313, with twenty-seven homers and 115 RBIs; Red Rolfe hit .311 and drove in eighty runs from second place in the batting order; and Tommy Henrich and Joe Gordon combined for forty-seven homers and 188 RBIs.

Yankees pitching again showed the American League's lowest earned run average (3.91), most complete games (ninety-one), and fewest runs allowed (710). At 21–7, Red Ruffing was the league's top winner; Lefty Gomez won eighteen (despite the distraction of a divorce from June O'Dea); Pearson won sixteen; and Spud Chandler, still bothered by a sore shoulder, won fourteen of twenty-three starts.

. . . . .

THE YANKEES again headed into the World Series as big favorites, this year over the Chicago Cubs. In another close, hard-fought National League race, the Cubs prevailed over Pie Traynor's Pittsburgh club, which finally was able to stay in contention all the way. At the end, the Cubs were two games better than the Pirates, but the Giants and Reds finished only five and six games back, respectively.

The post–Dizzy Dean St. Louis Cardinals endured their worst season in six years, finishing sixth, only a half-game ahead of Brooklyn and five and a half behind Casey Stengel's Boston Bees. Aside from big Johnny Mize

(.337, twenty-seven homers, 102 RBIs) and Joe Medwick, who batted .322, hit twenty-one homers, and led the league with 122 RBIs, the Cardinals couldn't generate much offense. But if they were never really in the race, at least they entertained—mostly off the field.

In the spring, Pepper Martin formed a hillbilly band consisting of himself, reserve outfielder Stanley "Frenchy" Bordogaray, and pitchers Bob Weiland, Lon Warneke, and Bill "Fibber" McGee. Calling themselves the Mississippi Mudcats and performing with guitar, banjo, washboard, and a couple of fiddles, they appeared on radio stations in St. Louis and around the league and occasionally at charity events. It all seemed harmless enough, but Joe Medwick, not getting along with manager Frisch and unhappy about things in general, wasn't amused by the Mudcats' shenanigans. "Instead of a ball club," growled Medwick, "we're supposed to be a traveling carnival. What is this anyway, a ball team or a bunch of clowns?"[14] For sure, it wasn't much of a ball team, and by long-established custom the manager got most of the blame. On September 10 Frisch was fired, and coach Miguel "Mike" Gonzalez took charge of the Cardinals for the remaining sixteen games.[15]

The Giants suffered from the fact that the arms of Carl Hubbell and Hal Schumacher were showing wear and tear. Prince Hal started twenty-eight games, won thirteen, but completed only twelve; King Carl started twenty-two games, finished thirteen, and had a 13–10 record in mid-August, when physicians examined his aching arm, found bone chips in his left elbow, and prescribed surgery. Hubbell left to have the operation done in Memphis and was lost for the season. Cliff Melton couldn't equal his twenty-win rookie season (and never would), collecting fourteen victories but losing the same number; Harry Gumbert, with a 4.01 earned run average, led the staff with fifteen wins. Dick Coffman had to relieve Terry's starters forty-eight times.

Burgess Whitehead underwent an appendectomy in the off-season, healed slowly, apparently worried himself into a nervous breakdown, and missed the whole season. Mel Ott dutifully moved from right field to fill another weak spot at third base; Ott, Joe Moore, and Harry Danning were the .300 hitters among Giants regulars, with Ott again leading the league with thirty-six homers.

Although they could score only 705 runs, the Giants were able to stay within five or six games of Pittsburgh and Chicago through August and into late September. But with Hubbell unavailable, they couldn't gain any ground and were still five out at the end of the season.

Pittsburgh scored only two more runs than the Giants but started the season with seven straight wins, later won thirteen in a row, and held the lead for nearly half the season—despite generally ragged starting pitching. The foursome of Cy Blanton, Jack Tobin, Russ Bauers, and Bob Klinger had a combined 52–38 record; what actually kept the Pirates on top was the valiant work of Mace Brown, a husky Iowan who relieved forty-nine times, saved five games, and on fifteen occasions held the opposition in check until the Pirates rallied to make him the winning pitcher.

The Waner brothers, especially Paul, were also starting to show some wear and tear. In fact, 1938 was Paul Waner's first sub-.300 season and marked the beginning of his protracted decline. But Arky Vaughan, still only twenty-six, batted .322, and Johnny Rizzo, a former Cardinals farm-hand, reached his big-league peak in his rookie season, with a .301 average, twenty-three homers, and 111 RBIs.

Bill McKechnie justified his reputation as one of baseball's best managers, keeping Cincinnati within a few games of first place until September 25, when both his Reds, beaten in Pittsburgh, and the Giants, who dropped a doubleheader in Boston, were eliminated from the pennant race. Frank McCormick, a tall New Yorker who'd had brief trials with the Reds before arriving to stay in the spring of 1938, played a competent first base, led the league in at bats (640), averaged .320, and drove in 106 runs while hitting only five homers. Big Ernie Lombardi led the league with a .340 average besides hitting nineteen homers and driving in ninety-five runs. As would be the case throughout his career, "The Schnoz" (so nicknamed for his heroic nose, or "Schnozzola") left people wondering what he might hit if he weren't so painfully slow that shortstops and third basemen played him in shallow left field.

Paul Derringer pitched more innings (307) than anybody in the National League and won twenty-one games—despite going through a bitter divorce. In midseason Warren Giles made what became one of the great deals in Cincinnati Reds history when he gave pitcher Al Hollingsworth, catcher Spud Davis, and $50,000 to the Phillies for infielder-turned-pitcher William "Bucky" Walters. Although Walters had compiled a dreary 38–53 record since going to the mound full-time in 1935 and was only 4–8 when he joined the Reds, McKechnie thought that Walters could bolster his staff. As in fact he did, winning eleven games during the remainder of the season.

But 1938 was also the year in which Johnny Vander Meer, a twenty-three-year-old Reds left-hander, became a national sensation. Disabled for much of August and September with an ear infection, Vander Meer showed an unimposing 15–10 record at season's end. But by then, the Prospect Park, New Jersey, native had gained lasting eminence for doing something unique in big-league annals: throwing back-to-back no-hit, no-run games.

Vander Meer's first no-hitter came in daylight at Crosley Field on Saturday, June 11, when he blanked the Boston Bees 3–0, aided by Lombardi's two-run homer. Often wild, that day he walked only three while striking out four. Four days later, in the first night game at Ebbets Field, Brooklyn, he did it again.

It was a Larry MacPhail extravaganza that turned out to be far more than MacPhail or anybody had expected. Speeches, marching bands, and foot races between various Dodgers and Jesse Owens, winner of four gold medals at the Berlin Olympic Games two years earlier, went on until 9:45, when Brooklyn's Max Butcher took the mound in full nightfall—as MacPhail had intended for maximum illumination.

More than two hours later, with Brooklyn batting in the bottom of the ninth inning and losing 6–0, hardly anybody in the standing-room-only crowd of 38,748 had left the ballpark. Although he'd walked ten men and had the bases full with two out, Vander Meer still hadn't yielded a base hit. Leo Durocher lifted a soft fly ball to center field for the final out, and Johnny Vander Meer had his slice of immortality.

That game and Brooklyn's remaining six night games drew 189,765, which boosted total season attendance for a seventh-place ball club to 663,087—nearly a 30 percent gain from 1937. Besides night baseball, MacPhail sought to collect customers by hiring Babe Ruth to coach at first base and entertain early arrivals by rapping a few balls in batting practice. Everybody on the team seemed to enjoy having the Babe around except Burleigh Grimes, who feared that Ruth wanted his job, and Durocher, who hadn't liked Ruth going back to their years as Yankees teammates in the late 1920s.

On one occasion Durocher executed a neat hit-and-run play that led to a Brooklyn score; a newspaper account had it that Ruth had signaled for the play. Durocher, who himself had put the sign on, was so furious that he got into a shoving match with Ruth in the locker room until Grimes separated them. "How the fuck could he call the play?" fumed Durocher. "He doesn't even know the fucking signs."[16] The Babe had wanted to get back into baseball, but having to put up with Durocher (whom he'd once dubbed "the all-American out") wasn't what he'd had in mind.

At the break for the All-Star Game, the afterglow of "Double No-Hit" Vander Meer's achievement was still warming Cincinnati fans, who that year had the added treat of hosting the game. Of course, Bill Terry picked

Vander Meer for the National League pitching staff and even named him to start. The left-hander pitched three scoreless innings, as did Chicago's Bill Lee. Mace Brown gave up a home run to Joe DiMaggio in the ninth inning, but the Nationals, helped by four American League errors, scored four times on Lefty Gomez, Johnny Allen, and Lefty Grove and gained their second All-Star victory.

By nightfall on Wednesday, September 25—with Vander Meer and mates as well as the Giants eliminated from the race—Pittsburgh held a two-and-a-half-game lead over the Chicago Cubs. They were no longer Charley Grimm's Cubs, because on July 20—even though Grimm's team had won seven games in a row—Philip Wrigley had fired "Jolly Cholly" and turned the team over to Gabby Hartnett. Grimm went upstairs to the radio broadcasting booth to provide commentary for Bob Elson's play-by-play accounts. At that point, the Giants held a slim lead over Pittsburgh, while Chicago was in third place, four and a half games out of first.

As in 1932, the Cubs changed managers in midstream and won a pennant. A good deal of the credit for that went to Dizzy Dean. Throwing at every speed but fast, pitching to spots, and using all the tricks he'd learned in six big-league seasons, Dean won his first two starts, but then—diagnosed as being afflicted with subdeltoid bursitis—didn't pitch for two months. When he returned to action (three days before Grimm's dismissal), he gained a four-hit, 3–1 decision over Boston; six days later he pitched a five-hitter in the nightcap of a doubleheader sweep of the Giants before 42,223 at Wrigley Field. In a game enlivened by a fight between Dick Bartell and Billy Jurges after they collided in the base path, Dean threw only eighty-eight pitches, relying on a sidearm curve and what John Drebinger described as "a tantalizing 'slider' that slid harmlessly off their bats as if it was operated on a string."[17]

Dean was no longer the wise-cracking braggart he'd once been. John Kieran characterized him by quoting a couplet from the poet Edwin Markham's "The Man with the Hoe": "The emptiness of ages in his face / And on his back the burdens of the world."[18] Yet over the balance of the season, Dean won three more starts and lost only once. Pitching in thirteen games and seventy-five innings, he won seven, lost one, and allowed fewer than two runs per nine innings. Dean could get batters out, said the Chicago sportswriter Warren Brown, because "many of them were continually off stride as they batted against his pitching movement rather than the ball which came toward the plate with all the fury of something blown out of a bubble pipe."[19]

Philip Wrigley may have gotten his $185,000 worth—both from Dean's infrequent but effective pitching and from the crowds he drew into Wrigley Field. But the real stalwart of the 1938 Cubs staff was Bill Lee, whose 22–9 record, 2.66 ERA, and nine shutouts were the majors' best; in September he ran off a string of thirty-nine scoreless innings. Clay Bryant won nineteen games; Tex Carleton, ten; and thirty-nine-year-old Charley Root pitched in forty-four games, won eight, and saved a like number. Larry French's 10–19 record belied his respectable 3.80 ERA and sparse offensive support.

Even more than in 1935, the Cubs lacked punch, collectively batting .269 and homering only sixty-five times. Ripper Collins led in circuit blows with thirteen; Stan Hack and American League castoff Carl Reynolds were the only men in the lineup to reach the .300 level. But then the National League as a whole averaged only .265 and scored nearly 1,200 fewer runs than the American League. Apparently, a deader National League ball had again worked its deadening effect.

Late in August, William Benswanger, president of the Pittsburgh franchise, was so confident of a pennant that he directed the construction of extra seats atop the Forbes Field grandstand and the issuance of press badges. When the pennant didn't happen, Benswanger would blame the North Atlantic hurricane of 1938. The huge storm assaulted the northeastern coast in mid-September, inundating Long Island and much of New England, killing some five hundred people, and disrupting baseball and much else from Philadelphia to Boston. (With rail service paralyzed in New England, the Cardinals had to fly from Boston to Newark and then take a train into New York.) "As we sat around hotel lobbies during the storm," lamented Benswanger of his Pirates, "a hot team cooled off and never regained its winning momentum."[20]

In any case, the Pirates had cooled off by Tuesday, September 27, when they began a showdown series in Wrigley Field with their lead over the Cubs reduced to a game and a half. As 42,238 looked on, both Dean and Jack Tobin pitched superbly. Dean held the Pirates scoreless until the ninth inning and then, with two on base, handed the ball to Lee and left with a two-run lead. Lee's first pitch was wild and let in a run, but then the Louisianian finally got the third out to save Dean's game. Afterward an exhausted Dean called his performance "the greatest of my life."[21]

The next day would become a historic one in Chicago baseball history. Hartnett used six pitchers and Pie Traynor three in a long struggle that was tied 5–5 with darkness closing over Wrigley Field. With two out in the bottom of the ninth and the umpires ready to stop play after that inning, the Cubs' manager came to bat against Mace Brown. Brown got two strikes on Harnett and then, instead of wasting a pitch, tried to get a curveball past him. But the seventeen-year veteran was ready for it and clubbed the ball on a line into the left-field bleachers to end the game. As Hartnett rounded the bases, a good portion of the crowd of 34,465 tumbled out of the stands, grabbed him at third base, and carried him to home plate.

In the visitors' clubhouse, the thirty-year-old Brown sat sobbing in front of his locker. "I stayed with him all that night," Paul Waner revealed years afterward. "I was so afraid he would commit suicide." The Cubs had taken only a half-game lead, and the teams would meet again the next day, but Harnett's "homer in the gloamin'," as it came to be called, would prove the decisive moment in the pennant battle. Said Hartnett later, "The heart was out of Pittsburgh."[22]

As in truth it seemed to be, because in the series finale on Thursday, before 42,628, the Cubs battered Russ Bauers and three successors for ten runs while Lee held the Pirates to one. The Cubs then entrained for St. Louis to close the season; the Pirates headed for Cincinnati.

Traynor's and Bill McKechnie's teams had the day off on Friday and waited for the score from St. Louis, where Carleton and French blew a five-run lead before the game was called for darkness at 7–7. Johnny Mize's homer beat Chicago in the opener of Saturday's doubleheader, but in the nightcap Charley Root gave up three early runs, pitched runless ball over the last six innings, and benefited from his teammates' seventeen-hit, ten-run attack. At Crosley Field, Pittsburgh scored six runs and drove out Bucky Walters, but four pitchers couldn't stop the Reds, who piled up seventeen hits and nine runs to put the Pirates two and a half games back and give the pennant to the Cubs.

In a meaningless Sunday game that closed the season, Paul Dean combined with rookie Mort Cooper to defeat Chicago 7–5—the younger Dean's third win without a loss since his recall from Rochester (where he'd been reassigned from Houston). The Pirates lost again to Cincinnati, which left the Cubs with an 89–63 record versus Pittsburgh's 86–64. In a stretch drive that was strikingly similar to those of 1932 and 1935, Hartnett's team had won twenty-one of its last twenty-five games and ten in a row before losing the opener in St. Louis on Saturday. It was a lastingly bitter disappointment for Pittsburgh fans, whose teams hadn't been that close to a pennant in eleven years—and wouldn't be again for another thirty-two.

On Monday, with an estimated 300,000 Chicagoans lining the streets, the triumphant home team rode in open automobiles from Wrigley Field to city hall, where a beaming Hartnett told everybody, "Hell, this is swell."[23]

But again the Cubs weren't prepared to be generous with their World Series money, which after a year's hiatus would again be enhanced by the radio networks' $100,000 fee for broadcast rights (purchased by the Gillette Safety Razor Company). As had happened to Rogers Hornsby in 1932, Charley Grimm, who'd managed the team through eighty-one games, was voted nothing at all.

· · · · ·

UNLIKE BABE RUTH and company in 1932, the 1938 Yankees could have cared less about the Cubs' stinginess. The Chicagoans were even more badly overmatched by the Bronx Bombers than the Giants had been the past two Octobers. When the Series ended five days and four games after it started, Ripper Collins could only say, "It's lucky we didn't get hurt."[24] It wasn't that bad—but it was pretty close.

More than 44,000 filled every seat and nook of Wrigley Field for the opener, which the Yankees won 3–1 behind Red Ruffing. Tommy Henrich was charged with a harmless error in the ninth inning on a ball that bounced up and hit him in the face—the Yankees' first error in Series play since 1936. But in the third inning, Cubs fielding lapses let in two runs, and that was pretty much the game. Lee struck out Gehrig twice; when umpire Charley Moran called him out in the eighth inning, the usually poised Gehrig ranted, got up in Moran's face, and had to be restrained by Joe McCarthy and coaches Earle Combs and Art Fletcher.

It was a harbinger of what would be a frustrating Series for Gehrig, who could manage only four singles in fourteen at bats. But if the rest of the Yankees hadn't really needed his bat during the regular season, they needed it even less against the Cubs. (It would be a tough Series for Moran as well; in game three, Joe Gordon's errant throw hit him in the mouth, knocked out his dentures, and necessitated two stitches on his upper lip.)

Game two was the last spotlighted start of Dizzy Dean's career. Again throwing sore-armed junk but keeping the Yankees off balance, Dean took a 3–2 lead into the eighth inning. New York's runs again had come as a result of a Chicago fielding mistake—this time a collision between third baseman Hack and shortstop Jurges on a ground ball that rolled into left field as two Yankees scored.

Dean later said that his arm had started hurting in the sixth inning, and he felt pain on every pitch after that. But he held on, getting the New Yorkers to overswing, sometimes sneaking one past with a little speed for a third strike. Then, with two out and one runner on base in the eighth inning, Frank Crosetti—never known for his power—timed one of Dean's slow balls and drove it into the left-field bleachers to put the Yankees ahead 4–3. Dean persuaded Hartnett to let him continue, but in the next inning DiMaggio hit one over the bleachers and into Waveland Avenue with Henrich aboard, at which point Dean exited in favor of Larry French. Johnny Murphy, who'd relieved Lefty Gomez after seven innings, set down the Cubs in their half of the ninth to end it 6–3. DiMaggio later said that Dean had tried to get "a fast ball that wasn't" past him. "I didn't have nothin'," Dean said a few years after that. "I had no license to beat anybody. But they could-a cut off my arm in that clubhouse if I'd a won that one."[25]

After a day's travel, the Series resumed before far less than a sellout crowd at Yankee Stadium—55,236 paid. Relying on his fast ball and change-up and, so he later said, throwing no more than half a dozen curves, Monte Pearson allowed five hits and two runs—one an eighth-inning homer by Joe Marty—while striking out nine. Clay Bryant pitched four scoreless innings before throwing a home-run ball to Joe Gordon, who also hit a two-run single in the next inning to give the Yankees a 4–1 lead and send Bryant to the showers. Bill Dickey tagged French for another homer in the ninth to make the final score 5–2.

Afterward McCarthy told reporters that Jacob Ruppert—bedridden with phlebitis at his Fifth Avenue apartment and absent from his first Yankees World Series—had asked for a sweep, and the players wanted to give it to him. Queried about whom he might choose to pitch the fifth game, McCarthy smiled and replied, "What in the hell are you talking about?"[26]

Game four, played before 59,487, justified McCarthy's feigned incredulity. Keyed by Crosetti's triple, the Yankees jumped on Lee in the second inning for three runs and scored another in the next inning on Henrich's homer off Charley Root. The Cubs reached Ruffing for one run in the fourth, and Ken O'Dea, subbing for the worn-down Hartnett, connected for a two-run homer in the top of the eighth to make the score 4–3. But in the bottom of the inning, the Yankees put the game out of reach with a four-run outburst. Tex Carleton wild-pitched one run across; Myril Hoag doubled in another; and, after Dean relieved Carleton, Crosetti's bloop double brought in two more runs before Dean got out of the inning. It would be Dean's last World Series appearance. (The last as well for Tony Lazzeri. Used sparingly by Grimm and Hartnett during the season, Lazzeri pinch-hit unsuccessfully in games three and four.)

Although he couldn't be there, Ruppert threw his usual victory party at the Commodore Hotel for players, wives, farm-club officials, baseball writers, and camp followers. While the Yankees talked about what they would do with their $5,815 apiece in Series money (versus $4,675 per Cub) and Lefty Gomez and June O'Dea let everybody know they'd reconciled, McCarthy hailed his team as the greatest ever. When somebody suggested to Ed Barrow that the Yankees might be too good, the curmudgeonly executive growled, "If the champions of the other league can't beat us, what can we do about it?"[27]

Lou Gehrig was acting out of character again, sitting astride a chair, laughing and mimicking himself riding a horse. Never much of a drinker, Gehrig this time more than held his own with the flowing booze, so much so that a teammate finally went over to Eleanor Gehrig and told her, "You'd better look after Lou. He's drinking triples, and he's really bombed."[28]

But if people wondered about Gehrig's behavior and his substandard season and Series, everything else looked good from a Yankees perspective. From his bed, Ruppert listened to the Junior World Series games between Newark and Kansas City, his two top farm clubs, which ended with Kansas City's seventh-game victory before a home crowd of more than 15,000. Ten other Yankees farm clubs had at least qualified for the four-team Shaughnessy playoffs; besides Newark and Kansas City, six had won pennants. It appeared that the Yankees would enjoy a steady influx of gifted youngsters and a continuing run of pennants, which was exactly what Ruppert expected.

"Why find fault with the Yankees because they represent the best in baseball?" the Colonel asked rhetorically later that year. "Major-league baseball should be of the highest type. That's what I want—the best. Every day I want to win. . . . I can't stand close games. They make me nervous. I like games where we win 10–0. Then I can sit back and enjoy myself."[29]

· · · · ·

MCCARTHY AND BARROW weren't about to stand pat. With Charlie Keller, a slugging outfielder, coming up from Newark, Myril Hoag was shipped to the Browns for pitcher Oral Hildebrand. The *New York World-Telegram's* Dan Daniel was certain that even if Jake Powell hadn't "embarrassed the New York club" with his "unfortunate and unintentional cracks" in that Chicago radio interview, he would still be on the trading block.[30] But for some reason, McCarthy decided to keep Powell, even though he would use him only thirty-one times in 1939.

Bill Terry and Horace Stoneham didn't stand pat, either. When their offer to buy Joe Medwick and Johnny Mize as a package (reportedly for $250,000) was refused by Branch Rickey, they traded Hank Leiber, Gus Mancuso, and Dick Bartell to the Cubs for Frank Demaree, Billy Jurges, and Ken O'Dea and paid Washington $20,000 and two minor leaguers for Zeke Bonura.

As usual, Larry MacPhail figured prominently in off-season baseball talk—what had come to be called the "hot stove league." In October he announced that Burleigh Grimes was out and that Leo Durocher, Brooklyn's thirty-three-year-old shortstop, would manage the team (which meant that Babe Ruth was out as well). And just before the December major-league meetings, MacPhail disclosed that the Dodgers were withdrawing from a five-year agreement signed in 1935 with the Giants and Yankees to ban radio broadcasts of the three teams' games. Doing play-by-play on Brooklyn's home and road games would be Red Barber, whom MacPhail had brought to Cincinnati to handle Reds games four years earlier. MacPhail sold broadcast rights to General Mills, Socony Vacuum, and New York's station WOR for $77,000.

Within a few weeks, the Yankees and Giants had decided that the money was too good to pass up and had negotiated their own radio deals. That meant that for the first time all sixteen big-league teams would have radio play-by-play coverage, although nearly all road games would be "re-created" in station studios based on minimal information teletyped from distant ballparks. General Mills (whose signature product was Wheaties breakfast cereal) sponsored every team except the two in Boston. As of the 1939 season, 7.3 percent of average franchise revenue would come from radio.

Both St. Louis teams as well as the bottom-dog Phillies announced managerial changes that October. The Browns dumped Gabby Street, under whose leadership the team had finished seventh, and hired Fred Haney, Toledo's manager since 1935; the Cardinals elevated Ray Blades, who'd played and managed in their organization since 1921, from Rochester. Frank Frisch found employment broadcasting Boston Red Sox and Bees games, thus joining Charley Grimm, Jack Graney (covering Cleveland), Harry Heilmann (working Detroit games), and Walter Johnson (doing play-by-play for Washington) as pioneer former ballplayers and/or managers who'd found a place in the broadcast booth. In Philadelphia, Gary Nugent replaced Jimmie Wilson (who joined Cincinnati as a coach) with James "Doc" Prothro, who'd managed in the Southern Association in Memphis and Little Rock.

At the December meetings, held in New York at the elegant Waldorf-Astoria, the American League executives—all but the Yankees—voted to follow the National Leaguers' lead in authorizing a maximum of seven night games for any teams that wanted to play at night; at that time, only Cleveland and the Philadelphia Athletics had expressed such a desire. The Giants had never been willing to play at night in either Cincinnati or Brooklyn, and now they reaffirmed their daylight-only policy, while the Yankees also declared that they wouldn't play at night anywhere.

Although the economy was still mired in the Roosevelt Recession—with the Works Progress Administration's rolls reaching a peak in October of 3,253,625 and business and industrial indexes hovering at around 85 percent of normal—it had been a surprisingly good year for baseball as a whole. The minor leagues continued their renaissance, with thirty-seven circuits starting and completing their seasons. Major-league attendance roughly equaled that of 1937, with the Yankees and Cubs each drawing close to 1 million paid.

So, after six years of austerely restricting rosters to twenty-three, the club owners voted unanimously to return to the pre-1932 twenty-five-man rosters. At the same time, though, they did away with the disabled list, so that whether a man was able to play or not, he had to be carried on the active roster. Once again, the joint rules committee voted to adopt a "uniform ball," which meant that the National League would readopt the ball in play in the American League during the previous season. Also, the rules committee reinstituted the sacrifice-fly rule that had been done away with following the 1930 season—although that would turn out be a one-year departure.

Jacob Ruppert died on January 13, 1939, at the age of seventy-one, from a phlebitis condition that had first been diagnosed the previous spring. His estate—including his brewery; extensive realty holdings; the Yankees, Yankee Stadium, and Yankees-owned minor-league franchises; his country manor in Garrison, New York; and various other properties—was estimated at between $70 and $100 million. His will named his two nieces and a young woman described as "his ward" as his heirs and put the Yankees organization in the hands of a four-man trusteeship that included younger brother George Ruppert. The trustees elected Ed Barrow as franchise president; George Weiss would continue as farm-system director and president of the Newark Bears.

Three weeks later, Lou Gehrig signed his 1939 contract for $36,000, taking the second cut of his career. Lefty Gomez, happily remarried and second-honeymooning at Niagara Falls, would be paid $20,000, as would Bill Dickey. Joe DiMaggio, initially seeking a refund on what he'd lost by missing the first part of the 1938 season, settled for $27,000, but Red Rolfe was offered (and eventually took) the same $15,000 he'd been paid in 1938, despite batting .311. Barrow's reasoning? Rolfe had driven in only eighty runs.

When Dizzy Dean did a post–World Series vaudeville stint with Bob Elson, he told an audience in Sioux City, Iowa, "If there is a father in this crowd who wants his boy to be a success in the major leagues, don't let him sign up with the Cardinals."[31] But Dean had no complaints about his current employer. In January he went to Chicago, looked at X rays supposedly showing his arm to be all right, and signed for $20,000.

Johnny Vander Meer, who'd not only pitched spectacularly but raked in substantial income from endorsements, saw his salary jump from about $5,000 to $12,000. That, as Vander Meer said decades later, "was unheard-of for most third-year players."[32] But Mel Ott, loyal to Bill Terry and ac-quiescent to a fault, agreed to take a $500 cut, to $19,500, despite having had a better year in 1938 than in 1937. Joe Medwick's salary was cut by $2,000 on the grounds that given the Cardinals' poor home attendance in 1938, the club just couldn't afford to pay him $20,000 again. Paul Waner accepted a 20 percent slash and signed for $12,000.

· · · · ·

TED WILLIAMS, all of twenty years old by the time he reported for the second time to the Boston Red Sox's Sarasota training site, was coming off a 1938 season in which he'd battered American Association pitching (.366, forty-three home runs, 142 RBIs). The Red Sox expected so much of the youngster that the previous December they'd traded Ben Chapman to Cleveland. Williams was cockier than ever and, if no heavier, appeared to have grown stronger. Calling himself "the Kid" (because he thought all great players ought to have memorable nicknames), Williams still wasn't much interested in anything besides hitting—he liked to stand in the out-field with the opposition at bat and use his glove for practice swings—but he dazzled onlookers with soaring drives beyond the fences. "Sure," a writer for *Baseball Magazine* said of him a few months later, "he's [as] crazy as the average youth of twenty bubbling over in good health and sitting atop the world."[33]

While young Williams's future seemed almost limitless, Lou Gehrig's looked increasingly bleak to those who watched him in St. Peterburg. A year earlier, in a piece in the *Sporting News*, Gehrig had suggested that simply dropping a pack of playing cards on the floor every morning and then picking each one up was sufficient to keep off excess poundage. By the spring of 1939, he could no longer manage that simple exercise—at least not without great difficulty. Dan Daniel, who usually wrote as the Yankees' unofficial cheerleader, said that "Gehrig really presents a problem. . . . He is quite bad. It seems he is having trouble with his legs." A couple of weeks later, Daniel was more specific: "He has pulled away from balls pitched right over the plate. His timing has been bad, he hasn't been able to bring his bat around fast enough. His running has been woeful, his fielding not so good."[34]

Joe DiMaggio, in his first full spring training, walloped the ball from the right side, and young Charlie Keller, whose muscles and beetle brows soon won him the nickname "King Kong," did the same from the left side. But even though Gehrig worked harder than he ever had, he still couldn't make himself right. He tried to stay upbeat, telling John Kieran with a grin, "They've got me starred in another thriller now. 'Buried Alive.' Yes, sir, the pallbearers have me dead and buried."[35] But he failed to reach ground balls and had trouble covering first base; when he made solid contact, the result was usually an easy roller or a bloop over the infield; and batting-practice pitchers worried that if they got the ball inside, he wouldn't be able to get out of the way.

Gehrig had a few encouraging days, such as when he drove in six runs on three singles against New Orleans and on the way back to New York homered twice over a short right-field fence in Norfolk. As always he was at first base on opening day, when Red Ruffing won a fine duel from Lefty Grove, 2–0, but twice Gehrig hit into double plays, and he also messed up a play in the ninth inning.

If at that point Gehrig's situation was still more a matter of perplexity than pathos, that of Monty Stratton had evoked sympathy throughout baseball. In 1937, his first full season with the White Sox, the lean, 6-foot 5-inch Stratton had won fifteen games, lost five, and registered an excellent 2.40 ERA. In 1938 he'd again won fifteen, and while his ERA swelled to 4.01, hardly anybody doubted that the farm boy from northeast Texas— still only twenty-six—could become one of the game's premier pitchers. One day in November, however, Stratton went hunting for rabbits with a pistol, stumbled, and shot himself in the right leg. In a period immediately before the advent of antibiotics, little could be done to prevent infection—

and then the onset of gangrene. Stratton's leg was amputated just below the knee.

Determined to return to baseball, the young right-hander had himself fitted with a prosthesis and nurtured ideas of coming back but eventually settled for a coaching sinecure with the White Sox. On May 1, 1939, the Chicago teams played a benefit game at Comiskey Park and raised $29,000 for Stratton. Dizzy Dean pitched four innings but left complaining that his arm was "weak and tired."[36]

If Dizzy Dean's arm was weak, Paul Dean's appeared to be completely gone; after one unhappy outing, he found himself again fighting humidity and mosquitoes in Houston. He now blamed his brother for his arm troubles, claiming that three years earlier Diz had "made me hold out [and] when I joined the club I was out of condition and tried to pitch when I hadn't trained enough. You know all the rest. I faded out with a sore arm." But he'd told Diz "to go his way and I'd go my way [and] from now on I was attending to my own affairs. I ain't hangin' onto Dizzy's apron strings any more."[37]

As for Diz, he was still able to pitch only as Gabby Hartnett's spot starter, but in that role he showed that he wasn't washed up. After making his first official appearance on May 16, in relief in a loss to Brooklyn, he pitched a splendid three-hit shutout five days later against Boston.

. . . . .

AS DIZZY DEAN, at twenty-nine, nursed his arm and career, at thirty-five Lou Gehrig decided to bring his career to an end. He later said that he had made his decision after an April 30 loss at Washington. In that game Buddy Myer hit a routine ground ball, which Gehrig scooped up and tossed to Johnny Murphy, covering first base for the out. In the dugout Murphy said, "Great play, Lou," and Gehrig wondered to himself, "Has it reached that stage?"[38]

On May 1, with Joe DiMaggio sidelined for a month with a torn knee ligament, the Yankees left for Detroit to begin their first swing of the western cities. Before the next day's game at Briggs Stadium, Gehrig went to Joe McCarthy and took himself out of the lineup—after 2,130 consecutive regular-season games. He had four singles to show for eight games and twenty-eight times at bat.

As team captain, Gehrig carried that afternoon's lineup to the umpires at home plate and then sat and watched his teammates slaughter the Tigers 22–2. Keller, Henrich, and Selkirk hit home runs, as did Gehrig's replacement—Ellsworth "Babe" Dahlgren, a right-handed San Franciscan who'd come up from Newark. When Dahlgren got back to the dugout after his homer, Gehrig jubilantly grabbed him and shouted, "Hey, why didn't you tell me you felt that way about it. I woulda got out of there long ago."[39]

A deft fielder, Dahlgren had trouble connecting consistently and, usually batting eighth, compiled only a .235 average in 144 games. But he did slap fifteen homers and drive in eighty-nine runs in a lineup that, especially with DiMaggio's return full time on June 7, had lost little of its explosiveness. In the first six games without Gehrig, the Yankees scored sixty-three runs. They won eight of ten games in the West and thirty-three of their first forty. Gehrig suited up at Yankee Stadium for every home game and continued to travel with the team and take the lineups to home plate. But after playing three innings in a night exhibition game at Kansas City on June 12 (with Vince DiMaggio in center field for the Blues), he left for Rochester, Minnesota, to be examined at the renowned Mayo Clinic.

The clinic's finding, released to the press after five days of exhaustive tests, was that Gehrig was "suffering from amyotrophic lateral sclerosis," an illness involving "the motor pathways and cells of the central nervous system and in lay terms is known as a form of chronic poliomyelitis (infantile paralysis)."[40] People at that time were generally familiar with poliomyelitis, which was a terrible crippling scourge, especially in children, but usually not fatal. So the reference "in lay terms" to polio no doubt led many to assume that while Gehrig was through as a ballplayer and might suffer some form of disability, his life wasn't necessarily threatened. Yet in fact this rare disease—ALS, in medical shorthand—knew no cure, no treatment, and no outcome but death, usually within about two years.

However little the disease was understood, the most admired and re-spected man in Yankees history had to be honored in some way. So the July 4 doubleheader with Washington at Yankee Stadium was the occasion for the most poignant day that any ballplayer would ever be given. With some 65,000 in the stands and Mayor LaGuardia, other dignitaries, and past and present teammates gathered near home plate, Gehrig shuffled to the microphone and, in his thick East Side brogue, spoke a simply eloquent valedictory for "the luckiest man on the face of the earth."[41]

. . . . .

IF GEHRIG'S PLIGHT evoked extreme pathos, what was happening on Long Island was a gigantic exercise in optimism, even as the Depression's grip remained firm. Throughout the 1938 season, the three New York teams had worn patches on their left uniform sleeves featuring the trylon and perisphere logo of the city's World's Fair, scheduled to begin the following spring. On Sunday, April 30, 1939, President Roosevelt officially opened the fair in an address before some 60,000 assembled in the Court of Peace within the vast fair complex. For those who weren't physically present, the three-hour ceremonies could be viewed on 9-inch television screens located in retail stores and a few New York–area homes, whose owners had paid around $600 apiece for their sets.

Television—soon to be available for the mass market, it was widely supposed—served to confirm a deeply held faith that progress was still possible through the wonders of technology. Even more of a hymn to progress was the fair's celebrated General Motors pavilion, with its huge moving model of "the world of the future" of 1960—a vision of multilayered superhighways; clean, well-designed cities; and a sky full of personally owned helicopters.

As the fair pointed to the future, official baseball sought to codify its official version of how baseball had come about. In the early years of the century, Albert G. Spalding—once a great pitcher, later a club owner, and still later a sporting-goods tycoon—had used his influence to bring about the formation of a blue-ribbon commission to inquire into baseball's origins. Chaired by onetime National League president Abraham G. Mills, the commission found as Spalding intended it to find, pronouncing that the game of baseball had been invented in May 1839 in the village of Cooperstown in upstate New York by young Abner Doubleday.

The commission's evidence was shaky at best, but in the years that followed the Doubleday version came to be generally accepted as accurate history by the press and baseball public. From time to time, a dissenter would pop up to insist that it was actually legend and myth—that, as Robert W. Henderson, an executive in the New York–Pennsylvania League, wrote in 1939, baseball was unmistakably derived from the ancient English game of rounders, and games called "base ball" were being played in various places in the United States as early as the 1820s.[42]

Henderson's effort to discredit baseball's official history was published shortly before that history was enshrined in brick, concrete, and glass in Cooperstown. Through the efforts of Alexander Clelland, director of a New York City immigrant-aid organization, National League president Ford Frick sought to promote a Cooperstown baseball historical museum—the nucleus for which would be a small collection of early artifacts in the town's possession. With financial backing from Stephen Clark, a wealthy philanthropist who was Clelland's employer, and with the endorsement of Commissioner Landis, the project went forward—the plan being that the museum's opening should coincide with baseball's mythical centennial and that the museum should feature a "Hall of Fame" of the game's greatest figures.

Beginning in 1936, the Base Ball Writers Association of America conducted a series of polls to choose the first class of Hall of Fame inductees. By 1939 twenty-one "immortals" had been chosen, and the building was completed. On June 12 some 10,000 people converged on Cooperstown for inaugural festivities. Landis, Frick, American League president William Harridge, and National Association president William G. Bramham cut the ribbons for what would officially be known as the National Baseball Hall of Fame and Museum.

Ten of the eleven living inductees—Babe Ruth, Honus Wagner, Tris Speaker, Napoleon Lajoie, Walter Johnson, Grover Cleveland Alexander, George Sisler, Cy Young, Eddie Collins, and Connie Mack—were present for the morning ceremonies. (Ty Cobb, who hated Landis and wanted to avoid having to be photographed with him, showed up late.) That afternoon, the celebrants adjourned to the local ballpark, called Doubleday Field, where, following exhibitions of "old-time" baseball, two squads of big leaguers, with Collins and Wagner acting as managers, played a six-inning game.

Even if no solid historical basis existed for siting the Hall of Fame at Cooperstown, New York, it was always a lovely place to visit (if never easy to reach), located in the foothills of the Catskill Mountains and by Lake Otsego (the Glimmerglass of James Fenimore Cooper's Leatherstocking Tales). In the decades to follow, tourists would come in swelling numbers to visit the Hall of Fame, view its growing collection of artifacts and exhibits, and witness the annual summertime ceremonies for new inductees. As James A. Vlasich has written, the Mills Commission "planted the seeds of the [Doubleday] legend; the 100th anniversary celebration nurtured it, and caused it to flower into fact. . . . Oddly, a celebration designed to recognize an important historical event had only helped to perpetuate a legend."[43]

As baseball looked to its past, its present continued to change—as did some of its attitudes. Whether to help out other clubs or to realize bigger road receipts, Ed Barrow surprised everybody by relenting on the Yankees' no-night-ball pledge. Two weeks after playing at night in Kansas City, the Yankees met the Athletics before a crowd of 33,074 in the fourth night game at Shibe Park. The veteran Philadelphia sportswriter Stoney McLinn, recalling Connie Mack's avowal a few years earlier never to play at night, observed that "time and science, hand in hand, do indeed march on."[44]

On June 1 the Phillies had played their first night game at Shibe Park, losing to Pittsburgh. Only about 8,000 were on hand, but that was still more than twice the Phillies' per-game average for the past several years. Later that month, the Indians inaugurated night baseball at Cleveland's big stadium, where 55,305 paid to see Bobby Feller pitch a one-hit, thirteen-strikeout victory over Detroit. The Chicago White Sox looked at nighttime attendance figures in Philadelphia and Cleveland (as well as in Cincinnati and Brooklyn), bowed to technological progress, and hurriedly installed lights at Comiskey Park. On August 14, about three weeks after owner Louis Comiskey's death (at fifty-three), the White Sox and the seventh-place Browns attracted some 30,000 to Chicago's initial big-league nighter; four days later, 46,000 paid to see the locals defeat Feller in eleven innings.

Baseball and television had their first mating on May 16, when NBC experimentally telecast (with one camera mounted on a platform off third base) a Princeton University–Columbia University game at Columbia's Baker Field. Murky reception and viewers' inability to pick up the baseball in flight didn't discourage NBC, which got Red Barber to sound out Larry MacPhail about having a big-league game telecast at Ebbets Field. MacPhail jumped on the idea, and on Saturday, August 26, two NBC cameras covered a Brooklyn–Cincinnati doubleheader. Barber ad-libbed commercials and did between-game interviews with Leo Durocher, Bill McKechnie, and Dolph Camilli. Although viewers again had trouble seeing the ball, MacPhail was so pleased that he promised to have regularly televised games in 1940.

. . . . .

WITH ALL THE OTHER baseball happenings that summer—not to mention bitter labor–management confrontations at home and increasingly ominous news from abroad—newspaper readers may have found it a bit harder to concentrate on the pennant races. But then in the American League, again there wasn't much of a race to concentrate on. At the All-Star Game break, the post-Gehrig Yankees—having recently totaled forty-three base hits and thirteen home runs in a 23–3, 10–0 doubleheader demolition of the Athletics—led the second-place Red Sox by six and a half games. In mid-July, Boston won seven of eight from the New Yorkers and moved to within five games, but they never got that close again. By August 28, after winning eight in a row and homering twenty-two times in their last ten games, the Yankees had stretched their margin over Joe Cronin's club to thirteen and a half.

As for the All-Star Game itself, it was another American League victory, its fifth in seven years. Some 63,000 at Yankee Stadium watched a well-enacted contest in which Bill Lee gave up a home run to DiMaggio and two other runs in the middle innings, and then Bobby Feller relieved Tommy Bridges to pitch three and one-third innings of shutout ball and preserve a 3–1 win.

Gehrig served as honorary captain of the American League All-Stars and, except for a follow-up examination at the Mayo Clinic in August, continued to be with the Yankees as they pulled away from the rest of the league. On September 16, by scoring seven times in the last two innings to overcome Detroit 8–5, they became the third major-league team to collect four consecutive pennants.[45]

It may have been the easiest of the four. The Yankees' 106–45 record left them seventeen games ahead of Boston. Committing only 126 errors, they led the majors with a .978 fielding average. New York pitchers threw fifteen shutouts and permitted but 556 runs. Red Ruffing (21–7) again topped the staff, but six other pitchers won at least ten games, and Johnny Murphy recorded nineteen saves. (Second-year man Steve Sundra was undefeated in eleven decisions before losing on the last day of the season.) New York's overall runs-scored-to-runs-allowed margin was an extraordinary 2.72.

With 462 official at bats, Joe DiMaggio won his first batting crown with a .381 average, besides homering thirty times and driving in 126 runs. George Selkirk enjoyed his best year overall (.306, twenty-one homers, 101 RBIs), Bill Dickey put in another good season (.302, twenty-four homers, 105 RBIs), Red Rolfe batted .324, and Joe Gordon had twenty-eight homers and 111 RBIs. In his rookie season, Charlie Keller came to the plate only 398 times but batted .334 and drove in eighty-three runs.

In August, after the Yankees swept a three-game series in stifling heat in Washington, Bucky Harris proclaimed Joe DiMaggio "the greatest ballplayer I ever saw." More than his bat, it was DiMaggio's fielding—how "he just materializes out of thin air" in the deep reaches of the outfield—that dazzled the Senators' manager.[46]

Besides DiMaggio and his Yankees mates, the American League showcased an abundance of star power. Despite being increasingly troubled by sinusitis and disabled in the last two weeks of the season by an appendectomy, Jimmie Foxx led the majors with thirty-five home runs and batted .360; Hal Trosky, who battled the same summertime upper-respiratory affliction, batted .335 with twenty-five homers and 104 RBIs; Hank Greenberg had thirty-three homers to go with a .312 average and 112 RBIs; and Bob Johnson, soldiering along with the lamentable Athletics, was one of the league's most productive hitters (.338, twenty-three homers, 114 RBIs).[47]

The talk of much of baseball, though, was the Kid in Boston. In his rookie season, Ted Williams gave every promise of fulfilling his announced ambition: to be the greatest hitter who ever lived. In 1939 Williams batted .327, led everybody in the major leagues with 145 RBIs, and cracked thirty-one home runs. Some of his homers, moreover, carried as far as Ruth, Foxx, or anybody else had hit them, such as one in Detroit on May 4 that cleared the Briggs Stadium right-field roof. Already showing the fastidious eye that would characterize his career, Williams also walked 107 times.

Williams turned twenty-one in August, but Bobby Feller was still only twenty when he closed out a season in which he led the American League in wins (twenty-four), innings (297), and complete games (twenty-four) and the majors in strikeouts (246). (Perhaps comparably impressive was the record of Washington's Emil "Dutch" Leonard, a right-hander who threw almost nothing but knuckleballs and garnered twenty of his club's sixty-six victories.)

. . . . .

ALTHOUGH THE TWO MAJOR LEAGUES were now supposed to be using the same ball, the American League continued to be the power-oriented circuit, while the National League continued to feature pitching and defense. Moreover, the Nationals obviously offered more stirring pennant races and maybe a greater number of colorful and combative personalities.

In Brooklyn, for example, Larry MacPhail and Leo Durocher proved a volatile but successful combination. MacPhail made shrewd trades and picked up American League retreads here and there, and Durocher (still at shortstop most of the time) managed a rebuilt team to an 84–69 record that pulled in nearly 1 million paying customers. Along the way, Durocher repeatedly got thrown out of games and had a fight with the Giants' Zeke Bonura.

As he had everywhere, Bonura hit well for the Giants, but Bill Terry, who'd been a premier first baseman himself, couldn't abide Bonura's fielding flaws and finally benched him. A different problem was Burgess Whitehead, who couldn't recover his competitive drive, sometimes didn't show up for games, and batted only .239 before Terry finally sent him home to Lewiston, North Carolina. Carl Hubbell won eleven games, but the surgery he'd undergone the previous year hadn't brought back his arm (which now hung at his left side with the hand twisted inward, the legacy of thousands of wrenching screwballs). Nobody else from the 1936 and 1937 league champions could win consistently except Harry Gumbert, who gave up a lot of runs but won eighteen times.

The Giants would end up in fifth place, winning only three games more than they lost, but over the first half of the season they seemed to have a chance for their fourth pennant of the decade. Although Cincinnati shot out to a big early lead, the Giants trailed them by only a few games on July 15, when they lost to the Reds at the Polo Grounds in a game that Harry Danning, for one, would always remember as the season's turning point. In the eighth inning, with Cincinnati in front 6–4, center fielder Harry Craft pulled a pitch down the short left-field line that plate umpire Lee Ballanfant ruled fair—for a two-run homer. Catcher Danning (who had the same view as Ballanfant), left fielder Joe Moore, Terry, and other Giants swarmed around Ballanfant and base umpires John "Ziggy" Sears and George Magerkurth to protest the call. Danning and Moore were ejected, but before that, Magerkurth (6 feet 4 inches, 240 pounds) and Billy Jurges (5 feet 11 inches, 175 pounds) spat on each other and then traded swings.

The Reds won the game 8–4 and took a six-and-a-half-game lead over New York. Ford Frick suspended Jurges for ten days and fined him $150; Magerkurth drew a like penalty; Moore, Danning, and Terry were fined $50 apiece. With Jurges unavailable, Lou Chiozza occupied shortstop but quickly suffered a broken leg; before Jurges returned to the lineup, the Giants had lost nine straight games and fallen out of contention. Craft's disputed homer did, though, result in a change at the Polo Grounds that would eventually be adopted in all the big-league parks: the attachment of 3-foot-wide screens to the foul poles on the fair-territory side so that any ball hit to the other side of the poles would have to be judged foul.

After coming so close in 1938, Pittsburgh, with the worst pitching in the league besides that of the Phillies, fell apart in August and September and tumbled all the way to sixth place. For the defending champion Cubs, it was a thoroughly disappointing season. Dick Bartell was unhappy in his new surroundings and played poorly, Hank Leiber was injured much of the time, and the Cubs led the league in errors. Bill Lee posted nineteen wins; Gabby Hartnett also got decent work from Larry French and Claude Passeau (acquired from the Phillies in May for cash and three players). But Hartnett and Philip Wrigley were at odds on various matters, and in mid-July, Harnett and Dizzy Dean had a falling out over a mysterious cut on his pitching arm that Dean had incurred in a New York hotel room. (Dean said that he had cut it on a table reaching for the telephone; others thought that Patricia Dean had hit him with something). Dean won two more starts to run his record to 6–0 and then lost his last four decisions of the season. The Cubs finished in fourth place, a half-game behind Brooklyn.

The surprise of the National League was the St. Louis Cardinals, who climbed all the way to second place, four and a half games from the top at the end. Frenchy Bordogaray was gone, the Mississippi Mudcats were defunct, and Ray Blades's team offered St. Louis fans nothing but serious baseball. Batting .294 (best in the National League since Gabby Street's 1930 champions), the Cardinals also led the league in runs scored. Joe Medwick spent the season griping about his salary, sometimes fielding indifferently, and bickering with Blades, but at bat he was still dangerous, averaging .332 and driving in 117 runs. Johnny Mize was even more dangerous, gaining the batting title with a .349 mark and leading the league with twenty-eight homers, while right fielder Enos "Country" Slaughter, a compact, left-hand–swinging North Carolinian in his second big-league season, batted .320.

Blades was considerably ahead of his time in the way he used his pitching staff, allowing his hurlers to complete only forty-five games. Curt Davis, who led the staff with twenty-two wins and thirteen complete games, also pitched in relief eighteen times and saved seven games; right-hander Bob Bowman and left-hander Clyde Shoun each relieved fifty-one times and saved nine games apiece. Sportswriters around the league wrote critically of Blades's frequent pitching changes, but withal Blades got more out of his staff and the rest of his team than anybody had expected.[48]

Bill McKechnie's Cincinnati Reds, a good fourth-place club in 1938, blossomed into the Queen City's first pennant winner in twenty years. By early June, the Reds had such a big lead that their fans were already writing and phoning in to reserve World Series tickets. Following the All-Star Game, they won sixteen of twenty games and opened a twelve-game bulge over St. Louis. But then the Cardinals made things interesting.

In the first half of August, St. Louis ran off an eleven-game winning streak. After the Cardinals swept a Sunday doubleheader from the Phillies before an overflow 40,807 at Sportsman's Park, Cincinnati's lead had shrunk to six and a half games. Within another month, the Cardinals had pruned it to three games; when the two teams split a doubleheader in Cincinnati and the next day Bill McGee threw a shutout to defeat Bucky Walters, the Reds led by only two and a half, with four games to play. But on Thursday, September 28, in the series finale, Paul Derringer gave up fourteen hits but held the Cardinals to three runs, while the Reds got to rookie Max Lanier, Davis, and Bowman for eight hits and five runs. When Derringer struck out Medwick and Mize to end the game, Bill McKechnie became the first manager to direct three pennant winners with three different teams.[49]

Hardly an outstanding ball club, the 1939 Cincinnati Reds were none-theless good enough to win ninety-seven games and, playing at home in the majors' smallest city, to attract 961,604 paying fans—second only to Brooklyn in the National League that year.[50] One reason they won was the acquisition of third baseman Bill Werber, who came over from the Phila-delphia Athletics for $25,000 and solidified McKechnie's infield. Werber, a Duke University graduate, had refused to take a $1,500 pay cut and ma-neuvered Connie Mack into selling him to Cincinnati, where his 1938 salary was restored. (After the season. Werber gave the $1,500 back to the Reds. "It was the principle of the thing," he later said.)[51]

Frank McCormick and Ernie Lombardi furnished most of the Reds' power. McCormick averaged .332, batted in 128 runs to lead the league, and knocked eighteen homers; after winning a batting title the previous year, Lombardi hit only .287 but slugged twenty homers. Harry Craft batted only .257 but hit thirteen homers and played a far-ranging center field, while Wally Berger, after bouncing from the Bees to the Giants to the Reds, hit fourteen in part-time duty. Ival Goodman, who'd homered thirty times in 1938, dislocated his shoulder in the All-Star Game and managed only seven, although he batted .323.

Mostly the Reds won with pitching—or, rather, with two pitchers. Bucky Walters's 319 innings were the most in the majors; Paul Derringer's 301 were the second most. The erstwhile infielder won twenty-seven games, lost eleven, and had a majors'-best 2.39 ERA; Derringer won twenty-five and lost seven with a 2.93 ERA (all the while worrying about an $8,100 judgment that one Robert E. Condon had secured in a New York court for being roughed up by Derringer in a Philadelphia hotel three years earlier).

Walters and Derringer carried an otherwise undistinguished staff that got little help from 1938 phenom Johnny Vander Meer, who struggled all season with his control and could do no better than a 5–9 record. Although the whimsical Lee Grissom won only nine, rookie Eugene "Junior" Thompson and second-year man Lloyd "Whitey" Moore won thirteen apiece.

Moore, from Ohio's Tuscarawas Valley, also tried Bill McKechnie's patience. On the night before the start of the decisive series with the Cardinals, Moore got drunk, headed his automobile down a railroad track, and barely missed colliding with a train. After going to the Cincinnati city jail at 2:00 A.M. to bail Moore out, McKechnie wanted to know, "Dammit Whitey, why'd you do it?" The best Moore could come up with was, "I thought it was a road."[52]

. . . . .

LOU GEHRIG was still in uniform on Wednesday, October 4, when the Yankees and Reds opened the World Series in New York before 58,541. Gehrig didn't take the lineup to home plate because, surmised Dan Daniel, Joe McCarthy wanted "to save Lou the ordeal of appearing before the vast crowd with that hitch in his step." But Gehrig was apparently still in good spirits; when National League umpires John "Beans" Reardon and Ralph "Babe" Pinelli came over to say hello, he joked, "How does it feel to sit down with champions for a change?"[53]

Red Ruffing's arm had been aching over the last part of the season; he hadn't won a game since early September and hadn't pitched in two weeks before he started the Series opener. But the big right-hander from Nokomis, Illinois, allowed the Reds only four hits and one run and retired the last fifteen batters he faced. Paul Derringer also pitched superbly, but in the fifth inning the Yankees scored when Wally Berger fielded Dahlgren's hit in left field and threw the ball to second base, whereupon Joe Gordon, who'd stopped at third, beat second baseman Linus "Lonnie" Frey's throw to the plate. The Yankees won it in the bottom of the ninth on Charlie Keller's triple off Ival Goodman's glove in deep right-center field and Bill Dickey's single. A few minutes later, before police could shoo reporters out of the visitors' clubhouse, Ernie Lombardi threw down his mitt and hurled his chest protector across the room, and Derringer screamed at Goodman, "You're supposed to make that play in the majors."[54]

The next day, with about 1,200 more people on hand, Monte Pearson held the Reds hitless until, with one out in the eighth inning, Lombardi singled. Pearson finished with a two-hit shutout, taking only one hour and twenty-seven minutes to defeat Bucky Walters 4–0. The Yankees scored three times in the fourth, starting when Dahlgren doubled, was sacrificed to third, and scored on Crosetti's ground out. Rolfe singled and scored when Keller blooped a double past Berger. DiMaggio's infield hit sent Keller to third, whence he scored on Dickey's single. Dahlgren's homer in the next inning ended the scoring.

With a day off for travel, the Series resumed on Saturday at Crosley Field, where a late-season extension of the grandstand upper deck to the foul lines had enlarged its capacity. With 32,723 (including New York mayor LaGuardia) watching in eighty-two-degree sunshine, Keller (two homers for four RBIs), DiMaggio (a homer for two RBIs), and Dickey (a homer with the bases empty) assaulted Junior Thompson for seven runs before Lee Grissom and a penitent Whitey Moore could shut down the New Yorkers. The Reds made ten hits (all singles) and got three runs in the first two innings off Lefty Gomez and Bump Hadley, but then Hadley held Cincinnati scoreless the rest of the way. At the Netherland Plaza, where the Yankees were lodging, a fan asked Gehrig whether they couldn't ease up a little. "What do you want us to do," snapped Gehrig, "play like the White Sox of 1919?"[55]

With another Yankees Series sweep seemingly inevitable, McKechnie came back with Derringer; McCarthy started Oral Hildebrand, a nine-year big leaguer who'd made a 10–4 record that season. The game was scoreless for six innings, with Hildebrand, his side paining him, giving way to Steve Sundra to start the fifth. New York scored twice in the seventh when first Keller and then Dickey connected for home runs. But Cincinnati went ahead 3–2 in the bottom of that inning on an error, a double by Al Simmons (picked up from the Boston Bees in August), an infield out, a walk, a single by backup catcher Willard Hershberger (batting for Derringer), and another single by Bill Werber.

With Johnny Murphy on the mound, the Reds made it 4–2 in the next inning when Goodman doubled and Lombardi singled. But to start the ninth, Walters, in relief of Derringer, gave up singles to Keller and DiMaggio. The slow-footed Dickey hit a double-play grounder to Frey, but shortstop Billy Myers dropped Frey's toss—the Reds' first error of the Series—and Keller scored. Gordon beat out an infield hit to send DiMaggio home with the tying run before Walters retired Dahlgren and Murphy.

Murphy kept the Reds from scoring in the bottom of the ninth, setting up one of the strangest half-innings in Series history. Walters walked leadoff man Crosetti, who took second on Rolfe's sacrifice and moved to third when Myers again erred, fumbling Keller's grounder. DiMaggio then lined a hit to right field that scored Crosetti; when Goodman let the ball get through his legs, Keller also scored, in the process bowling over Lombardi and planting a knee in his groin. As the big catcher lay momentarily disabled, DiMaggio saw his chance, raced for the plate, and scored as Lombardi lunged too late to get the hook-sliding Yankee.

That made it 7–4, New York, which is the way it ended—although Murphy sustained the suspense by giving up singles to Goodman and McCormick to start the bottom of the tenth. But Lombardi fouled to Dickey, Simmons flied out to Keller, and Crosetti squeezed Berger's soft liner. It was a World Series that would always be remembered for that one play, when Lombardi lay on his face while DiMaggio headed for home—"the snooze of the Schnoz," somebody dubbed it.

Going back to 1927, the Yankees had won twenty-eight of their last thirty-one games in World Series competition. The first team to garner four-straight Series titles, they left a lot of people just shaking their heads. Moaned former National League president John Heydler, "Is this thing never going to change? No club can be as good as the Yankees have shown themselves to be in recent Series against our teams." Others were in awe of the New York juggernaut. Fred Lieb predicted that "fans, still unborn, thumbing through the records of this decade, will ask: 'Could any team be that good?' "[56]

As other Yankees sang "The Beer Barrel Polka" (which had become something of a team anthem), Lou Gehrig sat alone in a corner of the visitors' locker room. He was voted a full share from the players' pool—again augmented by the sale of radio rights—and so received $5,614 for doing little since April 30 but be with the team. On October 16, in accordance with his wishes, he received his outright release.

Meanwhile a Cincinnati municipal judge found Whitey Moore guilty of driving while intoxicated, fined him $3, suspended his driver's license for six months, and remanded him to the city's workhouse for three days. But when Moore left the workhouse, he could look forward to receiving his full Series share of $4,282, which just about equaled his season's salary.

. . . . .

ALL THAT SUMMER OF 1939, as visiting baseball teams and millions of other people toured the New York World's Fair, they'd been struck by the sight of the flag at the Republic of Czechoslovakia's pavilion flying at half-mast—signaling Nazi Germany's extinction of that country's independence the previous spring. By the time the 1939 World Series was played, the Polish pavilion was being dismantled, because during the previous month Poland had fallen before the German blitzkrieg. France and Great Britain, although unable to help the embattled Poles, had declared war on Adolf Hitler's Germany, while on the other side of the world a huge conflict had been raging for more than two years between Japan, bent on creating an Asian empire, and the bitterly divided people of China.

But by the end of September 1939, after two years of the Roosevelt Recession, the *New York Times's* business index had finally climbed back to the 100 mark. Again people were leaving the WPA rolls for jobs in the private sector; again it appeared that the economy was in the process of recovery. And this time—boosted by orders from Britain, France, China, and later the Soviet Union for armaments, petroleum, steel, and other necessities for war and by the Roosevelt administration's determination to rebuild American military capability—the recovery would be sustainable. Good times—the best times in a long time—were finally on the way.

Yet the good times would ultimately become war times for Americans, too. Sooner or later, what was happening in 1940 and 1941 in the world beyond the United States would reach virtually everybody in some way, including that tiny segment of the population consisting of men who made their livings in professional baseball. Over the past decade, the erratic course of the Great Depression had been the chief external circumstance affecting their lives. It might be instructive to pause in the narrative and look more closely at what that decade was like for somebody who happened to possess exceptional skills at hitting, throwing, and catching a baseball.

CHAPTER 8

Baseball Lives

I N JANUARY 1938, when Grover Cleveland Alexander was notified that
he'd gained the necessary three-fourths majority in the Base Ball Writers
Association's Hall of Fame selections, he said, "The Hall of Fame is fine,
but it doesn't mean bread and butter. It's only your picture on the wall."[1]
The fifty-year-old Alexander—who'd won 373 games and thrown ninety
shutouts over twenty big-league seasons—had spent the previous summer
managing a semipro club in Springfield, Illinois, and now worked as a
greeter in the owner's bar. Meanwhile, at a Brooklyn nightclub, a tuxedoed
Hack Wilson, still only thirty-eight, was also chatting up customers, besides
doing a song-and-dance number with a tall chorus girl.

At the 1938 World Series games in Yankee Stadium, veteran sportswriters and even a few older fans may have recognized two elderly men
who were working as ushers. One was seventy-eight-year-old Arlie Latham,
who'd been a famous third baseman in the 1880s and later one of John
McGraw's coaches; the other was Bill Dahlen, sixty-eight, once considered
the National League's premier shortstop.

The predicament of such men—men who'd had lengthy playing careers
at salaries substantially above what most people earned—was fairly common in a time before players were able to wring a pension program out of
the club owners. As Waite Hoyt (who'd quickly found a home in radio)
wrote in 1941, baseball was a fine profession, but it had major drawbacks.
It was an expensive way of life that usually involved the maintenance of
two residences, especially if one had children of school age. Hoyt estimated

that a player averaging $10,000 per year for ten years could manage to end up with savings of only about $30,000. If he put his money into some of kind of business enterprise, his lack of experience might very well doom him to failure. The problem with "baseball as a life's work," Hoyt concluded, was that "it takes the player's best years and trains him for nothing else."[2]

. . . . .

HOYT MIGHT HAVE ADDED that the temptations awaiting healthy, well-paid young men away from home half the time frequently produced marital discord. In the summer of 1931, the wife of Hoyt's old Yankees teammate Joe Dugan (recently released by Detroit) sued in a New York court for separate maintenance, on the grounds that "Jumping Joe" drank, gambled, and chased other women. Hoyt took the stand to say that the bad behavior was about fifty–fifty between husband and wife, but Dorothy Pyle Hoyt testified in support of the charges against Dugan, after which she herself left for Reno for six weeks to establish residence so she could file for divorce from Hoyt under Nevada law.

Although the national divorce rate in the 1930s was far below what it would be within another generation (in part because unless one could afford to go to Reno, a divorce was harder to obtain), quite a lot of disharmonious domestic news made its way into the baseball press. Besides Hoyt and Dugan, such other luminaries as Lefty Gomez, Paul Derringer, Ben Chapman, and Jimmie Foxx had their marital difficulties publicized.

To be sure, club officials and baseball writers usually cooperated to keep really messy stuff from becoming public. As Dick Bartell described players' relations with the press in his day, "You could confide in a writer. . . . They weren't looking for scandal or gossip to print. Players' private lives were not considered fair game. The press was concerned with the game and what happened on the field. That was their beat."[3] What Bartell neglected to add was that with teams usually paying the expenses of writers on road trips, the scribes weren't likely to do a great deal of derogatory reporting about what players said or did.

Yet "baseball Annies" ("groupies," in a later generation's argot) had long been and still were a source of trouble. In June 1933, about a year after Billy Jurges was wounded in his Chicago hotel room in a struggle with a former woman friend, another young woman, named Lillian Eloise Mitchell, brought suit for $50,000 in a Chicago court against Cleveland first baseman Harley Boss. Mitchell claimed that following a party in a Cleveland hotel room earlier that season, Boss had torn her clothes and assaulted her. Boss countersued for slander, and in July a Chicago jury believed his version of what had happened: that Mitchell had gone to his room; he kissed her; she told him, "My time is valuable"; and, apparently not wanting to be rushed, he showed her the door.[4]

Harley Boss (who couldn't hit big-league pitching and was back in the minors by 1934) no doubt would have fit the last of three types of players with whom Willis Johnson, traveling secretary of the St. Louis Browns, said he had to deal. One type was the quiet, frugal men who tended to business and gave no trouble. Then there were the chronic complainers who expected special favors, such as loans from Johnson when they came up short on road trips. The third and most vexatious type consisted of fun lovers who'd never outgrown their boyhoods.

According to Billy Rogell, Rudy York, from a little town in Alabama, was an incorrigible fun lover. "I roomed with this goddamn Rudy York," Rogell reminisced. "He was the silliest bastard I ever met in my life." York was like "a lot of these southern boys—goddamn, they got up there, they'd go crazy. . . . All night long that goddamn phone was ringing. He knew every whore in New York." Charley Gehringer, who later also roomed with York, remembered that several times York set mattresses on fire by going to sleep with his cigarette still burning.[5]

York also was a heavy drinker (who died at fifty-six), as were many other ballplayers. Of course, after 1933 liquor was legally available in all forms in every big-league city. Prohibition had never kept ballplayers who really wanted to drink from doing so, although they couldn't do it in public places. "They didn't have cocktail parties or beer in the clubhouse," Joe Cronin recalled of Prohibition days. "A lot of players were not drinking at all. Of course if a guy wanted to find it, he found it." The *Washington Post's* Shirley Povich remembered that "there were all kinds of speakeasies in Washington. As many as you liked. . . . On the road, if you couldn't find a drink yourself you could always ask the bell captain. He could always find you a drink."[6]

If drinking among ballplayers was common, tobacco use in some form was almost universal. Although cigarettes had long been ruefully referred to as "coffin nails," as yet medical researchers hadn't found (or really looked for) a link between cigarette smoking and cardiopulmonary diseases. With cigarettes shrewdly marketed as symbols of both sophisticated, graceful living and rugged, manly activity (as well as functioning as seemingly essential props in motion pictures), taking up smoking became a rite of passage for young men and an acceptable indulgence for an increasing number of women.

Ballplayers smoked as much as and maybe even more than people in the general population, with cigars and pipes apparently favored by older players, managers, and coaches, and cigarettes the weed of choice for younger athletes. Players smoked before, after, and often during games— although under directives in force throughout Organized Baseball they weren't supposed to smoke in uniform within view of people in the stands. So Joe DiMaggio ducked into the runway behind the dugout to have a cigarette (and half a cup of coffee) nearly every half-inning. When Goose Goslin drove home Mickey Cochrane with the deciding run in the 1935 World Series, winning pitcher Tommy Bridges, similarly concealed, was pulling on a cigarette. That Series prompted advertisements in newspapers and magazines across the country professing that "19 of 22 of the Tigers smoke Camels," as well as testimonials from various Detroit players that Camels "don't get my wind" and "never upset my nerves."[7]

Many players also continued to load up with chewing tobacco (more leaf-cut than plug-cut by the 1930s) whenever they took the field. Chewing was probably more common among players from rural and small-town backgrounds than among city boys, but the image of a tough-looking competitor with a big cud in his cheek was so familiar that many American boys grew up convinced that serious baseball playing and tobacco chewing went together. In truth, spitting tobacco juice—spitting in general—had long been (and would long continue to be) basic to baseball's uniquely stylized movement.

. . . . .

DESPITE THE EXPANSION of publicly financed schooling over the past quarter-century and the proliferation of high schools and high-school graduates, many Depression-era ballplayers still had quite limited educations. Probably few were any more geographically literate than Roy "Peaches" Davis. A native Oklahoman who pitched at Nashville in 1935, Davis was to join the Cincinnati Reds the next spring. With the other Reds players, Davis received a letter from Larry MacPhail informing him that the team would train in Puerto Rico and inquiring whether he preferred to take an aircraft or a boat to reach the island. Replied Davis, "I prefer to drive down."[8]

Young men from rugged working-class backgrounds continued to be numerous at all levels of Organized Baseball. Typically, they'd made it

through grade school and maybe a year or two of high school before dropping out to go to work and support themselves. Thus they pretty much
bypassed adolescence—that supposedly critical phase of maturation on
which twentieth-century psychiatrists and psychologists, preoccupied with
the lifestyles of the middle class, had become fixated.

Chuck Klein, for example, born on a truck farm outside Indianapolis,
quit school to work for four years in an East Chicago steel mill, where he
played for the mill's baseball team and eventually signed with Evansville in
the Three-I League. "Players talk about double-headers on hot summer
days," commented Klein in 1930. "They should stand an eight hour shift
in a steel mill, without even time off for lunch."[9]

Adam Comorosky, a ten-year big-league outfielder with Pittsburgh and
Cincinnati (1926–1935), went to work at the age of twelve as a breaker boy
in a mine at Swoyerville, Pennsylvania. Mine work, observed Comorosky,
"teach[es] you values. If you're ever lucky enough to get a good job outside,
you value that job." His own experience in the mines of southeastern Ohio
made Ralston "Rollie" Hemsley, who became Bobby Feller's favorite
catcher after his trade from the Browns, "realize what a soft thing baseball
is. I wish some of these players . . . had to work all day in a mine for $6—
they'd realize how lucky they are."[10]

Earl Webb, who hit a record sixty-seven doubles in 1931 for the Boston
Red Sox, went to work in the coal mines in Tennessee at the age of twelve
and later spent a dozen years in the minor leagues before finally making it
to the big time to stay with the Chicago White Sox in 1927. Red Ruffing
was another product of the coal mines: he dropped out of grammar school
in Nokomis, Illinois, and took a job tending a mine ventilation system.
Ruffing lost four toes on his left foot when it was caught between two coal
cars—a happenstance that turned the big redhead toward a pitching rather
than an outfielding career.

Still another former miner was Danny Taylor, whose baseball odyssey
up to 1932 provides something of a case study in what many young ballplayers had to go through. At the age of thirteen, Taylor went down into
the mines at Lash, Pennsylvania. Four years later, he moved up to a choice
job as a weigher, but Taylor was determined to leave the mines and make
a career in baseball. Signed by a Pittsburgh scout out of local semipro ball,
he failed in Flint, Michigan, married, went back to his weigher's job, and
then signed with Buffalo in the International League. Sold by Buffalo to
Washington, he was successively optioned to Memphis, drafted by Brooklyn, sent back to Memphis, sold to the Chicago Cubs, sent down again to

Reading (where he led the International League in batting), brought back up to the Cubs, and finally, now a father, traded to Brooklyn in mid-1932. (Released by Brooklyn in 1936, he drifted back to the minors, where he spent a couple more years.)

Native Chicagoan Phil Cavaretta signed with the Cubs at the end of his junior year at Lane Technical High School. After spending most of the 1934 season with Peoria (Three-I League) and Reading (International League), he came up to the Cubs to stay and played in the 1935 World Series. Why did he leave school? Cavaretta explained that his father, an immigrant, was out of a job, and "it was up to me to go out and try to make a buck."[11]

Three of the more interesting baseball lives of the Depression era were those of Johnny Allen, Bill Zuber, and Edwin "Alabama" Pitts. Following the death of his father when Allen was seven, his mother placed her three children in an orphanage operated by the Southern Baptist Convention in Thomasville, North Carolina. Allen lived there for nine years, working at the orphanage's 600-acre farm and dairy. After leaving at seventeen, he held several clerking jobs at hotels in North Carolina and Virginia, but his prowess as a semipro pitcher-outfielder got him into professional ball, first in the Piedmont and South Atlantic Leagues and then, after the Yankees bought his contract, at Jersey City and Toronto. He went up to the Yankees to stay in 1932 at age twenty-six.

Bill Zuber, a husky pitcher whose eleven-year American League career began with Cleveland in 1936, was raised in Middle Amana, one of seven Amana religious colonies scattered across Iowa. Growing up, young Zuber had no games to play in an environment where piety and work governed peoples' lives. But later on, he started playing semipro ball and, in the common circumstance, signed on with a minor-league team and was eventually acquired by a big-league outfit. Although Zuber made his living in the secular world, every off-season he returned to Middle Amana to drive a tractor, tend cattle and hogs, and live according to the colony's strictures.

Early in June 1935, Alabama Pitts was about to be paroled from Sing Sing prison in Ossining, New York, after serving a term for having robbed a New York City grocery store at gunpoint. Pitts had knocked a lot of irretrievable baseballs over the walls in prison-league competition, and the Albany Senators, occupying last place in the International League, wanted to sign him to a $200-per-month contract. Pitts's parole board was agreeable, but National Association president William G. Bramham vetoed the idea on the grounds that no association franchise should employ a convicted felon. With sympathy for Pitts's cause growing in the press, Commissioner Landis stepped in, overruled Bramham (who claimed that Landis had earlier endorsed his ruling), and cleared Pitts to play anywhere within Organized Baseball. "Reputable people," said Landis, "have expressed to me their belief that there has been a complete reformation in Pitts' character."[12]

On Sunday, June 23, Pitts made his debut before 7,752 in Albany in a doubleheader with Syracuse. Although he made two hits in his first appearance, it was soon evident that he couldn't handle tough professional pitching. After batting .233 over the remainder of the season, he drew his release and dropped out of Organized Baseball. Six years later, Pitts was fatally stabbed during a quarrel in a North Carolina dance hall.

At the same time that Landis, the Albany owners and fans, and a great number of other people who followed Pitts's case saw nothing wrong with a paroled convict playing within Organized Baseball, nobody in a position of authority was ready to come out for the abandonment of the color line. Yet if all players from Class D to the major leagues still had to be certifiably Caucasian, their particular ethnic backgrounds changed significantly during the 1930s.

· · · · ·

THE PERIOD saw a substantial influx of players of eastern and southern European ancestry—sons of people who'd come to the United States as part of the great tide of "New Immigration" beginning in the 1880s. Migrating from Italy, Greece, Romania, Poland, Russia, and the multiethnic Austro-Hungarian Empire, these later arrivals, unlike earlier immigrants from northern and western Europe, who'd been mostly Protestant and largely English-speaking, spoke in a multiplicity of languages and dialects and were Roman Catholics, Eastern Orthodox Christians, or Jews. In language, religion, personal habits, and often physical appearance, they were different from (and often considered inferior to) settled, "old-stock" Americans.

So while Anglo-Saxon (English), Celtic (Scottish, Welsh, and Irish), and German names continued to predominate, big-league rosters came to include a growing number of players with names such as Comorosky, Ogrodowski, Vosmik, Urbanski, Kowalik, and Bejma (Polish); Niemiec and Kreevich (Serbian); Medwick (Hungarian); Kampouris (Greek); Krakauskas (Lithuanian); and even Coscaret (Basque). Some players Anglicized or otherwise simplified their names, of whom the best-known was Aloys Szymanski, who became Al Simmons when he entered professional ball. Others were John Bolinsky (Joe Boley), Anthony Pietruszka (Tony Piet), Joseph Dimaria (Frank Demaree), Harold Troyavesky (Hal Trosky), and, maybe oddest of all, Peter Jablonowski, who as Pete Appleton pitched for seven big-league teams over fourteen years.

Baseball players altered their names for the same reason as did immigrants and their offspring in other areas of American life: the United States was a country in which not only racial but ethnic and religious prejudices and stereotypes had always been and continued to be basic to the way people looked at and understood one another. And while the National Pastime was supposed to exemplify the expansive, democratic American way of life, inherited attitudes died very slowly—if they ever did die.

Any player with even a fraction of American Indian ancestry, for example, was still called "Chief" and usually presumed to have peculiar ways—and probably a weakness for strong drink. In what was supposed to be a salutary article on Elon Hogsett, "the Cherokee pitcher" (Hogsett was one-quarter Cherokee), *Baseball Magazine*'s Clifford Bloodgood assured readers that the Detroit left-hander didn't possess a quiver and bow, wasn't wrapped in a blanket, and wasn't "leaping up and down brandishing a tomahawk fiercely threatening butchery."[13]

Because there had never been more than a few Jewish players, their presence in the major leagues had always drawn special attention. Relatively little notice was given to Mississippian Buddy Myer's Jewishness or that of Newark native Moe Berg (perhaps because, during fifteen major-league seasons with five teams, Berg played in a grand total of 662 games). But much attention focused on New Yorker Hank Greenberg and only somewhat less on Californian Harry Danning and Wisconsinite Morrie Arnovich. By 1938 Danning was being described as the Giants' "long sought Jewish hero" as well as "one of the best liked among fans and fellow players, a great credit to his race." Arnovich, an outfielder who enjoyed a couple of good years with the Phillies, was unmistakably Jewish, thought the editor of *Baseball Magazine*: "He looks the part, dark complexioned, thick black hair, prominent nose."[14]

But what occasioned the most commentary was the rapidly growing number of Italian-American players. Before 1930 a few had made it to the majors, such as Ping Bodie (né Francesco Pezzolo), who played in the American League from 1911 to 1921. But Tony Lazzeri, a Yankees rookie in 1926, was really the first outstanding Italian-American player. A steady stream of Italian Americans followed Lazzeri, so many that by the mid-

1930s sportswriters were suggesting that they must possess a natural affinity for baseball—the same thing said about Irish Americans when they populated big-league rosters in the 1890s and early 1900s. "The Tonies take to baseball quicker than they take to spaghetti," commented a major-league manager in 1932. Once upon a time, he added, players were "all Pats," but "nowadays I can't even get a player on my team with the nickname of Pat."[15]

A year earlier, the *Sporting News* had announced that "the Italians have found baseball and they like it" and that soon the "sons of Caesar" would challenge the Irish "to prove their racial superiority." Italians, wrote Dan Daniel in 1936 (Joe DiMaggio's rookie season), were "an agile race, a sturdy, enduring and durable people, quick to learn and aggressive to the highest degree."[16]

Ethnic stereotyping was particularly pronounced where Italian-American players were concerned. For years Joe DiMaggio was "Giuseppe" in Daniel's columns, and in its July 1936 cover story on DiMaggio, *Time* attributed his "solemn, almost embarrassing humility" to his being "like many young brothers in large Italian families." Henry Luce's other weekly magazine, the vastly popular *Life*, reported that DiMaggio "speaks English without an accent" and "never reeks of garlic." That kind of thing continued in DiMaggio's second season, with, for example, Dan Parker of the *New York Daily News* observing that the Yankees' young star was a strong guy even "before taking aboard his cargo of pasta fagiole."[17] (It ought to be noted, though, that stereotyping could also be a matter of how one was willing to be perceived. Just as a couple of generations later well-to-do white Southerners might call themselves "rednecks," DiMaggio seemed to take satisfaction in his teammates' referring to him as "Daig" or "the Big Dago.")

Lou Smith of the *Cincinnati Enquirer* referred to Vince DiMaggio as "the stoop-shouldered, spaghetti-strangler," while the Pittsburgh reporter Charles J. "Chilli" Doyle wrote of Johnny Rizzo, "When you look at his thick chest, his pearly teeth and his raven locks, you might surmise that he had landed with one of the late Italian quotas, although he has yet to see the land of Mussolini." In St. Petersburg in the spring of 1939, Sam Breadon didn't know what to make of Cardinals rookie infielder Joe Orengo: "He's an Italian from San Francisco—or maybe he's a Spaniard—somebody says he's a Greek. If they can't figure out a man's name, they call him a Greek."[18] (Breadon actually had it right the first time.)

Melo Almada, a native of Huatabampo, Mexico, played for four full seasons (1935–1938) in the American League, with Boston, Washington, and St. Louis, before he was released by Brooklyn in 1939; and over the decades, a trickle of ballplayers from Cuba—all supposedly of unbroken European ("pure Castilian") ancestry—had performed within Organized Baseball. Probably the best known had been Mike Gonzalez, who was mostly a backup catcher in a seventeen-year playing career and then a coach and scout for the Cardinals, and Adolfo Luque, who posted twenty-seven wins in 1923 for Cincinnati and 193 in a twenty-year career with three clubs. By the late 1930s, a few more Cubans and other Latin Americans were coming into the major leagues—a development largely attributable to the efforts of Baltimorean Joe Cambria, who invested in both minor-league and black franchises and scouted the Caribbean region for the Washington Senators.

Cambria's first Latin American signee was the Cuban Roberto "Bobby" Estalella, who put in three years (1935–1936, 1939) as a part-time outfielder for Washington and, after a year in the American Association, went back up to the Browns. Estalella was still with Washington in spring training 1939, as were the Cubans Rene Monteagudo and Robert Ortiz and the Venezuelan Alejandro "Alex" Carrasquel. Washington controlled about ten other Cubans in the minor leagues.

Although describing the stocky Estalella as "gorilla-shaped," the journalist Bob Considine otherwise wrote sympathetically of the difficulties that Washington's Latin American contingent encountered. Estalella had been a regular target for American League hurlers "of that peculiar big-league mold which is almost psychopathically opposed to Roberto and his coffee-colored colleagues." So, "isolated by their lack of English, brutally snubbed by the dumber portions of Clark Griffith's predominantly southern ball club, the Washington aliens are among the unhappiest lot of athletes in the kingdom of sports." Senators manager Bucky Harris had to warn his American players to stop making slurs on the Latins in training camp. "They're all good boys, these foreigners," said Harris, "and the first punk who shows any resentment will get a fine slapped on him."[19] Carrasquel was the only one of the four players who finished 1939 with Washington; the Venezuelan won five games and lost nine and went on to pitch for seven seasons for the Senators.

But Spanish-speaking players were hardly alone in having to put up with insults and indignities. Bench jockeys zeroed in on physiognomy, walk, talk, marital difficulties, and whatever else they could make use of—but most of all one's ancestry. As Hank Greenberg put it, "Everybody got it. Italians were wops. Germans were krauts, and the Polish players were dumb polacks. Me, I was a kike or a sheeny or a mockey. . . . They reserved a little extra for me."[20] (Greenberg might have added that for city boys such as himself, Southerners were usually "hillbillies.")

. . . . .

AS BALLPLAYERS' ETHNICITY CHANGED, so did their geographic origins. Those who wrote about players' backgrounds often confused their birthplaces with where they grew up—as with Dick Bartell and Wally Berger, both Chicago-born Californians, and Schoolboy Rowe, Texas-born but Arkansas-reared. But whereas earlier in the century players had come predominantly from the northeastern and older midwestern states, by the 1930s a substantial shift toward the South and West had taken place.

One survey published early in 1934 put the number of Texans among all those listed on major-league rosters at thirty-six, Californians at thirty-five, and Illinois natives at thirty-four. Three years later, a survey of 225 players from thirty-five states identified nineteen Californians, eighteen Texans, fifteen each from Illinois and New York, fourteen each from North Carolina and Pennsylvania, twelve Ohioans, ten each from Oklahoma and Missouri, nine Louisianians, and eight each from New Jersey and Tennessee. Aside from a couple of Canadians, the remaining seventy-three in the survey were scattered among thirty-seven states. At that time, Al Lopez was the only native Floridian in the majors.

According to a study by Bill Bryson published the next year, only 13.8 percent of established big leaguers had grown up as residents of major-league cities; another 11.3 percent came from cities of more than 250,000. Small towns and rural communities—locales of less than 2,500 population—had produced an imposing 37 percent. Curiously, fifty-three of eighty-four pitchers in Bryson's study came from small towns and villages.

From the 1930s on, California's mild climate and burgeoning population would produce more major leaguers than any other state. Lefty O'Doul, Joe Cronin, Babe Herman, and Dick Bartell were already in the big time before 1930; subsequently, such notables as Lefty Gomez, Larry French, Frank Demaree, Wally Berger, Monte Pearson, Babe Dahlgren, Bobby Doerr, and Ted Williams came out of the Golden State. The biggest single concentration of big leaguers was in the San Francisco Bay area, which spawned O'Doul, Cronin, Bartell, Pearson, Dahlgren, and a steady flow of Italian-American players, including by 1940 Joe, Vince, and Dominic DiMaggio, Ernie Lombardi, Frank Crosetti, Tony Lazzeri, Dolph Camilli,

Cookie Lavagetto, Dario Lodigiani, and Joe Orengo. (But "sons of Caesar" came from all parts of the country. Gus Mancuso and Johnny Rizzo, for example, grew up in Houston; Zeke Bonura was from New Orleans; Lou Chiozza was born in Tallulah, Louisiana, and lived in Memphis.)

. . . . .

MUCH WAS MADE in the baseball press of the number of "college men" coming into the big leagues. That usually referred to players who hadn't actually graduated from college but had attended for a year or two, played college baseball, and then signed a professional contract and abandoned pursuit of a degree. Moreover, figures on college men in the majors varied not only from time to time but from source to source.

As early as 1929, according to *Baseball Magazine*, forty-six players with at least some college background (about 12 percent) were on big-league rosters. Five years later, the *Sporting News* put the number of ex-collegians in the National League alone at forty-four, led by the Phillies with nine and the Giants with eight. About one-third of the forty-four had earned degrees. In 1935 Bill Bryson in *Baseball Magazine* wrote that of 226 "star players," forty-four had attended "some college or other"; the next year, Bryson identified seventy former collegians on the total roll (368) of major leaguers. Forty-five of the seventy were in the American League, with the White Sox and Detroit listing eight each. At that point, according to Bryson's information, only Cincinnati had no college men at all.[21]

Front-rank big leaguers who'd attended college but hadn't graduated included Lou Gehrig, who dropped out of Columbia University in his junior year; Mickey Cochrane, who did the same at Boston University; and Hank Greenberg, who left New York University after only one semester. Bump Hadley attended Brown University; Mace Brown, the University of Iowa; Tommy Bridges, the University of Tennessee; Larry French, the University of California (Berkeley); Tex Carleton, Texas Christian University; Bill Lee, Louisiana State University; and Zeke Bonura, Loyola University of New Orleans.

But by the mid- and late 1930s, more big leaguers than ever had become legitimate college and university degree holders. From an academic standpoint, the most impressive were Burgess Whitehead (B.A., University of North Carolina), the first big leaguer to wear a Phi Beta Kappa key, and Monte Weaver, who had earned an M.S. in mathematics from the University of Virginia by doing his thesis on the vectorial angle of the curve ball.

Other notable diploma-holding big leaguers included Bill Werber from Duke University; Buddy Myer from Mississippi State Agricultural College; George Earnshaw, a Swarthmore College graduate; Eldon Auker, who finished at Kansas State; Claude Passeau, who held a degree from Millsaps College, in Jackson, Mississippi; Marvin Owen, a graduate of Santa Clara College; Luke Appling, a product of Oglethorpe College, in Atlanta; and Hal Schumacher, who had the company of most of his Giants teammates at St. Lawrence University's 1933 commencement.

Red Rolfe, who'd attended exclusive Exeter Academy before going on to play baseball and earn his B.A. at Dartmouth College, went up to the Yankees to stay in 1934. Several more college graduates subsequently joined the Yankees. Joe Gordon finished his degree at the University of Oregon after his second big-league season; Charlie Keller had graduated from the University of Maryland when he went up from Newark in 1939; and Marvin Breuer held a degree in civil engineering from the Missouri School of Mines when he joined the New York pitching staff the same year.

In August 1939, Cleveland promoted from Buffalo the hotshot middle-infield combination of Lou Boudreau and Ray Mack. Shortstop Boudreau had starred in both basketball and baseball at the University of Illinois, and had finished his degree despite being declared ineligible for his senior year when it became known that the Indians were paying his widowed mother $100 per month to ensure his services. Second baseman Mack (né Mlcknovsky) was a native Clevelander who gained a B.S. from that city's Case Institute of Technology.

The presence of so many college men occasionally prompted comments about how much ballplayers had changed, and some people weren't sure that was a good thing. In 1935 the Seattle sportswriter Royal Brougham sarcastically observed that "the grimy, unshaven, rough-and-ready of the old days is on his way out, and baseball is wearing a white collar, slacks and a daisy in its lapel." A few years later, Bill Terry expressed a longing for "the old-fashioned, insatiable player who would walk half the day to play a ball game." George Levy, former megaphone announcer at Yankee Stadium, thought that players were "more efficient, colder now. . . . [They] give you the impression they have a job to do, and they go in there and do it and get away as quickly as possible." Whether one liked it or not, Joe McCarthy believed that contemporary players had to be treated differently. While he'd blown off plenty of steam managing in the minors, McCarthy said in 1938, "The time when a manager used to talk to his players as though he were driving a bunch of mules is pretty well past."[22]

. . . . .

IF DEPRESSION-ERA BALLPLAYERS as a whole were better educated, more businesslike, and less amenable to verbal harangues, few of them were paid enough that they could afford to remain idle in the off-season. Some picked up extra cash by barnstorming in the fall, but most players pursued a great variety of off-season occupations. In the early 1930s, Phillies pitcher Phil Collins worked as a butcher in Chicago; Washington third baseman Joe Judge ran an automobile-repair shop in the District of Columbia; Cincinnati pitcher Eppa Rixey sold insurance; Ad Liska, who pitched for the Senators and Phillies, worked in a Philadelphia jewelry store; and Dazzy Vance operated a hotel and served as a fishing and hunting guide in Homosassa Springs, Florida. Clarence Mitchell, who finally retired in 1932 after eighteen big-league seasons as a left-handed spitballer, owned a farm in Nebraska, where he trained greyhounds to chase and catch coyotes, whose pelts he sold locally. After he finally made it to the majors, Jim Turner continued to run a milk-delivery business with his uncle in Nashville.

For minor leaguers, some source of off-season income was a necessity. Jim Bivin, who had a 2–9 record for the 1935 Phillies and was sold to Baltimore, spent the winter of 1935/1936 working on a freighter operating between the East Coast of the United States and British ports. Four years later, a number of minor leaguers residing in New York State took advantage of that state's unemployment compensation program and drew $50 to $60 per month in benefits. But when Cleveland third baseman Ken Keltner, who'd been paid $7,500 during the 1939 season, applied for unemployment compensation in Ohio, he came under fire in the baseball press. After his application was rejected, Keltner lamely claimed that the whole thing had been a gag, but Dan Daniel, for one, insisted that Indians owner Alva Bradley ought to give Keltner "a going over."[23]

Often ballplayers sought to help out their families in the midst of hard times. In 1932, for example, Woody English was paid $14,000 and gained a World Series loser's share. With his season's earnings he, paid $8,000 in cash for a farm outside Newark, Ohio, for his grandparents and made a $2,500 down payment on a house in Newark for his mother before indulging himself with a new Packard convertible. Burgess Whitehead used his 1934 World Series share to help his parents keep their tobacco farm in Tarboro, North Carolina, and Blondy Ryan, whose father was a policeman in Lynn, Massachusetts, spent his 1933 Series check on a house for his parents. Billy Rogell's salary, which topped out at $15,000 in 1935, supported not only his wife and himself but his wife's parents and his unemployed brother's family.

Ballplayers of that day tended to be outdoor types who spent much of the off-season fishing and hunting. Tramping through woods and over hills, maybe playing some golf, watching one's weight, and staying out of saloons were usually considered sufficient in the way of off-season conditioning, although urban residents sometimes worked out at local YMCAs. But arduous regimens designed to build muscle mass were anathema in baseball circles, where the conventional wisdom held that it wasn't mass but suppleness that mattered.

Jimmie Foxx was especially renowned for his powerful upper-body build, but in 1934 the Athletics' young strongman said that he didn't want to "[run] the risk of becoming musclebound." While he played off-season golf and did other exercises "that tend to give me a muscle tone and quick muscular coordination," he avoided "anything that I would call heavy exercise . . . which develops muscle at the expense of agility."[24]

. . . . .

WAITE HOYT might point out the drawbacks of a career in professional baseball, but for Foxx and others with the ability and good fortune to make it to the major leagues, a way of life awaited them that few people—and hardly anybody of modest education and family background—could possibly aspire to. In a 1937 *American Mercury* piece. Gerald Holland didn't exaggerate a great deal when he described a big-league ballplayer's life as "a never-never land of lower berths and club cars, beauty-rest mattresses, awe-stricken barbers and adoring women, Florida sunbaths, thick steaks and pie à la mode, alert medics and zealous trainers—topped each fortnight by a pay check for more money than exists in the workaday world of bookkeepers, soda-fountain attendants, and streetcar conductors."[25] Holland might have added that the daily $3.50 to $4.00 meal allowance on road trips was a day's pay for half the country's working people.

Yet decades later, ballplayers also remembered what it was like in the era of an inviolate reserve clause, no pension benefits, and, perhaps most vividly, no air-conditioning. Players especially hated to go to St. Louis in July and August and have to deal with the suffocating heat. Billy Herman remembered that the Cubs might take a night train from Chicago, arrive in St. Louis early the next morning, and check in at their hotel, which hadn't cooled off much during the night. They would eat breakfast in a hot dining room and try to get a few hours' sleep before going out to Sportsman's Park, where they played on a field made rock hard and nearly denuded from being used by both Browns and Cardinals.

The game over, "you take your shower, but there's no way you can dry off; the sweat just keeps running off of you." Back to a steamy hotel room. "But the dining room isn't much better, so you order room service and stay right there and eat." Later, unable to sleep in the heat, "you get up and pull the sheet off the bed and soak it with cold water and go back and roll up in a wet sheet; but it dries out after an hour or two, and you have to get up and soak it again." After four days in St. Louis, on to Cincinnati, "and it's the same thing. For eight days you haven't had a decent night's sleep."[26]

. . . . .

WHATEVER DISCOMFORTS and hardships big leaguers such as Billy Herman had to put up with, life at the top was always better than life in the minor leagues. Jobs and pay in the minors rapidly diminished as leagues folded in the early Depression years, but the minors' revival and expansion in the mid- and late 1930s did nothing to improve working conditions. In the upper minors, teams usually traveled in day coaches rather than Pullmans; in the lower minors, they rode cramped, creaky buses over bumpy two-lane roads, sometimes for hundreds of miles. A good player might pull down about $400 per month for a season of five or five and a half months in the International League and American Association and seven months in the Pacific Coast League. At the Class C or D level the pay would be $60 to $75 per month for a season of about four and a half months.

Minor-league ball—with its lesser pay, tough travel conditions, and, in the lower minors, inferior lighting systems—became a career for scores of aging players who may or may not have ever spent time in the Big Show.[27] It seems a safe assumption that from 1973 on, plenty of them would have been welcomed into the American League as designated hitters. As it was, men who consistently hammered strong minor-league pitching but had bad legs or weak throwing arms or just found it difficult to field a position stayed in the minors for season after season, sometimes decade after decade.

Five standout minor-league hitters from the 1930s serve as examples. After dividing the 1929 season between Cleveland and Milwaukee, Joe Hauser was a thirty-one-year-old first baseman when he landed in Balti-

more in the International League. Hauser had spent five years with the
Philadelphia Athletics (1922–1924, 1926, 1928), interrupted first by a near-
career-ending leg fracture and then by a season in Kansas City. With the
Athletics, Hauser had hit as many as twenty-seven home runs, but with
Baltimore the left-handed Hauser took advantage of a short right-field
fence at Oriole Park and in 162 games drove out an Organized Baseball–
record sixty-three homers. Hauser's home-run output dropped to thirty-
one in 1931 (although that was still enough to lead the league), and he was
sold to Minneapolis in the American Association. At Nicollet Park, he could
aim at another short right-field barrier, and over five seasons he slammed
208 homers, including sixty-nine in 1933 to break his own record and set
a mark that would stand for twenty-one years. After six years as player-
manager at Sheboygan in the Wisconsin State League, Hauser ended his
playing career with minor-league totals of 399 homers and 1,353 runs batted in.

Whereas Hauser was of modest size (5 feet 10 ½ inches, 175 pounds),
Russell "Buzz" Arlett was a big guy, a switch-hitting outfielder–first baseman who'd been a promising young pitcher in the Pacific Coast League
until he hurt his arm. From 1923 to 1930, Arlett averaged .354, drove in
1,192 runs, and hit 237 homers for Oakland. It was Arlett's bad luck finally
to make the majors in 1931, the year the ball was deadened. Drafted by
the Philadelphia Phillies, he batted respectably (.313, eighteen homers,
seventy-two RBIs), but he didn't have much of a throwing arm and covered
little ground in left field. For 1932 he was back in the minors with Baltimore, where he cracked fifty-four homers, followed by thirty-nine the next
year. Sold down to Birmingham in the Southern Association and then purchased by Minneapolis, he teamed with Joe Hauser to form one of the
most potent tandems in minor-league history. Both were released following
the 1936 season; Arlett hung on in Organized Baseball through six years of
managing in the lower minors. Over eighteen seasons in the minors, he hit
432 homers and drove in 1,786 runs, besides gaining 108 victories pitching
in the Pacific Coast League.

Another heavy-hitting former pitcher was Smead Jolley, who from 1926
to 1929, with San Francisco, hit as many as forty-five homers, drove in as
many as 188 runs, and successively batted .346, .397, .404, and .387. Purchased by the Chicago White Sox, Jolley hit above .300 in three of four
American League seasons, but his outfielding gaffes became legendary (including one occasion when a ball went through his legs, hit the fence, and
rolled back through his legs on the rebound). Back in the Pacific Coast

League by 1934, with Hollywood, he pummeled pitchers in that circuit as well as the International League, Southern Association, and Western International League for eight more years. All told, Jolley made 3,037 minor-league hits, homered 337 times, drove in 1,593 runs, had a .366 average, and won six batting championships.

Oscar "Ox" Eckhardt appeared in a total of twenty-four big-league games in a sixteen-year professional career, during which he won three Pacific Coast League batting titles and another in the Texas League, and averaged .367. Nick Cullop played in 128 major-league games (mostly with Cincinnati in 1930 and 1931) and spent twenty-five years in the minors. Cullop never won a batting title, but he hit 420 homers and drove in 1,857 runs—the most RBIs by any minor leaguer. Once asked why he never made it to the majors to stay, he was fairly philosophical: "I could have helped some teams, but not the ones I went to. Then after you've been around awhile, up and down, you get tagged as a guy who can't make it when you really can, if given a chance."[28]

For one reason or another, Hauser, Arlett, Jolley, Eckhardt, and Cullop were all "tagged" as either not having or no longer having big-league credentials. Frank Shellenback, however, stayed in the Pacific Coast League from 1920 to 1938 because the rules were changed on him.

As a nineteen-year-old right-hander, Shellenback went up to the White Sox from Milwaukee in 1918—a season when, with players leaving for military service or to work in wartime industry, big-league clubs scrambled to keep their rosters filled. Shellenback managed a 9–12 record with a 2.66 earned run average for a sixth-place team, but the next year he was back in the American Association, in Minneapolis. The young pitcher's favorite weapon had become the spitball, which was outlawed effective with the 1920 season. Although designated spitballers (including Shellenback) could continue to use the pitch for the remainder of their careers, minor leaguers couldn't bring it with them into the majors. So spitballer Shellenback put in nineteen years in the Pacific Coast League, during which he pitched for four teams, managed two, won 295 games, and lost 178. Organized Baseball's last legal spitballer, Shellenback finally quit pitching to become a coach for the Cardinals and subsequently the Red Sox.

. . . . .

IF SHELLENBACK and other fine ballplayers experienced frustration at being held out of the majors, and if their pay, travel, lodging, and food left much to be desired, the fact remains that just about anybody within all-white Organized Baseball had it better than ballplayers on the other side of the color line. Times were harder and life was tougher in every respect in black professional baseball, yet leagues operated, the competition was intense, the overall caliber of play was high, and millions of African Americans faithfully followed the fortunes of teams and players. Black baseball was always off to one side within the vast national baseball universe, but in the hard times of the 1930s—the last full decade of segregated professionalism—it may have been at its best.

CHAPTER 9

Shadowball

IN THE SUMMER OF 1939, the *Sporting News*, whose masthead proclaimed it to be the "baseball paper of the world," carried a feature article on contemporary major leaguers with names such as Krakauskas, Bordagarary, Kamporuis, Chiozza, Estalella, and Lodigiani, with the advisory that the names weren't "typographical errors" but "just so many members of the nation's greatest force of democracy—baseball, the national game—the melting pot of the sons of all languages, the caldron of equal big opportunity."[1]

That was a true statement as far as it went. What the *Sporting News*'s encomium ignored was the total exclusion from Organized Baseball of roughly 10 percent of this country's population as well as black and racially mixed athletes from other countries. It also ignored the fact that by that time Leroy "Satchel" Paige—a tall, lean, semiliterate, thirty-four-year-old native of Mobile, Alabama—was, apart from Babe Ruth, possibly the best-known baseball player in the Western Hemisphere. Because his skin was black, Satchel Paige practiced his marvelous pitching talents outside Organized Baseball.

Such was baseball reality in the American 1930s, the last decade of all-white Organized Baseball. Voices of protest had been raised over the years—in fact, they became more numerous and vehement in the thirties. In 1931, for example, the Chicago journalist Westbrook Pegler (a racial liberal subsequently made anathema by political liberals for his anti–New Dealism) denounced "the craziest wrong in baseball." Black Americans,

Pegler pointed out, had been in this country "for more generations than many of the Caucasians who make up the [major] league teams." Pegler wondered at a situation in which "colored athletes" competed with whites at the intercollegiate level, but "professional ball players must be protected by a regulation which the magnates haven't the gall to put on paper."[2]

Pegler referred to the unwritten but universally accepted policy within Organized Baseball—dating from the late nineteenth century—not to issue contracts to players with any detectable African ancestry. So in the twentieth century, black baseball players had gone their separate way, just as black teachers, attorneys, physicians, musicians, moviemakers, and professionals of other types had done.

. . . . .

DURING THE FIRST DECADES of the century, independent black professional teams proliferated across the United States, and by the mid-1920s two professional leagues were in operation. The Negro National League (NNL), organized in 1920 under the aegis of Andrew "Rube" Foster, co-owner of the powerful Chicago American Giants and once an outstanding pitcher, was based in midwestern and midsouthern cities. The Eastern Colored League (ECL), formed three years later, operated in Pennsylvania, Maryland, New Jersey, and the New York City area.

Black baseball was able to share in the general prosperity of the 1920s, and beginning in 1924 the two leagues staged their version of the World Series, with the NNL's Kansas City Monarchs defeating the ECL's Hilldale Club of Darby, Pennsylvania, five games to four. Staged in Philadelphia, Kansas City, Baltimore, and Chicago, that inaugural interleague series set the pattern that would be followed in black postseason competition.

Rube Foster, the dominating figure in the NNL, was a hard-headed businessman but also a visionary. His long-range ambition may have been to elevate black baseball to the point that it could command recognition as a third, separate-but-equal major league. But in 1926, probably afflicted by paranoid schizophrenia, Foster became so ill that his family committed him to the state insane asylum at Kankakee, Illinois, where he died four years later at age fifty-one.

Although the original NNL remained in business into the first years of the Great Depression, the league suffered from the loss of Foster's leadership and direction. Meanwhile the ECL—a shakier outfit that was dependent on booking arrangements controlled by the white New Yorker Nat

Strong—disbanded even before the 1928 season got under way. A successor called the American Negro League (ANL), consisting of mostly the same clubs, lasted for only one season. So as of 1930, organized black baseball consisted of the NNL—with teams in Chicago, Kansas City, St. Louis, Memphis, Birmingham, Detroit, Nashville, and Cincinnati—and a precariously operating lesser circuit called the Texas-Louisiana League, with teams in New Orleans, Houston, San Antonio, Waco, Dallas, and Port Arthur.

If the Great Depression was an ordeal for most white people, for black Americans it was virtually a disaster. The collapse of the cotton economy left the rural South, where a substantial majority of black people still lived, in desperate circumstances. Meanwhile, in the northern cities and industrial towns to which more than 700,000 African Americans had migrated in the 1920s, black unemployment soared. By 1932 the jobless rate among black Detroiters had reached 75 percent; among black Pittsburghers, 69 percent. As of the spring of 1935, 3 million black Americans—one in every four—were dependent on some form of public assistance.

Life in the North was better for black people, most of all in being generally free of lynchings and other forms of violence to which white Southerners continued to resort in their determination to maintain racial supremacy. But prejudice—mostly extralegal but deeply ingrained and inherited by successive generations of European immigrants—was also basic to race relations outside the South. White audiences in the North, for example, were just as captivated as white Southerners by the nightly radio program *Amos 'n' Andy*, broadcast to the nation out of Chicago and featuring a running parody of black urban life by Freeman Gosden and Charles Correl—two white men. Protests organized by the black press and civic organizations that *Amos 'n' Andy* was spurious and degrading were unavailing.

Black people in the North usually couldn't register at the better hotels, couldn't eat in the better restaurants, and couldn't rent apartments or buy homes in white neighborhoods. Although young black women and men sometimes attended integrated colleges and universities and a sprinkling of black athletes competed in northern intercollegiate competition, discrimination could crop up anywhere and in almost any circumstance.

The understanding throughout Organized Baseball was that no player with even the faintest trace of black ancestry was to be employed. Thus in 1936, when pitcher Tomás de la Cruz, supposedly a "pure Castilian" Cuban, reported to the Albany International League club and showed his passport to manager Al Mamaux, the manager became agitated. Mamaux told a reporter that Joe Cambria, who owned the Albany franchise and had scouted and signed de la Cruz, would be thrown out of baseball, because "he's got a Negro playing on this club." Mamaux calmed down when de la Cruz translated his passport, which specified *pelo negro*—black hair.[3]

. . . . .

APART FROM SIMPLE PREJUDICE, seemingly good, practical reasons for excluding African Americans from Organized Baseball weren't hard to come by. For one thing, the standard split-season format in Negro-league competition not only looked minor league but invited suspicion that the first-half winner would deliberately play below par to ensure some extra money from a postseason series with a different second-half leader. In many respects, moreover, black baseball replicated the semiorganized and often disorganized character of early white professional ball as it had developed in the 1860s and 1870s.

Many black professional clubs operated outside organized leagues, and the leagues that did exist were loosely run affairs, with their affiliates playing most of the time against nonleague outfits or against each other in games that didn't count in the standings. (Occasionally players had to ask spectators whether they were playing a league game.) Season schedules were frequently disregarded in favor of more attractive playing dates elsewhere; players might sign contracts but weren't bound by a reserve clause and often jumped from one club to another; umpires were usually local men hired on a per-game basis; and figures on teams' win–loss records and individual player performances were haphazardly reported.

On that last matter, the complaint of John H. Clark, secretary of the second Negro National League (formed in 1933), was a common one. Club owners, said Clark, simply would not see to the systematic reporting of game accounts or even game scores. When information did reach the league's central office by telegraph, it was usually of the bare-bones variety. Behaving "more like first-year sandlot promoters than big league owners," operators of black baseball franchises failed to understand that reliable statistics on the accomplishments of teams and players helped generate fan interest. "Because this phase of the game has gone unrecognized," Clark lamented, "is one of the genuine reasons why the status of Negro players cannot be proved. . . . The only way to put Negro baseball on a par with what we call major leagues is to keep records of performances, relay the same information to the public and play fair with the press."[4]

But what Clark wanted never really happened within black baseball, to the undying frustration of reporters compiling their baseball write-ups in the weekly editions of black newspapers (and of historians subsequently trying to structure narratives of black baseball). As Hall of Famer Buck Leonard put it in his old age, "We never kept proper statistics, so there's no permanent record, and you're liable to get a different story from each one of us. It's just what we can remember—and pass along."[5]

A widely shared belief in white baseball circles was that black baseball was little better than a racket in which the controlling forces were underworld characters and booking agents. That belief had much truth behind it. Especially during the Depression years, vice lords who directed the illegal numbers traffic in the black districts of northern cities commonly financed professional baseball teams. As for booking agents, such people as Nat Strong in New York (up to his death in 1935), Abe Saperstein (better known for his Harlem Globetrotters basketball tourists) in Chicago, and Eddie Gottlieb in Philadelphia were maligned but probably necessary figures in the affairs of black baseball. The fact was that Negro-league clubs made most of their money in games with white semipro clubs and in specially arranged matchups with each other that were usually put together by booking agents, who of course took a percentage of ticket sales.

White semipro outfits were nearly everywhere in the thirties. Most were sponsored by local business interests and consisted of employees who played avocationally. But in a number of well-organized semipro leagues, with teams playing three or four times a week from May to September, a star performer could supplement what he made at his regular job (if he had one) by as much as $400 to $500. By 1940 the National Baseball Congress, established in 1934, claimed 25,000 affiliated teams and 500,000 players nationwide.

The best-known eastern semipro circuit was the Metropolitan Baseball Association (MBA), which included as many as nine New York–area clubs. Although Sam Rosner's Bushwicks had the largest and best-lit playing facilities, other strong MBA teams included the Bay Parkways, Barton Nighthawks, and Cedarhurst. MBA teams regularly met black professional clubs—and usually were able to hold their own.

Booking agents also put together special events such as games between black teams at Yankee Stadium, the Polo Grounds, and other Organized Baseball venues. Although Jacob Ruppert and Ed Barrow viewed black baseball with contempt, by 1930 they were no longer willing to pass up the extra money to be made by letting black teams into Yankee Stadium. On Sunday, July 6, the stadium hosted its first black baseball, when some 15,000 mostly African-American fans attended an ANL doubleheader between the New York–based Lincoln Giants and the Baltimore Black Sox, with a portion of the proceeds going to the benefit fund of the Brotherhood of Pullman Car Porters. Two months later, the Lincoln Giants met the Homestead Grays in another Yankee Stadium doubleheader, as part of a migrating ten-game series for the mythical eastern championship, of which the Grays won six.

The take (usually 10 percent) that went to major-league and upper-minors owners who rented ballparks to Negro-league teams wasn't insignificant, especially in the Depression years. By the end of the 1930s, every big-league venue—with the exception of Sportsman's Park in St. Louis, Wrigley Field in Chicago, and the two ballparks in Boston—was being used at least occasionally for Negro-league games, as were such upper-minors plants as Oriole Park in Baltimore, Rickwood Field in Birmingham, Swayne Field in Toledo, Ruppert Stadium in Newark, and Muehlebach Field, long the home grounds of the Kansas City Monarchs. For such marginally operating franchises as the Washington Senators, Chicago White Sox, and Philadelphia Athletics, rent collected from black teams did much to defray expenses. The rich Yankees, though, added to their profits by making not only Yankee Stadium but Ruppert Stadium and Muehlebach Field, homes of their top-level farm teams, available to Negro leaguers.

. . . . .

DESPITE THE DIFFICULTIES involved in getting reliable quantitative data on black baseball, what we do know provides a convincing argument for the wealth of talent available on the other side of the color line—if at any time before 1946 Organized Baseball had been willing to tap it. In the spring of 1930—citing an eight-game barnstorming series the previous fall between the Chicago American Giants and a team that included four-time batting champion Harry Heilmann plus Bing Miller and Art Shires, won by the American Giants, six games to two—W. C. Hueston, Rube Foster's successor as president of the first NNL, submitted that his league played at least Class AA–grade baseball.

Hueston was probably very close to the mark. It's conceivable that if Foster had been able to carry on and if the Depression hadn't struck, the first NNL might have built on its promising beginnings and attracted enough patronage and capital to gain recognition from—if not integration into—Organized Baseball. As it was, the league started to fall apart in 1930, when at season's end J. L. Wilkinson and Thomas Y. Baird, Kansas City's white owners, withdrew the Monarchs.

For the next six years, the Monarchs would remain unaffiliated. From April into November, they would play two hundred or more dates with league teams, independent black clubs, the House of David, white semipros, and Dizzy Dean's and other aggregations of white professional "all-stars."

The most prominent independent black club in the East was the Homestead Grays, named for its origins in a steel-mill suburb south of Pittsburgh. Owned by Cumberland W. "Cum" Posey, an austere, imperious graduate of Penn State College, the Grays had a long history in black baseball, including membership in the short-lived ANL. Although he was well known as a womanizer, publicly Posey sought to project an image of respectability and propriety for both himself and his ball club. Like the New York Yankees, the Grays were supposed to be a cut above other outfits—better paid, better dressed, better behaved both on and off the ball field. In short, they were to act and play like the class of black baseball.

The Grays were the top road attraction in the East and drew respectable crowds at home—in games at Forbes Field when the Pirates were away and occasionally on midsummer late afternoons following Pirates home games. On July 24, 1930, for example, the Grays met the Monarchs at Forbes Field in an afternoon game and again that evening under the shadowy illumination and amid the noise and smoke from the Monarchs' gasoline-powered portable lighting system. That was the beginning of a sixteen-game tour from Pennsylvania through Ohio, Indiana, and Illinois that climaxed with an epic pitching duel in Kansas City.

On August 3, under the Monarchs' lights at Muehlebach Field, forty-five-year-old "Smoky Joe" Williams, nearing the end of more than two decades as a black professional, took the mound for the Grays against twenty-three-year-old Chet Brewer, already in his sixth season with the Monarchs. The generic spitball was still legal in black professionalism (and would be until 1938); with both pitchers using "everything but a blacksmith's file," Williams struck out twenty-seven batters, and Brewer, nineteen.[6] In the twelfth inning, the Grays' Oscar Charleston walked and scored the game's only run on the game's only hit beyond the infield—a double by Chaney White.

Of course, the Monarchs' series with the Grays had nothing at all to do with the 1930 NNL schedule. Within the league, the Monarchs played forty-five games during the first half of the split season but only twenty in the second half. But practices that would have been unthinkable (because intolerable) in Organized Baseball were commonplace in the world of black baseball.

As for the NNL season itself, the St. Louis Stars, first-half winners, defeated the Detroit Stars in a poorly attended postseason series and claimed the NNL championship. Featuring Norman "Turkey" Stearnes, one of black baseball's premier power hitters, the Detroit club operated under the controversial ownership of a haberdasher named John Roesink, described by a *Pittsburgh Courier* correspondent as "a member of the superior Nordics." Roesink had built a ballpark in suburban Hamtramck, but he irked black fans by refusing to install drinking fountains, hiring only white umpires, stationing only white people at the turnstiles and concession windows, and withholding advertisements from " 'shine' papers."[7]

Early in October the Chicago American Giants—with the addition of Oscar Charleston from the Grays, Satchel Paige from the Baltimore Black Sox, and a couple of others—took three of four games from a collection of white professionals that included future Hall of Famers Harry Heilmann and Charley Gehringer as well as Lefty O'Doul, Art Shires, and Earl White-hill. In the finale, on Monday night, October 6, the twenty-four-year-old Paige had his first encounter with white big leaguers, winning 7–6 with relief help in the ninth inning.

For 1931, with the ANL out of business, the NNL remained the sole organized black professional league in a rapidly worsening economy. In a six-club setup, the St. Louis Stars reportedly won both halves, although no final standings were published for either half. After twelve seasons, the league that Rube Foster had put together and made work sputtered to an inglorious end.

So for the 1932 season the dwindling number of African Americans who could still afford baseball tickets gave most of their attention to such independent clubs as the Monarchs, ranging over the middle part of the country; the newly formed New York Black Yankees, underwritten by the renowned tap dancer Bill Robinson and appearing several times in Yankee Stadium (with Nat Strong and Jacob Ruppert each taking 10 percent off the top); a revived Hilldale Club, managed by future Hall of Famer William "Judy" Johnson; a group of bearded black and racially mixed players called the Cuban House of David, owned by a Miami promoter named Syd Pollock; and most of all the emerging rivalry for Pittsburgh supremacy between the Homestead Grays and the upstart Crawfords.

. . . . .

IN THE 1920s the Crawfords (or Craws, to their followers) had grown from a junior team into the semipro Crawford Giants.[8] They'd functioned as something of a farm club for the Grays until 1930, when William A. "Gus" Greenlee took them over and set out to make the Pittsburgh Craw-

fords the best thing in black baseball. Thirty-four years old that year, Greenlee was a native South Carolinian who'd come north, entered the numbers
game, and eventually become king of the hill, both figuratively and literally.
Greenlee controlled numbers trafficking in black Pittsburgh, whose 55,000
residents were concentrated in the Hill district on the city's north side. By
the early Depression years, with the income from his numbers operations
and a string of speakeasies, he was probably the wealthiest black Pittsburgher.

Nicknamed "Big Red" (because his mixed-race ancestry gave him a light
complexion and reddish hair), Greenlee quickly put together a competitive
ball club, although they lost twice to the lordly Grays. But by mid-1931
he'd wooed the stellar battery of Satchel Paige and Bill Perkins away from
the Cleveland NNL club, and he was gathering other established professionals almost weekly. Having to use a public-school facility called Ammon
Field as their home grounds, the Crawfords did their important business
elsewhere, such as another couple of games versus the Grays at Forbes
Field, which the Grays again swept.

For the next six years, Greenlee would have a profitable but often frustrating relationship with the peripatetic Satchel Paige. Late in September,
for example, Paige switched over to the Grays as a hired gun to pitch in a
series at Forbes Field with the Baltimore Black Sox, which had themselves
brought in Hilldale's Herbert "Rap" Dixon, a hard-hitting outfielder, and
the versatile Cuban Martin Dihigo, who was at home whether in the infield,
in the outfield, or on the mound.

Not only the NNL but a number of independently operating teams
folded up following the 1931 season. Cum Posey tried to promote a Grays-
anchored successor to the NNL called the East-West League, which also
included Hilldale, Cleveland, Cincinnati, Baltimore, and Newark. But in
the bottom year of the Depression, Hilldale's experience was typical: a team
that had averaged 1,844 admissions for twenty-six home dates in 1926 could
do no better than 340 for eleven dates in 1932. By late June, the East-West
League had disbanded. The six-member Negro Southern League made it
through a half-season and into twelve games of the second half and then
went ahead with a championship series, won from Nashville by Cole's
American Giants (Rube Foster's old club), now owned by Robert Cole, a
white Chicago florist and mortician.

· · · · ·

THAT SAME YEAR Gus Greenlee, with money few people of any color
possessed, began assembling an extraordinarily talented ball club. With

Paige under contract (more or less), Greenlee raided the Grays for Oscar Charleston, who'd starred for seventeen years with various teams and now became the Crawfords' manager and first baseman. Jud "Boojum" Wilson, a stocky third baseman, and Ted Radcliffe (nicknamed "Double Duty" because he sometimes pitched and sometimes caught) also deserted Cum Posey, and after the East-West League folded Judy Johnson and Rap Dixon joined the Crawfords from Hilldale. Outfielder James "Cool Papa" Bell, probably the fastest man in baseball, arrived from the Detroit Stars, which had disbanded after John Roesink's ballpark burned. But Greenlee's prize acquisition was Josh Gibson, a twenty-one-year-old catcher who'd joined the Grays from the junior Crawfords in 1930. Since then, the powerfully muscled youngster had consistently awed spectators with home runs that traveled as far as Babe Ruth's, Jimmie Foxx's, or anybody else's.

Greenlee also paid for the construction of the first wholly black-owned baseball park. Located on Bedford Avenue on the Hill, supposedly costing $100,000, and seating about 6,000, Greenlee Field was nearly filled on Friday, April 29, when the Crawfords opened the season by losing 1–0 in ten innings to the Black Yankees, Jess Hubbard outpitching Paige. The Crawfords then boarded their new $10,000 Mack bus (equipped with sleeping berths) and embarked on a grand tour through the southern states. They were gone for three and a half months, playing almost daily on manicured diamonds in big cities and on small-town fields that were little more than cow pastures. When they returned to Greenlee Field for another series with the Black Yankees, Paige pitched a 6–0 no-hitter.

Greenlee's vision was much like Rube Foster's. He wanted to make black baseball independent of white capital and booking agents, and he wanted black people to embrace "Race baseball" as their own and quit giving preference to games between whites. But he also liked having white fans at Greenlee Field and wherever else the Crawfords played, which meant that, like everybody else in black baseball, he understood that most people would rather see a white team play a black team than a game between two black teams.

So while the Crawfords and the Grays met nineteen times in 1932 at Greenlee and Forbes fields, the Crawfords played lots of games against white semipro outfits. In Jamestown, Pennsylvania, for example, they batted against Hugh Bedient, who'd pitched in the 1912 World Series. The House of David travelers brought their lights into Greenlee Field and showed off Grover Cleveland Alexander for a couple of innings. The Bushwicks packed Dexter Park for a matchup between Paige and Stan Baumgartner, a onetime Athletics starter and a budding Philadelphia sportswriter.

And then there were the autumnal barnstorming encounters between black and white professionals. Following the 1932 major-league season, Casey Stengel organized a team that included, among others, Woody English, Danny Taylor, Roy Parmelee, Larry French, and Hack Wilson. They met the Crawfords in seven games in York, Altoona, Pittsburgh, and Cleveland. On October 1 Paige held the big leaguers to two runs and struck out fifteen, while the Crawfords slammed Parmelee for fourteen hits and ten runs. The Crawfords won four other games in the series; Stengel's team, only two.

By then, Cum Posey had developed an abiding hatred for Greenlee, not only because of Greenlee's player raids but because he aspired to dominate Pittsburgh's black baseball, just as he dominated the Hill's numbers traffic. Although Greenlee was contemptuous of Posey's pretenses to respectability, he also needed the Grays in the new league he was putting together. Posey, in turn, couldn't afford to be shut out of the circuit, so both the Grays and the Crawfords became charter members of the new Negro National League, established in Chicago in January 1933.

. . . . .

UNLIKE THE MIDWESTERN- and midsouthern-based original NNL, the second NNL scattered its affiliates from the Chesapeake Bay to the Great Lakes. Besides Greenlee's Crawfords and Posey's Grays, it included Cole's American Giants, the Detroit Stars, the Nashville Elite Giants, the Baltimore Black Sox, and the Columbus Blue Birds. It was an ambitious undertaking, especially in the middle of the Depression, but its prospects would have been considerably stronger if Wilkinson and Baird hadn't remained convinced that their Monarchs would make more money by staying independent.

Not long before the league season began, several prominent sportswriters allowed themselves to be quoted on the need to drop the color line in Organized Baseball. Dan Parker, Jimmy Powers, and Heywood Broun of New York and Gordon Mackey of Philadelphia all agreed that, as Parker put it in a letter to the *Pittsburgh Courier*'s Chester Washington, "by all means, let the Negro ball player play in organized baseball." But a statement by Sam Watters, vice president and secretary of the Pittsburgh Pirates, was little less than mind-boggling: "Exceptional playing ability and living habits are the main attributes and requirements for positions on major league ball clubs. And I don't believe that race, creed or color have ever entered into the selection of the players on big league clubs."[9] Like many other people within Organized Baseball, Watters probably believed that.

The first season of the new-edition NNL was a rocky one. Columbus dropped out in August and was replaced by Cleveland; Baltimore soon quit as well. But a far bigger blow came with the departure of the Grays after Posey raided Detroit for a couple of players, and Greenlee convinced the rest of the league representatives to suspend the Grays. So after a brief second venture into league baseball, Posey's Grays resumed their independent ways.

The season ended in confusion. Over its first half, fifth-place Detroit played thirty-three league-certified games; fourth-place Nashville, twenty-three; and third-place Baltimore, only twenty. Cole's American Giants, with a 21–7 record, edged the Crawfords (20–8) for the first-half championship, but the Crawfords, by sweeping a doubleheader from Nashville at Cleveland's Lakefront Stadium on October 1, apparently won the second half. Convinced that his club had already proved its superiority, Greenlee refused a postseason series with the American Giants and then a couple of months later cavalierly declared the Crawfords NNL champions.

One lasting achievement came out of the second NNL's first season. On Sunday, September 10, two months after the inaugural major-league All-Star Game, Greenlee, Chicago's Robert Cole, and Nashville's Tom Wilson pooled their money and influence to stage a comparable game—the first in what would become the biggest annual event in black baseball. Also played at Comiskey Park (as it always would be) and dubbed the East-West Game, the contest matched not only players in NNL teams but players from independent clubs—all elected by fans voting on ballots printed in the *Pittsburgh Courier* and *Chicago Defender*.

Although the three Monarchs electees didn't appear because of a booking in Wichita, the game still showcased most of the ranking black professionals of the day. Under overcast skies (which were blamed for a turnout of only about 15,000), big George "Mule" Suttles of the American Giants, a thirteen-year veteran, hit a two-run homer off the Crawfords' Sam Streeter to spark an 11–7 West victory. American Giants left-hander Willie Foster (younger brother of the late Rube) pitched all nine innings for the West. Greenlee, Cole, and Wilson paid White Sox president Louis Comiskey $2,500 and split a $3,000 profit among themselves. The players were reimbursed for travel expenses but paid nothing.

Henry D. Farrell of the *Chicago Daily News* watched the game and enthused over "the boy, Oscar Charleston" (age thirty-six), who Farrell believed could play for at least ten big-league teams, and Suttles, who possessed not only power but "everything in the way of speed and agility." "With a plentiful supply of adult calcimine," concluded Farrell, "a bunch of major league owners who are now on their knees might have their prayers answered."[10]

If one watched games in the California League, which a Los Angeles promoter named Joe Pirrone operated for several years in November and December, still further confirmation was available of the strong talent level in black baseball. Tom Wilson assembled a team he called the Royal Colored Giants to compete in the four-team league, which staged its games in White Sox Park, home of the local black team of that name. Turkey Stearnes, Cool Papa Bell, Mule Suttles, and Willie Wells (the American Giants' superb shortstop) were some of the players who teamed with Satchel Paige to win the league title. Paige was reported to have finished with a 16–2 record, with 229 strikeouts in 140 innings; Bell led the league in batting (.362 in forty-three games); Suttles led with fourteen homers. Although most of the white players in the league were minor leaguers and semipros, the Pirates' Larry French and Brooklyn's Hollis Thurston, both Californians, and Buck Newsom, who'd won thirty games in the Pacific Coast League that year, were among the pitchers who lost to the Negro leaguers.

. . . . .

FOR THE 1934 SEASON, the Crawfords, the American Giants, Nashville, and Cleveland were carryover members; Newark and Philadelphia were added; and for the second half of the season Baltimore and the Bacharach Giants of Atlantic City also came in. The Monarchs continued to remain aloof from league competition, while the Grays were given NNL "associate membership," which allowed them to book games with league members but not at Forbes Field.

Meanwhile such southern teams as the Birmingham Black Barons, Memphis Red Sox, New Orleans Crescents, Atlanta Black Crackers, and Monroe (Louisiana) Monarchs offered a brand of ball not much below that of the NNL, while Syd Pollock's Cuban Stars and Ethiopian Clowns traversed the country. Another outfit called the Zulu Jungle Giants, dressed in grass skirts and makeup, set a new standard for tastelessness.

The number of league games that NNL teams played in 1934 varied from twenty-five for the Newark Dodgers to forty-six for the Crawfords, with the Cleveland Red Sox playing within the league only five times during the season's second half. Back in the twenties, in the heyday of the first NNL, teams had regularly played as many as ninety league games—in other words, a schedule that approached Organized Baseball standards. In the thirties, though, most of the money was to be made in black-versus-white competition and in specially booked black matchups, with league schedules never taken with great seriousness.

The pace was often mind-numbingly hectic. On June 24, for example, the Craws had an afternoon doubleheader with the Bushwicks and then another at 8:00 P.M. with the Bay Parkways. The next day, they boarded their bus for a 6:00 P.M. date in Philadelphia with the Kensingtons, followed by an 8:30 game in Highstown, New Jersey. If there was profit in such engagements, there wasn't much glory, especially if the white teams happened to win.

Absent a reserve clause in players' contracts (if they signed a contract at all), black professionals were usually free to desert their nominal franchise obligations and sell their exceptional skills wherever they could command the most money. Gus Greenlee tried to keep Satchel Paige on a tether, but given the fact that as early as 1934 Paige had become a lucrative attraction in his own right, it always had to be a loose one.

In July, for example, Paige and Bill Perkins (whom he preferred to pitch to rather than Josh Gibson) left the Crawfords and hired on with the House of David to play in the eighteen-team tournament staged annually by the *Denver Post*. The hirsute Davids went through seven games undefeated to take the championship, with the Kansas City Monarchs, the first all-black team to compete in the tournament, losing 2–0 to Spike Hunter in the deciding contest. Before that, though, Paige, pitching with a phony red beard, had won three times in eight days, including a brilliant duel with Chet Brewer. Besides his up-front fee, Paige took his share of the $7,500 prize money.

Paige was back with the Crawfords in time to relieve teammate Harry Kincannon in the sixth inning of the East-West Game and shut down the West's hitters the rest of the way. Meanwhile Cool Papa Bell scored the game's only run in the bottom of the sixth, coming all the way home from second base on Jud Wilson's infield hit. Again the players got nothing but expenses; Louis Comiskey's rental fee came to $4,700.

Paige's absence weakened the Crawfords, who finished second to Cole's American Giants in the first half-season but dropped to third, behind the Philadelphia Stars and Nashville, during the second half. In the championship series—which the American Giants interrupted for three games in Toledo with the American Association Mudhens—the Stars won four of seven games.

Philadelphia's ace was Stuart "Slim" Jones, a 6-foot 6-inch, twenty-year-old right-hander who seemed destined to become one of black baseball's greatest. On September 9, in a four-team doubleheader at Yankee Stadium that drew some 27,000, the American Giants defeated the Black Yankees in the opener; then Paige and Jones dueled to a 1–1 standoff, called after nine innings for darkness. Two weeks later, in another Yankee Stadium four-team extravaganza that drew 20,000, Paige and Jones met again, with Paige outpitching the youngster 3–1. Sadly, Jones was already a hopeless drunk; for the next four seasons, he pitched infrequently and ineffectively, and in the winter of 1939, at age twenty-five, he was found frozen to death on a Philadelphia street.

With the NNL season over, Paige was on the road with an assortment of Negro leaguers who met the Dean brothers' mostly minor-league and semipro "All-Stars" in Oklahoma City and points north and east. Then both Dizzy Dean and Paige headed for Los Angeles, where Paige would pitch for a California League entry (sponsored by Tom Wilson) that again included Turkey Stearnes, Mule Suttles, Cool Papa Bell, and Willie Wells. In one memorable matchup Paige and Dean battled for twelve scoreless innings, until the Negro leaguers pushed across a run. Dean had struck out fifteen, and Paige seventeen, including such California big leaguers as Frank Demaree, Dolph Camilli, and Wally Berger. At season's end, the Negro leaguers had again proved to be the class of the California League competition.

· · · · ·

IN 1935, benefiting from the mild economic upswing in the northern cities, the NNL managed to get through both halves of a season in which all eight members started and finished and played about sixty games apiece. Having acquired a Pittsburgh underworld figure named Rufus "Sonnyman" Jackson as his partner in the Grays, Cum Posey sought and received re-admission into the NNL. By that time, Posey had largely rebuilt the Grays, his star attraction now being a South Carolina–born first baseman named Walter "Buck" Leonard.

The 1935 NNL consisted of the Crawfords, Grays, American Giants, Philadelphia Stars, Columbus Elite Giants, Newark Dodgers, Brooklyn Eagles, and New York Cubans. Numbers-rackets money had become a bigger than ever factor in NNL operations. Besides Gus Greenlee and Tom Wilson (who had numbers operations in Nashville and later Baltimore), the New York Cubans were owned by Alejandro "Alex" Pompez, who ran the numbers game in Harlem, while the Brooklyn Eagles were the property of Ed Manley, numbers boss in Newark.

The 1935 Pittsburgh Crawfords were undisputed NNL champs. After running away with the first half with a 26–6 record, they finished second to the New York Cubans in the second half and then defeated player-manager Martin Dihigo's formidable ball club in a seven-game series for the pennant. Charleston, Gibson, Bell, Johnson, and company then barnstormed their way to Mexico City, where they played several times against Mexican professional and amateur teams before tying one game and losing two to a team of big leaguers that included Jimmie Foxx, Heinie Manush, Earl Whitehill, and an aging Rogers Hornsby.

But whatever success the Crawfords enjoyed in 1935 came without reliance on Satchel Paige. Supposedly having signed a two-year contract with Greenlee for $350 per month, Paige instead took off for faraway Bismarck, North Dakota, where a local automobile dealer named Neil Churchill had hired him to pitch for Churchill's semipro team. Besides Paige, Churchill recruited pitcher-catcher Ted Radcliffe, catcher Quincy Trouppe, and pitchers Barney Morris and Hilton Smith from black professional ranks.

Typically fielding a lineup of five blacks and four whites, Bismarck won about seventy-nine games that season. Paige's 27–2–2 record was made mostly against regional semipro competition, although he faced the House of David five times and the Kansas City Monarchs twice. Churchill entered his team in both the newly organized National Baseball Congress tournament in Wichita and the *Denver Post* competition. Although he yielded nine hits, Paige also struck out fourteen to win the championship game at Wichita 2–1 over the Halliburton Cementers of Duncan, Oklahoma. In Denver, Paige again led his team through seven straight victories, winning four complete games and striking out sixty-four in thirty-eight and two-thirds innings.

The Monarchs also hired Paige for a couple of outings against the Deans' mostly minor-league barnstormers. In Kansas City on October 7, the Dean brothers and Columbus's Mike Ryba combined to top Paige and the Monarchs 1–0. After that, the Deans traveled eastward for games with a Negro-league ensemble that included the Crawfords' Gibson, Bell, and pitcher Leroy Matlock, all just back from Mexico, as well as Jud Wilson and several other tough competitors. Gibson smacked a titanic homer off Diz at York, Pennsylvania, but Dean shut out the Negro leaguers and young Johnny Taylor of the Philly Stars in the opener of an October 17 doubleheader at Yankee Stadium, swept by the Deans' "All-Stars" before 17,000.

Then Diz and Paige were again off to Los Angeles for another round of California League matchups. Dean's teammates on the coast included Joe Hauser, Larry French, and a faded Hack Wilson, while Paige's team— again fronted by Tom Wilson—included the Grays' Buck Leonard and Jerry Benjamin, the Philly Stars' Jud Wilson, and the American Giants' Turkey Stearnes. On Halloween, working seven innings, Dean again defeated Paige, who left after four innings, 5–4.

After helping win the California League, Buck Leonard was off to Puerto Rico, where he and Homestead teammates Ray Brown and Vic Harris joined Brooklyn's Leon Day and Newark's Ray Dandridge to form a "Brooklyn Eagles" team that captured that island's winter-league championship. In the title game Brown, a Wilberforce College graduate who was also Cum Posey's son-in-law, pitched the "Eagles" to victory over Martin Dihigo and the Cuban Almendares club. (But black weeklies in the United States also reported Dihigo's three-hit, 5–1 win over the Cincinnati Reds' Paul Derringer, three other pitchers, and a patched-together lineup and the win by the "Eagles" over the Cincinnati spring trainees a couple of days later.)

On the Pacific coast, meanwhile, Paige stayed around to pitch still another victory against a team of California major and minor leaguers. That one included Joe DiMaggio, who would shortly leave for Florida to join the Yankees. Although there's some question about how the celebrated rookie fared against Paige, he was widely quoted in the black press to the effect that Paige was the best pitcher he'd ever faced.

But if Paige's ability to draw people into ballparks anywhere and anytime he put on a uniform was unmatched since Babe Ruth's drawing power in his heyday, he made few real friends within black baseball. A year earlier, in the wake of Paige's departure for Bismarck, Ed Harris of the *Philadelphia Tribune* had written that for all his crowd appeal, "to his teammates, he's usually a pain where you don't want to be kicked. . . . Anything he wants is his and he takes it. . . . Ol' Satch just goes off and does what Ol' Satch wants." A few years later a Negro-league pitcher who'd played both with and against Paige put it another way: "First, he's just plain unreliable. . . . Second, Satchel is out for himself. . . . So he makes sure he does well. But he doesn't care about the rest of his teammates. They are just his supporting cast."[11]

And while Paige's conduct off the field wasn't publicized, his promiscuous adultery was well known to baseball people on both sides of the color line. Thus for all his acknowledged ability, he also provided a convenient stereotype: the wenching, wastrel black player whose behavior couldn't measure up to what was supposedly expected of white professionals.

· · · · ·

PRESUMABLY ALL WAS WELL with the Pittsburgh Crawfords in the spring of 1936. Paige made up with Greenlee and rejoined the team, which would compete in what began as a six-team NNL, with Columbus and Brooklyn having been dropped. Besides the Crawfords and Grays, the league would now be made up of Tom Wilson's Elite Giants (relocated to Washington and renting Griffith Stadium), the Philly Stars, the New York Cubans, and the Newark Eagles. Ed Manley and his wife, Effa, had abandoned Brooklyn, purchased the Newark franchise (which they renamed the Eagles), and worked out an agreement with the New York Yankees to use Ruppert Stadium when the International League Bears were on the road.

A few years earlier, James "Soldier Boy" Semler, another entrepreneur with business interests that didn't invite close scrutiny, had bought the Black Yankees from Bill Robinson. Tenants of Yankee Stadium, the Black Yankees had the potential to become black baseball's most prosperous franchise, and Greenlee and associates brought them into the NNL for the second half of the 1936 season. But Semler had mismanaged his operation, trading away his best young talent and, under the so-called cooperative plan, paying his players on a game-by-game basis out of gate receipts. They played only fifteen official NNL games during the season's second half, winning eight.

In a season-opening Grays–Cubans doubleheader on May 10, 1936, at Dyckman Oval on 214th Street in Manhattan, Paige outlasted Chet Brewer 8–4, and Sam Steeter won over the Cubans' Johnny Taylor in the second game. Josh Gibson homered once in the opener, twice in the nightcap. Still, with strong support in Harlem, including the patronage of such black musical celebrities as Cab Calloway, Louis Armstrong, and Lionel Hampton, the Cubans' prospects looked good.

A few days later, though, owner Alex Pompez—under indictment for tax evasion in New York district attorney Thomas E. Dewey's ongoing anti-rackets campaign—fled to Europe. Returning early the next year, Pompez would hide out for a time in Newark and then flee again—this time to Mexico. With shrinking finances and an uncertain future, the Cubans finished fifth in the first half of the 1936 NNL season, and fourth in the second half.

Paige stayed with the Crawfords most of the time in 1936, although in August he headed up a powerhouse cast of fourteen black professionals drawn from the Crawfords, Grays, and Elite Giants that entered the *Denver Post* tournament. They overmatched everybody and easily gained the $5,093 first-place purse. Besides Paige, the "Negro League All-Stars" included Gibson, Bell, Streeter, Ray Brown, and the Elite Giants' stellar second baseman, Sammy T. Hughes, and hard-hitting outfielder Bill Wright. It was one of the most talented ensembles in black baseball history.

That year's East-West Game drew 26,400 to Comiskey Park—the biggest crowd so far. The West, consisting entirely of players from the Monarchs and American Giants, lost 10–2 to an East team numbering only Crawfords and Elite Giants. Paige made what had become his obligatory appearance, pitching the last couple of innings for the East. For the first time, Greenlee, Cole, and Wilson didn't split all the profits, part of which went into an emergency fund to help clubs meet their payrolls—notably the "co-op" Black Yankees and the orphaned Cubans.

Paige was away in Texas in September, pitching for a semipro team, but he flew to New York to throw a shutout on September 24 against the Black Yankees before some 20,000 at the Polo Grounds after Washington had bested Philadelphia in the first game of a gala doubleheader. The occasion was a benefit staged for the blind and indigent old prizefighter Sam Langford, with former heavyweight champions Jack Johnson and Jack Dempsey, along with Jesse Owens, fresh from his track-and-field triumphs at the Berlin Olympics, on hand to take their bows.

That show pretty much closed down the NNL season, because what should have been a championship series between the Washington Elite Giants, who barely edged the Philadelphia Stars in the first half, and the Craws, easy second-half winners, was called off. The Stars, supported by Cum Posey, contested the first-half standings on the grounds that the Elite Giants had refused to make up two scheduled games that had been rained out.

· · · · ·

SUCH ANTICS continued to disgust much of the black baseball press. Wrote the *Pittsburgh Courier's* Rollo Wilson, "The club owners are as bewildered men in a huge cavern. . . . They grope in blind alleys and bump their (fortunately for them) hard heads against the walls which have resisted those impacts these many years."[12] In truth, how could the NNL be considered an authentic league in the absence of established and consistently honored ways of determining its champion?

The ballplayers themselves didn't seem to attach great importance to who won particular pennants. As an elderly Judy Johnson put it, "There was always sun shining someplace."[13] From the mid-1930s on, an increasing number of black professionals played year-round: in the United States in the summer; in Cuba, Puerto Rico, the Dominican Republic, Mexico, or Venezuela in the winter. In 1936/1937, for example, Buck Leonard, Ray Dandridge, Leon Day, Vic Harris, Slim Jones, and Ray Brown were among the NNL players making up a team that again competed in the Puerto Rican winter league; the Black Yankees' Bill Holland and Barney Brown pitched in Venezuela; and Willie Wells, Bill Perkins, and Craws infielder Harry Williams, among others, played in Cuba.

That winter, the NNL owners elected Greenlee president and Ferdinand Q. Morton of New York commissioner and dropped the New York Cubans from the league. Effa Manley, representing her husband's relatively well-heeled and increasingly competitive Newark Eagles, now became an assertive voice in NNL affairs.

One of the most fascinating personalities in Negro-league history, Effa Brooks Manley was a very light skinned, exceptionally attractive woman in her mid-thirties who was presumed to be African American. She, however, claimed to be the out-of-wedlock daughter of a white Philadelphia businessman and a white seamstress who subsequently married a black man named Brooks. In any case, she lived all her life among black people, although until she met Abe Manley, she said, "I was not accepted into the better circles of Negro society."[14]

Effa Manley was what would later be regarded as an activist. Outside baseball, she raised money for the National Association for the Advancement of Colored People's campaign against lynching and joined demonstrations for equal employment opportunities for black people in Newark's downtown stores. Inside baseball, she tried to reduce the clout of Gus Greenlee and Tom Wilson (whom she considered Greenlee's stooge) and inveighed against white booking agents, most notably Eddie Gottlieb, who now owned the Philadelphia Stars outright.

. . . . .

MEANWHILE, a group of midwestern and southern entrepreneurs—apparently sharing the widespread, if mistaken, belief that the Depression was about over—came together in Indianapolis and formed a rival organization called the Negro American League (NAL). J. L. Wilkinson and Tom Baird brought their Monarchs into the new league, which also included the Chicago American Giants, Indianapolis Athletics, Birmingham Black Sox, Memphis Red Sox, Detroit Stars, St. Louis Stars, and Cincinnati Tigers. Abe Saperstein was officially named booking agent for NAL teams; Robert R. Jackson of Chicago would be the NAL's first president; Wilkinson would serve as league secretary.

It all looked pretty good on paper. After a parade by their booster club to Muehlebach Field, the Monarchs opened a three-game weekend series with the American Giants. Willie Foster shut them out on Saturday, but the Monarchs swept a Sunday doubleheader, with Hilton Smith tossing a no-hitter in the opener. It soon became apparent that the other six NAL clubs were overmatched against the Monarchs and American Giants. Kansas City beat out the American Giants by a half-game in the season's first half; no official standings were published for the second half, but Chicago was declared the winner. In what was publicized as a championship series, the Monarchs won four, lost one, and tied one.

For Gus Greenlee—without whom the NNL wouldn't have happened (at least not in 1933)—things started to go bad in the spring of 1937. Josh Gibson refused the money that Greenlee offered and became a holdout, whereupon Greenlee traded him as well as the aging Judy Johnson to the Homestead Grays for catcher Lloyd "Pepper" Bassett and infielder Henry "Jake" Spearman, plus $2,500 in cash. Greenlee also sold Harry Kincannon, who'd been a Crawfords pitching mainstay for several years, to the Black Yankees. It had become obvious by then that for all he'd invested and all the ballyhoo that had gone into promoting his cherished Craws, "Big Red" had tired of losing money on the ball club.

But it was about to get worse. Late in April, former New York Cubans Martin Dihigo and Lazaro Salazar journeyed north to recruit Satchel Paige to pitch in the Dominican Republic for the Ciudad Trujillo team, sponsored by dictator Rafael Trujillo. Paige's example was enough to induce others to follow. Subsequently, Cool Papa Bell, Harry Williams, shortstop Sammy Bankhead, and four other Crawfords, as well as Josh Gibson, Bill Perkins, and Jake Spearman from the Grays; pitcher Bob Griffith from Washington; and Chet Brewer, late of the New York Cubans, hired on with teams in the Dominican League. A total of fourteen players left NNL clubs to play a two-month season at salaries ranging from about $1,500 for the season for most American recruits to $2,200 for Gibson and probably at least $3,000 for Paige.

The idea was that most of the talent would concentrate on Trujillo's team, that it would win the league championship, and that the dictator's prestige would be enhanced and his enemies cowed. Which is generally the way it worked out. With Paige, Gibson, Bell, Griffith, Williams, and Bankhead combining with Cuban standouts Salazar and Tetelo Vargas, the Dominican star Enrique Latigua, and Petrucho Cepeda, Puerto Rico's home-run king, Los Dragones of Ciudad Trujillo finished first in the four-team league. They then defeated San Pedro de Macorís in a tough seven-game series for the championship, with Sammy Bankhead's homer winning the deciding contest for Paige. The *norte americanos* were quickly on their way back to the United States to finish out the baseball summer.

Baseball in general and black baseball even more so have always lent themselves to tall stories. Subsequent accounts of the climactic encounter with San Pedro de Macorís had Paige's team sequestered in jail cells the night before to keep them out of trouble, a win-or-die message communicated to the team, and soldiers with rifles lining the foul lines as Paige struggled to victory over both the opposition and a fearful stomachache. Little of that happened, but the Dominican episode became a centerpiece in a rapidly expanding Paigian folklore, to which nobody contributed more than Paige himself.

It wasn't folklore, though, that about 15 percent of the NNL's players had taken off with the season barely under way. Commissioner Morton wrote to Senator Robert F. Wagner of New York to protest the "stealing" of NNL players. Men in his league, complained Morton, ought to be satisfied with an average wage of $250 per month for a four-month season. It didn't seem to occur to Morton that the pay levels he cited might have been at the heart of the problem.

Gibson rejoined the Grays just before the NNL's first half ended and stayed for the remainder of the season. Homestead won the first half with a 21–9 record, as compared with 19–14 for Newark, which boasted what was hailed as the "dream infield" of Mule Suttles at first, Dick Seay at second, Willie Wells at shortstop, and Ray Dandridge at third. The gutted Crawfords were fifth, ahead of only the Black Yankees. The second half ended in disarray, with no official standings reported by the league office. Declared the NNL pennant winners, the Grays borrowed Dandridge, Wells, and pitcher Terris McDuffie from the Newark Eagles and met a combined Monarchs–American Giants squad in a nine-city postseason series that was little more than a traveling exhibition.

For black fans, neither indeterminate split-season competition nor migrating postseason series could ever equal the appeal of the annual East-West Game. The game of August 8, 1937—the first interleague matchup—was graced by Chicago mayor Edward J. Kelly, who threw out the first ball and then shared a box with NAL president Jackson. The East won 7–2, with the Grays' Buck Leonard homering for the East and the Monarchs' Ted Strong hitting one out for the West. The American Giants' Ted Trent took the loss; the Craws' Monty Morris, the East's starter, got credit for the win.

Meanwhile Paige was again leading a team of topflight black professionals to victory in the *Denver Post* tournament. Composed mostly of players who'd been in the Dominican League, the "Trujillo All-Stars" lost the opener of a decisive doubleheader to the Halliburton Cementers, with little Jimmy Walkup, who'd pitched briefly in the American League ten years earlier, outlasting Paige 6–4. But Leroy Matlock of the Crawfords coasted to an 11–1 win in the nightcap to give the Negro leaguers the tournament trophy and $5,179 in prize money.

Paige kept the team together for a tour that took it to Chicago for a brace of games with the semipro Duffy Florals and then to Philadelphia and New York to meet the Philadelphia Stars in contests promoted by Gus Greenlee at the Polo Grounds and Yankee Stadium. On Sunday, September 19, before a Polo Grounds crowd of 22,500 (including Thomas E. Dewey), young Johnny Taylor, pitching for a collection of NNLers, held the "Trujillo All-Stars" hitless, while Paige gave up a two-run homer to Washington's Jim West. A week later, though, Paige got his revenge, as his team bombed Taylor for nine runs before some 25,000 at Yankee Stadium.

The Dean brothers, both afflicted with sore arms, wouldn't be going barnstorming with Paige or anybody else. So before leaving for parts west to pitch for various teams, Paige apparently took it easy for a while among admirers in Harlem and may even have attended some of the 1937 Yankees–Giants World Series. In any case, following the Giants' third-straight loss, he sent a telegram to Bill Terry: "Giants seem to be having trouble. Try Ethiopian pitchers." (Two months later, Chester Washington, sports editor of the *Pittsburgh Courier*, sent his own wire to Pirates manager Pie Traynor, touting Gibson, Leonard, Paige, Bell, and Ray Brown as the "answer to your prayers right here in Pittsburgh.")[15]

· · · · ·

BOTH NEGRO LEAGUES realigned for 1938, and in both the spitball and other "trick pitches" were finally outlawed. In the NNL, Tom Wilson moved his Elite Giants to Baltimore, where they would rent the International League ballpark; black fans in the national capital had to watch an awful team that won only one league game before folding. The NAL dropped Cincinnati, Detroit, and St. Louis and added the Atlanta Black Crackers and Jacksonville Red Caps, although Jacksonville withdrew even before the halfway point.

The Grays—a disciplined, well-drilled outfit that was powered by the one–two punch of Leonard and Gibson—easily won the NNL's first half, and while no standings were published for the second half, the league office eventually announced that the Grays had led the remaining four clubs. The Memphis Red Sox and Atlanta Black Crackers were surprise winners in the NAL, but league president Jackson canceled their championship series because of the unavailability of Ponce de Leon Park, which the Black Crackers rented from the Southern Association Crackers.

The caliber of play in both Negro leagues was definitely below what it had been in 1937. Despite a lot of angry talk about permanently banning the Dominican deserters, the club owners ended up only fining them a week's pay. But 1938 brought more defections—to the Dominican Republic, Cuba, Venezuela, and most of all Mexico. Some who left wouldn't reappear in the Negro leagues for years.

In the spring of 1938, after supposedly signing with Newark and suggesting that Effa Manley become his "sideline girlfriend," Satchel Paige decided that he wouldn't pitch for the Eagles after all, even for the $5,000 that Abe Manley was willing to pay him.[16] For a time, he talked about playing in Argentina (which would have made him something of a baseball pioneer, inasmuch as that country had never shown much enthusiasm for the game). The Manleys secured a state court injunction to prevent Paige from jumping his contract, but the celebrated pitcher ignored that and left—not for Argentina but for Mexico, where Cool Papa Bell, Chet Brewer, Quincy Trouppe, and various lesser lights from the Negro leagues were already plying their skills in the strong professional circuit controlled by the wealthy Pasquel brothers. In May, the Manleys were able to convince the other NNL club owners to adopt a permanent ban on Paige.

As they had in the other Spanish-speaking countries, black players from the United States found conditions in Mexico generally to their liking. Besides being paid more, they lived in better hotels and apartments; went to whatever bars, restaurants, and other public places they wished; and didn't always have to worry about saying or doing the wrong thing—as every black person had to do in the cities and towns of the American South. As Johnny Taylor put it after he jumped to Mexico the next year, "Playing in the Negro

League, you were going in the back door. But in Mexico they treat you royally. No segregation."[17]

Back home, Jake Powell's witless remarks in his late-July radio interview at Comiskey Park produced a furor in the black press, nowhere more so than at the *Chicago Defender*, which was published on the city's South Side in the heart of black Chicago and not far from Comiskey Park. Frank A. "Fay" Young, sports editor of the *Defender*, called for Powell's banishment from baseball and a boycott of the Yankees and Ruppert's Beer by New York's black fandom. "Nothing in recent years," Young wrote, "has stirred the Race population . . . as did Powell's insult to our race. . . . My race is not pacified by the 10-day fine [*sic*] and Judge Landis and Powell's boss don't need to think we are."[18]

The Powell episode emphasized how much Organized Baseball would have to overcome if the doors to black ballplayers were ever to be opened. Yet black baseball itself continued to invite criticism and ridicule from both sides of the color line for its squabbling club owners, lack of professional umpiring staffs (and frequent players' assaults on umpires), nonchalant attitude toward schedules, piecemeal records, and various other shortcomings. The NNL, resignedly wrote Wendell Smith, a young reporter for the *Pittsburgh Courier*, was just as bad as white baseball people said—"nothing but a farce."[19]

The biggest gate receipts still came not from league games, but from matchups with white semipros and big days booked by Abe Saperstein or Eddie Gottlieb. On Sunday, May 29, for example, a crowd of 15,000 jammed Dexter Park for a Bushwicks–Crawfords doubleheader. Waite Hoyt (just released by Brooklyn) threw seven hitless innings, but the Craws scored three runs off his successor, while Theolic Smith held the Bushwicks to two runs. In the nightcap the Craws drove George Earnshaw from the mound after the former American League ace had given up twelve hits and six runs in six innings. And on Sunday, July 26, the Craws, Black Yankees, Elite Giants, and Stars simply ignored the league schedule in favor of a four-team doubleheader booked by Gottlieb that drew 18,000 to Yankee Stadium.

The East-West Game, played on August 21, lacked Satchel Paige, but it drew another record crowd—around 30,000—to Comiskey Park. The NALers won 5–4, the key moment coming when the Craws' Sammy Bankhead, playing center field, let a drive by Memphis's Neil Robinson get through his legs for what was scored as a three-run, inside-the-park homer.

Lloyd Lewis, then a reporter for the *Chicago Daily News* and later a best-selling author, attended that East-West Game. He judged the caliber of play to be a little above that of Class AA ball and a little below that of the major leagues. What particularly impressed Lewis was the black players' speed. "The bases were run with a swiftness and daring absent from the white man's game for 20 years," he wrote. The Negro leaguers reminded him of "the game when it was in its golden age, the days of McGraw and Tinker and Cobb and Chance." But Lewis was put off by the "trace of non-professionalism" when players made one-handed catches, especially Monarchs first baseman Ted Strong, who "insists upon 'showboating' with his glove."[20]

Testimonials to the quality of play in black baseball came from other white observers. In September the *New York Daily News*'s Jimmy Powers asked Waite Hoyt and several other former major leaguers who'd competed against black professionals to name the men they considered good enough to play in the majors. Seventeen were named, including Gibson, Wells, Leonard, Paige, Dihigo, and Johnny Taylor. Meanwhile Dizzy Dean, in an interview for the *Chicago Tribune* that was reprinted in virtually every black newspaper in the country, touted Paige as the best pitcher in all baseball.

But Paige was considerably less than that in the fall of 1938. His arm went lame in Mexico, and when he returned to the United States, inasmuch as he was barred from the NNL, he sought out J. L. Wilkinson in Kansas City. Wilkinson assigned Paige to the Monarchs' second team, sometimes billed as the Junior Monarchs and at other times as one of the many incarnations of Satchel Paige's All-Stars.

While Paige toured small towns in the central United States with the Monarchs' seconds, pitching a couple of innings at a time, Syd Pollock's Ethiopian Clowns—with players listed as "Askari," "Kalihari," "Tarzan," "Selassie," "Impo," and the like—entertained black and white fans in Atlanta and Jacksonville in games with the Black Crackers and Red Caps.

After the 1938 season, the era of Gus Greenlee in baseball history came to an end. Having invested heavily, lost heavily, and seen his once-splendid Crawfords reduced to mediocrity, Greenlee had his ballpark razed and turned over the property (which he'd leased from the city) to the Pittsburgh Housing Authority, which planned to build a project on the site. In February 1939 he resigned as NNL president and sold the Crawfords to investors in Toledo, who kept the name Crawfords as well as Oscar Charleston as manager.

Alex Pompez, eventually taken into custody by Mexican officials and extradited back to New York, struck a deal with District Attorney Dewey:

he would testify against a Tammany Hall bigwig who'd been receiving pay-offs from gangsters in exchange for pleading guilty to a misdemeanor charge and receiving a sentence of two years' probation. From here on, said the debonair Pompez as he watched the 1938 East-West Game, he intended to stick to baseball: "The money may not be as fast, but it is much less troublesome in the end." Pompez's rehabilitation seemed complete when he reorganized his Cubans club and gained reentry into the NNL. As Mark Ribowsky has noted, Pompez's record was of little concern to "his fellow blackball owners, who were after all not so different from him."[21]

. . . . .

BESIDES THE CUBANS, the 1939 NNL consisted of the Grays, Newark, Baltimore, Philadelphia, and the Black Yankees. For once, the NNL abandoned the split season and adopted the Shaughnessy playoff format, which had become standard throughout Organized Baseball's minor leagues. The Grays, with a 33–14 record, finished five games ahead of Newark over the regular season. In the playoffs, third-place Baltimore eliminated Newark three games to one, and the Grays did the same to fourth-place Philadelphia. But then the Elite Giants—sparked by Bill Wright, Sammy T. Hughes, and an eighteen-year-old catcher named Roy Campanella—won the single pennant-deciding game 2–0, played at Yankee Stadium on September 28.

The NAL started the season with the Monarchs, American Giants, Memphis, St. Louis, Cleveland, and Indianapolis, but Indianapolis dropped out almost as soon as the season began. The Toledo Crawfords, late of Pittsburgh, joined the league for the season's second half. The Monarchs were first-half winners; apparently the St. Louis Stars led the field in the second half, but no standings were published. In any case, the Monarchs and the Stars met in a postseason series, which Kansas City won three games to two.

As always the East-West Game was the highlight of the season. Booked by Abe Saperstein, the second interleague spectacle attracted an officially tabulated attendance of 39,489—the biggest crowd to see Negro leaguers in action up to then. Many people came to Chicago on special trains from as far away as Memphis, Nashville, and Little Rock. Apparently at ease in unfamiliar surroundings, American League president William Harridge sat through the game alongside league presidents Ferdinand Q. Morton and J. M. Martin. Getting home runs from Memphis's Neil Robinson and St. Louis's Dan Wilson, the West scored four times in the last two innings off

the Grays' Roy Partlow; Memphis's Ted Radcliffe got the win. (A second
Gottlieb-booked East-West Game, held at Yankee Stadium six weeks later,
drew 16,000 and was a 10–2 walkover for the East, highlighted by Gibson's
bases-loaded triple.)

Losses to the Mexican League continued to decimate NNL and NAL
rosters. By 1939 such front liners as Johnny Taylor, Ray Dandridge, Willie
Wells, Leroy Matlock, Bert Hunter, and Bill Wright had also opted for many
pesos over a modest number of dollars. The biggest catch the Pasquels
hadn't yet made was Josh Gibson. In that off-season of 1939/1940, the big
slugger came no closer to Mexico than Cuban and Puerto Rican winter
ball, but few people expected that Cum Posey could count on his loyalty
indefinitely.

. . . . .

BY THE LATE 1930S, so many white players had competed against so
many black professionals in barnstorming series and semipro ball (or had
watched Negro-league encounters such as the Grays' late-afternoon games
at Forbes Field) that a great deal of knowledge of particular players was
current within white baseball circles. The consensus was that while quite
a few Negro leaguers were of big-league caliber, most weren't. Harry Danning, who played against some of the best black professionals in the California League, later estimated that Negro-league teams had only two or
three topflight players apiece. "The guys who were outstanding," said Danning, "were great because they played against mediocre players."[22]

Lest Danning's remarks be dismissed, one ought to take into account
some interviews that Sam Lacy of the *Baltimore Afro-American* conducted
in August 1939 with managers Vic Harris of the Homestead Grays, Jud
Wilson of the Philly Stars, and Felton Snow of the Baltimore Elite Giants.
Lacy asked each manager how many of his contemporaries were actually
ready for the majors. "It's like this," said Harris. "We do have some good
ballplayers among us, but not nearly as many fit for the majors as seems to
be the belief." Wilson's view was that "there are some fellows who could
probably make it, but at least half of them wouldn't because they are too
old." He went on to name thirteen players—all NNLers or former NNLers
now playing in Mexico. Snow took a different tack, expressing a view that
was common among both white baseball people and better-educated
blacks: "We've got so many guys who just wouldn't act right. Some of these
fellows who are pretty good out there on the diamond would give you a

heartache elsewhere. . . . You see, there are so many men who get $3 or $4 in their pockets, and right away, they want to tell 'the man' where he can go."[23]

That same summer, the *Pittsburgh Courier*'s Wendell Smith talked to all eight National League managers and forty National League players, asking each how he felt about having black players in Organized Baseball. Impressed with his interviewees' familiarity with black baseball, Smith also observed a general lack of resistance to the idea. The white players almost invariably cited Satchel Paige and Josh Gibson as ready right now for the big leagues. Manager Casey Stengel of the Boston Bees was more reminiscent, recalling the abilities of black stars from earlier in the century, such as "Bullet Joe" Rogan, John Donaldson, and the Cuban right-hander Jose Mendez. Yet Stengel, like Felton Snow, was skeptical about the attitudes that black players might bring into Organized Baseball.

Most of Smith's interviewees were northern-born. Although he found the views of the Oklahoman Pepper Martin surprisingly liberal, Arkansan Paul Dean brushed him off when Smith approached him in the lobby of the Schenley Hotel. Carl Hubbell, another native Oklahoman, praised the talents of Paige and Gibson, but the great Giants left-hander still favored a separate league for blacks "that could be built up." By contrast, Pirates manager Pie Traynor, a Massachusetts native, spoke without reservation: "I have seen countless numbers of Negro ballplayers who could have made the grade in the majors." Traynor didn't understand "why the ban against Negro players exists at all."[24]

As usual Leo Durocher, Brooklyn's brash young manager (also a Massachusetts native), was hyperbolically outspoken: "Sure, I've seen plenty of colored boys who could make the grade in the majors. Hell, I've seen a million." But the remarks of Tennessean Bill Terry, manager of the reigning National League champions, were doubtless closer to the controlling assumptions at Commissioner Landis's office and elsewhere within Organized Baseball. Blacks, Terry thought, would never play with whites in the major leagues because of "the problem of mingling socially with the other players and traveling about the country together."[25]

Smith predictably concluded from his interviews that "the big league owners have misinformed the public by stating that their employees would object to Negro ball players in the majors." But Jud Wilson, who'd been through everything Jim Crow baseball had to offer, saw it another way: "It will never be, because the big league game, as it is now, is over-run with Southern blood."[26] Wilson exaggerated—no more than a third of any major-league roster in the late 1930s consisted of southern-born players—but his was a common explanation and, for whites, a convenient rationalization for maintaining the color line.

. . . . .

MEANWHILE, the Negro leagues got along as best they could. Infighting went on as usual in the NNL, with Alex Pompez deserting the Manleys and the Black Yankees' Semler to join Eddie Gottlieb and Cum Posey in electing Tom Wilson league president. That prompted Randy Dixon, a young *Pittsburgh Courier* columnist, to publish an open letter to Wilson complaining about NNL affairs in general. "I shouldn't use the word 'league,' " grumbled Dixon, "because a league is supposed to represent several things, not any of which are present in your Negro National League setup."[27]

Now dividing their Sunday games between Forbes Field and Griffith Stadium in Washington, the "Washington-Homestead Grays" finished first again in the 1940 NNL with a 28–13 record, versus Baltimore's 25–14 and Newark's 25–17. Ray Brown won twenty-four of twenty-eight decisions, but he didn't have Gibson as a battery mate. In April the man hailed as the Babe Ruth of the Negro leagues and, after Paige, black baseball's foremost gate attraction left to play in Venezuela, taking pitcher Roy Partlow with him. According to Cum Posey, Gibson had received a $1,000 bonus and would be paid $700 per month in Venezuela.

As for Paige, the Manleys still insisted that he was the property of the Newark Eagles and ought not to be pitching for anybody else in either league. In June, though, they agreed to an arrangement whereby Paige would remain Kansas City property in exchange for the transfer from the NAL's Toledo-Indianapolis Crawfords of infielder John "Buzz" Clarkson and pitcher Ernest "Spoon" Carter. Paige, still working his arm back into shape, remained with the Monarchs' second team until late in the season, when J. L. Wilkinson brought him back for a couple of outings in Detroit and Chicago. His arm fully recovered, Paige worked nine innings both times, throwing a three-hitter against the American Giants and striking out ten.

Although Paige was already the one figure in black baseball with whom white fans everywhere were familiar, that summer he received his first national exposure in the white press—as, for that matter, did black baseball in general. In June, *Time* ran a condescending and often erroneous piece about "Satchelfoots" (as the magazine inexplicably christened him) but acknowledged that "many a shepherd of a limping major club has made no secret of his yearning to trade more than a couple of buttsprung outfielders for colored players of the caliber of Satchelfoots Paige."[28]

The next month, the weekly *Saturday Evening Post* carried a longer article by Ted Shane that dealt mostly with Paige but also with the makeup and ambience of black baseball. Shane described the black game as "much more showmanlike than white baseball. . . . Their baseball is to white baseball as the Harlem stomp is to the sedate ballroom waltz. . . . They play faster, seem to enjoy it more than white players." Paige, Shane wrote, had "apelike arms" and the "Stepinfetchit accent in his speech," but "behind his sleepy eyes his brain works shrewdly." Paige's greatness was widely recognized; Dizzy Dean had put a price tag of $200,000 apiece on him and Gibson. But the Negro leagues also had "other players of DiMaggio or Foxx caliber," including Buck Leonard, "the Lou Gehrig of Negro ball."[29]

With the veteran Hilton Smith heading a strong pitching staff, manager Andy Cooper's well-balanced Monarchs hadn't really needed Paige in 1940 NAL competition. They won the first half with a 12–7 record and were declared second-half winners as well, although no final standings were published. Cum Posey claimed that he'd offered to pit his Grays against the Monarchs in the first black World Series since 1927, but Wilkinson and Tom Baird had turned him down.

For the second year in a row, Eddie Gottlieb promoted five four-team doubleheaders at Yankee Stadium, with the August 4 event the first to match clubs from the different leagues (St. Louis–New Orleans versus Baltimore, Memphis versus the Black Yankees). But, as always, the East-West Game was the season's centerpiece. About 25,000 spectators, some 15,000 fewer than in 1939, witnessed the most lopsided game in the series' history: an eleven-run pounding of Memphis's Eugene Bremmer and three successors, while Philadelphia's Henry McHenry, the Cubans' Poppa Ruiz, and the Grays' Ray Brown shut out the West on five hits.[30]

As Tom Wilson's team (basically his Elite Giants minus Roy Campanella) again competed in the California League and such stalwarts as the Grays' Buck Leonard and Ray Brown; Baltimore's Campanella; and Newark's Monte Irvin, Buzz Clarkson, and Lenny Pearson performed in Puerto Rico, the NAL and NNL club owners had reason to look forward to black baseball's best year since the late 1920s.

. . . . .

BY THE BEGINNING OF 1941, the Roosevelt administration had won from Congress a rearmament program that was rapidly putting Americans back to work in steel mills, rubber factories, aircraft plants, shipyards, and the rest of an expanding war-economy infrastructure. This time the Depression really was coming to an end, and people had money in their pockets for just about everything, including baseball tickets. Jobs were opening up for black people as well, although A. Phillip Randolph, president of the Brotherhood of Pullman Car Porters, had to threaten a mass march on Washington to pressure Roosevelt into creating the Fair Employment Practices Commission (FEPC). (The FEPC's efforts to minimize discrimination in hiring and pay scales would be only partly successful.)

In 1941 Satchel Paige was again blowing batters away and performing as the top individual attraction in all of baseball. Although contracted to the Monarchs, he was still free-lancing much of the time. On May 15, before a Yankee Stadium crowd of 20,000 that included Mayor Fiorello LaGuardia, Paige opened the NNL season by pitching the Black Yankees to a 5–3 victory over the Philly Stars. (Paige got the publicity, but Chet Brewer pitched a better game in the nightcap, throttling the Black Yankees for the Stars, 4–1.) In June, Paige and still another band of his All-Stars met the Ethiopian Clowns in a Sunday doubleheader at Crosley Field, Cincinnati. Between his Monarchs salary and his fees for appearances elsewhere, Paige was likely the best-compensated ballplayer in the world.

But the pay was also good in Mexico—so good that the outflow of talent continued. Cum Posey thought he had Josh Gibson tied up for the 1941 season, but the brawny catcher, thoroughly aware of his own value by now, parlayed his Grays contract into a fatter deal in Mexico and left to play for the Vera Cruz Blues.[31] For the eight-month Mexican League season, Gibson would be paid $6,000, which was a record straight salary for a Negro leaguer. Gibson's teammates with Vera Cruz included Willie Wells, Johnny Taylor, and Ray Dandridge. Other stellar black professionals in Mexico that season included Theolic Smith, Leroy Matlock, Bill Wright, and Bill Perkins (Mexico City); Sammy T. Hughes and Roy Welmaker (Torreon); Cool Papa Bell, Sammy Bankhead, and Quincy Trouppe (Monterrey); Ted Strong and Bert Hunter (Puebla); and Buzz Clarkson (Tampico). All told, about twenty-five Negro leaguers were playing south of the border.

Despite their absence and what was undoubtedly diminished quality of play, black baseball shared in the prosperity of the last peacetime baseball season and commanded its biggest crowds in more than a decade. The Chicago American Giants' ancient wooden ballpark having burned over the winter, the Comiskey heirs agreed that besides profiting from the East-West Game, they would rent Comiskey Park to the American Giants for nighttime and Sunday dates when the White Sox were on the road. Even

Walter O. Briggs, the haughty owner of the Detroit Tigers, finally acknowledged the extra money to be had from renting to black teams; early in August a crowd of 27,949 watched a Grays–Elite Giants doubleheader at Briggs Stadium—the first black baseball on the Tigers' home field since 1921.

Although the 1941 American Giants prospered in their new surroundings and were still a strong team, how they or anybody else did in the NAL can't be determined, because standings weren't published for either half of the season. By contrast, the NNL again made it through a whole season—a split one for 1941—with its membership intact and fairly reliable figures on league standings. Even without Gibson, the Grays were able to come out on top, easily taking the first half with a 17–9 record and then winning three of four games from the Cubans, who played only six official league games (winning four) in the second half.

More than anything else, the 1941 East-West Game, with Satchel Paige again available to excite fan interest, testified that the Depression was fading and better times were ahead in black baseball. The players, who'd never been paid anything except expenses for their services, threatened to strike unless they were cut in on the gate receipts. They finally agreed to take $50 apiece and make way for the foremost spectacle thus far in black baseball annals. The paid attendance of 50,256 was not only bigger than that of the first major-league All-Star Game eight years earlier but one of the biggest turnouts in all of baseball that season.

The Newark Eagles' young Monte Irvin, later a New York Giants star, remembered singing a number written by Count Basie and recorded by Jimmy Rushing called "Goin' to Chicago" as he rode the train taking him and two teammates to the game: "Goin' to Chicago. I couldn't wait. . . . You didn't go to Chicago to sleep. By comparison, I found out later, the big league All-Star Game wasn't nearly as much fun." The atmosphere at Comiskey Park was festively black. "The fans started arriving early, while we were out on the field," another player recorded in his diary. "They were dressed, I tell you. The men had on their Sunday best suits, some guys with zoot suits. The ladies had on big hats and tight dresses and jewelry. Everybody watched everybody else and took turns trying to look finer than their neighbors. I guess a lot of folks had brought liquor in with them, and a lot had brought food. . . . In the East-West game people come to have a good time."[32]

The game itself wasn't especially memorable. The East jumped out to a two-run lead on Buck Leonard's homer, added six more in the fifth inning, and won 8–3. The Eagles' Terris McDuffie, the Cubans' 5-foot 7-inch Dave Barnhill (who'd formerly hurled for the Ethiopian Clowns as "Impo"), and three successors held the West batters at bay; Paige made his required appearance with the game lost, pitching two scoreless innings.

Later that month, Syd Pollock's roundly criticized Ethiopian Clowns won the annual *Denver Post* tournament, defeating the Bona Allens of Buford, Georgia, in the second game of a doubleheader after the Bona Allens had won the opener. The Georgia team's pitchers included former big-leaguers Johnny Lanning and Cletus "Boots" Poffenberger and future big-leaguer Sig Jakucki; the Clowns' ace was Roosevelt Davis, a seventeen-year professional whose Clowns sobriquet was "Macou."

There was an element of show business in much of what went on outside Organized Baseball—in, for example, the House of David's long hair and beards and their juggling acts or in Paige's stunt in games with weak semi-pro clubs of calling in his fielders before he struck out the side. But while Pollock's Clowns were mostly good athletes and played competitive ball, they were first and last entertainers. Apart from their pseudo-African titles and jabberings, they'd come to be known for their "shadowball" routine, wherein, with remarkable timing and deftness (but minus a ball), they pantomimed pregame fly shagging and infield practice. But if that pregame pantomime was the particular speciality of the Ethiopian Clowns, "shadowball" could serve as a metaphor for all of black professional baseball, which had always performed in the shadows of the National Pastime.

That fall Josh Gibson—a famous man within those shadowed circumstances—came back to Pittsburgh after a Mexican League season in which his Vera Cruz Blues team won the pennant with a 67–35 record and he was credited with a .374 batting average, thirty-three home runs, and 124 runs batted in. While he was away, Cum Posey had sued him for $10,000 for breach of contract, won his suit in a local court, and as compensation taken possession of Gibson's house on the Hill. A somewhat chastened Gibson met with Sonnyman Jackson (who could apply muscle Posey lacked) and signed a two-year contract in exchange for the return of his house.

On that fairly tawdry note, the pre–World War II history of the Negro leagues might be brought to an end. Within another few weeks, the Japanese attack at Pearl Harbor would plunge the United States formally into the conflict. During the war years, older players such as Paige, Gibson, Leonard, Ray Brown, and Hilton Smith would continue to ply their trade in the Negro leagues. Others such as Dandridge and Bell would remain in Mexico, while others (Willie Wells, Roy Welmaker) would eventually return north to finish their careers. Still others—younger Negro leaguers such as Newark's Monte Irvin and Max Manning—would enter the armed forces, where they would serve their country under the same Jim Crow practices that had kept them out of Organized Baseball. On the home front, Paige on several occasions took no pay for pitching in games that served as war-bond rallies and raised money for war charities.

Black baseball would enjoy its best times during the war years. As Paige said, "Everybody had money and everybody was looking around for entertainment."[33] In the fall of 1942, the NNL and NAL finally reestablished the black World Series, featuring a legendary confrontation between the Monarchs' Paige and the Grays' Gibson. By war's end, the shadows that had hung over black baseball since before the turn of the century were starting to lift; late in 1945 Jackie Robinson, a Monarchs infielder and former multisport collegiate star on the Pacific coast, was signed to play in the Brooklyn Dodgers organization. In the postwar era, the color line would fall throughout Organized Baseball, yet for nearly all those who'd played through the hard times of the 1930s, it would be too late.

CHAPTER 10

Recovery and War, 1940–1941

LARK GRIFFITH wasn't called the Old Fox for nothing. At the major leagues' December 1939 meetings in Cincinnati—amid much mewling about Yankees domination—Griffith convinced representatives of six other American League franchises (the Yankees abstaining) to adopt his proposed rule: henceforth no team would make an exchange of players with the reigning league champion except when a player was put on waivers. Sputtered Branch Rickey, "They've gone communistic in that league. Socialistic, I should say—trying to curtail enterprise."[1] The club representatives in Rickey's league voted down a similar motion.

Of course, much of the Yankees' success resulted from emulating what Rickey had started: fashioning a farm system and developing young players in the minors. By 1940 the St. Louis Cardinals owned or had working agreements with thirty-two minor-league teams. Brooklyn and Detroit had twelve farm teams each; the Yankees, eleven; the Boston Red Sox, nine. But if the necessity to build farm systems had become conventional wisdom in both leagues, poorer franchises such as Washington, the Boston Bees, the St. Louis Browns, and the two Philadelphia clubs had to rely exclusively on working agreements, which frequently shifted from year to year.

Only the Chicago Cubs still tried to operate in the old way, seeking to buy players (in an increasingly tight market), taking whatever was available in the annual draft of eligible minor leaguers, and trading with other National League teams. Philip K. Wrigley owned the Los Angeles franchise and ballpark, but the Angels were operated in such a way that the Cubs actually had to buy their players. Only Tulsa in the Texas League, with which the Cubs had formed a working agreement, truly functioned as a Cubs farm team.

Rickey would always insist that the expansion of the Cardinals' and others' farm systems had saved the minors in the Depression years. Whether one bought Rickey's argument or not, the fact remained that despite the Roosevelt Recession the minors had recovered splendidly from the doldrums of 1932 and 1933. In 1939 forty-one minor leagues attracted approximately 18.5 million customers, up some 300,000 from the previous year and a new record for the kind of professional baseball that most people still paid to see. North Carolina could qualify as the minors' unofficial capital; for the 1940 season, the Tarheel State would have twenty-six teams in four leagues.

. . . . .

DESPITE THEIR MONOTONOUS SUCCESS on the field and their productive network of farm teams, the Yankees seemed to some observers to be behind the times. In running away with a fourth-straight American League pennant, the New Yorkers had been outdrawn at home by both Brooklyn and Cincinnati, clubs thoroughly committed to nighttime play. Ed Barrow was still defiant on that subject. The Yankees had been willing to play at night on the road to help other American League clubs, said Barrow, "but never will you see night ball in the Stadium. The thing will die out. Night ball is not baseball. . . . The stunt will wear out its welcome."[2]

Yet the trend was clearly in the other direction. The forty-two night games played in the major leagues in 1939 attracted 987,955 customers, with Brooklyn (206,000) and the White Sox (205,265) leading the way. In November, despite Bill Terry's conviction that "we are catering to a fickle attendance in staging an unnatural attraction," Giants president Horace Stoneham announced that he was spending $166,000 to illuminate the Polo Grounds.[3] Shortly thereafter, Pittsburgh president William Benswanger revealed that Forbes Field was also being equipped for nighttime play.

Said Connie Mack resignedly, "None of us . . . are particularly pleased with the arrival of the night game, but we cannot close our eyes to the demands of the public." Yet Larry MacPhail, night ball's originator in the majors, cautioned against too many games under the lights. "If you play more than one night game a week," argued MacPhail, "you will overdo it. . . . You cannot cheapen the sport and get away with it."[4]

The St. Louis Browns were anxious to "overdo it"—if that's what playing more than seven nighters amounted to. So was the Cardinals' Sam Breadon, who'd complained for some time that St. Louis couldn't support two big-league teams but was finally willing to split with Browns owner Donald Barnes on the cost of putting up lights in Sportsman's Park. But whereas the Cardinals would adhere to the league limit of seven night games, the American League voted to allow the indigent Browns to play up to fourteen nighters.

Players might grouse that night baseball interfered with their meal routines, disrupted their sleep patterns, and even bothered their eyes, but as Lloyd Waner put it, "Nocturnal ball is bad for the players, but good for the gate receipts."[5] The 1940 big-league schedule would have ten of the sixteen teams playing seventy-seven night games in eight ballparks.

Tom Yawkey had no interest in night ball at Fenway Park (and wouldn't for another seven years), but he continued to modify the facility otherwise. In the 1939/1940 off-season—mainly to accommodate the left-hand–hitting Ted Williams—low-fenced bullpens for both home and visiting teams were built in front of the huge right-field bleachers, which cut the distance to straightaway right by 23 feet. And while Billy Evans was building a network of minor-league affiliates, Yawkey's money was still available for promising acquisitions, such as the $40,000 paid to San Francisco for bespectacled center fielder Dominic DiMaggio, the youngest (and smallest) of the ball-playing DiMaggios.

Baseball had already made the DiMaggio family one of the nation's most familiar, and now Joe DiMaggio's wedding, within a few days of his brother's sale to the Red Sox, became a gaudy media spectacle. A huge, unruly mass of people jammed and surrounded Saints Peter and Paul Church in San Francisco's North Beach district, where on November 19 DiMaggio married a twenty-year-old blonde actress named Dorothy Arnoldine Olson. A Minnesota native who'd taken the show-business name Dorothy Arnold, she'd met DiMaggio two years earlier in New York during the filming of *Manhattan Merry-Go-Round*, in which the ballplayer had a small speaking part.

. . . . .

A VERY TIRED JOKE about getting married was that a husband thereby acquired his ball and chain. To Kenesaw Mountain Landis's way of thinking, farm-system baseball attached a figurative ball and chain to young ballplayers. The commissioner's spring 1938 directive that freed seventy-four players in the Cardinals organization had outraged Branch Rickey, embarrassed Sam Breadon, and made sensational news, but it hadn't really hurt a talent-loaded system that was nearly three times bigger than anybody else's. Of the twenty-five players on St. Louis's 1939 roster, only five hadn't come up through its farm system.

But in January 1940. Landis dealt a truly damaging blow to the Detroit Tigers when he made free agents of ninety-one players currently in their organization. That left the Tigers with only forty-three minor leaguers still under their control and cost them an estimated $500,000 worth of players. Moreover, Landis directed that Detroit pay a total of $47,250 to fifteen players who'd been sold to other organizations. And while Landis's action against the Cardinals had cut loose only one future major leaguer, five players listed on the Tigers' 1940 spring roster were now free agents.

Landis reconsidered the case of rookie pitcher Paul "Dizzy" Trout and decided that the Tigers had handled his assignments legally. Two freed pitchers would have inconsequential careers in the National League. But outfielder Roy Cullenbine received $25,000 for signing with Brooklyn, and Landis voided Detroit's recent trade of Benny McCoy, a highly regarded young infielder, to the Athletics for outfielder Wally Moses. Thus to get McCoy, Connie Mack had to come up with $45,000 from the franchise's skimpy cash reserves.

That spring—as players, coaches, managers, sportswriters, and quite a number of wives and small children migrated to the training sites from Florida to southern California—the war in Europe was six months old; the Asian conflict had been going for some twenty months. The American news media (which now included network radio) paid relatively little attention to the vast Sino-Japanese struggle, while in western Europe, in what was labeled the "Phony War," the Anglo-French and German forces had yet to engage each other in significant operations.

Since November, however, Finland's stubborn resistance to the Soviet Union's unprovoked invasion had won great sympathy in the United States and sparked a series of aid-to-Finland rallies across the nation. Organized Baseball officially joined in by staging two games—on March 10 in Los Angeles and a week later in Tampa—between squads made up of players from teams training in the two states. The games raised about $30,000 for the Finnish Relief Fund, although by the time Bobby Feller pitched for the American Leaguers versus the National Leaguers in Florida, the exhausted Finns had yielded to Soviet demands, and the war had ended.

Earlier that month, the *Sporting News* had received a letter from Genbrugge, Belgium, from a young Belgian citizen and baseball enthusiast named Frank du Cypar, who enclosed a check to cover his subscription for the next three years and affirmed that he was a Yankees fan. Within another two months, du Cypar's homeland was being stormed by German forces driving through the Low Countries into France. The Phony War was over; the German conquest of western Europe—completed with the collapse of French resistance by the end of June—would leave Britain standing alone against Nazi power.

Yet whatever one felt about what was happening in Europe and Asia, it was all still happening a long way from American shores. Recently developed opinion polls (which had added a new dimension to American public discourse) indicated that while sentiment was decidedly anti-German and anti-Japanese, an overwhelming majority of citizens thought that the United States ought to stay out of war anywhere. By the spring of 1940, the principal indicators of commercial and industrial activity, which had advanced the previous autumn with the outbreak of the European conflict, had again slipped below the one hundred mark; more than 9 million Americans were still unemployed. For readily understandable reasons, people still tended to view events at home as affecting their lives more than anything happening abroad.

So for tens of millions of Americans that spring of 1940, what still held more interest than anything else beyond their own immediate circumstances was the coming baseball season—the first since 1925 to open without Lou Gehrig in the Yankees lineup. The previous December, the Base Ball Writers Association of America had voted to waive its rule that a player had to be retired for five years to be eligible for election to the Hall of Fame and had unanimously elected Gehrig. The Yankees also permanently retired his uniform number (four)—the first player to be so honored by any club. Gehrig himself, although stooped and tiring easily, accepted an appointment as a parole commissioner for New York City from Mayor La Guardia.

. . . . .

THAT SPRING, the Cincinnati Reds, defending National League champions, gathered farther south than any other team, doing their early conditioning in Havana. There, for a guarantee of $6,000, they played to a loss, a win, and a tie against a picked team of Cuban professionals managed by the venerable Adolfo Luque. In the first game of the series, Johnny Vander Meer gave up a 500-foot home run to Alejandro Crespo, a husky outfielder who would soon join the Negro National League's New York Cubans (and later have a long career in Mexico). Five of the Cuban players, wrote the *Cincinnati Enquirer*'s Lou Smith, were "blacker than the well known eight ball," but the Cubans' speed—"jackrabbits in uniform," in Smith's description—was their most impressive quality.[6]

As usual, unhappy players weren't hard to find that spring. At Catalina Island, the Cubs' sumptuous spring base, Bill Lee, who'd been paid $25,000 and won nineteen games in 1939, protested to everybody who'd listen about having to accept a $5,000 reduction in salary. (In fact, Lee's career had already gone into irreversible decline; over the next two seasons, his combined record would be 17–31.) Joe Medwick thought that after batting .332 in 1939 he deserved better than another contract for $18,000, but of course he eventually signed it. Zeke Bonura complained to Bill Terry about being cut by $5,000 and was told, "You'll take $10,000 or leave it."[7] Bonura signed but then aired his grievance in the press, whereupon Terry sold him to Washington (where he stayed only until July, when Clark Griffith peddled him to the Cubs). Still another player facing a dubious future that spring (or so he thought) was Harold "Pee Wee" Reese, a flashy shortstop purchased by Brooklyn from Louisville. Although great days awaited Reese with the Dodgers, at the time the young Kentuckian didn't like his prospects. "That's the last place in the world I'd want to go to," he said. "All you ever read about is guys getting hit in the head by fly balls. . . . I don't want to go there."[8]

For others, though, things were definitely looking up. The previous fall Pie Traynor, who, as one reporter put it, "treated his men a lot better than they treated him," had been fired at Pittsburgh.[9] Now, in San Bernardino, California, Frank Frisch was happy to be out of the broadcasting booth and back on the field as Traynor's successor. Drafted by the Giants in the off-season, Paul Dean was also happy to be back in the majors, as was Tex Carleton, who'd had a big year with Milwaukee that got his contract purchased by Brooklyn for $10,000. And accompanied by his black chauffeur-valet and Chow dog, Dixie Walker arrived in Clearwater, Florida, confident that after six injury-plagued seasons in the American League, he'd finally gotten his career on track with the Dodgers.

Hank Greenberg, coming off a season in which he'd hit twenty-five fewer home runs and batted in thirty-four fewer runs than in 1938, struck a deal with the Detroit front office: he would agree to move from first base to left field, thereby making a secure place in the lineup for Rudy York;

but if he had to learn how to chase fly balls, then he wanted more money—$40,000 to be precise. After some haggling, the Tigers agreed to pay Greenberg the biggest salary since Babe Ruth's.

For the 1940 season, Greenberg and everybody else who swung a bat on a regular basis could expect to have their averages reduced by at least a few points. After a year's trial, the joint major-leagues rules committee (whose decisions were governing throughout Organized Baseball) had decided to repeal the sacrifice fly. For 1940 a caught fly that resulted in a tag-up and score from third base would again be just another out.

Hank Greenberg was at the peak of his career, but Carl Hubbell would struggle to win eleven games (while losing twelve) and never again win more than eleven. Dizzy Dean, once Hubbell's great rival for National League pitching supremacy, disembarked at Catalina Island three weeks late and full of complaints about his $10,000 salary. Dean also predicted that Gabby Hartnett—with whom he'd been on the outs since the previous summer—wouldn't finish the season as Cubs manager. When Hartnett fined him $100 for being late for a train at Topeka, Kansas, and then wouldn't give him permission to visit his father in Dallas or his mother's grave in Arkansas, Dean publicly referred to his manager as "tomato face" and "pickle puss." Commented Philip Wrigley, "We bought insubordination when we bought Dean."[10]

A discouraging season awaited Dean. After being hit hard in several starts in April and May, he found himself demoted to Tulsa, where he packed people into ballparks wherever he took the mound, worked 142 innings, and fooled enough Texas League hitters to compile an 8–8 record. But late in August, when he returned to the Cubs, he would still be throwing his "nothin' ball," and his baseball future was as unpromising as ever.

Both Carl Hubbell and Dizzy Dean belonged to the old school of pitchers who were expected to finish what they started—and expected as much of themselves. But by 1940, the trend was increasingly toward the use of pitchers who were paid to work largely or entirely in relief. That dismayed Honus Wagner, who put the blame on the lively ball, which made it harder for pitchers to coast with a lead. "Unless the pitcher gets a break," said Wagner, "soon it will be a parade of two, three and four-inning pitchers. . . . And the more relief pitchers you have in a game, the longer and drearier the game."[11]

. . . . .

THE OLD HALL OF FAMER spoke more prophetically than he could have imagined, but the baseball of 1940 still offered plenty of strong-armed, durable hurlers. Twenty-one-year-old Bobby Feller began the 1940 season before 20,187 shivering Chicagoans by doing something not done before (or since): pitching a no-hit, no-run game on opening day. The same day, in the season opener in Washington, the Red Sox's Lefty Grove pitched perfect ball for seven innings until Ted Williams muffed a fly in left field. Grove had to settle for a two-hit, 1–0 victory over knuckleballer Dutch Leonard. In the locker room, Grove gave the young Californian the kind of chastisement he'd given other erring teammates in the past. Much of Boston's numerous sports press corps also got on Williams's case, and his long-running feud with the "knights of the typewriter," as he came to call the Boston writers, was under way.

Williams's persistent brassiness and self-centeredness didn't win him any friends. Although the previous winter he'd dressed up for a black-tie dinner in his honor given by the Boston writers, from then on he disdained neckties of any kind—at a time when ballplayers seldom appeared in public without them. "I've found out," cracked Williams, "that you don't have to wear a necktie—if you can hit." Later that season, stung by something that had been written about him, he was quoted as saying that he was underpaid (at $12,500) and that he'd rather be a fireman in San Diego than a ballplayer in Boston. That prompted the waggish Jimmy Dykes to outfit his White Sox players with toy firemen's helmets and have them yell "Fireman! Save my child!" whenever Williams came to bat.[12]

But if sensitive and moody, "the Kid" could hit. Although he missed ten games with minor injuries, Williams whacked twenty-three home runs, drove in 113 runs, batted .344, and led the majors with 134 runs scored. (In September he appeared on the cover of *Life*; inside, a photo layout showed Williams, clad only in swim trunks, demonstrating his batting form.) Williams, Jimmie Fox, Bobby Doerr, and player-manager Joe Cronin powered a lineup that scored lots of runs and kept the Red Sox in contention over the first half of the season. But Boston's pitching was shaky (as it would be most of the time for the next twenty years). Lefty Grove—perhaps the first pitcher to become truly obsessive about reaching three hundred career victories—laboriously accumulated seven more wins to end the season with 293. Only two Boston pitchers won as many as twelve games for a team that finished tied with Dykes's White Sox for fourth place.

For the fourth time in five springs, Joe DiMaggio wasn't ready to start the season. Hampered by a leg injury, the newlywed didn't get into the lineup until May 7, at which point the Yankees had lost their last eight games and occupied last place. Top-heavy favorites to win another pennant,

Joe McCarthy's club floundered week after week, with everybody but DiMaggio (who batted .352 to win his second-straight title), Charlie Keller, and Joe Gordon finding base hits hard to come by. Lefty Gomez battled arm troubles and pitched only twenty-seven innings; Monte Pearson was generally ineffective, as was Spud Chandler. Red Ruffing was still the staff's bellwether, winning fifteen games, but as the season progressed, McCarthy increasingly gave the ball to his younger moundsmen: Atley Donald, Marvin Breuer, Ernie "Tiny" Bonham, and left-hander Marius Russo. It was the beginning of June before the Yankees reached the .500 mark; early in August they were still in fifth place, nine and a half games out of first.

Dan Daniel thought he'd identified "the paramount factor" behind the Yankees' inability to win consistently. Pointing to the off-season marriages of DiMaggio, Chandler, and Russo, those in recent years of Red Rolfe and Frank Crosetti, and upcoming nuptials for a couple of other Yankees, Daniel believed that so much matrimony had been bad for the team (although he didn't specify whether it was a matter of wives' spats with each other or husbands' emotional distraction or maybe even physical debilitation).[13]

In the *New York Daily News*, Jimmy Powers suggested something even more outlandish: the disease that afflicted Lou Gehrig, wrote Powers in an August 18 column, had spread to other Yankees; the ball club had been hit by a "mass polio epidemic."[14] Enraged, Gehrig sued Powers and the *Daily News* for $1 million; Bill Dickey and other Yankees subsequently filed their own suits. Five weeks later, the newspaper printed a front-page retraction and apology.

By then the Yankees had climbed into the thick of the tightest American League pennant race since 1908. Although Boston and the White Sox dropped off the pace in August, Cleveland and Detroit stayed within a few games of each other week after week.

The 1940 Indians weren't the heavy hitters of past years. Little Roy Weatherly was the team's only .300 batter; shortstop Lou Boudreau, its only hundred-plus-RBI man. Hal Trosky, once the team's slugging leader, battled migraines and sinusitis and drove in only ninety-three runs. It was a ball club that played sound defense and relied on Bobby Feller's mound heroics. Feller followed up his opening-day no-hitter with twenty-six more victories against eleven losses. Besides leading the majors in wins, Feller also started the most games (thirty-seven), completed the most (thirty-one), worked the most innings (320), struck out the most batters (261), and allowed the fewest earned runs (2.61). Left-hander Al Milnar, a native Cleve-

lander, posted an 18–10 record; Al Smith, another left-hander who'd once
been with the Giants, won fifteen.

Overall, the 1940 Detroit Tigers probably weren't as strong as the 1934
and 1935 teams, but Hank Greenberg was at the top of his game, pounding
forty-one homers and driving in 151 runs to go with a .340 average. Charley
Gehringer batted .313 in his last good season; second-year man Barney
McCosky batted .340 and led the majors in hits (two hundred) and triples
(nineteen); and Rudy York fully justified Greenberg's displacement from
first base by batting .313, clouting thirty-three homers, and driving in 134
runs. Dick Bartell, who'd arrived from the Cubs the previous December
in a waiver swap for Billy Rogell, batted only .235 but steadied the infield
and enlivened the clubhouse and dugout.

Schoolboy Rowe, although no longer as durable as he'd once been, came
back from arm troubles to win sixteen games, while the aging Tommy
Bridges won twelve and Al Benton, a big left-hander, made forty-two appearances, all in relief, and saved seventeen wins. Detroit's ace was Buck
Newsom (or "Bobo," as he also liked to be called), who'd shuttled from the
Red Sox back to the Browns in the off-season of 1937/1938 and then gone
to the Tigers in May 1939 in a ten-player deal. Although he missed several
starts with a broken thumb, Newsom still won twenty-one and lost only six,
with a 2.83 ERA. On September 25, in the first game of a doubleheader
with the White Sox, he was the winning pitcher in relief; then he rested
for a few minutes, warmed up again, and threw a complete-game 3–2 victory in the nightcap.

Newsom, a burly, garrulous North Carolinian, was also good copy. After
winning his thirteenth game in a row on July 13 in Washington, he took
exception to something written by Robert Ruark, a reporter for the *Washington News*, and belted Ruark on the chin in the Griffith Stadium visitors'
locker room. Offered only $300 as compared with Feller's $1,500 for a
breakfast cereal endorsement, he insisted that not only was he a better
pitcher, but "I got more color and he ain't—and, what's more, I can do
imitations." For the *New York Times*'s John Kieran, "Bobo will do until
another Dizzy Dean comes along."[15]

Newsom could also be contrary. That summer Joe McCarthy, for reasons never wholly explained, declined to manage the American League All-
Stars. Joe Cronin, subbing for McCarthy, announced that Red Ruffing
would start the game at Sportsman's Park, St. Louis. "Buck starts, or he
doesn't pitch," growled Newsom. "To hell with the All-Stars."[16] Eventually,
though, he calmed down, relieved Ruffing, and pitched three scoreless

innings. By then the game was lost, because Boston's Max West had tagged Ruffing for a three-run homer in the first inning. The Nationals went on to win 4–0, with Paul Derringer and four successors yielding only three hits in the first All-Star Game shutout.

At the break, only a half-game separated Detroit and Cleveland. For many years thereafter, aging Cleveland fans would remain convinced that the Indians would have won their first pennant in twenty years if they'd been able to get along with their manager. They couldn't. In mid-June, following a bad road trip, the players organized a full-fledged revolt against Oscar Vitt.

It had been building for two years, ever since Vitt's first season in Cleveland. Sarcastic, easily agitated, and, in Lou Boudreau's description, "upbeat and inspirational to our face, but mean and spiteful behind your back," Vitt gradually lost his players' confidence.[17] He seems to have had an especially bad effect on Jeff Heath, who'd had an outstanding rookie year in 1938, slumped the next season, and in 1940 batted only .219 in one hundred games.

Eleven veteran players eventually went to Indians president Alva Bradley with their complaints: Vitt "dealt double" with them, showboated with the press, raged at them during games, made light of them in comparison with his 1937 Newark Bears powerhouse. Bradley listened politely, assured the "boys" that he'd check into what they'd told him, and urged them to keep everything to themselves.

The next morning, though, the *Cleveland Plain Dealer* headlined both the fall of Paris to the Germans and reporter Gordon Cobbledick's scoop on what he called "an act without known parallel in baseball history." The *Cleveland Press*'s Franklin "Whitey" Lewis subsequently labeled the revolt "the screwiest situation that ever arose in the history of the Major Leagues." Two days later, after the Indians swept a doubleheader from the unfortunate Athletics at Lakefront Stadium, Bradley met with the players (with Vitt absent) and got them to sign a retraction of whatever critical remarks they'd made about their manager. "Oscar hasn't got a friend on the club," Bradley confided to an associate.[18]

Their uprising over (at least for the time being), the Indians became a hot ball club, winning eight games in a row and moving into first place. On August 21, after another hot streak, they led Detroit by five and a half games. Yet at best, Vitt and his players were operating under what one Cleveland writer called "an armed truce." And both hometown fans and people in ballparks around the American League demonstrated their contempt for the Cleveland "crybabies," not only by offering verbal ridicule but by throwing baby bottles, rattles, and other objects on the field. In Detroit, Tigers partisans stood in the street outside the Indians' hotel singing "Rockabye, Baby" for most of one night; that afternoon they hung diapers on a clothesline above the visitors' dugout. Because he was team captain, Hal Trosky was wrongly assumed to be the ringleader of the revolt against Vitt; Jimmy Dykes took to calling him "Trotsky."[19]

In newspapers around the league, the Indians were derided as "boo hoo boys," "half Vitts," "lollypop boys," and a "bawl team." The *Chicago Tribune* captioned a photo of Vitt: "His boys have put away their rattles and teething rings." Traveling salesmen representing Cleveland firms even reported increased customer resistance; in the grand parade at the American Legion's annual convention in Boston, shouts of "Crybabies! Crybabies!" followed Cleveland Legionnaires down Boylston Street.[20]

Early in September, while Cleveland was losing a three-game series in Detroit that reduced its lead to one game, several Indians regulars met in Johnny Allen's room and apparently agreed to ignore Vitt's signals and use their own. As Feller remembered it, "We decided to go around Vitt. We worked with his coaches. . . . We used our own set of signals, worked our own strategy during games and ignored the head man as much as we could."[21]

Their new system evidently didn't work very well, because the Indians went on to lose six in a row. Yet the Tigers played inconsistently and couldn't build much of an advantage. Meanwhile the Yankees had caught fire and drawn to within a few games of first place, although they crippled their chances by losing a doubleheader in St. Louis on Sunday, September 16, before 17,247, the Browns' biggest daylight crowd since 1927. By beating the Indians in two of three games in Detroit, on September 19 to 21, the Tigers assumed the lead for good; when they came into Cleveland for a season-ending three-game set, they led the Indians by two games and New York by two and a half and needed to win only once to clinch the pennant.

Friday, September 26, was ladies' day at the big stadium by Lake Erie; nearly half the crowd of 45,553 consisted of women. Their presence did nothing to keep things under control; fruit and vegetables fell on the Tigers during pregame practice, and when Greenberg caught Roy Weatherly's first-inning fly the section reserved for women in the left-field stands barraged him with whatever could be thrown. Two innings later, a Clevelander pushed a basket of tomatoes and beer bottles over the top of the left-center-field fence and into the Detroit bullpen, where it landed on catcher George "Birdie" Tebbetts's head and knocked him unconscious. At that point, Vitt took the loudspeaker-system microphone to plead for order.

By the late innings, the crowd had quieted considerably, as Detroit's 2–0 lead—gained in the fourth inning when Rudy York pulled a pitch from Feller down the left-field line into the seats at the 320-foot mark—continued to hold up. That was one of only three hits allowed by the sturdy young Iowan. But the Indians couldn't score on manager Del Baker's surprise starter: a lean, thirty-year-old right-hander from West Virginia named Floyd Giebell, who'd pitched only once since coming up from Buffalo a couple of weeks earlier. Giebell gave up six hits but also struck out six and left six Cleveland runners on base. Dick Bartell remembered that the Indians "were so tight, they were swinging at everything, way outside, bounced up to the plate, and all."[22]

In Philadelphia, the Yankees had been eliminated when Athletics right-hander Johnny Babich defeated them for the fifth time that season. The Tigers lost both Saturday and Sunday games at Cleveland, with Baker using mostly substitutes. Detroit finished at 90–64, versus Cleveland's 89–65 and New York's 88–66. For the first time since 1935, a team other than the Yankees would represent the American League in the World Series.

. . . . .

ALTHOUGH FEATURING an extraordinary number of fracases and some truly strange episodes, the 1940 National League season provided far less suspense. Cincinnati encountered relatively little trouble repeating as pennant winners, although with the season a week old the Reds found themselves sitting on chairs near third base at Crosley Field, forced from their dugout as waters from Mill Creek, a tributary of the flooding Ohio River, seeped into the field-level boxes and onto the field. With much of the ballpark under water, the next two days' games had to be called off despite mild temperatures and bright sunshine.

Leo Durocher's Brooklyn ball club made it interesting for much of the season. The Dodgers won their first nine games and twelve of their first fourteen, including Tex Carleton's no-hitter against the Reds. The hated "Jints" stayed in contention over the first half of the season, with Paul Dean, pitching mostly in relief, making a comeback of sorts. But Bill Terry's team fell apart in August and September and sank all the way to sixth place, the Giants' worst finish since 1932. Home attendance dropped by about

200,000; turnouts for night games at the Polo Grounds were disappointing except for August 7, when 54,000 showed up for Mel Ott Night. After the popular Louisianian was showered with gifts, the Dodgers hammered Hubbell for an 8–4 win. The Cubs made an avant-garde fashion statement by stepping out in new sleeveless and zippered uniform shirts, but their unconventional attire didn't keep them from becoming a lackluster outfit that could do no better than fifth place and draw only 543,000 customers into Wrigley Field. Frank Frisch brought color and vitality to the Pirates, who had the league's certified batting champion in little Debs Garms (although he had only 358 official at bats) and by a late-season rally improved by ten games over 1939 to finish fourth.[23]

Ray Blades started his second season as Cardinals manager with the same propensity for lineup juggling and pitcher changing for which he'd been criticized the previous season. In St. Louis's first thirty games, Blades used eighty-six pitchers. On May 5, at Sportsman's Park, he and Durocher combined to use a record thirty-nine players before the Dodgers won it with four runs in the ninth inning. Five weeks later, with the team in sixth place with a 14–24 record, Sam Breadon fired Blades and promoted Billy Southworth, who'd managed in the Cardinals organization for thirteen years, from the Rochester farm club. (Blades hadn't been an active player since 1934, but Breadon had saved money by putting him under a player's contract, so that he could be released with only ten days' pay.)

Southworth continued to use Clyde Shoun frequently in relief, but he also put him into the starting rotation. Shoun ended up with fifty-four appearances, five saves, and a 13–11 overall record. Mort Cooper, Bill McGee, and Lon Warneke were Southworth's other starters. Big Johnny Mize had one of his finest seasons, leading the majors with forty-three homers and driving home 137 runs; Terry Moore and Enos Slaughter also had strong years at bat.

After May 10, when Junior Thompson pitched a complete-game victory at St. Louis while Brooklyn lost to Philadelphia, Cincinnati was never out of first place. Bucky Walters and Paul Derringer didn't have to carry as much of the load as they had in 1939 because Thompson won sixteen decisions, Jim Turner (acquired in a trade with Boston) won fourteen, and Joe Beggs, a former Yankees farmhand whom Bill McKechnie used frequently in relief, won twelve and saved seven. Whereas in 1939 Walters and Derringer had combined for fifty-two wins, in 1940 they won forty-two. With nineteen home runs and 127 RBIs, Frank McCormick was again the Reds' main offensive force, although Ernie Lombardi led the club with a .319 batting average in 376 at bats before he was disabled. More than anything else, the Reds' 100–53 record—which left them twelve games better than runner-up Brooklyn—was the result of stout pitching and tight defense. They won forty-one games by one run; their staff ERA was a majors'-lowest 3.05; and they set a new big-league mark by erring only 117 times.

After Billy Southworth took over, the Cardinals played .608 baseball to finish in third place, four games behind Brooklyn. On August 18 Durocher's Dodgers closed to within four games of Cincinnati, but two days later they dropped a doubleheader in St. Louis, while the Reds scored three runs in the bottom of the ninth inning to defeat the Giants at Crosley Field. That pushed Cincinnati's lead back to five and a half games; exactly one month later, the Reds clinched the pennant in Philadelphia with their ninth consecutive victory and twenty-third in twenty-seven tries. Johnny Vander Meer—beset by poor control and relegated to Indianapolis in June—doubled to drive in the go-ahead run in the top of the thirteenth inning and then gave way to Beggs, who wrapped it up.

But if the Dodgers didn't win anything, "dem Bums" and their pugnacious manager grabbed the headlines much of the time. While the Giants faded into mediocrity, the National League's most belligerent rivalry came to center on the Dodgers and Cardinals. On June 12 Larry MacPhail acquired the long-sought Joe Medwick, sending $125,000 and four second-line players to the Cardinals for Medwick and Curt Davis, a twenty-two-game winner in 1939 but 0–4 so far in 1940. The next day, when American Airlines deposited Medwick and Davis at La Guardia Field, the slugging outfielder declared, "I'm the happiest guy in the world."[24]

Five days later, Medwick, Durocher, Billy Southworth, and Cardinals right-hander Bob Bowman found themselves sharing an elevator in the Hotel New Yorker, where Durocher lived and the Cardinals stopped on their trips into New York. Durocher and Bowman exchanged insults and almost came to blows before they reached the lobby. That afternoon at Ebbets Field, Bowman was Southworth's starter. In Brooklyn's first at bats, Dixie Walker singled and scored on a double by Cookie Lavagetto, who came home on Joe Vosmik's single. Bowman then threw a fast ball that hit Medwick squarely in the left temple. As Medwick lay in the batter's box, MacPhail stormed onto the field, screaming curses at Bowman and the Cardinals' dugout until he was restrained by Brooklyn players and herded into the stands by the umpires. With several Dodgers threatening Bowman, Southworth removed him from the game, which ended in an eleven-inning, 7–5 win for St. Louis.

Often surly and always self-absorbed, Medwick had never been popular with his Cardinals teammates. Although a photograph shows Bowman dashing to the plate to see about him—hardly the reaction of a pitcher who'd really tried to hurt somebody—MacPhail, Durocher, the Dodgers players, and the 6,500 or so fans present that Tuesday were convinced that Bowman and the Cardinals had been out to get Medwick. Sam Breadon, though, pointed out that when the Dodgers had been at Sportsman's Park the previous month nobody had complained when Brooklyn's Hugh Casey plugged Don Padgett, Johnny Mize, and Enos Slaughter.

Although he quickly regained consciousness, Medwick spent the next three days under observation at Caledonian Hospital. There he was questioned by an assistant state's attorney, who quickly dropped the far-fetched notion that Bowman might be charged with assault. Meanwhile National League president Ford Frick questioned Southworth, Durocher, Bowman, MacPhail, and several others about what had happened. On Wednesday night 31,249 Brooklynites, expecting to see trouble of some kind, packed Ebbets Field. Durocher and Cardinals catcher Arnold "Mickey" Owen almost came to blows after Owen slid hard into Pete Coscaret at second base; otherwise, nothing extraordinary happened in an 8–3 Brooklyn win. The next morning, Owen was notified by Frick's office that he was fined $50 and suspended for four days.

Pee Wee Reese, the Dodgers' prize rookie shortstop, had been disabled by a pitch from Chicago's Jake Mooty three weeks earlier, and on June 23 the Giants' Billy Jurges was felled and hospitalized when he was hit in the head by Bucky Walters. (A distraught Walters went to Jurges's bedside to apologize.) Ever the innovator, MacPhail proposed that ballplayers—or at least his Dodgers—start wearing some kind of protective headgear at bat. Durocher disagreed, believing that if a batter were wearing a helmet, he would become even more of a target for pitchers. Frank Frisch was contemptuous: "The game's become sissy enough, anyway. No, I wouldn't have my men go for those bonnets. They'd look like a bunch of six-day bike riders who'd lost their bicycles."[25] Bill Terry, Billy Southworth, Bill McKechnie, and the Phillies' Doc Prothro were also quoted in opposition to helmet wearing. But MacPhail hadn't given up on the idea.

If Durocher and his men didn't go looking for trouble, it nonetheless found them with remarkable regularity. Late in July, in the opener of a doubleheader sweep by Cincinnati at Ebbets Field, the Reds' Lonnie Frey knocked over Pete Coscaret on a slide into second base, whereupon Brooklyn pitcher Whitlow Wyatt ran to the base and stood over Frey, repeatedly slapping him on the head with his glove until the umpires intervened. After that melee, John McDonald and Gabe Paul, road secretaries, respectively, for the Dodgers and the Reds, had a shouting match, and Frick visited both locker rooms between games in an effort to calm things down. A few days later, Brooklyn catcher Ernest "Babe" Phelps tangled with Pittsburgh's Arky Vaughan; Frick hit both players with $25 fines.

Then, on Monday, September 16, the kind of thing that seemed peculiarly suited to Ebbets Field occurred. Cincinnati built its lead over Brooklyn to ten games by defeating the Dodgers 4–3 in ten innings. The winning run scored after umpire Bill Stewart called out a Cincinnati runner at second base and then had his call reversed by George Magerkurth, who ruled that Coscaret had dropped the ball. Magerkurth listened to Durocher's tirade and then ordered him to the clubhouse.

When Joe Beggs set down the Dodgers to end the game, Frank Genano, a chubby, 5-foot 5-inch petty thief out on parole from the state vocational school at West Coxsackie, ran onto the field, jumped Magerkurth, and actually had the brawny umpire on the ground and was pummeling him when a park attendant and a couple of spectators pulled him off. In the aftermath, Genano went back to West Coxsackie, while Durocher had to pay a $100 fine for agitating the crowd against Magerkurth.

. . . . .

IF THE GENANO–MAGERKURTH FRAY was opéra bouffe, the death six weeks earlier of Cincinnati's Willard Hershberger had elements of genuine tragedy. Late in July, Ernie Lombardi had suffered a severe ankle sprain—so severe that the big catcher could hardly walk on the foot and would play little until the World Series. So Hershberger, a nice-looking, rather slightly built, thirty-year-old bachelor who'd backed up Lombardi since his acquisition from the Yankees organization in 1938, had to move behind the plate full time.

"Hershy," as his teammates called him, was never a home-run threat, but in 1939 he'd batted .345 in sixty-three games and in the current season was again above .300. Although popular with his peers and especially with the Reds' women fans, he was an incessant worrier, a hypochondriac who traveled with bottles of pills and nose drops, a gun collector who carried a pistol in his suitcase, and a man haunted by the suicide of his father, who'd killed himself with a shotgun when Hershberger was a high-school senior in Fullerton, California.

The pressure of catching every game and calling every pitch in the midst of a pennant race apparently became too much for Hershberger. In a night game at the Polo Grounds on July 31, the Giants scored four times on Bucky Walters with two out in the bottom of the ninth inning to beat the Reds 5–4. The game-winning blow was Harry Danning's two-run homer.

August 1 was an off day for the Reds in Boston. Third baseman Bill Werber talked Hershberger into taking in a movie, during which Hershberger kept fidgeting and leaving his seat to stroll the lobby. He blamed himself for Walters's defeat the previous night, saying, "That sort of thing doesn't happen when Lombardi's catching. I must have called for the wrong pitches."[26]

The next day, in the nightcap of a doubleheader loss to the Bees, Hershberger was hitless in five at bats and failed to field a ball topped in front of the plate; pitcher Whitey Moore barely got to it in time to throw out the Boston runner. When Bill McKechnie asked Hershberger if something was wrong, the catcher replied, "Yes, plenty. I'll tell you all about it after the game."[27] That evening, in the manager's room at the Copley Plaza Hotel, he sobbed as he talked about his father's death, about his own thoughts of suicide, about how he wasn't hitting and was letting the team down. McKechnie believed that he'd finally worked his troubled ballplayer into a better mood, because they ordered dinner, Hershberger ate well, and afterward he sat in the hotel lobby joking with teammates.

But at breakfast the next morning, when the *Cincinnati Enquirer's* Lou Smith sought to draw him out, Hershberger was unresponsive. Later he told Bill Baker, his roommate and the Reds' third catcher, that he was sick and would join the team later; when Gabe Paul called from the ballpark as the Reds and Bees readied for another doubleheader, he said the same thing. Worried, McKechnie pressed the gimpy Lombardi into service, waited until the first game was a couple of innings old, and then asked Dan Cohen, a Cincinnati fan traveling with the team, to go see about Hershberger.

Finding Hershberger's door locked, Cohen got a maid to let him into the room. There he discovered a gruesome sight: shirtless but otherwise fully clothed, Hershberger sat on the bathroom floor amid neatly arranged towels, his back against the tub, his throat slit, a safety razor nearby. A medical examiner subsequently put the time of Hershberger's death at about 2:30 P.M.

It later came out that Hershberger had made careful preparations for ending his life. Before the Reds had embarked on the present road trip, he'd taken out a life-insurance policy, payable to his mother, and had asked outfielder Lew Riggs, with whom he shared an apartment in Cincinnati, to take care of his automobile and finances if anything should happen to him. He'd also repeatedly talked about suicide to Riggs and Bill Baker. When reporters queried McKechnie about the reason for Hershberger's act, the Cincinnati manager would only say, "It has nothing to do with anybody on the team. It was something personal. He told it to me in confidence, and I will not utter it to anyone. I will take it to my grave."[28]

Although shaken by their teammate's suicide, the Reds were seasoned professionals whose uppermost concern was gaining another pennant and another World Series check. While Hershberger's body was being shipped across the continent for burial (in Presbyterian services) at Visalia, California, McKechnie had coach Jimmie Wilson, who'd caught a total of seven games over the past two years, placed on the active-player roster. The forty-year-old Wilson and Bill Baker divided the catching chores for the remainder of the season, as the Reds, threatened by Brooklyn for a couple of weeks in August, pulled away from the competition.

· · · · ·

THE MUTUAL BROADCASTING SYSTEM again paid $100,000 for radio rights to the World Series and sold exclusive advertising time to the Gillette Safety Razor Company. Red Barber and Gene Elson did play-by-play, with Mel Allen (né Melvin Israel), a young Alabaman who'd begun working Yankees games that year, providing pregame commentary. Floyd Giebell, Detroit's pennant-clinching hero, watched from the grandstand because he'd joined the Tigers too late in the season to be eligible for Series play.[29] George Magerkurth also sat out the Series, even though it was his turn to umpire under the majors' four-year rotation. But big "Mage" agreed to pass up the Series and the extra money so that Bill Klem, who was retiring after thirty-six years as baseball's premier umpire, could do one more postseason classic. Such generosity wasn't shared by the Cincinnati players, who voted Johnny Vander Meer a one-third Series share, only to be ordered by Commissioner Landis to make it a full one.

Klem, working the Series opener behind the plate, had plenty of blue-suited company. For the first time in Series history, six umpires—one at each base, one down each foul line—would be on the field. But if the umpires might have appeared overmanned, the Reds were definitely undermanned, with Jimmie Wilson doing the catching instead of rookie Baker and the still-hobbled Lombardi and Eddie Joost covering second base in place of Lonnie Frey, who'd broken his right big toe when he managed to drop the lid of a dugout water cooler on it.

The most competitive World Series in six years began on Wednesday, October 2, in front of 31,793 at Crosley Field. Bobo Newsom held Cincinnati to two runs while his mates, helped by two Reds errors, scored five times in the second inning off Derringer and went on to win 7–2. Detroit right fielder Bruce Campbell, an eleven-year American Leaguer who'd fought off three attacks of meningitis, clouted a two-run homer in his league's tenth consecutive Series victory. Early the next morning, Newsom's sixty-eight-year-old father died of a heart attack at the Netherland Plaza Hotel. While Newsom's relatives left with the body for North Carolina, the grieving pitcher announced that he was staying with the team through the Series.

That afternoon, the Reds won their first game in Series competition since 1919. After a shaky first inning, Walters settled down to throw a three-hitter. Cincinnati came out on top 5–3, with Jimmy Ripple—a onetime Giants mainstay obtained late in August from Brooklyn for the $7,500 waiver price—tagging Schoolboy Rowe for a two-run homer in the third inning to put the Reds ahead for good. Afterward the two teams hustled for their train and were off to Detroit, where the Series would continue without a break.

With 52,877 filling Briggs Stadium, the third game established the Series's seesaw pattern. Rudy York and Pinky Higgins spoiled the Series debut of thirty-seven-year-old Jim Turner by each slamming two-run homers in the seventh inning. The Reds reached Tommy Bridges for ten hits and scored three times in the last two innings, but the smallish, curveballing Tennessean held on to come out with a 7–4 win, his fourth (and last) in Series play. Still obviously favoring his ankle, Lombardi made his only start of the Series, catching seven innings and hitting a double before giving way to Baker.

Cincinnati evened it behind Derringer, who walked six Tigers but limited them to five hits and two runs, while the Reds collected eleven hits and scored five times on Dizzy Trout, Clay Smith, and Archie McKain. Ival Goodman was the Reds' batting leader with a single, a double, and two RBIs. But on October 6, with 55,189 on hand, Newsom came back to pitch the finest game of his long career: a three-hit shutout, all three hits being singles. The Tigers landed a thirteen-hit, eight-run barrage on Thompson, Moore, Vander Meer, and Johnny Hutchings, including Hank Greenberg's three-run homer.

Back in Cincinnati the next day, the Reds drew even when Walters again mastered the tough Detroit lineup and Rowe again couldn't do the job. Rowe gave up two runs and retired only one batter before leaving in favor of Johnny Gorsica. In the sixth inning, the Reds scored another run on Gorsica; then Walters, an ex-infielder who could still swing the bat, homered in the eighth off young Fred Hutchinson to make the final margin 4–0.

Whereas the previous three games at Crosley Field had drawn full houses, only 26,769 showed up for the decisive meeting. Del Baker sent Newsom back to the mound with only a day's rest, and the rustic right-hander was able to keep the Reds from scoring for six innings. Derringer was also very tough, yielding only an unearned run in the third, when Detroit catcher Billy Sullivan scored on Bill Werber's errant throw to first base. Then, in the bottom of the seventh, Frank McCormick and Jimmy Ripple tied the game with back-to-back doubles. After Jimmie Wilson sacrificed Ripple to third, shortstop Billy Myers first bunted foul on an intended squeeze play and then drove Barney McCosky back to the center-field fence for his fly ball, which sent Ripple home with the go-ahead run. Newsom retired the side and also set down the Reds in the eighth, but the Tigers couldn't get anything started against Derringer. Former Cleveland star Earl Averill, batting for Newsom, ended the Series by grounding out, Joost to McCormick.

The Series made each of the Reds $5,782 richer; each Tiger went home with $3,519. Nobody had earned his money more than Jimmie Wilson, a portly, middle-aged, ostensibly retired catcher who despite aching legs squatted behind the plate for six games, made six singles in seventeen at bats, and stole the only base of the Series. Now back in the limelight after five desultory seasons managing the Phillies and two years as McKechnie's aide, Wilson soon signed with the Cubs to succeed Gabby Hartnett, who, contrary to Dizzy Dean's prediction, at least had lasted out the season.

. . . . .

As everybody with the barest knowledge of Cleveland baseball matters had long expected, Oscar Vitt was fired a few weeks after the season ended. Roger Peckinpaugh, a Cleveland native who'd managed the Indians from 1928 to 1933, was willing to leave a secure position with the American League's Promotion Bureau and return to what was generally considered a managers' graveyard.

Although Cincinnati's 1940 attendance was nearly 130,000 below the previous season's, the Reds' World Series victory was a bracing experience for the National League, which hadn't had a Series winner since 1934. That a club other than the Yankees won in the other league was also bracing for baseball in general, apparently even for Yankees fans. Whereas in 1939 the Yankees had admitted slightly more than 900,000 ticket holders to Yankee Stadium, in 1940 they fell just short of 1 million.

Overall majors attendance was the highest since 1930. The Tigers led everybody at 1,078,352, while the runner-up Indians, despite still playing more than half their home games in little League Park, set a franchise record by topping 900,000. The White Sox outdrew the Cubs for the first time in twenty years, attracting 660,336 to Comiskey Park, including nearly 215,000 for seven night games. Playing fourteen night dates and rising from the bottom to sixth place, the Browns drew 239,591, double their 1939 home attendance, while the last-place Athletics played before 432,145 at Shibe Park, their best attendance in seven years. The American League totaled 5,433,791 paying customers, more than 1 million above its previous high in 1924.

With smaller aggregate seating capacity, dreary showings by the Giants and Cubs, and not much of a pennant race, the National League—led by Brooklyn with 977,093—drew about 1 million fewer people than the American League. Despite their strong play in the season's second half, the Cardinals could interest only about 330,000 people into coming to Sportsman's Park. Together, the third-place Cardinals and the sixth-place Browns attracted about 100,000 fewer fans than did the fourth-place White Sox alone.

Even more bracing that autumn and winter was the steadily improving American economy. Although France had been knocked out of the war, purchase orders from Great Britain—for everything from aircraft, tanks, and artillery pieces to steel, petroleum, and grains—mounted week by week. And as the United States aided Britain's war effort it also rearmed itself and fueled its economy. While some 8.5 million workers were still unemployed, by the first week in September 1940 the *New York Times*'s business index had reached 105.3. By the following March it had climbed to 121.5, which was actually above the peak level of activity for 1929, the last pre-Depression year. By May 1941 the index for steel production had reached 131; automobile output was at 117.3. Recovery, long-sought but always elusive under the New Deal, was finally at hand in the circumstances of another world war.

But if the economic news was good, operators of baseball franchises from Class D to the majors worried about the effects of the Selective Service Act, passed by the Congress in September. The nation's first peacetime conscription law, it required the registration of all men between the ages of twenty-one and forty-six. Much was made in the baseball press of registration by such luminaries as Bucky Walters, Bobby Feller, and Hank Greenberg at local offices of the new Selective Service Administration.

The December National Association and major-league meetings, in Atlanta and Chicago, respectively, produced more than the usual commodity trading in players. Brooklyn paid the Cardinals $65,000 and threw in an aging Gus Mancuso and a minor-league pitcher to get Mickey Owen, the fiery young catcher who'd squared off with Leo Durocher the previous June. The Reds handed the regular shortstop job to Eddie Joost and traded Billy Myers to the Cubs for a couple of bench riders, while Cleveland sold Johnny Allen to the Browns and traded Ben Chapman to Washington for pitcher Joe Krakauskas. The Yankees, no longer bound by the "Griffith rule," began regrouping by selling Monte Pearson to Cincinnati, Bump Hadley to the Giants, Babe Dahlgren to the Bees, and Jake Powell to San Francisco. Pepper Martin ended his colorful big-league career and became manager of the Cardinals' Sacramento farm club. Three future Hall of Famers were in transit. Pittsburgh gave Paul Waner his outright release, and although the three-time batting champion quickly signed with Brooklyn, in May he would be sold to the Boston National Leaguers. Lloyd Waner, traded to Boston in May, would end the season with Cincinnati. And Detroit said good-bye to Earl Averill, who also had a brief stay in Boston before being sold to Seattle.

Even before the Chicago meetings, Larry MacPhail had made what would turn out to be the off-season's best deal when he gave the ever-needy Phillies $100,000 and three unneeded players for Kirby Higbe, a twenty-five-year-old right-handed South Carolinian who'd made a 26–34 record for a team that had won a total of ninety-five games over the past two seasons. Higbe was the latest in a long succession of deals with the Phillies involving big amounts of cash, which had enabled Gerald Nugent to keep his franchise afloat from season to season. In just four transactions from 1938 to 1940—for Bucky Walters, Dolph Camilli, Claude Passeau, and Higbe—Nugent netted $205,000.

Whatever his financial struggles, Nugent remained a full peer among big-league owners in Chicago. Among other matters dealt with, the owners extended Commissioner Landis's contract to 1946 and voted again to limit

night games to seven dates per team in both leagues. The National Leaguers were unanimous on the matter; the Browns' Donald Barnes, whose
fourteen night dates in 1940 had accounted for more than two-thirds of his
home attendance, was livid when he alone voted against reimposing the
seven-nighter rule. At the same time, Clark Griffith, whose seventh-place
Washington club had played before only 381,000, announced his surrender
on the question of night baseball. For 1941 the Senators would become
the eleventh major-league team to play at home under the lights.

· · · · ·

FOR SPRING TRAINING, Larry MacPhail sent his Dodgers to Havana,
where they received a fulsome *bienvenido* from Colonel Fulgencio Batista,
Cuba's political strongman, before checking in at the posh Hotel Nacional.
The Dodgers had games scheduled on the island with the Giants, the Red
Sox, Cleveland, and a team of top Cuban professionals, and they were also
to conduct clinics for young Cuban amateurs (who were all supposed to be
passably white).

Per MacPhail's instructions, a supply of plastic liners that would fit neatly
inside baseball caps had been shipped to Havana. Designed by Walter
Dandy, M.D., a brain specialist at Johns Hopkins University, the cap liners,
MacPhail avowed, would be worn by every player in the Brooklyn organization. Resigned to doing his boss's wishes, Leo Durocher ordered his
grumbling players to insert the liners in their caps and keep them there.

Kirby Higbe would always remember the Dodgers' stay in Cuba for the
friendship he and Hugh Casey struck up with Ernest Hemingway, who
took the two pitchers around to his favorite bars and invited them out to
his home for evenings of drinking and yarn swapping. During one late-
night session, Hemingway and Casey donned boxing gloves and started
flailing at each other, knocking over furniture and breaking glassware until
the author's wife broke up the party.

Van Lingle Mungo's stay in Havana turned out to be a short one. "He
drank a bit," Durocher once said of the South Carolinian, "a bit of everything."[30] On the night of March 9, Mungo imbibed far too freely at the
Hotel Tropicana bar and got into a fight with a cabaret dancer over the
dancer's partner (who happened to be his wife). When Mungo showed up
the next morning at Tropical Stadium bruised and hung over, Durocher
told him he was fined $200 and ordered him to report to the Dodgers'
Montreal farm team in Macon, Georgia. Whereupon Mungo returned to

the Hotel Nacional and engaged in a reprise of his 1937 furniture-wrecking escapade. The next day, he flew by Pan-American Clipper to Miami and boarded a train for Macon. Although MacPhail subsequently had him rejoin the Dodgers as they played their way north, after two brief relief appearances in April he would be back in Montreal.[31]

That spring, Louis Perini and two partners in a Boston construction business purchased a controlling interest in the city's National League franchise. Although they kept Casey Stengel as manager and Robert Quinn as president, they restored the name Braves and rechristened the ballpark Braves Field. But whether Braves or Bees, Stengel's team remained a punchless and pitching-poor outfit that seemed to have acquired a lease on seventh place.

The 1941 Phillies again would be even worse—all of nineteen games worse. But at least Hugh Mulcahy, who'd compiled a 42–82 record over six discouraging seasons with the Philadelphia National Leaguers, would be spared further indignity. On March 8, 1941, Mulcahy became the first big leaguer ordered to report for the one year of military training specified under the Selective Service Act.

By then, according to National Association president William G. Bramham, forty-one minor leaguers had entered military service. Bramham's records also showed that Frank Stewart, a Vancouver native who'd played briefly in the Pacific Coast League and umpired in the minors the past two years before entering the Canadian army, had been killed in Scotland in a bombing raid. Stewart thus became American baseball's first wartime casualty.

Unlike bachelor Hugh Mulcahy, married ballplayers such as Joe DiMaggio weren't initially affected by the draft law, nor were others such as Ted Williams, who could claim to be the sole support of his mother. DiMaggio appeared satisfied with his $35,000 contract when he reported to St. Petersburg, where onlookers were already buzzing about the flashy play of Phil Rizzuto, a little shortstop up from Kansas City. Williams breezed into Sarasota and interrupted a meeting of Boston baseball writers to announce that as far as he was concerned, bygones were bygones.

That spring, John Kieran paid a visit to Lou Gehrig. No longer able to walk, Gehrig had resigned his parole officer's position and now was confined to his house in Riverdale, New York. There Kieran found him sitting by an open window and tossing peanuts into the snow for a couple of pheasants the Gehrigs kept. Pointing to a first baseman's mitt on a shelf, Gehrig remarked that it was the biggest he'd ever used and that Jimmie Foxx had given it to him because "toward the last, when I couldn't bend over so well, I was having trouble getting in the low throws and short hops."[32]

· · · · ·

ON OPENING DAY in Washington, April 14, the capacity crowd stood as a recording of "The Star-Spangled Banner" blared over Griffith Stadium's loudspeaker system; then President Roosevelt tossed out the first ball. Playing "The Star-Spangled Banner" (which the Congress had officially recognized as the national anthem less than a decade earlier) would become standard across the major leagues and much of the rest of Organized Baseball during the course of the baseball season.

Other baseball-promoted displays of patriotic feeling accompanied growing anxiety that the United States was being drawn ineluctably into the war. Organized by various patriotic groups and sanctioned by the Roosevelt administration, Sunday, May 18, 1941, became I Am an American Day. In cities and towns across the country, the day featured martial airs, parades, and speeches; nearly everywhere baseball was played that Sunday, patriotic observances in some form preceded the first pitch. At Yankee Stadium, for example, 30,109 people listened to music by the Seventh Regiment Band, a speech by Bronx Borough President James J. Lyons, and the singing of "The Star-Spangled Banner" by the prima donna Lucy Monroe (who in the years ahead would make the anthem almost her personal signature).

On May 27 play was halted during night games at the Polo Grounds and in St. Louis while players, managers, umpires, people in the stands, and Americans across the country listened to a forty-five-minute radio address by the president proclaiming "an unlimited national emergency." Two weeks later American League president William Harridge announced that henceforth members of the military services in uniform would be admitted free of charge to all American League parks. On July 24 the Cardinals gave free admission to some 10,000 women who showed up with pieces of aluminum to donate to the War Department's collection campaign; by game time, a small mountain of aluminum had accumulated at the main entrance to Sportsman's Park.

· · · · ·

AS THE NATION geared up for war, the baseball season proceeded as usual. In 1941 the pennant races reverted to type: the Yankees reasserted their dominion over the rest of the American League, whereas in the National League, with Cincinnati struggling to score runs and falling out of the running by midseason, the race resolved itself into a bitter fight between Brooklyn and St. Louis.

The Dodgers got off to another fast start, winning twenty of their first twenty-six games, including five shutouts—by Whitlow Wyatt, Kirby Higbe, Luke Hamlin, Curt Davis, and Hugh Casey—over their first fourteen. Mickey Owen didn't hit much, but he gave Durocher the agility and aggressiveness he wanted behind the plate. The acquisition on May 6 of Billy Herman—for whom MacPhail paid the Cubs $65,000 and a couple of second-line players—gave Brooklyn the majors' finest infield: Dolph Camilli (who would lead the league in homers and runs batted in), Herman, Pee Wee Reese, and Cookie Lavagetto. The outfield of Dixie Walker, Pete Reiser, and Joe Medwick (even though he would never be the offensive force he'd been before his beaning) was tops in the league.

Reiser was the prize catch from Landis's liberation of Cardinals farmhands in 1938. A little under 6 feet tall but a strong 185 pounds, a left-handed batter and right-handed thrower, Reiser had come up in August of the previous season as an infielder. But Reiser's great speed had led Durocher to make him into a center fielder, which is where the twenty-two-year-old St. Louis native was positioned on opening day.

In that game, the Phillies' Ike Pearson nailed Reiser in the back of the head with a fastball. Although Reiser crumpled at the plate and was briefly hospitalized, he was back in the lineup within a week, with the medical assessment being that but for his plastic cap liner he would probably have been badly hurt. After that, MacPhail heard no more complaints about cap liners. Within a few weeks, moreover, the Cubs were wearing them and the Indians had ordered a batch, as bean balls continued to be a part of baseball life. By season's end, Pee Wee Reese, Mickey Owen, Reiser (again), Terry Moore, Frank McCormick, and Bill Dickey had all lost playing time after being hit in the head by pitches.

Reiser would go on to lead the National League in batting (.343), runs (117), triples (seventeen), and total bases (299). Hailed by Leo Durocher as "another Ty Cobb," he possessed what scouts called the "five tools" (ability to throw, field, run, hit, and hit for power), and he loved to play the game.[33] But he also played with utter abandon, seemingly oblivious to outfield walls, which in that time were constructed of unpadded concrete or metal. Later that season he crashed into the iron gate in deepest center at Ebbets Field in pursuit of a drive by the Cardinals' Enos Slaughter and was disabled for several games. It was the first in a succession of Reiser's encounters with walls, which together with his various other injuries would hamper and eventually shorten what might have been one of baseball's brightest careers.

However solid the 1941 Dodgers were, the Cardinals refused to be shaken. After winning eleven games in a row in May, they took a two-game lead over Brooklyn. Five weeks later, the Dodgers had moved back in front by three games, but by late July, after Brooklyn's doubleheader loss in Pittsburgh, St. Louis had retaken the lead. Little would separate the two teams from then on.

Whereas MacPhail had built the Dodgers through trades, waiver acquisitions, and about $350,000 in cash outlays, the 1941 Cardinals were almost entirely homegrown and cost Sam Breadon and Branch Rickey relatively little. Most of Billy Southworth's players had spent years working their way up through St. Louis's minor-league empire in competition with hundreds of other tough, determined youngsters. "Your typical Cardinal rookie," as characterized by Lloyd Lewis of the *Chicago Daily News*, "is a poor boy of rudimentary education, bursting with base hits and ambitions, a lean, whip-muscled kid who can throw and run all day. . . . He wants money, but more than that he wants to play baseball and play it always."[34]

The Dean brothers—"poor boys of rudimentary education" who'd once been the toast of St. Louis—had about come to the end of the road. In mid-May, the Giants (on their way to a fifth-place finish) sent Paul Dean back to the Cardinals along with Harry Gumbert and cash in exchange for Bill McGee, but the younger Dean was soon on his way to Sacramento, where he would throw his slow stuff for Pepper Martin's Solons. As for Dizzy Dean, after one start and a first-inning exit he was grateful to take a coach's job with the Cubs, at the same $10,000 salary he'd been paid as a player. Diz took his new duties seriously, too, drawing a ten-day suspension and $50 fine in June for rowing with umpire John "Beans" Reardon in a night game at Ebbets Field.

A month later, though, Dizzy and Patricia Nash Dean moved from Chicago to St. Louis, where Diz had been offered a job broadcasting both Cardinals and Browns games for station KWK. With his rambling reminiscences, cornpone humor, fractured grammar, and renditions of "The Wabash Cannonball," he quickly won a large and affectionate audience. Over the next quarter-century—especially after he began working network *Game of the Week* telecasts in the 1950s—"Ol' Diz" would come to enjoy greater fame and far greater riches than he'd ever known as a player.

A succession of injuries over the latter half of the season probably cost the Cardinals the pennant. Johnny Mize missed twenty-seven games with an assortment of ills, Terry Moore was disabled for nearly a month after a beaning by a Boston pitcher, Enos Slaughter missed most of August and September with a broken collarbone, and Mort Cooper had to have elbow surgery. But the Cardinals got sharp infield play from Frank Crespi at second base, Marty Marion at shortstop, and Jimmy Brown at third; and six pitchers won at least ten games, led by the veteran Lon Warneke and the rookie left-hander Ernie White. Another left-hander, twenty-year-old Howard Pollet, came up from Houston in time to win five of seven decisions, including two shutouts. As of August 30, when Warneke pitched a 2–0 no-hitter in Cincinnati, the Cardinals were again in first place.

That day, Warneke bested rookie Elmer Riddle, whose nineteen wins, together with a sixteen-win comeback by Johnny Vander Meer, were about the only positive outcomes for the Reds that year. The sagging fortunes of the defending world champions evidently worked their effect on Bill McKechnie, because on September 3, endeavoring to travel from Chicago to Pittsburgh for a night game, McKechnie boarded the wrong aircraft, landed in Detroit, got into a taxi, and told the driver "Forbes Field." Apprised of his whereabouts, the distracted Reds manager scrambled to get a flight to Pittsburgh, barely arriving in time for the game.

On September 4, when the Dodgers left for the western cities aboard a new Pennsylvania Railroad chrome and aluminum train, with each player having a compartment to himself, they held a three-game lead over the crippled Cardinals. Highlights of that western swing included winning two of three games in St. Louis (where, as Dixie Walker later related, "We won that series because we rode the younger St. Louis players into the jitters");[35] scoring five runs in the top of the seventeenth inning to defeat Paul Derringer in Cincinnati, with late-season pickup Johnny Allen pitching the first fifteen frames; and losing a game in Pittsburgh because umpire Magerkurth called a balk on Hugh Casey. Predictably, Durocher unleashed a verbal barrage on Magerkurth; predictably, Magerkurth ordered him out of the game. As the Dodgers' manager stormed through the corridor to the visitors' locker room, he smashed every lightbulb and then threw a chair through a window in the umpires' room. For all that, Durocher drew a $150 fine.

Arriving in Philadelphia only a game in front of St. Louis, the Dodgers went two and a half games up by sweeping a Saturday doubleheader from the Phillies behind Wyatt and Higbe, while the Cardinals lost to the sixth-place Cubs. The next day, St. Louis swept two from Chicago, as Stanley Musial, a twenty-year-old outfielder just arrived from Rochester, made four hits in five at bats and scored the winning run in the opener. At Shibe Park, with some 5,000 Brooklynites on hand (including movie stars George Raft and Betty Grable), the Phillies played before a rare full house. Before the first game of still another doubleheader, hundreds of Dodgers faithful wandered around the field; some even sat in the visitors' dugout and chatted with Durocher. Wrote Tom Meany of the New York daily *PM*, "Not since the Bolshevists took over the Imperial Gardens in St. Petersburgh [*sic*] . . . has the proletariat taken over as it did yesterday."[36] But the Dodgers could manage only a split with Doc Prothro's cellar dwellers.

As Durocher and his players traveled by train to Boston and hundreds of their fans flew to the city in nine chartered aircraft, the Cardinals split a doubleheader in Pittsburgh to fall back by a game and a half. Both contenders won the next day, but on September 25 St. Louis's hopes died at Forbes Field when Elbie Fletcher's two-run homer and Max Butcher's five-hit pitching overcame Ernie White, 3–1. At Braves Field, meanwhile, the Dodgers clinched their first pennant in twenty-one years. Reiser hit a two-run homer, and Wyatt pitched his seventh shutout of the season—two days before his thirty-fourth birthday.

A jubilant Larry MacPhail, following the game by radio in Brooklyn, headed for the 125th Street station in upper Manhattan, where he expected to board the train carrying the Dodgers to their victorious arrival at Grand Central Terminal. But Durocher and his players, anxious to get home, advised the conductor not to stop, which left MacPhail standing on the station platform as the train rolled by on its way to a greeting by thousands of Brooklynites. That evening, soused and seething, MacPhail told Durocher he was fired, although by morning he'd sobered up and taken it back.

On Sunday, September 28, the Dodgers closed the season before 12,870 at Ebbets Field by beating the Phillies for their one hundredth win. That pushed their season's home attendance to a majors'-best 1,215,253; sufficient profits had accumulated for MacPhail to finish paying off the franchise's long-standing debt to the Brooklyn Trust Company. The Dodgers had also made money for the fifth-place Giants, who drew 827,066 at the Polo Grounds, with nearly half of that total coming in games with Brooklyn.

On Monday "dem Bums" rode from Grand Army Plaza to Borough Hall as their fans screamed, pushed past mounted police, and threw themselves against the convertibles carrying Durocher and his men. "It was parade, carnival and mardi gras rolled into one," reported the *New York Times*, "unmatched in Brooklyn's history for sheer spontaneous madness."[37]

. . . . .

APART FROM the Yankees' resurgence, the 1941 American League season would be remembered for the loss of one of its top players to military service, the spectacular achievements of two others, and the death of Lou Gehrig. On June 2 the man who'd once seemed virtually indestructible finally succumbed to amyotrophic lateral sclerosis, seventeen days short of his thirty-eighth birthday. Inasmuch as the disease leaves one's mind alert while the paralysis of the body becomes total, dying of ALS "is like being a participant at your own funeral."[38] Coincidentally, the same evening that Gehrig died the Yankees arrived in Detroit, where twenty-six months earlier the Iron Horse had taken himself out of the lineup.

The next afternoon, with Joe McCarthy on his way back to New York to attend Gehrig's funeral, the Yankees lost 4–2 to Dizzy Trout. One of the Yankees' runs came on a homer by Joe DiMaggio—the twentieth-consecutive game in which the "Yankee Clipper," as the press had nicknamed him, had hit safely. At that point, with Bobby Feller dominating nearly every team he faced, Cleveland was in first place; with only five games separating the first six teams, the Yankees, at 25–21, were three and a half games behind the Indians and two behind the White Sox.

The defending league champion Tigers would end the season tied for fourth place, four games below .500. The reasons for Detroit's flop were manifold. After signing for $35,000, the biggest pitcher's salary up to then, Bobo Newsom had trouble getting anybody out; for the season he won twelve and lost twenty. Onetime aces Tommy Bridges and Schoolboy Rowe weren't much better. Charley Gehringer could manage only a .220 batting average in his next-to-last year in baseball; Rudy York still hit for power and drove in runs but lost forty-seven points on his batting average; and Dick Bartell, the team's sparkplug in 1940, quarreled with the front office over bonus money that he claimed was owed him and drew his release in May. (Bartell caught on with the Giants, with whom he would play for three more seasons.)

But most of all it was the induction of Hank Greenberg into the U.S. Army on May 8 that killed the Tigers. Although up to that point Greenberg was batting only .269 and had hit a couple of homers and driven in a dozen runs, with his departure, wrote John Kieran, "the Tigers might as well join the Ringling circus."[39] Assigned to basic training in Camp Chester, Michigan, Greenberg revealed to reporters that his 1941 contract had been for $55,000, of which he'd been paid $7,500 thus far. Now he would give up baseball's top salary for $50 per month in army pay.

On the night of May 28, Walter Johnson, on his third toss, cut a beam at home plate that triggered an electrical switch, illuminating Griffith Stadium for its first night baseball game. George Selkirk pinch-hit a bases-loaded eighth-inning homer to give the Yankees a 6–5 victory and disappoint about 25,000 customers.

By that time, Joe McCarthy had given up on his experiment of making a first baseman of Joe Gordon and had installed rookie Johnny Sturm, up from Kansas City, at the position. Phil Rizzuto subsequently took over at shortstop from Frank Crosetti, but otherwise it was the same everyday players McCarthy had used for the past two years. A competent fielder, Sturm hit with even less authority than Babe Dahlgren, while the careers of Red Rolfe and Bill Dickey were starting to tail off. But little Rizzuto batted .307, and the rest of the Yankees' lineup still packed plenty of power. As usual, the New Yorkers' 151 home runs led the majors, and they also set a record by hitting at least one homer in twenty-five straight games. Gordon had twenty-four; Tommy Henrich, thirty-one; Charlie Keller, thirty-three (with 122 RBIs); and DiMaggio, thirty (with a majors'-best 125 RBIs).

Also as usual, the Yankees' pitching and defense were superb. The 1941 team executed a record 196 double plays; its pitching staff allowed the fewest runs in the league and registered the second-lowest earned run average. Lefty Gomez regained form, winning fifteen times, as did Red Ruffing; Marius Russo, Spud Chandler, and wide-girthed Tiny Bonham won fourteen, ten, and nine, respectively; and Johnny Murphy saved fifteen games for a staff that still completed nearly half its starts. From mid-June to early August, the Yankees won forty-two of fifty-five games and left the rest of the league in the dust. Atley Donald pitched the clincher at Boston on September 4—the earliest date on which any team had wrapped up a pennant. At 101–53, New York outdistanced Boston by seventeen games and Chicago by twenty-four. Cleveland, with an overworked Feller winning only five times after August 3 (for an overall record of 25–13), slumped into a fourth-place tie with Detroit. (With Detroit out of the running early, the Griffith no-trades rule was repealed by the American League owners at the All-Star Game break.)

The surge that carried the Yankees to their fourth pennant in five years basically coincided with what, more than sixty years later, would still be widely recognized as the foremost individual attainment in baseball history: Joe DiMaggio's feat of hitting safely in fifty-six consecutive games. It became one of the most familiar stories in all of American sports, featuring several suspenseful last-at-bats, a couple of questionable scorer's calls, the theft (and return) of the hero's favorite weapon, successive milestones reached and passed (thirty games to set a new Yankees team record, forty-two games to break George Sisler's "modern" record, forty-five games to surpass Willie Keeler's almost-forgotten 1897 record), and finally the streak's end, enacted on the night of July 17 in Cleveland's big stadium, with 67,468 people looking on.

The Yankees won the game 7–4—their sixteenth victory in their last seventeen tries, thirty-first in their last thirty-six—and thereby extended their lead over the Indians to seven games. But the overriding story was that Al Smith and Jim Bagby held DiMaggio hitless in four at bats. Third baseman Ken Keltner made two outstanding plays—what many years afterward he described as "identical" backhanded stops against the foul line behind third base, followed by perfect throws to first baseman Hal Trosky. After the game, Keltner and his wife walked out of the stadium under police escort. "Joe had a lot of Italian friends in Cleveland," said Keltner, "and the club wanted to make sure I got to my car OK."[40]

DiMaggio hit safely the next day and went on to accumulate another streak of sixteen games. Over his fifty-six-game run, he'd batted .408, hit fifteen home runs, driven in fifty-five runs, scored an average of a run a game, and struck out only seven times. (For the whole season, DiMaggio fanned thirteen times in 541 official at bats.) Nothing up to that time had captivated the media and the sports public like DiMaggio's day-by-day performance—not Babe Ruth's sixty homers in 1927 (because the Babe himself seemed perfectly capable of breaking his own record the next year), not anything else. DiMaggio was no longer the Italian-American curiosity he'd been five years earlier but, as hailed in the hit song commemorating his streak, "Joltin' Joe DiMaggio." It didn't even seem to matter that, as revealed publicly by Lefty Gomez (his roommate on road trips), DiMaggio's principal reading matter consisted of comic books, especially the "Superman" and "Bat Man" series. If DiMaggio saw the latest edition of either of his favorites on a magazine rack, he had Gomez buy it for him. "He doesn't dare buy it himself," explained Gomez, "they all know him, you know."[41]

Because DiMaggio performed for the Yankees in the nation's media capital, was a multitalented player, and generally kept on good terms with the press (even if he rarely spoke in anything but banalities), his streak would dominate retrospective accounts of the 1941 season—including the fact that Washington's Cecil Travis outhit him .359 to .357. Yet eventually what Ted Williams did that year would come to have almost as much of a magical quality as DiMaggio's achievement.

For Williams (who turned twenty-three on August 30), it was a great year all around. His three-run homer off the facade of the Briggs Stadium right-field upper deck—struck off Claude Passeau with two out in the bottom of the ninth inning—won the ninth All-Star Game for the American League, 7–5. (Few people would remember Arky Vaughan's two homers and four RBIs for the National League cause.) That season, Williams perfected his amazing batting eye, walking 145 times in 143 games. But as he stayed above or near .400 week after week, the Boston press found reason to criticize his bases on balls, on the grounds that he was so occupied with protecting his batting average that he wouldn't try to help the team by swinging at pitches not clearly within the strike zone.

To be sure, Williams never seemed greatly concerned with the fortunes of most of his teammates. An exception was Jimmie Foxx, of whom the young Californian was genuinely fond. The 1941 season was Foxx's last productive one (.300, nineteen homers, 105 RBIs); early in the 1942 campaign, at age thirty-three, he would be rudely dumped on waivers to the Chicago Cubs. And while Williams had steered clear of the wrathful Lefty Grove after messing up Grove's game early in the previous season, he no doubt shared in the general satisfaction of Grove's three hundredth career victory on July 25 at Fenway Park, an inelegant 10–6 win over Cleveland. It would be the great left-hander's last.

Whatever animosity Williams may have nurtured over the years toward the Boston press, nothing seems ever to have affected his self-confidence. Early in September, after reaching Lefty Gomez for two doubles and a single at Yankee Stadium (while the Red Sox still lost 8–5), he told *PM*'s Bob Brumby, "I'll break every record in baseball. . . . I'll beat Gehrig's mark for runs batted in, Hornsby's and Cobb's batting record and Ruth's homers. I'm the boy to do it, too."[42]

Williams never did any of those things during his nineteen-year big-league career. But if he'd accomplished nothing else (and over those nineteen seasons, twice interrupted by military service, he would put up staggering numbers), what he did in 1941 was enough to gain him a large measure of immortality. Nobody since Bill Terry had batted .400; sixty years later nobody had done it since Williams.

Williams's three hits in that September 8 game at Yankee Stadium pushed his average to .413. After that he cooled off quite a bit, so that going into the final day of the season—on which the Red Sox would play a doubleheader in Philadelphia—his average stood at .3995. Boston manager Joe Cronin suggested that he sit out the two games and preserve what official statisticians would round out to .400 (as the Athletics' Wally Moses did that day to stay at .301). But to the prickly youngster's undying credit, he insisted on playing both games, in the opener of which he hit a homer and three singles, followed by a double and a single in the nightcap. At day's end, his average stood at .406. Williams had also increased his major's-leading totals in home runs (thirty-seven), runs (135), and slugging average (.735) and had upped his RBIs to 120.

. . . . .

FIVE YEARS LATER, Washington first baseman James "Mickey" Vernon would beat out Williams for the American League batting title. But in 1941, having just finished his first full season with the Senators, twenty-three-year-old Vernon had to stand in line all night to buy a bleachers seat for the third World Series game at Ebbets Field. The future two-time batting titlist didn't know anybody who could provide tickets; nobody at Ebbets Field recognized him.

By the time Mickey Vernon got to see his first Series game, the Yankees and Dodgers had garnered a victory apiece in New York City's sixth "subway series." The throng of 68,540 who watched the opener at Yankee Stadium on October 2 was the largest up to then in Series history. Joe McCarthy gave the ball to Red Ruffing, who held Brooklyn to six hits and two runs. Joe Gordon hit a solo homer off Curt Davis in the second inning; the Yankees added single runs in the fourth and sixth. The game's key play came in the seventh inning, when with one out the Dodgers scored their second run and had runners on first and second base. Durocher wanted the runners bunted over, but pinch-hitter Jimmy Wasdell missed the bunt sign and hit a pop foul, which Red Rolfe caught in front of the third base (visitors') dugout. Pee Wee Reese tried to advance to third, but Rizzuto, covering the bag, tagged him out to kill the rally.

Game two ended in the same 3–2 score, but this time Whitlow Wyatt throttled the Yankees, who finally lost a Series game after ten-straight wins. Brooklyn won it in the sixth inning when Gordon (who fielded spectacularly but occasionally messed up easy plays) threw wide to first on Dixie Walker's grounder. After Billy Herman singled, Murphy relieved starting pitcher

Spud Chandler and struck out Reiser but then gave up a run-scoring single to Camilli.

After a rainout, Ebbets Field was full on Sunday, as Brooklyn native Marius Russo pitched a four-hitter, holding the Dodgers runless until the bottom of the eighth, when Reiser drove in Walker. The Yankees had scored twice in the top of that inning on four straight singles off Hugh Casey, who replaced Fred Fitzsimmons in the seventh when Russo's drive hit him squarely in the knee. Although Reese caught the carom on the fly for the third out, Fitzsimmons, who'd shut out the Yankees on four hits up to then, couldn't continue.

For game four, Durocher finally sent twenty-two-game-winner Kirby Higbe to the mound, while Atley Donald got the call from McCarthy. By the end of five innings both had been driven out, and the Dodgers led 4–3 on the strength of Reiser's two-run homer. Casey relieved Johnny Allen in the fifth with the bases loaded, retired the side without a score, and did the same for the next three innings. To start the top of the ninth, Johnny Sturm grounded out to Coscaret (playing in place of Herman, who'd pulled a muscle in his side in the third game), and Red Rolfe tapped weakly back to Casey. Tommy Henrich worked the big right-hander to a three–two count; then something happened that would go down as the single most infamous moment in the history of the Brooklyn Dodgers.

Casey's next pitch was low and inside to the left-hand–batting Henrich, who swung and missed. But as cheers went up over Ebbets Field and from people gathered around radios all over Brooklyn, and as policemen scrambled onto the field to contain the crowd, Owen chased after the ball and Henrich ran safely to first. Owen later said that he had been looking for Casey's "smaller quick" curveball, but instead got "that big one," and it ticked off his mitt. "My fault."[43]

As one baseball writer put it, "Give those Yankees a reprieve and they climb right out of the electric chair and execute the warden."[44] It proved an apt metaphor. DiMaggio followed with a single, and after looking bad on two swings, Charlie Keller doubled off the screen atop the right-field wall, scoring both Henrich and DiMaggio. Dickey drew a base on balls, whereupon Gordon doubled off the left-field wall to drive in Keller and Dickey and put the Yankees ahead 7–4. After Rizzuto walked, Casey was finally able to get Johnny Murphy to ground out. Working his second inning in relief of Marvin Breuer, Murphy then easily retired Reese, Walker, and Reiser to end it.

Owen might get sympathy in some quarters, but not from the Yankees, still angered by his spikes-first leap into Rizzuto in game two as the short-stop tried to complete a double play. "He tried to cut Phil down," snapped Donald. "He played dirty ball." Added the usually taciturn DiMaggio, "As long there has to be a goat, I'm glad it was him. We're not a bit sorry for him."[45]

Game five, something of an anticlimax, was nonetheless a strong exhibition of pitching by the weathered Wyatt and the cherubic Bonham, whose looks belied his twenty-eight years. Bonham let the Dodgers have a run in the first inning but pitched hitless ball after the third. Gordon singled in Keller in the second to put New York ahead 2–1; Henrich added a bases-empty home run in the fifth. Wyatt, perhaps frustrated by his teammates' inability to score runs for him, had a confrontation with DiMaggio when, after flying out to Reiser, the Yankees' star passed the mound on his way back to the third-base dugout. Both dugouts emptied; players did the usual milling around before the umpires disbursed them.

Bonham retired the Dodgers on three pitches in the eighth and then set down Camilli, Medwick, and Wasdell (hitting for Reese) to clinch still another Yankees Series championship and nearly $6,000 for each team member. The Dodgers would have to console themselves with record losers' shares that came to $4,808 each.

That wasn't much consolation for Durocher, who endured a lot of second-guessing: for starting Davis rather than Wyatt or Higbe in game one, for holding Higbe back until game four, and, most of all, for not going to the mound to calm Casey after Owen's passed ball. While Durocher acknowledged that mistake ("I sat on my ass and didn't do anything"), he never explained it.[46]

· · · · ·

OVERALL, big-league attendance for 1941—nearly 10.5 million—closely reflected the nation's booming economy. The Cardinals doubled their home crowds, the bottom-rung Athletics increased theirs by 200,000, and even the Phillies, who managed to win only forty-three games, sold more tickets than they had since 1930. The general condition of the minor leagues was one of robust health, with forty-one circuits again starting and finishing the season.

Two months and two days after Joe DiMaggio gathered in Jimmy Was-dell's long fly to end the World Series, the Japanese struck the American fleet at Pearl Harbor in the Hawaiian Islands; within a few days Germany and Italy, in accordance with their military pact with Japan, had joined the war against the United States. For the first time since winning independence, this country would fight a war with formal military allies, not only Great Britain but also the Soviet Union, whose twenty-two months of self-deceiving neutrality (under its 1939 pact with Germany) had ended with the Third Reich's onslaught on the USSR's western republics the previous summer. Having weathered the worst of times in the Great Depression, baseball was about to confront a dramatically new set of circumstances in a time of war. Like nearly everything else in American life, baseball would never really be the same.

Postscript

BY THE FALL OF 1941—with the United States providing ever-increasing aid to Great Britain and the Soviet Union under the Lend-Lease program, cooperating in the British antisubmarine campaign in the North Atlantic, and stymied in its efforts to pressure Japan into withdrawing from China—most Americans, ballplayers included, seemed resigned to their country's full-scale involvement in the war. The Cardinals' Enos Slaughter, Ernie White, and Johnny Hopp, together with the Browns' Joe Grace, took off-season jobs at a small-arms factory in St. Louis; the Athletics' Sam Chapman and Benny McCoy joined the U.S. Navy; and Washington's Buddy Lewis volunteered for the Army Air Corps. At the beginning of December, Sergeant Hank Greenberg was discharged from army duty but placed in the active reserves, subject to immediate recall. Nearly three hundred minor leaguers were now in the armed forces, according to National Association president Bramham.

Yet in other respects, the affairs of baseball proceeded pretty much as usual. On October 3 Bobby Feller, pitching for an ensemble called Mike Gonzalez's All-Stars, kicked off a barnstorming tour with Satchel Paige and the Kansas City Monarchs at Sportsman's Park in St. Louis, where about 10,000 watched them work five innings apiece. With the All-Stars ahead 4–1, Feller and Paige gave way to Pittsburgh's Ken Heintzelman and the Monarchs' Hilton Smith, who kept the score unchanged. Meanwhile, in Los Angeles, Ted Williams played for Joe Pirrone's All-Stars against Buck Leonard and other Negro leaguers, who again appeared as Tom Wilson's Royal Giants.

At age forty-one, Lefty Grove, his three hundred wins safely in the record books, retired to his home in Lonaconing, Maryland, where everybody admired him. But when Mickey Owen, who owned a farm near Brookfield, Missouri, went into town for supplies, he was accosted by a local resident who told him that he'd really like to kick Owen's rear end for having missed that pitch in the World Series. Meanwhile Dizzy Dean, still hoping to resurrect his pitching arm, underwent treatments by a Philadelphia athletic trainer named Willie Clark, who'd invented a contraption called a "nervo-mulizer" that supposedly broke up adhesions and stimulated blood flow to tissues and nerves. It didn't work; Dean would have to stick to radio play-by-play.

In the major deals of the off-season, Pittsburgh traded Arky Vaughan to Brooklyn for Luke Hamlin, Jimmy Wasdell, Pete Coscaret, and Babe Phelps, and the Cardinals gave Johnny Mize to the Giants in exchange for $50,000 and three players. Joe Moore and Burgess Whitehead, stalwarts of the Giants' 1930s pennant winners, were sold to Indianapolis and Toronto, respectively. Ben Chapman's fiery big-league career ended with his release by the White Sox; the 1942 season would find him managing in the Piedmont League.

In the usual postseason round of managerial changes, Bill Terry finally moved into the Giants' front office full time and entrusted the team to Mel Ott, still only thirty-two and still one of the majors' top power hitters. At twenty-four and with a decade as a player still ahead of him, Lou Boudreau succeeded Roger Peckinpaugh in Cleveland, thereby becoming the last "boy manager." The woebegone Phillies replaced Doc Prothro with sixty-year-old John "Hans" Lobert, who'd been Prothro's coach.

In the spring of 1940. Henry Misselwitz, a Hollywood screenwriter who'd spent some time in Japan as a correspondent, had published a magazine piece describing that country's passion for baseball. Instead of devising their own terminology, the Japanese had simply adapted American baseball language, so that umpires yelled "Bauruu!" and "Strik-u!" and everybody got excited over a "Homuruno." Although as yet Japan didn't have a professional league, Misselwitz foresaw the day when American and Japanese baseball champions would meet in a true World Series. In any case, the two countries' love for the game ought to help promote mutual understanding and respect, because, concluded Misselwitz, "you can't hate a man you literally play ball with—not for long, anyway."[1]

Yet a year and a half later, the roving baseball comedian Al Schacht, having just returned by boat from an appearance at a Hawaiian baseball tournament, acknowledged worrying "if the waters of the Pacific are safe."[2] Within another couple of weeks, the Japanese had proved how treacherous those waters had become.

On December 8, with Pearl Harbor still aflame from the Japanese bombing twenty-four hours earlier, major-league owners and officials gathered at the Palmer House in Chicago for their annual winter meetings. Browns owner Donald Barnes arrived with a plan for moving his franchise to Los Angeles, where Philip Wrigley had agreed to sell his Pacific Coast League franchise and ballpark for $1 million. A group of local civic boosters had guaranteed to cover any losses that Barnes might incur if attendance didn't reach 500,000. A detailed study of airline schedules supposedly supported the feasibility of the move. But with the country going to war, all was confusion and uncertainty—and would be until a few weeks later, when President Roosevelt gave his famous "green light" sanction for baseball's continuation in wartime. So the Browns remained in St. Louis, where in 1944, under the managership of Luke Sewell (who'd replaced Fred Haney during the 1941 season), their assortment of overage and physically deferred players would win the only pennant in the franchise's fifty-two years in the American League.

If Pearl Harbor determined that the Browns would stay in St. Louis, it also gave Philip Wrigley an excuse for not lighting Wrigley Field, which he probably didn't want to do anyhow. Wrigley had purchased $185,000 worth of lights, steel towers, and wiring and had contracted to have installation work begun on December 8. With the nation at war, the Cubs' owner donated the materials to the War Department. It would be 1988, eleven years after Wrigley's death, before the first night game was played in his ballpark.

Two days after his discharge and a day after Pearl Harbor, Hank Greenberg, at age thirty, reenlisted. "We are in trouble," he said in a formal press statement, "and there is only one thing for me to do—return to the service. I have not been called back. I am going back of my own accord."[3] Greenberg wouldn't return to the Tigers until late in the 1945 season.

Bobby Feller was driving in his new Buick from Iowa to the majors meetings in Chicago to talk with Cleveland officials about his 1942 contract when he heard the news of the Japanese attack on his car radio. Upon his arrival, Feller told Indians general manage Cy Slapnicka to forget the contract; he was enlisting in the navy. "A lot of people thought I was crazy," recalled Feller in his autobiography. He didn't have to enlist; having been granted a deferment because his father was terminally ill, he could have continued playing for at least another season. "That wasn't the way most young men felt, though. . . . We were outraged about Pearl Harbor and what Hitler was doing in Europe."[4] So at the age of twenty-two, having already gained 107 victories (more than anybody at that age), Feller put his career on hold for what in his case would be nearly four seasons.

By the spring of 1942, forty-one players from the American League and twenty from the National League had entered military service. Not everybody was stirred by a compelling sense of patriotic duty. Despite taking quite a lot of public criticism, Joe DiMaggio, who had become a father in October 1941, stayed around to lead the Yankees to another pennant. With his marriage falling apart, DiMaggio joined the Army Air Corps in February 1943. Ted Williams topped the majors in batting average (.356) and virtually every other offensive category in 1942 before entering training to become a Marine pilot. Under a family hardship deferment, Stan Musial remained with the Cardinals through three consecutive National League pennants, two World Series victories, and the first of his seven batting titles before entering the navy following the 1944 season.

Some frontline performers—such as Lou Boudreau (arthritic ankles), Detroit left-hander Hal Newhouser (heart murmur), and the Cubs' slugging Bill Nicholson (diabetes)—continued playing under 4-F physical disqualifications. Others such as Luke Appling, Roger Cramer, and Dixie Walker were too old to be drafted by the time the Selective Service System began scraping the bottom of the manpower barrel in 1944. Others who were still older—Paul Waner and Mel Harder, for example—were able to hang on for a few more years as the available talent steadily dwindled.

Feller saw plenty of action aboard warships in both the Atlantic and Pacific theaters; Greenberg served with a B-29 bomber unit operating out of western China; and Harry Walker, Dixie's younger brother and the Cardinals' regular center fielder in 1942, was a combat infantryman during the Allies' push across western Europe. But most major-league players who entered the armed services stayed out of harm's way. In fact, many of them served their country mainly by playing baseball for service teams and in interservice all-star games. Of the approximately 400,000 Americans who gave their lives, only two were onetime big leaguers. Elmer Gedeon, a University of Michigan graduate who appeared in five games for Washington in 1939, was lost in air combat over France, and Harry O'Neill, a Philadelphia native who caught one inning for the Athletics, also in 1939, was killed on Iwo Jima.

Minor leaguers were more likely to experience combat, and many did.

One was a young left-handed pitcher named Warren Spahn, who reminded a Boston writer of Herb Pennock during the Braves' spring training at San Antonio in 1941. Optioned to the Three-I League, Spahn won nineteen games that season and seventeen in the Eastern League the next before going up to the Braves in time to make four appearances. Spahn spent the next three years in the infantry, seeing some of the war's toughest fighting in the Allied drive into Germany. When he returned to the Braves in 1946, he began a twenty-one-year career that would make him the winningest left-hander in history.

Larry MacPhail, restless as ever, took the war as the occasion for leaving the Brooklyn organization. Shortly after the Dodgers lost the pennant to the Cardinals on the last day of the 1942 season, MacPhail resigned to enter the army with a lieutenant colonel's commission. The franchise's directors quickly brought in Branch Rickey, who was ready to leave the Cardinals after several years of deteriorating relations with Sam Breadon. While other big-league executives were content to wait for the war's end and the return of their good players, Rickey busied himself signing young draftees and expanding the Dodgers' minor-league connections, so that by 1946 his farm system was second only to the Cardinals' in extent and number of players. In the postwar years, Brooklyn's superabundant minor-league network, in combination with Rickey's willingness to break down the color barrier and sign Jackie Robinson, Roy Campanella, and a succession of other gifted black players, would make the Dodgers the powerhouse of the National League.

More than anything before in their history or probably anything that would come afterward, World War II brought Americans together in a common cause and common national effort. The memory of a Long Beach, California, woman typified how her generation thought of the war: "The patriotism was so thick you could cut it with a knife."[5] The war not only ended the Great Depression but created the conditions under which a triumphant American people would enjoy an unprecedented and truly astonishing postwar prosperity—good times in which baseball would share fully. Although the Negro leagues went into sharp decline with the grudging acceptance of black professionals within Organized Baseball, the sport as a whole would experience its last great boom in the immediate pretelevision years.

By 1950 most of those who'd played in the Depression era were out of baseball; many were all but forgotten. They naturally envied the bigger salaries being paid in the postwar good times (just as the players of those years would envy what those who came after them would make). For ball-players in the Depression era, the professional game wasn't just how they wanted to make a living; for many of them, it was about the only way they could make a living. The players of those hard times would often look back on the baseball of their day as having been more rugged and generally more demanding than the game they watched in later decades. Billy Rogell, for one, was sure of it. "The competition was so much keener when I played," he said in 1986. "We got guys playing major-league ball today that we wouldn't have even let in the ballpark in my day. It's a lousy way to say it, but it's true. I played in the best era of baseball."[6]

If Rogell exaggerated, it was the pardonable foible of an old man who was proud of what he'd accomplished in baseball and proud of the men he'd played with and against. But then again, he just may have been right.

Notes

1. Past Times

1. A notable exception was the Pacific Coast League (often called the strongest of the minor leagues), based where the mild climate made possible a schedule varying from 180 to 200 games and extending from March to October.

2. Ruppert gained his own ballpark namesake when in 1932 the Yankees purchased the Newark International League franchise, and Ruppert acceded to renaming the local ballpark Ruppert Stadium.

3. I'll confess to considerable skepticism about the heights and weights at which baseball players are listed today. Given the current fixation on size, long-distance hitting, and ninety-five-mile-per-hour fastballs, it's not unlikely that many young athletes fudge on their size to influence scouts, coaches, and anybody else they feel they need to impress. Sports publicity people may even aid the process. The figures on the 1936 Yankees I take to be pretty accurate, although rookie Joe DiMaggio was listed as 2 inches shorter than his generally accepted height of nearly 6 feet 2 inches.

4. Here I'm using the 1936 Yankees spring-training roster of thirty-three players, including five catchers, and the 2000 Yankees regular-season roster of twenty-seven (including three players on the disabled list), which had only two catchers.

5. *Sporting News*, August 16, 1934, p. 1; *Baseball Magazine*, March 1934, p. 480.

6. Brent Kelley, *The Early All-Stars: Conversations with Standout Ballplayers of the 1930s and 1940s* (Jefferson, N.C.: McFarland, 1997), p. 38.

7. *Sporting News*, February 24, 1938, p. 4.

8. Richard Bak, *Cobb Would Have Caught It: The Golden Age of Baseball in Detroit* (Detroit: Wayne State University Press, 1991), p. 193.

9. Ibid., p. 268.

10. Kelley, *Early All-Stars*, p. 56.

11. *New York Times*, August 18, 1933, p. 11.

12. The period did see one fatality as a result of a batter's being hit in the head by a pitch. In 1936 twenty-year-old George Tkach, playing for Superior in the Class D Northern League, died after being hit by Alex Ufferman of Winnipeg.

13. Clifford Bloodgood, "Sheer Perseverance Has Made Tom Oliver," *Baseball Magazine*, July 1932, p. 377; Rick Van Blair, "Harry Danning: Catching Star of Another Era," *Baseball Digest*, October 1994, p. 64.

14. Bak, *Cobb Would Have Caught It*, p. 306.

15. Norman L. Macht, "Baseball of Another Era Left Some Golden Moments," *Baseball Digest*, August 1995, p. 63.

16. In August 1938, when Washington gave Wes Ferrell, one of the top pitchers of the decade, his outright release despite his 13–8 record for the season, Washington owner Clark Griffith (who'd worked thirty-nine complete games himself in the National League in 1895) explained that Ferrell "couldn't finish what he started. . . . Somebody had to finish the game for him" (*Sporting News*, August 18, 1938, p. 1).

17. Although rarely mentioned, another reason for shorter games in the 1930s was the absence of television, with its insistence on crowding a succession of commercials into each half-inning break. Such breaks today average nearly three minutes; in the thirties, even with the advent of radio sponsors, the break time was about half that.

18. Bob Smizik, *The Pittsburgh Pirates: An Illustrated History* (New York: Walker, 1990), p. 61.

19. Kelley, *Early All-Stars*, p. 37; Lawrence S. Ritter, *The Glory of Their Times*, rev. ed. (New York: Vintage, 1985), p. 279; Walter Langford, "Bill Werber: Star of Another Era," *Baseball Digest*, March 1988, p. 77.

20. *New York Times*, June 23, 1935, p. 3.

2. The Last Fat Year, 1930

1. Hank Greenberg, *The Story of My Life*, ed. Ira Berkow (New York: Times Books, 1989), p. 18.

2. F. C. Lane, "He Played a Lone Hand to the Limit," *Baseball Magazine*, August 1931, p. 421.

3. *Sporting News*, August 21, 1930, p. 5.

4. *Baseball Magazine*, September 1930, p. 434.

5. William Wrigley Jr., "Owning a Big-League Ball Team," *Saturday Evening Post*, September 13, 1930, p. 25.

6. *Chicago Tribune*, August 1, 1930, p. 17.

7. *St. Louis Post-Dispatch*, September 25, 1930, p. 16; Dick Bartell and Norman L. Macht, *Rowdy Richard* (Berkeley, Calif.: North Atlantic, 1987), p. 77.

8. Kyle Crichton, "The Great Hoiman," *Collier's*, August 19, 1932, p. 35.

9. Norman L. Macht, "Doc Cramer: He Remembers Playing for Connie Mack," *Baseball Digest*, January 1987, p. 98.

10. Before the 1923 season, Charles Comiskey did pay a reported $100,000 for Pacific Coast League star Willie Kamm. Kamm, a fine third baseman but not a strong

hitter, put in a thirteen-year American League career with Chicago and later Cleveland, but he never really justified his original price tag.

11. *New York Times*, May 3, 1930, p. 13.

12. F. C. Lane, "The Romance of Night Baseball," *Baseball Magazine*, October 1930, p. 483.

13. *New York Times*, June 27, 1930, p. 26; *Sporting News*, January 16, 1930, p. 4. One wonders what Spink might have thought about the abundance and variety of today's ballpark food—and the enormous amount of eating that goes on during games now played preponderantly at night.

14. *Baseball Magazine*, July 1930, p. 338.

15. William B. Mead, *Two Spectacular Seasons: 1930—The Year the Hitters Ran Wild; 1968—The Year the Pitchers Took Revenge* (New York: Macmillan, 1990), p. 59; Charles C. Alexander, *Rogers Hornsby: A Biography* (New York: Holt, 1995), p. 161; *New York Times*, May 15, 1930, p. 25.

16. John Thorn, "The 1930 Phillies," *National Pastime* 13 (1993): 73.

17. Many years later, Rhem claimed that he was actually suffering from food poisoning, that he was "sicker than I have ever been my life" when he woke up the morning of September 16. He didn't pitch in the series in Brooklyn, but he defeated Philadelphia 9–3 a few days later (John Thorn, "The Kidnapping of Flint Rhem," *National Pastime* 10 [1990]: 79–82).

18. *St. Louis Post-Dispatch*, October 1, 1930, p. 1B.

19. *St. Louis Post-Dispatch*, October 4, 1930, p. 3B.

3. Lean Years, 1931–1932

1. *Sporting News*, October 23, 1930, p. 7. Whereas Ruppert's title was honorary, T. L. Huston was a legitimate retired colonel in the U.S. Army Corps of Engineers.

2. "The Lively Ball Wins!" *Baseball Magazine*, January 1931, p. 467; "Modern Baseball, the Greatest Ever," *Baseball Magazine*, July 1931, p. 340.

3. The sacrifice-fly rule, first adopted in 1908, had initially pertained only to run-scoring flies, but in 1926 it was broadened to include flies on which runners tagged and moved up to second or third base as well.

4. In the absence of numbers on players' uniforms, spectators hadn't been totally without means of identifying them. Apart from the age-old practice of having the umpire-in-chief or somebody else bellow out the names of starting pitchers and catchers—the batteries—through a megaphone before the game started, since early in the century teams in the majors and upper minors, at least, had posted starting lineups by position and by assigned number on their scoreboards. Fans could then match the scoreboard numbers with the same numbers alongside players' names on their scorecards.

5. Quoted in *Sporting News*, April 23, 1931, p. 2.

6. *Sporting News*, May 21, 1931, p. 4; *Sporting News*, October 22, 1931, p. 4; "How Raised Stitches Raise a Baseball Argument," *Literary Digest*, May 30, 1931, p. 41; *New York Times*, June 25, 1931, p. 32.

7. Anthony J. O'Connor, ed., *Baseball for the Love of It: Hall of Famers Tell It Like It Was* (New York: Macmillan, 1982), p. 297.

8. *New York Times*, August 16, 1931, sec. 10, p. 2.

9. "A Fighting Pitcher Discusses His Trade," *Baseball Magazine*, November 1931, p. 544.

10. Gehrig would have won the home-run title with forty-seven if on April 26 teammate Lyn Lary hadn't thought Gehrig's drive into the center-field stands at Washington had actually been caught. Lary trotted to the third-base visitors' dugout while Gehrig crossed home plate and was called out for passing a runner. Lary's gaffe also cost the Yankees the game, 9–7.

11. Jim Kaplan, *Lefty Grove: American Original* (Cleveland: Society for American Baseball Research, 2000), p. 150.

12. *New York Times*, September 17, 1931, p. 32.

13. *Sporting News*, July 16, 1931, p. 1.

14. *Sporting News*, July 9, 1931, p. 1.

15. Rick Van Blair, "Jo Jo Moore Recalls Days with Old New York Giants," *Baseball Digest*, March 1990, p. 72.

16. *St. Louis Post-Dispatch*, October 8, 1931, p. 2B.

17. Although vaudeville had gone into decline with the advent of talking motion pictures at the end of the 1920s, baseball players still could nicely supplement their playing salaries with postseason appearances on the Loews, Keith-Albee, and other theater circuits.

18. George Vass, "Top Base Running Feats, Blunders in World Series," *Baseball Digest*, September 1985, p. 24.

19. Frederick G. Lieb, *Baseball as I Have Known It* (reprint, Lincoln: University of Nebraska Press, 1996), p. 197.

20. *St. Louis Post-Dispatch*, October 12, 1931, p. 4B.

21. *Sporting News*, December 10, 1931, p. 5.

22. *Baseball Magazine*, February 1932, p. 401; "The Spotlight on Sports," *Outlook*, January 27, 1932, p. 116; *Sporting News*, January 21, 1932, p. 4.

23. *Sporting News*, December 10, 1931, p. 1.

24. Eugene C. Murdock, *Baseball Between the Wars: Memories of the Game by the Men Who Played It* (Westport, Conn.: Meckler, 1992), p. 73.

25. Tommy Henrich and Bill Gilbert, *Five O'Clock Lightning: Ruth, Gehrig, DiMaggio, Mantle, and the Glory Years of the New York Yankees* (New York: Carol, 1992), p. 21; Bill Werber and C. Paul Rogers III, "A Veritable Who's Who of Managing," *Nine* 8 (1999): 89.

26. Joe Williams, "Busher Joe McCarthy," *Saturday Evening Post*, April 15, 1939, pp. 12, 77. In 1931 Chapman stole sixty-one times, the most in either league in eleven years.

27. *New York Times*, April 2, 1932, p. 8.

28. Although Vaughan grew up in California, he'd been born in Arkansas, thus the nickname "Arky."

29. Van Blair, "Jo Jo Moore Recalls," p. 73.

30. *Sporting News*, July 14, 1932, p. 1.

31. *Sporting News*, July 21, 1932, p. 4; "Is Baseball Getting Rougher?" *Literary Digest*, July 23, 1932, p. 35.

32. Charles C. Alexander, *Rogers Hornsby: A Biography* (New York: Holt, 1995), pp. 175–176.

33. *Sporting News*, March 23, 1933, p. 4.

34. Norman L. Macht, "Monte Weaver Recalls Pitching for Old Senators," *Baseball Digest*, May 1992, p. 56.

35. In its early years the stadium was usually called Lakefront. Subsequently it was Municipal Stadium and, in its final thirty years or so, Cleveland Stadium.

36. *Sporting News*, October 6, 1932, p. 1.

37. John P. Carmichael, *My Greatest Day in Baseball* (reprint, Lincoln: University of Nebraska Press, 1996), p. 5. Contrary to what one sees in conflated film footage supposedly depicting Ruth's "called shot" homer, in 1932 there were no tiered bleachers topped by a scoreboard at Wrigley Field. The current configuration dates from several years later.

38. *New York Times*, October 2, 1932, p. 9; *Sporting News*, October 6, 1932, p. 6.

4. The Leanest Year, 1933

1. *Sporting News*, October 13, 1932, p. 1.

2. *Sporting News*, November 10, 1932, p. 1.

3. Rud Rennie, "Changing the Tune from Gloom to Cheer," *Literary Digest*, June 16, 1934, p. 25.

4. *Sporting News*, January 5, 1933, p. 6; *Baseball Magazine*, June 1933, p. 290; *New York Times*, April 11, 1933, p. 24.

5. *Sporting News*, September 7, 1933, p. 4.

6. *Sporting News*, June 6, 1933, p. 2.

7. Bill McCullough, "Meal Ticket," *Saturday Evening Post*, July 3, 1937, p. 87.

8. Rick Van Blair, "Harry Danning: Catching Star of Another Era," *Baseball Digest*, October 1994, p. 64; Edward F. "Dutch" Doyle, "Baker Bowl: A Personal History," *National Pastime* 15 (1995): 28.

9. *Sporting News*, October 10, 1033, p. 3.

10. Charles C. Alexander, *Rogers Hornsby: A Biography* (New York: Holt, 1995), p. 186.

11. *Sporting News*, September 21, 1933, p. 3.

12. Charles C. Alexander, *John McGraw* (New York: Viking, 1988), p. 311. In that first All-Star Game, National Leaguers wore specially made gray road uniforms trimmed in navy blue, with "National League" lettered across the shirtfronts, while American Leaguers wore their individual white home uniforms. From then on, representatives from both leagues would wear the uniforms of their particular teams.

13. Ward also conceived of an annual preseason football game, pitting the reigning National Football League professional champions and a picked team of outstanding graduated college players. The first such game, in August 1934, between the Chicago Bears and the College All-Stars, took place at Chicago's mammoth Soldier Field, where it would continue to be played every year until it was discontinued in 1976.

14. Bruce Kuklick, *To Everything a Season: Shibe Park and Urban Philadelphia* (Princeton, N.J.: Princeton University Press, 1991), p. 72.

15. *Baseball Magazine*, February 1934, p. 386.

5. New Deal Baseball, 1934–1935

1. *Sporting News*, February 1, 1934, p. 1.

2. *Sporting News*, May 24, 1934, p. 4; *Sporting News*, May 31, 1934, p. 8.

3. *Sporting News*, March 1, 1934, p. 4; *New York Times*, April 1, 1934, sec. 3, p. 2.

4. Daniel M. Daniel, "Psychology Wins: The Cleveland Indians Move," *Baseball Magazine*, December 1933, p. 308.

5. Jim Kaplan, *Lefty Grove: American Original* (Cleveland: Society for American Baseball Research, 2000), p. 184.

6. Warren Brown, *The Chicago White Sox* (New York: Putnam, 1952), p. 146.

7. The 1934 All-Star Game generated $52,982 for the players' charity fund, for a total in excess of $100,000 for the first two games.

8. Bob Broeg, "Frankie Frisch: He Played the Game with Gusto," *Baseball Digest*, June 1993, pp. 66, 69.

9. *PM*, September 12, 1941, p. 31.

10. Doug Feldman, *Dizzy and the Gashouse Gang* (Jefferson, N.C.: McFarland, 2000), pp. 108–109.

11. *New York Times*, October 2, 1934, p. 26.

12. *St. Louis Post-Dispatch*, October 12, 1934, p. 2E; *New York Times*, October 3, 1934, p. 28.

13. Stan Grosshandler, "Last of the Old St. Louis Cardinals' Gas House Gang," *Baseball Digest*, June 1992, p. 66; Joseph Skrec, "Fame Forgotten," *National Pastime* 13 (1994): 95.

14. On June 4, 1934, when the Yankees traveled up to New Haven, Connecticut, for an exhibition game, Gehrig stayed behind in New York to have two front teeth pulled, thereby missing his first game of any kind in nine years.

15. *New York Times*, May 23, 1935, p. 30.

16. *New York Times*, March 7, 1930, p. 29.

17. Nicholas Dawidoff, *The Catcher Was a Spy* (New York: Pantheon, 1994), p. 117.

18. Hank Greenberg, *The Story of My Life*, ed. Ira Berkow (New York: Times Books, 1989), pp. 116–117.

19. *New York Times*, October 3, 1934, p. 26.

20. J. Roy Stockton, *The Gas House Gang and a Couple of Other Guys* (New York: Putnam, 1945), p. 64.

21. *St. Louis Post-Dispatch*, October 4, 1934, p. 2B.

22. Feldman, *Dizzy and the Gashouse Gang*, p. 157; *New York Times*, October 7, 1935, p. 4.

23. Norman L. Macht, "Eldon Auker: He Remembers How It Was in the 1930s," *Baseball Digest*, February 1993, p. 64.

24. Hugh Bradley, "The Whole Town Goes Crazy," *Baseball Magazine*, October 1939, p. 483.

25. *New York Times*, October 10, 1934, p. 28.

26. Rob Edelman, "On the Silver Screen," *National Pastime* 18 (1998): 54–55.

27. *St. Louis Post-Dispatch*, October 4, 1934, p. 20.

28. *New York Times*, October 11, 1934, p. 22; Frederick G. Lieb, *The Detroit Tigers* (New York: Putnam, 1946), p. 184.

29. *Sporting News*, October 25, 1934, p. 1.

30. *Baseball Magazine*, January 1935, p. 338.

31. Ibid.

32. Morris "Moe" Berg's fifteen-year career in the majors with six teams was spent mostly in the bullpen, where he entertained and often befuddled teammates with commentary on astronomy, classical Greek philosophy, the intricacies of Sanskrit, and other esoterica.

33. *Sporting News*, April 19, 1934, p. 4.

34. Don Warfield, *The Roaring Redhead: Larry MacPhail* (South Bend, Ind.: Diamond Communications, 1987), p. 58; David Pietrusza, *Judge and Jury: The Life and Times of Judge Kenesaw Mountain Landis* (South Bend, Ind.: Diamond Communications, 1998), p. 382; *Sporting News*, December 17, 1934, p. 3.

35. Salary figures reported by sportswriters were often on the money but often considerably off base. From 1935 on the most reliable figures were those released by the U.S. House Ways and Means Committee two years after each tax year, as required under the Revenue Act of 1935.

36. *Sporting News*, May 23, 1935, p. 1.

37. *Sporting News*, May 30, 1935, p. 3.

38. *Sporting News*, September 5, 1935, p. 6.

39. Detroit again hosted the Series opener because in 1934, with the national American Legion convention occupying most of the downtown hotel space in St. Louis, the first game had been moved to Detroit. Thereby, however, the National League forfeited its position in the pattern of alternating the opener between the two leagues.

40. Norman L. Macht, "Whatever Happened to All the Chatter on the Field?" *Baseball Digest*, January 1992, p. 47.

41. *Chicago Tribune*, October 5, 1935, p. 21; Pietrusza, *Judge and Jury*, p. 344.

42. Lawrence S. Ritter, *The Glory of Their Times*, rev. ed. (New York: Vintage, 1985), p. 288.

43. Macht, "Eldon Auker," p. 64.

44. *New York Times*, October 7, 1935, p. 32.

45. *Time*, October 7, 1935, p. 23.

46. Ritter, *Glory of Their Times*, p. 288.

6. Toward Recovery, 1936–1937

1. Paul Dean passed up the 1935 barnstorming season to be with his ailing new wife in Texas.

2. *New York Times*, March 19, 1936, p. 32.

3. When Yankee Stadium opened in 1923, the triple-tiered grandstands didn't touch either foul line. In 1928 Ruppert had the grandstand extended into left-center field.

4. The 1935 Pacific Coast League season was scheduled for 175 games. Pennant-winning San Francisco actually played 173 games; DiMaggio appeared in all but one.

5. *Sporting News*, March 12, 1936, p. 1.

6. *New York Times*, March 21, 1936, p. 21.

7. *New York Times*, April 15, 1936, p. 27.

8. *New York Times*, March 5, 1930, p. 30.

9. *Time*, July 13, 1936, p. 42.

10. Walter Langford, "Pinky Whitney: Star from Another Era," *Baseball Digest*, June 1988, p. 73. Klein returned to the Cubs on May 21, 1936, in a trade that also sent Fabian Kowalik to Philadelphia in exchange for pitcher Curt Davis and outfielder Ethan Allen.

11. *Sporting News*, September 17, 1936, p. 4.

12. *Sporting News*, October 1, 1936, p. 3.

13. *Sporting News*, July 9, 1936, p. 4.

14. *New York Times*, July 28, 1936, p. 14.

15. *New York Times*, August 2, 1936, p. 8.

16. Heywood Broun, "Broun's Page," *Nation*, September 12, 1936, p. 46.

17. *Sporting News*, October 8, 1936, p. 6.

18. Ballplayers of that era usually delayed their celebrating until they got to the clubhouse. That was especially the case at the Polo Grounds, where much of the crowd crossed the field at game's end and exited through the center-field gate to catch the Eighth Avenue elevated train.

19. Ray Robinson, *Iron Horse: Lou Gehrig in His Time* (New York: Harper Perennial, 1991), p. 217.

20. According to Stengel's biographer, Robert W. Creamer, the Stengels invested $10,000 in Texas oil and "made a very nice bundle" (*Stengel: His Life and Times* [New York: Simon and Schuster, 1984], p. 191).

21. *Sporting News*, October 1, 1936, pp. 4–5, 7.

22. *Sporting News*, March 4, 1937, p. 4.

23. *Sporting News*, April 8, 1937, p. 4; *New York Times*, April 4, 1937, sec. 4, p. 8.

24. *New York Times*, March 1, 1936, p. 23; *New York Times*, March 2, 1936, p. 25.

25. Tommy Henrich and Bill Gilbert, *Five O'Clock Lightning: Ruth, Gehrig, DiMaggio, Mantle, and the Glory Years of the New York Yankees* (New York: Carol, 1992), p. 6.

26. *New York Times*, May 25, 1937, p. 21; Dick Bartell and Norman L. Macht, *Rowdy Richard* (Berkeley, Calif.: North Atlantic, 1987), p. 202.

27. *New York Times*, May 20, 1937, p. 25.

28. Rick Van Blair, "Hall of Famer Dizzy Dean: He Was One of a Kind," *Baseball Digest*, July 1998, p. 76

29. *Sporting News*, June 19, 1937, p. 4; *New York Times*, June 3, 1937, p. 30; *New York Times*, June 5, 1937, p. 28.

30. Bartell and Macht, *Rowdy Richard*, p. 217.

31. Oscar Eddleston, "The '37 All-Star Game," *National Pastime* 17 (1997): 120.

32. *New York Times*, September 9, 1937, p. 28; *Sporting News*, September 15, 1937, p. 2; *Sporting News*, September 16, 1937, p. 1.

33. *Sporting News*, July 1, 1937, p. 4.

34. At this point it would be well to remember that saves wouldn't be given official recognition in pitching records until 1967, when a complicated scoring rule was adopted to give credit to pitchers who worked all or mostly in relief. Murphy's and Brown's achievements were generally understood at the time but not officially quantified.

35. Richard Bak, *Cobb Would Have Caught It: The Golden Age of Baseball in Detroit* (Detroit: Wayne State University Press, 1991), p. 237.

36. Stanley Frank, "Rough Riders of the Dugout," *Saturday Evening Post*, May 17, 1941, p. 86.

37. *Sporting News*, October 14, 1937, p. 4.

38. Tom Meany, "The New Minor League: The National?" *Saturday Evening Post*, March 19, 1938, p. 12.

7. Pathos and Progress, 1938–1939

1. *Sporting News*, February 11, 1937, p. 2; *Sporting News*, November 11, 1937, p. 9; Robert W. Creamer, *Babe: The Legend Comes to Life* (New York: Penguin, 1985), p. 405.

2. *Sporting News*, March 10, 1938, p. 4.

3. J. Roy Stockton, "The People's Choice: The National League," *Saturday Evening Post*, July 16, 1938, p. 68.

4. *Sporting News*, January 27, 1939, p. 4.

5. *New York Times*, March 23, 1938, p. 27.

6. *New York Times*, April 18, 1938, p. 18.

7. Ed Linn, *Hitter: The Life and Turmoils of Ted Williams* (Boston: Harcourt Brace, 1993), p. 82.

8. *Sporting News*, December 16, 1937, p. 9.

9. Tommy Henrich and Bill Gilbert, *Five O'Clock Lightning: Ruth, Gehrig, DiMaggio, Mantle, and the Glory Years of the New York Yankees* (New York: Carol, 1992), p. 42.

10. Joel Zoss and John Bowman, *Diamonds in the Rough: The Untold History of Baseball* (New York: Macmillan, 1989), p. 152.

11. David Pietrusza, *Judge and Jury: The Life and Times of Judge Kenesaw Mountain Landis* (South Bend, Ind.: Diamond Communications, 1998), p. 417.

12. Ibid., p. 416; *Dayton Daily News*, June 26, 1996, p. 11A.

13. "Why the Yankees Win," *Nation*, September 17, 1938, p. 258.

14. *Sporting News*, June 16, 1938, p. 2.

15. Gonzalez, a Cuban catcher who'd played with five National League teams, also did quite a lot of scouting for the Cardinals. He gained a measure of baseball immortality with one report on an infield prospect: "Good field, no hit."

16. Robert W. Creamer, *Baseball and Other Matters in 1941* (reprint, Lincoln: University of Nebraska Press, 2000), p. 51.

17. *New York Times*, July 24, 1938, sec. 5, p. 1.

18. *New York Times*, August 3, 1938, p. 24.

19. Warren Brown, *The Chicago Cubs* (reprint, Carbondale: Southern Illinois University Press, 2001), p. 166.

20. Frederick G. Lieb, *The Pittsburgh Pirates* (New York: Putnam, 1948), p. 263.

21. *New York Times*, September 28, 1938, p. 24.

22. Rick Van Blair, "The Pitcher Who Yielded Famous 'Homer in the Gloamin','" *Baseball Digest*, September 1994, p. 72; John P. Carmichael, *My Greatest Day in Baseball* (reprint, Lincoln: University of Nebraska Press, 1996), p. 98.

23. *Chicago Tribune*, October 4, 1938, p. 30.

24. *Chicago Tribune*, October 10, 1938, p. 20.

25. Joe DiMaggio, "Pitchers I Have Hit," *Collier's*, July 29, 1939, p. 34; Carmichael, *My Greatest Day in Baseball*, p. 15.

26. *Chicago Tribune*, October 10, 1938, p. 20.

27. *Sporting News*, October 13, 1938, p. 7.

28. Eleanor Gehrig and Joseph Durso, *My Luke and I* (New York: Crowell, 1976), p. 5.

29. Rud Rennie, "Stop Squawking!" *Collier's*, March 4, 1939, p. 11.

30. *Sporting News*, October 20, 1938, p. 1.

31. *Sporting News*, December 1, 1938, p. 9.

32. Clayton B. Crosley, "A Conversation with Johnny Vander Meer," *Baseball Research Journal* 13 (1984): 70.

33. Clifford Bloodgood, "They Call Him a Screwball," *Baseball Magazine*, August 1939, p. 403.

34. *Sporting News*, April 14, 1938, p. 4; *Sporting News*, March 23, 1939, p. 3; *Sporting News*, April 6, 1939, p. 1.

35. *New York Times*, March 28, 1939, p. 26.

36. *Sporting News*, May 11, 1939, p. 8. Stratton's attempt at a comeback in 1942 with Lubbock, Texas, in the Class D West Texas–New Mexico League was unsuccessful, but in 1946 he won eighteen games for Sherman in the Class C East Texas League and went on to pitch until 1953 for Texas entries in various other lower minor leagues.

37. *Sporting News*, March 30, 1939, p. 4.

38. *Sporting News*, May 11, 1939, p. 4.

39. *Sporting News*, October 19, 1939, p. 4; Joe Gergen, "Baseball's Most Amazing Streak of Durability," *Baseball Digest*, January 1984, p. 56. Dahlgren had once been the property of the Boston Red Sox and was slated to take over first base for 1935—until the acquisition of Jimmie Foxx.

40. Ray Robinson, *Iron Horse: Lou Gehrig in His Time* (New York: Harper Perennial, 1991), p. 258.

41. Ibid., p. 262.

42. Robert William Henderson, "Baseball's Father," *Current History*, June 1939, pp. 53–54.

43. James A. Vlasich, *A Legend for the Legendary: The Origin of the Baseball Hall of Fame* (Bowling Green, Ohio: Bowling Green Popular Press, 1990), p. 224.

44. *Sporting News*, May 25, 1939, p. 2. The June 26 Yankees–Athletics game was

the first home nighter the Athletics won (3–2), as Henry Pippen outpitched Bump Hadley. The Philadelphia inaugural had taken place on May 16, when in forty-six-degree weather only 15,108 showed up to see Connie Mack's team lose to Cleveland.

45. The previous four-time winners were the St. Louis Browns of the old major-league American Association (1885–1888) and John McGraw's New York Giants (1921–1924). Gehrig posed with the rest of the Yankees for the end-of-season team photograph, but he kept on his suit pants and street shoes and donned only uniform shirt and cap.

46. *Sporting News*, August 24, 1939, p. 16.

47. Bob Johnson, from Pryor, Oklahoma, was the younger brother of Roy Johnson, who was no longer in the majors by 1938.

48. In the American League, Clint Brown surpassed his own record with sixty-one appearances, saving eighteen games and compiling an 11–10 record.

49. In 1925 McKechnie had managed Pittsburgh to a pennant and World Series win over Washington; in 1928 his Cardinals were swept by the Yankees.

50. The 1939 Reds benefited from playing four more home games than the scheduled seventy-seven because of rainouts in the eastern cities that were made up in the West.

51. Norman L. Macht, "Bill Werber Recalls How It Was in the 1930s," *Baseball Digest*, November 1987, p. 89.

52. Bill Werber and C. Paul Rogers III, "A Veritable Who's Who of Managing," *Nine* 8 (1999): 100.

53. *Sporting News*, October 12, 1939, p. 3; *Cincinnati Enquirer*, October 5, 1939, p. 14.

54. *Sporting News*, October 12, 1939, p. 6.

55. Ibid., p. 7. Gehrig's reference was of course to the bribing of seven 1919 Chicago White Sox to throw that year's World Series to the Reds.

56. *Sporting News*, October 12, 1939, p. 3.

8. Baseball Lives

1. *Sporting News*, January 27, 1938, p. 4.

2. *Sporting News*, January 23, 1941, p. 3.

3. Dick Bartell and Norman L. Macht, *Rowdy Richard* (Berkeley, Calif.: North Atlantic, 1987), p. 156.

4. *Sporting News*, June 8, 1933, p. 8; *Sporting News*, July 13, 1933, p. 6.

5. Richard Bak, *Cobb Would Have Caught It: The Golden Age of Baseball in Detroit* (Detroit: Wayne State University Press, 1991), p. 274.

6. William B. Mead, *Two Spectacular Seasons: 1930—The Year the Hitters Ran Wild; 1968—The Year the Pitchers Took Revenge* (New York: Macmillan, 1990), p. 72. Shirley Povich, a sports reporter and columnist for the *Washington Post* for half a century, was once mistakenly listed in a volume of *Notable American Women*.

7. For example, *New York Times*, October 7, 1935, p. 14.

8. *Sporting News*, September 3, 1936, p. 3.

9. F. C. Lane, "The Coming Star of the National League," *Baseball Magazine*, October 1930, p. 493.

10. F. C. Lane, "A Pal for the Waner Boys," *Baseball Magazine*, February 1930, p. 401; George Kirksey, "When a Feller Needs a Fella," *Baseball Magazine*, June 1938, p. 334.

11. Rich Westcott, *Diamond Greats: Profiles and Interview with 65 of Baseball's History Makers* (Westport, Conn.: Meckler, 1988), p. 133.

12. David Pietrusza, *Judge and Jury: The Life and Times of Judge Kenesaw Mountain Landis* (South Bend, Ind.: Diamond Communications, 1998), p. 377.

13. Clifford Bloodgood, "Elon Hogsett, the Cherokee Pitcher," *Baseball Magazine*, July 1933, p. 365.

14. Ken Smith, "The Giants' Jewish Catcher," *Baseball Magazine*, March 1938, p. 474; Clifford Bloodgood, "Arnovich: A Superior Lad from Superior," *Baseball Magazine*, July 1939, p. 347.

15. "How Tony Gives a Latin Tone to Our National Game," *Literary Digest*, July 2, 1932, p. 37.

16. *Sporting News*, July 9, 1931, p. 4; Daniel M. Daniel, "Viva Italia!" *Baseball Magazine*, July 1936, p. 379. Daniel, whose given name was Daniel Margowitz, used the formal "Daniel M." when he wrote for magazines.

17. *Time*, July 13, 1936, p. 43; Charles C. Alexander, *Our Game: An American Baseball History* (New York: Holt, 1991), p. 177; *Sporting News*, September 9, 1937, p. 4.

18. *Cincinnati Enquirer*, March 5, 1940, p. 14; *Sporting News*, March 5, 1938, p. 3; *New York Times*, March 17, 1939, p. 20.

19. *Cincinnati Enquirer*, March 16, 1940, p. 14; Bob Considine, "Ivory from Cuba," *Collier's*, August 3, 1940, p. 19; *Sporting News*, March 16, 1939, p. 6.

20. Hank Greenberg, *The Story of My Life*, ed. Ira Berkow (New York: Times Books, 1989), p. 42.

21. Ralph W. Brewer, "Look at Them College Boys," *Baseball Magazine*, February 1930, p. 394; *Sporting News*, March 29, 1934, p. 5; Bill Bryson, "The Majors Go Collegiate," *Baseball Magazine*, July 1935, pp. 369–370; Bill Bryson, "Majoring for the Majors," *Baseball Magazine*, June 1936, pp. 319–320.

22. *Sporting News*, March 21, 1935, p. 5; Bill Terry, "Fly by Night," *Collier's*, April 20, 1940, p. 97; *Sporting News*, December 25, 1941, p. 11; *Sporting News*, November 24, 1938, p. 3.

23. *Sporting News*, December 7, 1939, p. 4.

24. "The Secret of Jimmy [*sic*] Foxx's Slugging Power," *Baseball Magazine*, September 1934, p. 394.

25. Gerald Holland, "Baseball and Ballyhoo," *American Mercury*, May 1937, p. 81.

26. Donald Honig, *Baseball When the Grass Was Real: Baseball from the Twenties to the Forties Told by the Men Who Played It* (New York: Coward, McCann, 1975), p. 148.

27. The use of the term "Big Show" in reference to the major leagues was fairly common in baseball parlance as far back as the 1930s. A later generation of players would usually shorten that to "the Show."

28. Eugene C. Murdock, *Baseball Players and Their Times: Oral Histories of the Game, 1920–1940* (Westport, Conn.: Meckler, 1991), p. 202.

9. Shadowball

1. *Sporting News*, July 13, 1939, p. 1.

2. *Sporting News*, November 5, 1931, p. 5.

3. *Sporting News*, March 11, 1937, p. 4.

4. *Pittsburgh Courier*, July 8, 1933, sec. 2, p. 5.

5. Anthony J. Connor, ed., *Baseball for the Love of It: Hall-of-Famers Tell It Like It Was* (New York: Macmillan, 1982), p. 208.

6. *Pittsburgh Courier*, August 9, 1930, sec. 2, p. 5.

7. *Pittsburgh Courier*, August 2, 1930, sec. 2, p. 4. "Shine," presumably from "shoe shine," being one of innumerable racial slurs of the time.

8. Apparently the source of the Crawfords' nickname was the Crawford Bath House, owned by the club's first sponsor.

9. *Pittsburgh Courier*, March 25, 1933, sec. 2, p. 5.

10. *Pittsburgh Courier*, September 16, 1933, sec. 2, p. 5.

11. Jim Reisler, ed., *Black Writers/Black Baseball: An Anthology of Articles from Black Sportswriters Who Covered the Negro Leagues* (Jefferson, N.C.: McFarland, 1994), p. 147; G. Edward White, ed., "A Diary of the Negro Leagues," *National Pastime* 17 (1997): 27.

12. *Pittsburgh Courier*, October 17, 1936, sec. 2, p. 4.

13. *There Was Always Sun Shining Someplace: Life in the Negro Baseball Leagues* (Refocus Productions/Southwest Texas Public Broadcasting Council, 1983), video.

14. Gail Ingham Berlage, "Effa Manley: A Major Force in Negro Baseball in the 1930 and 1940s," *Nine* 1 (1993): 164.

15. *Sporting News*, October 7, 1937, p. 9; *Pittsburgh Courier*, December 11, 1937, p. 17.

16. Mark Ribowsky, *Don't Look Back: Satchel Paige in the Shadows of Baseball* (New York: Simon and Schuster, 1994), p. 167.

17. John Holway, "The Kid Who Taught Satchel Paige a Lesson," *Baseball Research Journal* 16 (1987): 42.

18. *Chicago Defender*, August 6, 1938, p. 9.

19. *Pittsburgh Courier*, August 20, 1938, p. 17.

20. *Chicago Defender*, August 27, 1938, p. 8. Ted Strong spent the winter months playing professional basketball as a member of Abe Saperstein's Harlem Globetrotters, while veteran Negro-league infielder Clarence "Fats" Jenkins put in many off-seasons with the New York Renaissance, whom the Globetrotters eventually displaced as basketball's main barnstorming attraction.

21. *Chicago Defender*, August 27, 1938, p. 8; Mark Ribowsky, *A Complete History of the Negro Leagues, 1884 to 1955* (Secaucus, N.J.: Birch Lane, 1995), p. 240. Pompez attained full respectability in Organized Baseball when in the 1950s he became a scout for the New York Giants in the Caribbean region.

22. Lawrence S. Katz, *Baseball in 1939* (Jefferson, N.C.: McFarland, 1995), p. 154.

23. Reisler, *Black Writers/Black Baseball*, pp. 16–17.

24. *Pittsburgh Courier*, August 5, 1939, p. 16; *Pittsburgh Courier*, September 2, 1939, p. 16.

25. *Pittsburgh Courier*, July 22, 1939, p. 16

26. *Pittsburgh Courier*, September 2, 1939, p. 16; Reisler, *Black Writers/Black Baseball*, p. 16.

27. *Pittsburgh Courier*, February 17, 1940, p. 16.

28. *Time*, June 3, 1940, p. 44.

29. Ted Shane, "The Chocolate Rube Waddell," *Saturday Evening Post*, July 27, 1940, pp. 79–81. The June 2, 1941, issue of *Life* magazine also carried a picture layout on Paige.

30. The East-West series would continue until 1950.

31. The Vera Cruz Blues were actually based in Mexico City, along with the Mexico City Reds. Jorge Pasquel had a controlling interest in both clubs but named one of them after Vera Cruz, his hometown.

32. Ribowsky, *Complete History of the Negro Leagues*, p. 242; White, "Diary of the Negro Leagues," p. 28.

33. Charles C. Alexander, *Our Game: An American Baseball History* (New York: Holt, 1991), p. 193.

10. Recovery and War, 1940–1941

1. *Sporting News*, January 1, 1940, p. 12.

2. *Sporting News*, November 2, 1939, p. 1.

3. Bill Terry, "Fly by Night," *Collier's*, April 20, 1940, p. 97.

4. Edwin M. Rumill, "Baseball After Dark," *Christian Science Monitor Weekly Magazine*, March 30, 1940, p. 5.

5. Quoted in Harold Winerip, "Speaking of Night Ball," *Baseball Magazine*, August 1940, p. 398.

6. *Cincinnati Enquirer*, March 26, 1940, p. 12.

7. *Cincinnati Enquirer*, March 21, 1940, p. 16.

8. Lawrence S. Katz, *Baseball in 1939* (Jefferson, N.C.: McFarland, 1995), p. 56.

9. *New York Times*, March 26, 1940, p. 24.

10. *Sporting News*, April 18, 1940, p. 4.

11. Honus Wagner and George Kirksey, "Help! Help!—Help for the Pitchers," *Saturday Evening Post*, July 13, 1940, p. 60.

12. *Sporting News*, April 25, 1940, p. 2; Frank Graham, "Big League Hotfoot," *American Magazine*, October 1940, p. 116.

13. *Sporting News*, August 15, 1940, p. 2.

14. Ray Robinson, *Iron Horse: Lou Gehrig in His Time* (New York: Harper Perennial, 1991), pp. 269–270.

15. *Sporting News*, April 10, 1941, p. 12; *New York Times*, July 10, 1940, p. 24.

16. *Sporting News*, July 18, 1940, p. 4.

17. Lou Boudreau and Russell Schneider, *Covering All the Bases* (Champaign, Ill.: Sagamore, 1993), p. 26.

18. Charles C. Alexander, "The 'Cry-Baby' Cleveland Indians of 1940," *Nine* 5 (1996): 5–7.

19. Ibid., p. 8; Stanley Frank, "Rough Riders of the Dugout," *Saturday Evening Post*, May 17, 1941, p. 18.

20. Alexander, " 'Cry-Baby' Cleveland Indians," p. 8.

21. Ibid., p. 9.

22. Ibid., p. 11; Stan Grosshandler, "Floyd Giebell Recalls His Greatest Day in Baseball," *Baseball Digest*, April 1991, pp. 90–91.

23. As of 1940, one qualified for the batting title simply by appearing in one hundred games; Garms played in 103. Subsequently the rule became a minimum of four hundred official at bats and still later 511 total at bats, including walks, sacrifice flies, and bunts.

24. *New York Times*, June 14, 1940, p. 27.

25. *Sporting News*, June 27, 1940, p. 10.

26. Bill Werber and Harold Parrott, "A Ballplayer Boos Back," *Saturday Evening Post*, July 25, 1942, p. 46.

27. *Cincinnati Enquirer*, August 4, 1940, p. 27.

28. William Nack, "The Razor's Edge," *Sports Illustrated*, May 6, 1991, p. 64; James Barbour, "The Death of Willard Hershberger," *National Pastime* 6 (1987): 62–65. Ironically, only eight days before Hershberger's suicide the August 1940 issue of *Baseball Magazine* had appeared on the newsstands with a flattering article on him entitled "Lombardi's Understudy."

29. Giebell would pitch in seventeen games for the Tigers in 1941, with no decisions, before being returned to Buffalo. He never appeared in another game in the big leagues.

30. Rick Van Blair, "In the 1930s, Van Lingle Mungo Was a Scourge for N. L. Hitters," *Baseball Digest*, May 1996, p. 68.

31. Purchased by the Giants late in the 1942 season, Mungo pitched in forty-two games in 1943, was out of baseball in 1944, and ended his big-league career at the age of thirty-four with a fine 14–7 season for the Giants in baseball's last wartime season.

32. *New York Times*, March 14, 1941, sec. 5, p. 2.

33. *Sporting News*, June 12, 1941, p. 17.

34. J. Roy Stockton, *The Gas House Gang and a Couple of Other Guys* (New York: Putnam, 1945), p. 6.

35. *Sporting News*, December 25, 1941, p. 4.

36. *PM*, September 22, 1941, p. 32.

37. *New York Times*, September 30, 1941, p. 25.

38. Robinson, *Iron Horse*, p. 273.

39. *New York Times*, April 20, 1941, sec. 5, p. 2.

40. John Holway, "Who Was the Mystery Man at the End of DiMaggio's Streak?" *Baseball Digest*, June 1991, p. 47.

41. Russell Owen, "DiMaggio, the Unruffled," *New York Times Magazine*, July 13, 1941, p. 19.

42. *PM*, September 5, 1941, p. 31.

43. Norman L. Macht, "Why Did Mickey Miss the Ball?" *National Pastime* 11 (1992): 45.

44. *PM*, October 6, 1941, p. 28.

45. Robert W. Creamer, *Baseball and Other Matters in 1941* (reprint, Lincoln: University of Nebraska Press, 2000), p. 312.

46. Ibid., p. 311.

Postscript

1. Henry Misselwitz, "American Baseball Conquers Japan," *Living Age*, May 1940, p. 225.

2. *Sporting News*, November 20, 1941, p. 11.

3. *Sporting News*, December 18, 1941, p. 1.

4. Bob Feller and Bill Gilbert, *Now Pitching, Bob Feller* (New York: Carol, 1990), p. 116.

5. Studs Terkel, *"The Good War": An Oral History of World War II* (New York: Ballantine, 1985), p. 234.

6. Richard Bak, *Cobb Would Have Caught It: The Golden Age of Baseball in Detroit* (Detroit: Wayne State University Press, 1991), pp. 282–283.

SELECT BIBLIOGRAPHY

NEWSPAPERS

Call and Post (Cleveland), 1934–1941
Chicago Defender, 1932, 1937–1939
Chicago Tribune, 1932–1939
Cincinnati Enquirer, 1939–1940
Cleveland News, 1940
Cleveland Plain Dealer, 1932–1940
Cleveland Press, 1940
Dayton Daily News, 1996
New York Times, 1930–1941
Pittsburgh Courier, 1930–1941
PM, 1940–1941
Sporting News, 1929–1942
St. Louis Post-Dispatch, 1930–1934, 1940–1941

PERSONAL INTERVIEWS

Aloys "Ollie" Bejma, South Bend, Indiana, September 12, 1991
Elwood "Woody" English, Newark, Ohio, September 10, 1991
Travis Jackson, Waldo, Arkansas, December 5, 1985
John Welaj, Arlington, Texas, April 18, 1996

BOOKS

Alexander, Charles C. *John McGraw*. New York: Viking, 1988.
———. *Our Game: An American Baseball History*. New York: Holt, 1991.
———. *Rogers Hornsby: A Biography*. New York: Holt, 1995.

————. *Ty Cobb*. New York: Oxford University Press, 1984.

Allen, Frederick Lewis. *Since Yesterday*. New York: Harper & Row, 1940.

Allen, Lee. *The Cincinnati Reds*. New York: Putnam, 1948.

————. *The National League Story*. New York: Hill and Wang, 1965.

Bak, Richard. *Casey Stengel: A Splendid Baseball Life*. Dallas: Taylor, 1997.

————. *Cobb Would Have Caught It: The Golden Age of Baseball in Detroit*. Detroit: Wayne State University Press, 1991.

Bankes, Jim. *The Pittsburgh Crawfords*. Reprint, Jefferson, N.C.: McFarland, 2001.

Bartell, Dick, and Norman L. Macht, *Rowdy Richard*. Berkeley, Calif.: North Atlantic, 1987.

The Baseball Encyclopedia. 10th ed. New York: Macmillan, 1996.

Benson, Michael. *Ballparks of North America*. Jefferson, N.C.: McFarland, 1989.

Bevis, Charlie. *Mickey Cochrane: The Life of a Baseball Hall of Famer*. Jefferson, N.C.: McFarland, 1998.

Bolino, August P. *From Depression to War: American Society in Transition—1939*. Westport, Conn.: Praeger, 1998.

Bone, Robert S., and Gerald Grunska. *Hack: The Meteoric Life of One of Baseball's First Superstars: Hack Wilson*. Highland Park, Ill.: Highland, 1978.

Boston, Talmadge. *1939: Baseball's Pivotal Year*. Fort Worth, Tex.: Summit Group, 1994.

Boudreau, Lou, and Russell Schneider. *Covering All the Bases*. Champaign, Ill.: Sagamore, 1993.

Brashler, William. *Josh Gibson: A Life in the Negro Leagues*. Chicago: Ivan Dee, 2000.

Brown, Warren. *The Chicago Cubs*. Reprint, Carbondale: Southern Illinois University Press, 2001.

————. *The Chicago White Sox*. New York: Putnam, 1952.

Bruce, Janet. *The Kansas City Monarchs: Champions of Black Baseball*. Lawrence: University Press of Kansas, 1985.

Burk, Robert F. *Much More Than a Game: Players, Owners, and American Baseball Since 1930*. Chapel Hill: University of North Carolina Press, 2001.

Carmichael, John P. *My Greatest Day in Baseball*. Reprint, Lincoln: University of Nebraska Press, 1996.

Carter, Craig, ed. *Daguerreotypes*. 8th ed. St. Louis: Sporting News, 1990.

Chadwick, Bruce. *When the Game Was Black and White: The Illustrated History of the Negro Leagues*. New York: Abbeville, 1992.

Clark, Dick, and Larry Lester, eds. *The Negro Leagues Book*. Cleveland: Society for American Baseball Research, 1994.

Cohen, Stanley. *Dodgers! The First 100 Years*. New York: Carol, 1990.

Connor, Anthony J., ed. *Baseball for the Love of It: Hall-of-Famers Tell It Like It Was*. New York: Macmillan, 1982.

Cramer, Richard Ben. *Joe DiMaggio: The Hero's Life*. New York: Simon and Schuster, 2000.

Creamer, Robert W. *Babe: The Legend Comes to Life*. New York: Penguin, 1985.

———. *Baseball and Other Matters in 1941*. Reprint, Lincoln: University of Nebraska Press, 2000.

———. *Stengel: His Life and Times*. New York: Simon and Schuster, 1984.

Crepeau, Richard. *Baseball: America's Diamond Mind, 1919–1941*. Reprint, Lincoln: University of Nebraska Press, 2000.

Curran, William. *Big Sticks: The Batting Revolution of the Twenties*. New York: Morrow, 1990.

———. *Mitts: A Celebration of Fielding*. New York: Morrow, 1985.

———. *Strikeout: A Celebration of the Art of Pitching*. New York: Crown, 1995.

Daniel, W. Harrison. *Jimmie Foxx*. Jefferson, N.C.: McFarland, 1997.

Dawidoff, Nicholas. *The Catcher Was a Spy*. New York: Pantheon, 1994.

Debono, Paul. *The Indianapolis ABC's*. Jefferson, N.C.: McFarland, 1997.

Dewey, Donald, and Nicholas Acocella. *Encyclopedia of Major League Baseball Teams*. New York: HarperCollins, 1993.

DiMaggio, Dom, and Bill Gilbert. *Real Grass, Real Heroes: Baseball's Historic 1941 Seasons*. New York: Zebra, 1990.

Dixon, Phil, and Patrick J. Hannigan. *The Negro Leagues: A Photographic History*. Mattituck, N.Y.: Amerion, 1992.

Durso, Joseph. *Joe DiMaggio: The Last American Knight*. Boston: Little, Brown, 1995.

Echevarria, Roberto Gonzalez. *The Pride of Havana: A History of Cuban Baseball*. New York: Oxford University Press, 1999.

Eskenazi, Gerald. *The Lip: A Biography of Leo Durocher*. New York: Morrow, 1993.

Feldman, Doug. *Dizzy and the Gashouse Gang*. Jefferson, N.C.: McFarland, 2000.

Feller, Bob, and Bill Gilbert. *Now Pitching, Bob Feller*. New York: Carol, 1990.

Frisch, Frank, and J. Roy Stockton. *The Fordham Flash*. Garden City, N.Y.: Doubleday, 1962.

Gehrig, Eleanor, and Joseph Durso. *My Luke and I*. New York: Crowell, 1976.

Gershman, Michael. *Diamonds: The Evolution of the Ballpark*. Boston: Houghton Mifflin, 1993.

Graham, Frank. *The New York Yankees*. New York: Putnam, 1951.

Greenberg, Hank. *The Story of My Life*. Ed. Ira Berkow. New York: Times Books, 1989.

Gregory, Robert. *Diz: Dizzy Dean and Baseball During the Great Depression*. New York: Viking, 1992.

Henrich, Tommy, and Bill Gilbert. *Five O'Clock Lightning: Ruth, Gehrig, DiMaggio, Mantle, and the Glory Years of the New York Yankees*. New York: Carol, 1992.

Higbe, Kirby, and Martin Quigley. *The High Hard One*. Reprint, Lincoln: University of Nebraska Press, 1998.

Holway, John. *Blackball Stars: Negro League Pioneers*. Westport, Conn.: Meckler, 1988.

———. *Black Diamonds: Life in the Negro Leagues from the Men Who Lived It*. Westport, Conn.: Meckler, 1989.

———. *Josh and Satch*. Westport, Conn.: Meckler, 1991.

———. *Voices from the Great Black Baseball Leagues*. New York: Dodd, Mead, 1975.

Honig, Donald. *Baseball Between the Lines: Baseball in the Forties as Told by the Men Who Played It*. Reprint, Lincoln: University of Nebraska Press, 1993.

———. *Baseball in the '30s: An Illustrated History*. New York: Crown, 1989.

———. *Baseball When the Grass Was Real: Baseball from the Twenties to the Forties Told by the Men Who Played It*. New York: Coward, McCann, 1975.

Jordan, David M. *The Athletics of Philadelphia: Connie Mack's White Elephants, 1901–1954*. Jefferson, N.C.: McFarland, 1999.

Kaplan, Jim. *Lefty Grove: An American Original*. Cleveland: Society for American Baseball Research, 2000.

Kashatus, William C. *Connie Mack's '29 Triumph: The Rise and Fall of the Philadelphia Athletics Dynasty*. Jefferson, N.C.: McFarland, 1999.

Katz, Lawrence S. *Baseball in 1939*. Jefferson, N.C.: McFarland, 1995.

Kavanagh, Jack. *Ol' Pete: The Grover Cleveland Alexander Story*. South Bend, Ind.: Diamond Communications, 1996.

———. *Walter Johnson*. South Bend, Ind.: Diamond Communications, 1995.

Kavanagh, Jack, and Norman Macht. *Uncle Robbie*. Cleveland: Society for American Baseball Research, 1999.

Kelley, Brent. *The Early All-Stars: Conversations with Standout Baseball Players of the 1930s and 1940s*. Jefferson, N.C.: McFarland, 1997.

———. *Voices from the Negro Leagues: Conversations with 52 Standouts of the Period 1924–1960*. Jefferson, N.C.: McFarland, 1998.

Kennedy, David M. *Freedom from Fear: The American People in Depression and War, 1929–1945*. New York: Oxford University Press, 1999.

Kuklick, Bruce. *To Everything a Season: Shibe Park and Urban Philadelphia*. Princeton, N.J.: Princeton University Press, 1991.

Lanctot, Neil. *Fair Dealing and Clean Playing: The Hilldale Club and the Development of Black Professional Baseball, 1910–1932*. Jefferson, N.C.: McFarland, 1994.

Lansche, Jerry. *The Forgotten Championships: Postseason Baseball, 1882–1981*. Jefferson, N.C.: McFarland, 1989.

Leutzinger, Richard. *Lefty O'Doul*. Carmel, Calif.: Carmel Bay, 1997.

Levine, Peter. *Ellis Island to Ebbets Field: Sport and the American Jewish Experience*. New York: Oxford University Press, 1992.

Lewis, Franklin. *The Cleveland Indians*. New York: Putnam, 1949.

Lieb, Frederick G. *Baseball as I Have Known It*. Reprint, Lincoln: University of Nebraska Press, 1996.

———. *The Boston Red Sox*. New York: Putnam, 1948.

———. *The Detroit Tigers*. New York: Putnam, 1946.

———. *The Pittsburgh Pirates*. New York: Putnam, 1948.

———. *The St. Louis Cardinals*. Reprint, Carbondale: Southern Illinois University Press, 2001.

Lieb, Frederick G., and Stan Baumgartner. *The Philadelphia Phillies*. New York: Putnam, 1953.

Linn, Ed. *Hitter: The Life and Turmoils of Ted Williams*. New York: Harcourt
    Brace, 1993.

Lowry, Philip J. *Green Cathedrals*. Reading, Mass.: Addison-Wesley, 1992.

MacFarlane, Paul, ed. *Daguerreotypes of Great Stars of Baseball*. St. Louis:
    Sporting News, 1981.

Mayer, Ronald A. *The 1937 Newark Bears*. Union City, N.J.: Wise, 1980.

McNary, Kyle P. *Ted "Double Duty" Radcliffe*. Minneapolis: McNary, 1994.

McNeil, William F. *The Dodgers Encyclopedia*. Champaign, Ill.: Sports, 1997.

Mead, William B. *Two Spectacular Seasons: 1930—The Year the Hitters Ran Wild;
    1968—The Year the Pitchers Took Revenge*. New York: Macmillan, 1990.

Moore, Jack B. *Joe DiMaggio: A Bio-Bibliography*. Westport, Conn.: Greenwood
    Press, 1986.

Murdock, Eugene C. *Baseball Between the Wars: Memories of the Game by the
    Men Who Played It*. Westport, Conn.: Meckler, 1992.

———. *Baseball Players and Their Times: Oral Histories of the Game, 1920–1940*.
    Westport, Conn.: Meckler, 1991.

O'Connor, Anthony J., ed. *Baseball for the Love of It: Hall of Famers Tell It Like It
    Was*. New York: Macmillan, 1982.

Okkonen, Marc. *Baseball Uniforms of the 20th Century*. New York: Sterling, 1991.

Okrent, Donald, and Harris Lewine. *The Ultimate Baseball Book*. Boston:
    Houghton Mifflin, 1984.

O'Neal, Bill. *The Texas League*. Austin, Tex.: Eakin, 1987.

———. *The Pacific Coast League, 1903–1988*. Austin, Tex.: Eakin, 1990.

Overmyer, James. *Effa Manley and the Newark Eagles*. Metuchen, N.J.: Scarecrow,
    1993.

Peterson, Robert. *Only the Ball Was White: A History of Legendary Black Players
    and All-Black Professional Teams*. Rev. ed. New York: McGraw-Hill, 1984.

Pietrusza, David. *Judge and Jury: The Life and Times of Judge Kenesaw Mountain
    Landis*. South Bend, Ind.: Diamond Communications, 1998.

———. *Lights On! The Wild Century-Long Saga of Night Baseball*. Metuchen,
    N.J.: Scarecrow, 1997.

Povich, Shirley. *The Washington Senators*. New York: Putnam, 1954.

Reisler, Jim, ed. *Black Writers/Black Baseball: An Anthology of Articles from Black
    Sportswriters Who Covered the Negro Leagues*. Jefferson, N.C.: McFarland,
    1994.

Rendle, Ellen. *Judy Johnson: Delaware's Invisible Hero*. Wilmington, Del.: Cedar
    Tree, 1994.

Rhodes, Greg, and John Eradi. *Cincinnati's Crosley Field: The Illustrated History
    of a Classic Ballpark*. Cincinnati: Road West, 1995.

Rhodes, Greg, and Mark Stang. *Reds in Black and White: 100 Years of Cincinnati
    Images*. Cincinnati: Road West, 1999.

Ribowsky, Mark. *A Complete History of the Negro Leagues, 1884 to 1955*.
    Secaucus, N.J.: Birch Lane, 1995.

———. *Don't Look Back: Satchel Paige in the Shadows of Baseball*. New York:
    Simon and Schuster, 1994.

————. *The Power and the Darkness: The Life of Josh Gibson*. New York: Simon and Schuster, 1996.

Rickey, Branch. *The American Diamond: A Documentary History of the Game of Baseball*. New York: Simon and Schuster, 1965.

Riess, Steven A., ed. *Sports and the American Jew*. Syracuse, N.Y.: Syracuse University Press, 1998.

Riley, James A. *Dandy, Day, and the Devil*. Cocoa, Fla.: TK, 1987.

Ritter, Lawrence S. *The Glory of Their Times*. Rev. ed. New York: Vintage, 1985.

————. *Lost Ballparks: A Celebration of Baseball's Legendary Fields*. New York: Viking, 1992.

Robinson, Ray. *Iron Horse: Lou Gehrig in His Time*. New York: Harper Perennial, 1991.

Rogosin, Donn. *Invisible Men: Life in the Negro Leagues*. New York: Atheneum, 1983.

Ruck, Rob. *Sandlot Seasons: Sport in Black Pittsburgh*. Urbana: University of Illinois Press, 1987.

Seidel, Michael. *Streak: Joe DiMaggio and the Summer of '41*. New York: Penguin, 1989.

————. *Ted Williams: A Baseball Life*. Reprint, Lincoln: University of Nebraska Press, 2000.

Shatzkin, Mike, ed. *The Ballplayers: Baseball's Ultimate Biographical Reference*. New York: Morrow, 1990.

Singletary, Wes. *Al Lopez: The Life of Baseball's El Señor*. Jefferson, N.C.: McFarland, 1999.

Smelser, Marshall. *The Life that Ruth Built: A Biography*. Reprint, Lincoln: University of Nebraska Press, 1995.

Smizik, Bob. *The Pittsburgh Pirates: An Illustrated History*. New York: Walker, 1990.

Spink, J. G. Taylor. *Judge Landis and Twenty-five Years of Baseball*. New York: Crowell, 1947.

Starr, Bill. *Clearing the Bases: Baseball Then and Now*. New York: Kesend, 1989.

Staten, Vince. *Ol' Diz: A Biography of Dizzy Dean*. New York: HarperCollins, 1992.

Stein, Fred. *Mel Ott: The Little Giant of Baseball*. Jefferson, N.C.: McFarland, 1999.

Stockton, J. Roy. *The Gas House Gang and a Couple of Other Guys*. New York: Putnam, 1945.

Sullivan, Neil. *The Minors: The Life and Times of Baseball's Poor Relation from 1876 to the Present*. New York: St. Martin's Press, 1990.

Terkel, Studs. *"The Good War": An Oral History of World War II*. New York: Ballantine, 1985.

Thomas, Henry. *Walter Johnson: Baseball's Big Train*. Washington, D.C.: Phenom, 1995.

Thorn, John, et al., eds. *Total Baseball: The Official Encyclopedia of Major League Baseball*. 7th ed. Kingston, N.Y.: Total Sports, 2001.

Tygiel, Jules. *Past Time: Baseball as History*. New York: Oxford University Press, 2000.

Vlasich, James A. *A Legend for the Legendary: The Origin of the Baseball Hall of Fame*. Bowling Green, Ohio: Bowling Green Popular Press, 1990.

Voigt, David Quentin. *American Baseball*. Vol. 2, *From the Commissioners to Continental Expansion*. Norman: University of Oklahoma Press, 1970.

Warfield, Don. *The Roaring Redhead: Larry MacPhail*. South Bend, Ind.: Diamond Communications, 1987.

Watkins, T. H. *The Hungry Years: A Narrative History of the Great Depression*. New York: Holt, 1999.

Wecter, Dixon. *The Age of the Great Depression, 1929–1941*. New York: Macmillan, 1948.

Werber, Bill, and C. Paul Rogers III. *Memories of a Ballplayer: Bill Werber and Baseball in the 1930s*. Cleveland: Society for American Baseball Research, 2001.

Westcott, Rich. *Diamond Greats: Profiles and Interviews with 65 of Baseball's History Makers*. Westport, Conn.: Meckler, 1988.

Wheeler, Lonnie, and John Baskin. *The Cincinnati Game*. Wilmington, Ohio: Orange Frazier, 1988.

White, G. Edward. *Creating the National Pastime: Baseball Transforms Itself, 1903–1953*. Princeton, N.J.: Princeton University Press, 1996.

Williams, Ted, and John Underwood. *My Turn at Bat*. 2d ed. New York: Simon and Schuster, 1988.

Zingg, Paul J., and Mark D. Medeiros. *Runs, Hits, and an Era: The Pacific Coast League, 1903–1958*. Urbana: University of Illinois Press, 1994.

Zoss, Joel, and John Bowman. *Diamonds in the Rough: The Untold History of Baseball*. New York: Macmillan, 1989.

ARTICLES

Alexander, Charles C. "The 'Cry-Baby' Cleveland Indians of 1940." *Nine* 5 (1996): 1–17.

"America Cries Play Ball in a Recovery Year." *Literary Digest*, April 14, 1934, pp. 30–31.

Anderson, Arthur O. "Bean Balls and Helmets." *Baseball Magazine*, October 1940, pp. 497–498.

Barbour, James. "The Death of Willard Hershberger." *National Pastime* 6 (1987): 62–65.

Barrow, Edward Grant, and Arthur Mann. "Baseball Cavalcade." *Saturday Evening Post*, April 24, 1937, p. 34.

"Baseball Precedent." *Literary Digest*, February 8, 1936, p. 37.

Berg, Moe. "Pitchers and Catchers." *Atlantic Monthly*, September 1941, pp. 282–288.

Berlage, Gail Ingham. "Effa Manley: A Major Force in Black Baseball in the 1930s and 1940s." *Nine* 1 (1993): 162–184.

Beverage, Dick. "A Forgotten Boston Pennant Race." *National Pastime* 15 (1995): 13–18.

"Big League Baseball." *Fortune*, August 1937, pp. 36–45.

Bjarkman, Peter C. "First Hispanic Star? Dolf Luque, Of Course." *Baseball Research Journal* 19 (1990): 28–32.

Black, C. M. "Carl Hubbell." *Scribner's Magazine*, April 1938, pp. 23–28.

Bloodgood, Clifford. "A Big-League Castoff Who Broke a Record." *Baseball Magazine*, May 1932, p. 555.

———. "Arnovich: A Superior Lad from Superior." *Baseball Magazine*, July 1939, p. 347.

———. "Elon Hogsett, the Cherokee Pitcher." *Baseball Magazine*, July 1933, p. 365.

———. "Lucky Guy." *Baseball Magazine*, February 1941, p. 414.

———. "Mace Brown to the Rescue." *Baseball Magazine*, October 1938, p. 526.

———. "A Milkman and a Bee." *Baseball Magazine*, March 1938, p. 440.

———. "Sheer Perseverance Has Made Tom Oliver." *Baseball Magazine*, July 1932, p. 377.

———. "A Star Rookie of 1933." *Baseball Magazine*, February 1934, pp. 407–408.

———. "They Call Him a Screw Ball." *Baseball Magazine*, August 1939, pp. 403–404.

———. "Time of Game." *Baseball Magazine*, May 1936, pp. 543–544.

Bowman, Larry G. "The Monarchs and Night Baseball." *National Pastime* 16 (1996): 80–83.

———. "To Save a Minor League Team: Night Baseball Comes to Shreveport." *Louisiana History* 38 (1997): 185–202.

Boynton, Bob. "One Team, Two Fields." *National Pastime* 16 (1995): 51–54.

Bradley, Hugh. "The Whole Town Goes Crazy." *Baseball Magazine*, October 1939, pp. 483–484.

Brewer, Ralph W. "Look at Them College Boys." *Baseball Magazine*, February 1930, p. 394.

Broeg, Bob. "Frankie Frisch: He Played the Game with Gusto." *Baseball Digest*, June 1993, p. 65.

———. "Relief Pitchers Were Once Low Men on the Totem Pole." *Baseball Digest*, June 1987, p. 50.

Broun, Heywood. "Broun's Page." *Nation*, September 12, 1936, p. 46.

Bryson, Bill. "League of Nations." *Baseball Magazine*, July 1938, pp. 365–366.

———. "Majoring for the Majors." *Baseball Magazine*, June 1936, pp. 319–320.

———. "The Majors Go Collegiate." *Baseball Magazine*, July 1935, pp. 369–370.

———. "No Runs, No Hits—No Baseball." *Baseball Magazine*, May 1939, p. 552.

———. "Small Town Boys Make Good." *Baseball Magazine*, June 1938, p. 323.

———. "The .300 Club: It's Exclusive Again." *Baseball Magazine*, December 1941, pp. 305–306.

Burr, Harold C. "All Teeth and Tonsils." *Baseball Magazine*, November 1939, pp. 539–540.

———. "The Brothers DiMaggio." *Baseball Magazine*, July 1941, pp. 367–368.

———. "The Free Agents Go to Market." *Baseball Magazine*, April 1940, pp. 485–486.

Cardello, Joseph. "Dazzy Vance in 1930." *Baseball Research Journal* 25 (1996): 127–130.

Carleton, Tex, and Stanley Frank. "Pride Pitching." *Collier's*, August 10, 1940, p. 9.

Clark, Dick, and John Holway, "1930 Negro National League." *Baseball Research Journal* 18 (1989): 81–86.

Cobbledick, Gordon. "Break Up the Yankees!" *Collier's*, February 25, 1939, p. 19.

Considine, Bob. "Ivory from Cuba." *Collier's*, August 3, 1940, p. 19.

———. "One-Two Punch." *Collier's*, September 28, 1940, p. 12.

Crichton, Kyle. "The Great Hoiman." *Collier's*, August 19, 1932, p. 24.

Crissey, Harrington "Kit." "The Splendid Splinter's Splendid Finish." *National Pastime* 12 (1992): 53–54.

Crosley, Clayton B. "A Conversation with Johnny Vander Meer." *Baseball Research Journal* 13 (1984): 69–70.

Curran, William. "Dodgers End Hubbell's Record Streak." *National Pastime* 14 (1994): 61–65.

Daniel, Daniel M. "Major Leaguers Tack on Service Stars as Players Answer Call of Uncle Sam." *Baseball Magazine*, May 1942, pp. 533–534.

———. "Psychology Wins: The Cleveland Indians Move." *Baseball Magazine*, December 1933, pp. 307–308.

———. "Vander Meer, Rookie of the Year." *Baseball Magazine*, August 1938, pp. 389–390.

———. "Viva Italia!" *Baseball Magazine*, July 1936, pp. 347–348.

———. "We Cheer for Martin, and We Sing of Grimes." *Baseball Magazine*, December 1931, pp. 291–292.

Debs, Victor Jr. "Randy Gumpert." *National Pastime* 19 (1999): 91–94.

Derby, Richard E., and Jim Coleman. "House of David Baseball." *National Pastime* 14 (1994): 7–10.

DiMaggio, Joe. "Pitchers I Have Hit." *Collier's*, July 29, 1939, p. 17.

Doyle, Edward F. "Dutch." "Baker Bowl: A Personal History." *National Pastime* 15 (1995): 24–31.

Eddleston, Oscar. "The '37 All-Star Game." *National Pastime* 17 (1997): 119–120.

Edelman, Rob. "On the Silver Screen." *National Pastime* 18 (1998): 52–55.

Escher, John. "Baseball Madness in Brooklyn." *American Mercury*, September 1939, pp. 79–84.

Evans, Billy. "Baseball from the Bleachers." *Saturday Evening Post*, July 27, 1935, pp. 12–13.

———. "Big-League Over-head." *Saturday Evening Post*, August 5, 1933, pp. 16–17.

Felber, Bill. "Neck and Neck in the Stretch: The Great Race of 1935." *National Pastime* 4 (1985): 60–64.

Feldman, Jay. "Benny McCoy." *National Pastime* 13 (1994): 39–41.

"A Fighting Pitcher Discusses His Trade." *Baseball Magazine*, November 1931, pp. 543–544.

Frank, Stanley. "As Good as He Has to Be." *Saturday Evening Post*, March 16, 1940, p. 37.

————. "Iron Man in a Mask." *Saturday Evening Post*, June 17, 1939, p. 17.

————. "Rough Riders of the Dugout." *Saturday Evening Post*, May 17, 1941, pp. 18–19.

Gaven, Michael. "Meet the Playoff Man." *Baseball Magazine*, June 1938, pp. 319–320.

Gehrig, Mrs. Lou. "Baseball Bride." *Collier's*, June 1, 1935, p. 14.

Gergen, Joe. "Baseball's Most Amazing Streak of Durability." *Baseball Digest*, January 1984, p. 53.

Givens, Horace. "Hal Schumacher Recalls the Old New York Giants." *Baseball Digest*, January 1984, p. 67.

Gould, James M. "Is Radio Good for Baseball?" *Baseball Magazine*, July 1930, pp. 341–342.

Graham, Frank. "Big League Hotfoot." *American Magazine*, October 1940, p. 53.

Grosshandler, Stan. "Floyd Giebell Recalls His Greatest Day in Baseball." *Baseball Digest*, April 1991, pp. 90–93.

————. "Last of the St. Louis Cardinals' Gas House Gang." *Baseball Digest*, June 1992, pp. 66–68.

"Hard Times Hit the Minors." *Literary Digest*, July 30, 1932, p. 37.

Harper, Walter N. "Big Lombardi's Understudy." *Baseball Magazine*, August 1940, p. 418.

————. "Player Protection." *Baseball Magazine*, June 1941, pp. 304–305.

Henderson, Robert William. "Baseball's Father." *Current History*, June 1939, pp. 53–54.

Henrich, Tom, and Richard Nickas. "Joe Gordon." *Baseball Research Journal* 28 (1999): 41–43.

Hofmann, Herbert F. "Schoolboy Rowe and the 1934 Tigers." *National Pastime* 16 (1997): 62–66.

Holl, James P. "Buckeye Bush League: The Ohio State League, 1936–1941." *Timeline*, July–August 1999, pp. 18–29.

Holland, Gerald. "Baseball and Ballyhoo." *American Mercury*, May 1937, pp. 81–87.

Holtzman, Jerome. "Babe Ruth's Last Stand Still a Vivid Memory." *Baseball Digest*, August 1992, pp. 63–65.

Holway, John. "Dandy at Third: Ray Dandridge." *National Pastime* 1 (1982): 7–10.

————. "The Kid Who Taught Satchel Paige a Lesson." *Baseball Research Journal* 16 (1987): 36–44.

————. "Who Was the Mystery Man at the End of DiMaggio's Streak?" *Baseball Digest*, June 1991, pp. 45–47.

"How Raised Stitches Raise a Baseball Argument." *Literary Digest*, May 30, 1931, p. 41.

"How Tony Gives a Latin Tone to Our National Game." *Literary Digest*, July 2, 1932, p. 37.

Hoyt, Waite, and Stanley Frank. "Why the American League Wins." *Saturday Evening Post*, April 2, 1938, pp. 16–17.

"Is Baseball Getting Rougher?" *Literary Digest*, July 23, 1932, pp. 33–35.

Jacobs, Jane, and Douglas Jacobs. "Dexter Park." *Baseball Research Journal* 19 (2000): 41–45.

Karst, Gene. "The Great Days, the Great Stars." *National Pastime* 2 (1982): 48–51.

———. "Spring Training Pioneers." *National Pastime* 6 (1987): 22–27.

Kavanagh, Jack. "Dizzy Dean vs. Carl Hubbell." *Baseball Research Journal* 21 (1992): 33–35.

Keller, David M. "Oh Johnny! Forgotten Baseball Legend." *Timeline*, March–April 1998, pp. 34–43.

Kirksey, George. "Baseball's Circus Man." *Baseball Magazine*, October 1938, pp. 515–516.

———. "When a Feller Needs a Fella." *Baseball Magazine*, June 1938, pp. 309–310.

Knight, Tom. "George Magerkurth." *National Pastime* 12 (1993): 13–15.

Lane, F. C. "Baseball Problems of the Winter Meetings." *Baseball Magazine*, December 1933, pp. 291–292.

———. "The Coming Star of the National League." *Baseball Magazine*, October 1930, pp. 492–493.

———. "He Played a Lone Hand to the Limit." *Baseball Magazine*, August 1931, pp. 395–396.

———. "The Home Run King of the National League." *Baseball Magazine*, May 1930, pp. 539–540.

———. "A Pal for the Waner Boys." *Baseball Magazine*, February 1930, pp. 401–402.

———. "The Romance of Night Baseball." *Baseball Magazine*, October 1930, pp. 483–486.

———. "Slashing Baseball Salaries." *Baseball Magazine*, February 1932, pp. 401–402.

———. "The Sweeping Success of Night Baseball in the Minors." *Baseball Magazine*, January 1937, pp. 369–370.

Langford, Walter. "Bill Werber: Star of Another Era." *Baseball Digest*, March 1988, pp. 77–84.

———. "An Interview with Glenn Wright." *Baseball Research Journal* 19 (1990): 71–76.

———. "Pinky Whitney: Star from Another Era." *Baseball Digest*, June 1988, pp. 69–73.

———. "Travis Jackson: He Captained McGraw's Giants." *Baseball Digest*, September 1984, pp. 89–95.

Lewis, Allen. "The Year When National League Hitters Went Wild." *Baseball Digest*, August 1985, pp. 74–76.

Lewis, Jerry D. "Where the Big Leaguers Come From." *Baseball Magazine*, January 1934, pp. 363–364.

Liley, Thomas. "Whit Wyatt: The Dodgers' 1941 Ace." *National Pastime* 11 (1992): 46–47.

Litwin, Sandy. "Anatomy of a Streak." *Baseball Research Journal* 16 (1997): 104–106.

"The Lively Ball Wins!" *Baseball Magazine*, March 1931, p. 467.

Lundquist, Carl. "The Magnificent Yankee." *National Pastime* 11 (1992): 34–37.

Macht, Norman L. "Baseball of Another Era Left Some Golden Memories."
    Baseball Digest, August 1995, pp. 61–63.

———. "Bill Werber Recalls How It Was in the 1930s." *Baseball Digest*,
    November 1987, pp. 87–89.

———. "Doc Cramer: He Remembers Playing for Connie Mack." *Baseball Digest*,
    January 1987, pp. 96–100.

———. "Eldon Auker: He Remembers How It Was in the 1930s." *Baseball Digest*,
    February 1993, p. 62.

———. "Monte Weaver Recalls Pitching for Old Senators." *Baseball Digest*, May
    1992, p. 538.

———. "Whatever Happened to All the Chatter on the Field?" *Baseball Digest*,
    January 1992, pp. 46–49.

———. "Why Did Mickey Miss the Ball?" *National Pastime* 11 (1992): 44–45.

MacPhail, Lee. "A Year to Remember, Especially in Brooklyn." *National Pastime*
    11 (1992): 41–43.

Mann, Arthur. "Part-time Baseball: The Semipros." *Collier's*, August 24, 1940, p. 18.

McCullough, Bill. "Meal Ticket." *Saturday Evening Post*, July 3, 1937, p. 11.

McGowen, Roscoe. "Little Man, Swat Now." *Baseball Magazine*, July 1941,
    pp. 357–358.

———. "That Family Man, Camilli." *Baseball Magazine*, September 1939,
    pp. 457–458.

Meany, Tom. "The New Minor League: The National?" *Saturday Evening Post*,
    March 19, 1938, pp. 12–13.

Meany, Tom, and Bill McCullough. "Once a Dodger." *Saturday Evening Post*,
    March 6, 1937, pp. 12–13.

Merin, Samuel. "An Italian Baseball Guide." *Baseball Magazine*, March 1934,
    pp. 463–464.

———. "Those Poling Poles." *Baseball Magazine*, May 1935, pp. 559–560.

Michel, Henry John. "First Baseball Telecast Wasn't Ready for Prime Time."
    Baseball Digest, November 1989, pp. 40–41.

Misselwitz, Henry. "American Baseball Conquers Japan." *Living Age*, May 1940,
    pp. 222–225.

"Modern Baseball, the Greatest Ever." *Baseball Magazine*, July 1931, pp. 339–340.

Nack, William. "Lost in History." *Sports Illustrated*, August 19, 1996, pp. 73–85.

———. "The Razor's Edge." *Sports Illustrated*, May 6, 1991, p. 52.

Nelson, Don. "The Hapless Braves of 1935." *National Pastime* 2 (1982): 10–13.

Nicholson, W. G. "When Baseball Owners Reigned in the 1930s and 1940s,
    Baseball Was Hardly a Get-Rich-Quick Venture for Players." *Sports History*,
    May 1989, p. 12.

Owen, Mickey, and Charles Dexter. "The Mystery of the Missed Third Strike."
    Collier's, April 18, 1942, p. 19.

Owen, Russell. "DiMaggio, the Unruffled." *New York Times Magazine*, July 13,
    1941, p. 9.

Owen, Viola, "The RBI Record of the Battalion of Death." *National Pastime* 21 (2001): 44–47.

Pearson, Monte. "Secrets of a Champion Pitcher." *Popular Mechanics*, May 1939, pp. 674–677.

"Pennant for a Price: Tom Yawkey and the Boston Red Sox." *Literary Digest*, December 21, 1935, p. 35.

Rabinowitz, Bill. "No Charity for Baseball." *Sports History*, September 1989, pp. 24–35.

Rennie, Rud. "Changing the Tune from Gloom to Cheer." *Literary Digest*, June 16, 1934, p. 25.

———. "Free Agent." *Collier's*, July 17, 1937, p. 17.

———. "Stop Squawking!" *Collier's*, March 4, 1939, p. 11.

Reynolds, Quentin. "The Frisco Kid." *Collier's*, June 13, 1936, p. 22.

———. "The Making of a Hero." *Collier's*, April 23, 1938, pp. 50–51.

———. "Pop-off Kid." *Collier's*, August 5, 1939, p. 14.

———. "Who's Goofy Now?" *Collier's*, May 2, 1936, p. 22.

Rives, Bob. "Good Night." *National Pastime* 13 (1998): 21–24.

Rolfe, Robert A. "Red." "More than Base Hits." *Collier's*, August 17, 1940, p. 13.

Roper, Scott. "Uncovering Satchel Paige's 1935 Season." *Baseball Research Journal* 23 (1994): 51–54.

Ross, Mike. "Tragedy and Triumph: Bobo Newsom's 1940 World Series." *National Pastime* 10 (1990): 75–78.

Rumill, Edwin M. "Baseball After Dark." *Christian Science Monitor Weekly Magazine*, March 30, 1940, p. 5.

"Satchelfoots." *Time*, June 3, 1940, p. 44.

"Satchel Paige, Negro Ballplayer, Is One of Best Pitchers in Game." *Life*, June 2, 1941, pp. 90–92.

Sayama, Kazuo. " 'Their Throws Were Like Arrows': How a Black Team Spurred Pro Ball in Japan." *Baseball Research Journal* 16 (1987): 85–88.

Schulian, John. "Laughing Outside." *Sports Illustrated*, June 26, 2000, pp. 90–92.

"The Secret of Jimmy [*sic*] Foxx's Slugging Power." *Baseball Magazine*, September 1934, pp. 393–394.

Shane, Ted. "The Chocolate Rube Waddell." *Saturday Evening Post*, July 27, 1940, p. 20.

———. "Big Red." *American Magazine*, August 1939, pp. 44–45.

Shaver, John W. "The Cubs: Baseball's Contribution to Successful Management." *Factory and Industrial Management*, October 1929, pp. 840–842.

Singlais, Neil. "Wally Berger: Home Run Hitter of Another Era." *Baseball Digest*, December 1987, pp. 93–95.

Skrec, Joseph. "Fame Forgotten." *National Pastime* 13 (1994): 94–96.

Smith, Ken. "The Giants' Jewish Catcher." *Baseball Magazine*, March 1938, p. 444.

Stockton, J. Roy. "The People's Choice: The National League." *Saturday Evening Post*, July 16, 1938, pp. 14–15.

Sumner, Jim. "Almost Perfect." *National Pastime* 13 (1994): 51–54.

Swart, Steve. "Lou Gehrig on the Radio." *National Pastime* 17 (1997): 13–16.

Swope, Tom. "Baseball's Brightest Success Story." *Christian Science Monitor Weekly Magazine*, September 23, 1939, p. 7.

Tekulsky, Joseph D. "Elmer Gedeon." *National Pastime* 14 (1994): 68–69.

Terry, Bill. "Fly by Night." *Collier's*, April 20, 1940, p. 23.

Terry, Bill, and Arthur Mann. "Terrible Terry." *Saturday Evening Post*, January 29, 1938, pp. 5–7.

"Texas—Mother of Baseball Stars." *Literary Digest*, April 6, 1935, p. 34.

Thom, John. "The Kidnapping of Flint Rhem." *National Pastime* 10 (1990): 79–82.

———. "The 1930 Phillies." *National Pastime* 13 (1993): 71–75.

Thompson, Dick, "The Wes Ferrell Story," *National Pastime* 21 (2001): 96–124.

Thornley, Stew. " 'Unser Choe': Hauser's Double 60." *Baseball Research Journal* 20 (1991): 20–22.

Tomlinson, Gerald. "A Minor-League Legend: Buzz Arlett, the Mightiest Oak." *Baseball Research Journal* 17 (1988): 13–16.

Tompkins, Christopher. "I Think He's Just Grand." *Baseball Magazine*, March 1938, pp. 462–463.

Touraugeau, Dixie. "Grove's Grandest Groove." *National Pastime* 19 (1999): 85–90.

Trevor, George. "But It Isn't Cricket." *Outlook*, April 9, 1930, p. 503.

"Two Young Yankees from College." *Literary Digest*, June 30, 1934, p. 32.

Van Blair, Rick. "Hall of Famer Dizzy Dean: He Was One of a Kind." *Baseball Digest*, July 1998, pp. 74–76.

———. "Harry Danning: Catching Star of Another Era." *Baseball Digest*, October 1994, pp. 63–66.

———. "In the 1930s, Van Lingle Mungo Was a Scourge for N. L. Hitters." *Baseball Digest*, May 1996, pp. 68–73.

———. "Jo Jo Moore Recalls Days with Old New York Giants." *Baseball Digest*, March 1990, pp. 72–73.

———. "Opposing Pitchers Couldn't Stop Him but a War Did." *Baseball Digest*, July 1994, p. 56.

———. "The Pitcher Who Yielded Famous 'Homer in the Gloamin'.' " *Baseball Digest*, September 1994, p. 72.

Vass, George. "Top Base Running Feats, Blunders in World Series." *Baseball Digest*, September 1985, p. 18.

Vaughn, Gerald F. "Mexico's Year of Josh Gibson." *National Pastime* 12 (1992): 53–56.

Wagner, Honus, and George Kirksey. "Help! Help!—Help for the Pitchers." *Saturday Evening Post*, July 13, 1940, pp. 20–21.

Ward, John L. "A College Professor Who Pitches Winning Ball." *Baseball Magazine*, February 1933, p. 403.

———. "The Home Run Rookie of the Chicago White Sox." *Baseball Magazine*, September 1934, pp. 449–450.

———. "When the Arc Lights Blazed at Cincinnati." *Baseball Magazine*, July 1935, p. 351.

Werber, Bill, and Harold Parrott. "A Ballplayer Boos Back." *Saturday Evening Post*, July 25, 1942, p. 23.

Werber, Bill, and C. Paul Rogers III. "A Veritable Who's Who of Managing." *Nine* 8 (1999): 86–103.

White, G. Edward, ed. "A Diary of the Negro Leagues." *National Pastime* 17 (1997): 25–29.

Wigley, Brian J., et al. "Willard Hershberger and the Legacy of Suicide." *National Pastime* 20 (2000): 72–76.

Williams, Joe. "Busher Joe McCarthy." *Saturday Evening Post*, April 15, 1939, pp. 12–13.

———. "Deacon Bill McKechnie." *Saturday Evening Post*, September 14, 1940, p. 39.

"Williams of Red Sox Is Best Hitter." *Life*, September 1, 1941, pp. 43–44.

Winerip, Harold. "Speaking of Night Ball." *Baseball Magazine*, August 1940, pp. 397–398.

"Winter Glimpses of Famous Baseball Stars." *Baseball Magazine*, April 1931, pp. 505–506.

Wrigley, William, Jr. "Owning a Big-League Ball Team." *Saturday Evening Post*, September 13, 1930, pp. 24–25.

VIDEOTAPES

1937 World Series Plus 1937 Spring Training and Lefty Gomez Interview. Rare Sportsfilms TM Video, 1994.

1939 American League Film: "Touching All Bases." Rare Sportsfilms TM Video, 1999.

There Was Always Sun Shining Someplace: Life in the Negro Baseball Leagues. Refocus Productions/Southwest Texas Public Broadcasting Council, 1983.

Index

A. G. Spalding and Brothers (baseball manufacturer), 29, 37
Adams, Charles F., 103, 118
African Americans. *See* black Americans
alcoholism, among ballplayers, 187
Alexander, Dale, 66
Alexander, Grover Cleveland, 30, 174, 185, 213
All-Star Games: of 1933, 71–72; of 1934, 84; of 1935, 107; of 1936, 123; of 1937, 137; of 1938, 160–161; of 1939, 176; of 1940, 248–249; of 1941, 272
All-Stars (Dean brothers' postseason team), 218, 219–220. *See also* Joe Pirrone's All-Stars; Mike Gonzalez's All-Stars; Satchel Paige's All-Stars; Trujillo All-Stars
Allen, Johnny, 56, 59, 91, 117, 124, 142, 154, 190, 267, 274
Allen, Mel (Melvin Israel), 257
Almada, Melo, 143, 193–194
Almendares, Cuba, team in, 134, 220
Altrock, Nick, 73
American Giants. *See* Chicago American Giants

American League: attendance, 35, 260; batting statistics in, 29; champions of, rule on trades with, 239; competitiveness of, 150; night games in, authorization for, 168; numbered uniforms in, 38; power orientation of, 177. *See also* pennant races
American Negro League (ANL), 206
Ammon Field (Pittsburgh), 212
Amos 'n' Andy (radio program), 206
amyotrophic lateral sclerosis (ALS), 172, 269
Andrews, Ivy, 144
Angels. *See* Los Angeles Angels
Appleton, Pete (Peter Jablonowski), 192
Appling, Luke, 124, 154, 280
Arlett, Russell "Buzz," 201
Arnold, Violet, 60
Arnovich, Morrie, 192
Athletics. *See* Indianapolis Athletics; Philadelphia Athletics
Atlanta Black Crackers, 216, 227
Atlanta Crackers, 115
Atlantic City Bacharach Giants, 216
attendance: at All-Star Games, 72, 84, 107, 176; at East-West Games, 222,